THE ABBEY REBELS OF 1916

Acknowledgements

I am grateful to Aideen Howard, the Abbey Theatre's former literary director, for directing my attention to the Abbey's commemorative plaque. The staff of the Abbey, particularly its archivist Mairéad Delaney, tolerated my (unsolicited) obsession with this remarkable institution's early history, and kindly allowed me to reproduce documents from its wonderful archive.

Appropriately, for a book inspired by a memorial, my initial focus on how a revolutionary movement emerged from a cultural revival increasingly gave way to an interest in historical memory, and questions about representations and ownership of the past. Although most of what we now know about the Abbey is filtered through the lens of W. B. Yeats and Lady Gregory, the voices of the theatre's less prominent founders, who had their own aspirations and agency, deserve to be better known. I am grateful to the descendents of some of the individuals who feature in this book for responding to queries or offering assistance, including Dan Ford, Colbert Kearney, Dave Kenny, Declan Kiberd, Dualta Ó Broin and Kevin Stanley.

I would like to acknowledge the assistance of the archivists and librarians, some of whom work in difficult conditions in underfunded institutions, who facilitated my requests. These include Niall Bergin and Aoife Torpey (Kilmainham Gaol); (the wonderful) Mary Broderick, Frances Clarke, Glen Dunne, James Harte, Berni Metcalfe (National Library of Ireland); Catriona Crowe and Aideen Ireland (National Archives); Sandra Heise, Lar Joye, Finbar Connolly (the National Museum of Ireland); Padraic Kennedy and the staff of the Military Archives; Barry Houlihan (Hardiman Library, NUIG); the staff of the Lilly Library; Sinéad McCoole (Jackie Clarke Collection, Ballina Public Library); Keith Murphy (National Photographic Archive); and the staff of the New York Public Library.

Jennie Carlsten collaborated with me in developing this project from its inception as an Arts and Humanities Research Council-funded documentary proposal, undertook photo research, and kindly read the manuscript. Ciara O'Dowd shared her valuable research with me. Others who offered help or advice include Nicholas Allen, Douglas Appleyard, Marie Coleman, Hugh Denard, Sé Merry Doyle, Chris Fox, Ruth Hegarty, Keith Jeffery, Roy Foster, Peter Gray, Michael Hewitt and DoubleBand Films, Laura McAtackney, Bill McCormack, Jason McElligott, Kevin McGarry, Patrick Maume, James Moran, Jimmy Murphy, Will Murphy, Éanna Ó Caollaí, Tom Reilly, Mark Reynolds, Fidelma Slattery, and C. P. Smythe. The creative vision of Conor & David and the professionalism of the staff at Gill & Macmillan, particularly Conor Nagle, Catherine Gough and the unflappable Jen Patton, helped to make this book a reality.

This book is dedicated to my wife, Selina, and my daughters, Sofia and Ava, whose love and support make everything possible.

THE ABBEY REBELS OF 1916

A Lost Revolution

Fearghal McGarry

Gill & Macmillan

Gill & Macmillan
Hume Avenue, Park West, Dublin 12
www.gillmacmillanbooks.ie

© Fearghal McGarry 2015

978 0 7171 6881 1

Designed in Ireland by WorkGroup
Edited by Seirbhísí Leabhar
Indexed by Adam Pozner
Printed by BZ Graf. S.A. Poland

This book is typeset in *Fedra Serif B*
and *Berthold Akzidenz Grotesk*.

5 4 3 2 1

For Selina, Sofia and Ava

Contents

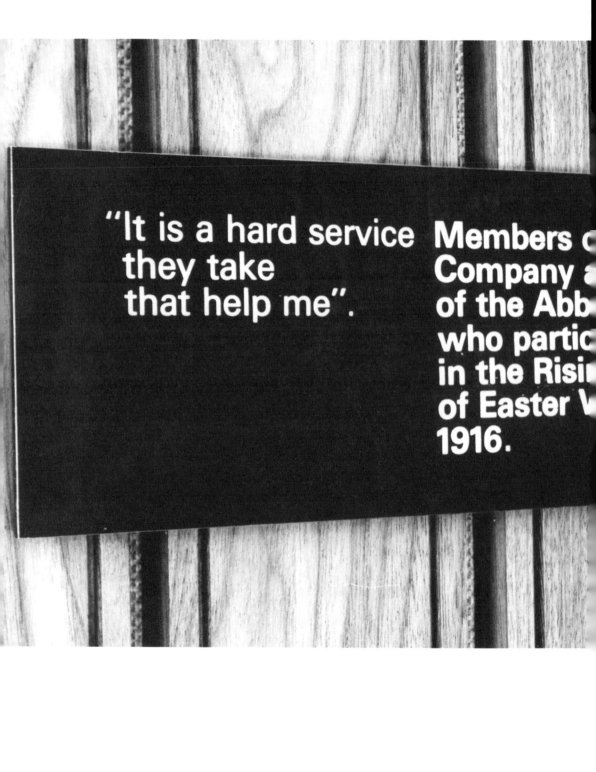

"It is a hard service they take that help me".

Members o
Company a
of the Abb
who partic
in the Risi
of Easter V
1916.

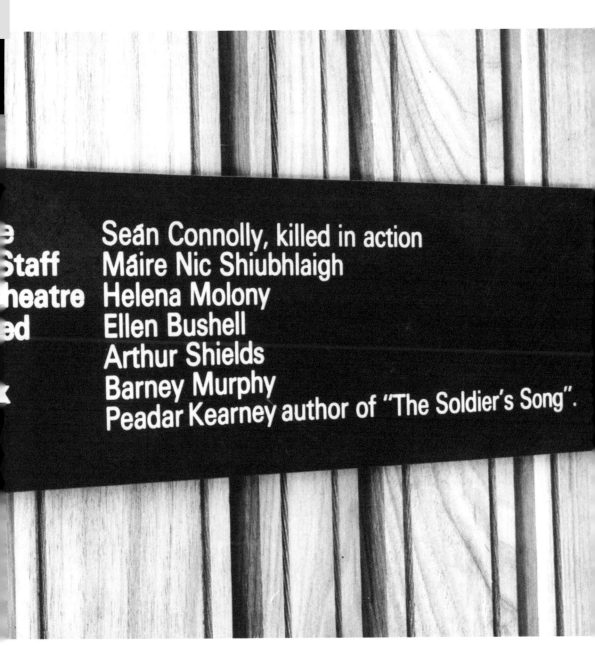

e
Staff
heatre
ed

Seán Connolly, killed in action
Máire Nic Shiubhlaigh
Helena Molony
Ellen Bushell
Arthur Shields
Barney Murphy
Peadar Kearney author of "The Soldier's Song".

Unveiled to mark the reopening of the theatre in 1966, the Abbey's commemorative plaque was inscribed with a quotation from *Cathleen ni Houlihan*, the play most identified with the cultural revival's revolutionary impact (AT).

They shall be remembered for ever,
They shall be alive for ever,
They shall be speaking for ever,
The people shall hear them for ever.

—W. B. Yeats, *Cathleen ni Houlihan* (1902)

Chapter 1

Hard service

1916 in 1966

(L–R), The Taoiseach, Seán Lemass, Christine Shields (daughter of Arthur Shields), and Gypsy Kenny (sister of Máire Nic Shiubhlaigh) at the unveiling of the plaque on 23 July 1966. Gypsy was one of several 1916 veterans whose names were omitted from the plaque (HL, T13/B/350).

On 23 July 1966 the Taoiseach, Seán Lemass, attended a ceremony at the Abbey Theatre to pay tribute to seven rebels who had fought in the Easter Rising of 1916. A modest plaque unveiled in the vestibule honoured these remarkable individuals. Helena Molony was the first Irishwoman of her generation to be imprisoned for a political offence when she was arrested for protesting against King George V's visit to Ireland in 1911. Intimately involved in the planning of the Rising, she had hidden copies of the Proclamation under her pillow as she slept at Liberty Hall the night before the rebellion. Arthur Shields, who became a Hollywood star in later life, had fought with James Connolly at the General Post Office, and was among the last rebels to surrender at Moore Street. Máire Nic Shiubhlaigh, one of the founding members of the Irish National Theatre Society, had been the Abbey Theatre's first leading lady. Peadar Kearney, a veteran of the Fenian movement, wrote the words to 'The Soldier's Song', the marching song which epitomised the spirit of the Irish revolution and was later adopted as the national anthem. Responsible for the opening attack of the Easter Rising, one that bore more than a passing resemblance to a scene from the Robert Emmet plays in which he had often performed, Seán Connolly had led a small band of poorly armed men and women into Dublin Castle, the headquarters of the British administration in Ireland. Shot on the roof of City Hall, he became the first rebel to die.

In other respects, though, the Abbey's rebels were ordinary people, or, more accurately, people from ordinary backgrounds. They were working-class Dubliners, followers rather than leaders, whose role on the historical stage seemed to come to an end after Easter Week. The details of their lives had been largely forgotten by 1966. After the Rising, Ellen Bushell had returned to the Abbey Theatre's box office, where she worked for another three decades. Little was known of the fate of the former stage hand Barney Murphy, who had fought with Ned Daly's 1st Battalion at the Four Courts, although he was still remembered at the Abbey as 'the prompter who had no belief in actors' pauses'.[1] Even the better-known among them, such as Nic Shiubhlaigh and Kearney, had faded from public memory, to the disappointment of their own families.

Only two of the seven remained alive in 1966. Helena Molony, frail and wheelchair-bound, attended the ceremony. She died several months later. Unable to travel from California because of his poor health, Arthur Shields was represented by his daughter, Christine, who addressed the gathering. Relatives of the deceased rebels attended what was described as a 'brief, dignified, ceremony'. The presence of Máire Nic Shiubhlaigh's sister Patricia ('Gypsy'), her brother Frank and the 86-year-old stage carpenter Seán Barlow represented the Abbey's last living links to the turn-of-the-century revival from which this extraordinary theatre had emerged.[2]

The memorial's inscription – 'It is hard service they take that help me' – came from *Cathleen ni Houlihan*, the play which more than any other work in the Abbey's repertoire symbolised the link between the cultural revival and the political revolution that followed. Set in 1798, the Year of the French, it tells the story of Michael Gillane, who abandons his young bride to follow a

Portrait of Máire Nic Shiubhlaigh (1904) by John Butler Yeats (1839–1922), father of W.B. Yeats (NGI).

Seán Connolly as Robert Emmet.
Radical amateur dramatic companies
lost few opportunities to re-enact the
United Irishmen's insurrections of
1798 and 1803 (NMI, HE/EW/4446).

wronged old woman, Cathleen, who has come to his farmhouse to appeal for help in securing the return of her 'four beautiful green fields'. By renewing the insurrectionary tradition, his martyrdom transforms Cathleen into a young girl with 'the walk of a queen', ensuring that Michael is 'remembered for ever'.[3] Yeats's powerful evocation of the willingness of young men to die for Ireland was widely believed to have revived separatist ideals among the revolutionary generation that brought about 1916. Although the play's electrifying debut (when Maud Gonne's personification of the cause of Ireland created a sensation) preceded the founding of the Abbey, *Cathleen ni Houlihan* came to symbolise its potent legacy. 'No other theatre', one scholar has claimed, has 'been so directly involved in the rise of a nation'.[4]

Yeats, admittedly, had a hand in promoting this appealing notion. Accepting the Nobel Prize for Literature in Stockholm in 1923, he insisted that the political revolution had been a product of the literary revival in which he and the Abbey's others founders, Lady Gregory and Edward Martyn, had played such a central role. He cultivated this idea throughout his life, most powerfully in lines learnt by later generations of schoolchildren: 'Did that play of mine send out | Certain men the English shot?'[5] But Yeats was not the first to suggest the connection. Even before the Rising, the Irish Party politician Stephen Gwynn had famously asked whether 'such plays should be produced unless one was prepared for people to go out to shoot and be shot'.[6] Encountering Yeats on the street, as Dublin lay in ruins, the journalist P. J. Little recalled that, 'by way of a joke, I said to him that I would tell the British authorities that he, with his *Cathleen ni Houlihan*, was responsible for the Rising.'[7]

There were intriguing connections between the play and the event it was believed to have inspired. The role of Cathleen on the Abbey's opening night had been played by Máire Nic Shiubhlaigh, who went on to perform in what she described as 'the greatest drama of all' at Easter, 1916.[8] Among the 'certain men' whose death kept Yeats awake towards the end of his life was Seán Connolly, whose final performance at the Abbey was in its March 1916 production of *Cathleen ni Houlihan*. Unknown to Yeats, the press on which the Proclamation was reportedly printed had been kept hidden – beside Arthur Shields's rifle – under the stage of the Abbey. And, as chance would have it, *Cathleen ni Houlihan* was due to be performed the day the rebellion began. Fearing it might further incite the people, the Abbey's manager, St John Ervine, cancelled the performance after he heard the first shots.

Ben Bay's depiction of a 1907 production of *Cathleen ni Houlihan* (1902). Yeats's remarkably popular play was staged by the Abbey on over 350 occasions between the opening of the theatre in December 1904 and the Easter Rising (NLI, PD 2159/TX/3/1).

There were, moreover, wider parallels between the Rising and theatre. The rebellion was choreographed by a seven-man military council that included three playwrights and a theatre-founder. The symbolic nature of the spectacle they staged at Easter, which conveyed an understanding of 'the political value of theatre and of the theatricality of politics', was instantly grasped by many contemporaries.[9] Some even mistook the insurrection's opening actions for improvised street theatre, while one visitor to Liberty Hall assumed that the preparations for the Rising were a rehearsal for a play.[10] Joseph Holloway, the Abbey's best-known patron, initially mistook the Proclamation (signed by two of the Irish Theatre's founders) for a playbill.[11] In retrospect, none of this was surprising: the climactic performance at the GPO was 'the result of intense rehearsals conducted since the turn of the century'.[12]

Although 'no previous Irish insurrection had been mounted in such avowedly theatrical terms', not all rebels appreciated the symbolism. 'Looking at it from the inside (I was in the GPO)', Michael Collins griped, 'it had the air

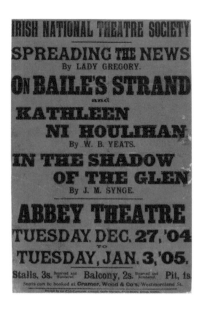

Aptly, in the light of its incendiary reputation, *Cathleen ni Houlihan* had been scheduled to play on Easter Monday, 1916. T. H. Nally's *The Spancel of Death* was finally performed, to little acclaim, at Boston College in 1986 (AT).

Opening night. The Abbey's striking posters and programmes were characterised by bold type and clear layout. They were often printed by printers with radical political connections (NLI, EPH F158).

Founded by the Irish National Theatre
Society in 1904, the Abbey Theatre
was the product of a collaboration
between Yeats's Irish Literary
Theatre and the Fay brothers' Irish
National Dramatic Company (AT).

of a Greek tragedy about it'.[13] Collins had a better understanding of military
strategy than of the power of myth. It was precisely because of its tragic arc,
culminating in the British authorities' vengeful finale, that the Rising came
to symbolise the triumph of failure, rendering it the most important event
of modern Irish history. After the revolution, in a tacit acknowledgement of
the Abbey's political significance, it became the first theatre in the English-
speaking world to receive a state subsidy. Supporters of the Irish National
Theatre – such as its long-serving managing director, Ernest Blythe – were
rarely slow thereafter to draw attention to the Abbey's role in raising 'the
fighting spirit of the people ... making possible the hard military and political
effort which secured the establishment of a sovereign Irish state.'[14]

 The historical reality, explored by this book, is just as interesting as the
myth. Most of those honoured in 1966 had broken with the Abbey before the
Rising as a result of their political beliefs. In contrast to its 'elitist, reformist,
Ascendancy' management,[15] the players and staff members of the Abbey
Theatre were mostly working-class Catholics. Many of them were radicals,
committed to revolutionary ideals such as feminism and socialism. By 1966,
however, these ideals had been largely forgotten, as was the important role
played by Inghinidhe na hÉireann in founding the theatre. Attesting to Yeats's
success in writing himself into the narrative of an event in which he had
played no part was the routine description of the Rising as 'a terrible beauty'
by 1966. Similarly, the press reported how the purpose of the ceremony at the
Abbey was to honour the seven rebels who took 'part in the fighting for which
the tone of so many Abbey plays had conditioned the nation'.[16]

Production for the first time on any Stage of On Baile's Strand and Spreading the News. on Tuesday, 27th December, 1904. and every evening till Tuesday, 3rd January, 1905.

ON BAILE'S STRAND, A PLAY IN ONE ACT, BY W. B. YEATS.

CUCHULLAIN, the King of Muirthemne	F. J. Fay
CONCOBAR, the High King of Ullad	George Roberts
DAIRE, a King	Arthur Sinclair
FINTAIN, a blind man	Seumas O'Sullivan
BARACH, a fool	W. G. Fay
A YOUNG MAN	P. MacSiubhlaigh
YOUNG KINGS and OLD KINGS	Maire Ni Gharbhaigh, Emma Vernon, Sara Algood, Doreen Gunning, R. Nash, N. Power, U. Wright, E. Keegan.

SCENE—A Great Hall by the Sea close to Dundalgan.

Costumes designed by Miss Horniman.

SPREADING THE NEWS, A COMEDY IN ONE ACT, BY LADY GREGORY.

BARTLEY FALLON	W. G. Fay
Mrs. FALLON	Sara Algood
Mrs. TULLY	Emma Vernon
Mrs. TARPEY	Maire Ni Gharbhaigh
SHAWN EARLY	J. H. Dunne
TIM CASEY	George Roberts
JAMES RYAN	Arthur Sinclair
JACK SMITH	P. MacSuibhlaigh
A POLICEMAN	R. S. Nash
A REMOVABLE MAGISTRATE	F. J. Fay

SCENE—The Outskirts of a Fair.

On Tuesday, Thursday, and Saturday, 27th, 29th, and 31st December, On Baile's Strand will be followed by :—

KATHLEEN NI HOULIHAN, A PLAY IN ONE ACT, BY W. B. YEATS

KATHLEEN NI HOULIHAN	Marie Nic Shiublaigh
PETER GILLANE	W. G. Fay
BRIDGET GILLANE, his Wife	Sara Algood
MICHAEL GILLANE } his Sons	P. MacSiubhlaigh
PATRICK GILLANE }	U. Wright
DELIA CAHEL	Maire Ni Gharbhaigh

SCENE—A Cottage near to Killala, in 1798.

On Wednesday and Friday, 28th and 30th December, and on Monday and Tuesday, 2nd and 3rd January, On Baile's Strand will be followed by :—

IN THE SHADOW OF THE GLEN, A PLAY IN ONE ACT, BY J. M. SYNGE.

DAN BURKE, Farmer and Herd	George Roberts
NORA BURKE, his Wife	Maire Nic Shiublaigh
MICHAEL DARA, a Young Herd	P. MacSiubhlaigh
A TRAMP	W. G. Fay

SCENE—The last Cottage at the head of a long glen in County Wicklow.

The next production will be a new play in three acts, by J. M. Synge.

Excerpt from the Abbey's first programme. Máire Nic Shiubhlaigh and her brother, Proinsias, performed on the Abbey's opening night, as did Edward Keegan, another of the 1916 veterans overlooked in 1966 (AT).

In official commemoration, the dead are often little more than props, trapped in myths of others' making. The ceremony at the Abbey formed part of a broader remembrance of 1916 which saw one of the most revolutionary moments in Irish history reimagined by a conservative state, obscuring from view some of its most radical features, such as the role played by women and socialists.[17] It was not only these impulses that were overshadowed in 1966: so too was the role of other 1916 veterans associated with the Abbey – such as Edward Keegan and Marie Perolz – who had been omitted from the memorial. After 1966 the memory of their involvement in 1916 would further recede, as the Abbey's memorial began generating its own history, demonstrating how commemoration reconfigures the past that it recalls.

This book explores the story of the Abbey's rebels rather than the Abbey's representation of 1916, although the two narratives occasionally intersect. It has two aims. The first is to scrape away the layers of myth and memory that shroud the rebellion in order to assess the Abbey's rebels within their own historical context. The second is, more or less, the opposite: to explore how the historical Rising was reimagined – through commemoration, cultural representation and memory – as the foundational myth that has shaped not merely Ireland's politics but also its culture and identity over the past century. Rather than assuming a 'binary opposition between history and myth', this approach acknowledges how the significance of 1916 resides in the blurred boundaries between history and memory.[18]

The opening section of this book explores the radicalisation of the Abbey's rebels during the period Yeats described as the 'long gestation', the years of separatist marginalisation and cultural revival between the fall of Parnell in 1891 and the Home Rule crisis of 1913. It traces the rebels' path to the GPO, focusing in particular on how theatre shaped their revolutionary activism. The central section of the book reconstructs Easter Week and its aftermath, exploring how tensions between revolutionary expectations and realities were present from the outset. The final part explores one of the least considered aspects of the independence struggle: the experience of veterans after their guns fell silent. It traces the growing divergence between their hopes for liberation and the more prosaic outcome of the revolution. Although their efforts set in train the transformation that followed, the Ireland that emerged was not what they anticipated. Like most revolutionaries, they reaped little reward for their sacrifices. In contrast to the best-known veterans of the Rising, who secured a place among the state's ruling elite, most died in obscurity and poverty. In predicting this 'hard service', as in much else about Ireland's revolution, Yeats had been prescient. Their Rising remained nonetheless a defining experience, one they felt compelled to remember in different ways throughout their lives – a process the final chapters explore.

Part I:

Before

All that I have said and done,
Now that I am old and ill,
Turns into a question till
I lie awake night after night
And never get the answers right.
Did that play of mine send out
Certain men the English shot?
Did words of mine put too great strain
On that woman's reeling brain?
Could my spoken words have checked
That whereby a house lay wrecked?
And all seems evil until I
Sleepless would lie down and die.

—W. B. Yeats, 'The Man and the Echo'

Chapter 2

Máire Nic Shiubhlaigh

1883–1903

Máire Nic Shiubhlaigh (1883–1958)
by John Butler Yeats (AT).

... From the very start we felt that we must have a theatre of our own. The theatres of Dublin had nothing about them that we could call our own. They were empty buildings hired by the English travelling companies and we wanted Irish plays and Irish players. When we thought of these plays we thought of everything that was romantic and poetical, for the nationalism we had called up – like that every generation had called up in moments of discouragement – was romantic and poetical.

—W. B. Yeats, 1923[1]

When I see that play I feel it might lead a man to do something foolish. —George Bernard Shaw to Lady Gregory, following the London performance of *Cathleen ni Houlihan*, 1909[2]

Of the Abbey's seven rebels, Máire Nic Shiubhlaigh was the most closely bound up with the theatre's origins in the wider cultural ferment of *fin de siècle* Dublin. This period witnessed not only a flourishing of Irish-Ireland activism but also a remarkable wave of political agitation, encompassing the centenary of the 1798 Rebellion, protests against royal visits in 1900 and 1903, and support for the Boer Rebellion in South Africa. These campaigns led to the emergence of such radical political organisations as Cumann na nGaedheal and its successor, Sinn Féin. Along with their opposition to the political compromises of John Redmond's Irish Party, these organisations shared a commitment to the importance of strengthening Irish identity through cultural revival. In the light of the Irish Republican Brotherhood's decline, and of the lack of electoral opposition to the Home Rule movement, cultural activism assumed a greater importance for many militant nationalists than either conventional politics or traditional republicanism. Although the revival appeared to have achieved little by 1909, when Sinn Féin fell into decline, the importance of this period in radicalising the revolutionary generation is illustrated by the experiences of the Abbey's rebels.

Born in Dublin in 1883, the daughter of Matthew Walker, a printer, and Marianne Doherty, a dressmaker, Mary Elizabeth Walker was one of many of her generation drawn into politics through cultural activism. After joining the Gaelic League in 1898, she graduated to the radical women's organisation Inghinidhe na hÉireann (Daughters of Ireland) on its formation in 1900. A militant organisation that advocated the attainment of a republic through insurrectionary violence, Inghinidhe na hÉireann had a preoccupation with cultural pursuits which, as described by Máire, was characteristic of the advanced nationalist movements of the day:

> We used to hold classes and debates, encouraging the study of Irish history, music, literature and art, and for those of us who were interested in acting there was a small dramatic company. At the time this was producing tableaux vivants at the Antient Concert Rooms, a small theatre in Brunswick Street – 'living pictures' – very popular just then, showing a scene from some period in Irish history or illustrating some legend or patriotic melody.[3]

In her memoir, *The Splendid Years*, Máire recalled the Dublin of her youth as a place 'full of earnest young people, all of them anxious to do something useful for Ireland'.[4] Inghinidhe na hÉireann formed part of a broader renaissance that produced (with the publication of Arthur Griffith's *The Resurrection of Hungary* in 1904) not only a new nationalism but also the invention of modern Irish theatre and radical developments in literature and art. Among those who watched Máire rehearse in shabby halls were W. B. Yeats, a young James Joyce and George Russell (Æ), the kindly 'poet, journalist, artist and mystic'. Her memoir conveys the fusion of culture and politics that characterised bohemian Dublin:

> Dublin bristled with little national movements of every conceivable kind: cultural, artistic, literary, theatrical, political. I suppose a generation arriving amidst the bickering of parliamentarians, of Parnellites and anti-Parnellites, had turned from politics and begun at last to seek a national expression elsewhere. Everyone was discussing literature and the arts, the new literature that was emerging. Everywhere, in the streets, at ceilidhes and national concerts, anywhere that crowds gathered, one met enthusiasts, young people drawn from every side of the city's life, leaders or followers of all the little clubs and societies that were appearing every day. The parent group was the Gaelic League, which was non-political and non-sectarian and strove principally for the revival of the language; but there were other bodies like Cumann na nGaedheal, the immediate forerunner of Sinn Féin, whose leader was Arthur Griffith; smaller clubs which combined social with political activities; circles devoted to industrial and agricultural development; and from the beginning there had been societies for the foundation of an Irish theatre.

This recollection echoes the 'long gestation' described by Yeats in his influential Nobel speech: the turning away of a younger, idealistic generation from constitutional nationalism, their work for the revival of Irish culture and identity, and the shift to a revolutionary commitment that resulted.

The importance of amateur theatrical groups within this milieu is striking. 'Most of us came out of nationalist clubs in Dublin, or were connected in some fashion with the nationalist movement', Máire recorded. 'Almost everyone in the Irish theatre was, during its first years'. The overlap between theatre and politics was particularly evident within Inghinidhe na hÉireann's National Players: 'We met every week and discussed plays. Alice Milligan had written some plays and it was suggested that we should put on two of her plays … Everyone was writing plays at the time'.[5] The women who learnt to act at Inghinidhe na hÉireann's classes at the York Street Workman's Club included not only future leading lights of Dublin theatre – including Molly and Sara Allgood – but also such revolutionaries as Marie Perolz and Helena Molony.

Although cultural activism exercised an important politicising impact on Máire, other radicalising influences lay closer to home. Her militant nationalism and commitment to the Irish language – she was one of the first actors to use an Irish form of her name for her stage name – were products of her family background. Her father, Matthew, proprietor of the *Carlow Vindicator*, had been denounced from the pulpit, and his children turned away from the church on Confirmation day, before he was finally run out of Carlow for backing Parnell when the Irish Party split.[6] He moved to Dublin, joining the *Daily Express* as one of the city's first Linotype operators and, later, working as a compositor for the *Irish Times*. He set up the Tower Press in Cornmarket and, benefiting from the patronage of nationalist societies, established the Gaelic Press in Upper Liffey Street.[7] This business was responsible for printing many of the radical newspapers known as the 'mosquito press', as well as subversive broadsheets and ballads that circulated through Dublin's revolutionary underground. It was not only Matthew's political radicalism but his unusually egalitarian outlook which accounted for his daughters' political activism. The support offered by both parents, the writer Padraic Colum believed, also made it possible 'for the younger girls to move, casually it seemed, into the theatre'.[8]

The friendship between the Walker family and the Fay brothers also facilitated this transition. In 1900 Máire joined an elocution class taught at the Coffee Palace Hall in Townsend Street by the theatre-obsessed accountant Frank Fay. She became a protégée of Frank and his brother Willie:

> I learned to recite … I was brought to concerts at St Theresa's Hall and the Father Matthew, anywhere I could get an audience, and he [Frank] would come with me to prompt. Whenever a good play came to Dublin I was taken to see it.[9]

In 1901 Inghinidhe na hÉireann's dramatic company was placed under the brothers' guidance. Advocates of a national theatre, the Fays saw in its players the raw material for a movement that might depict 'life through Irish eyes'.[10] Willie, an electrician reputed to know more about his hobby than his trade, had extensive experience staging productions in Dublin. His taciturn brother specialised in recitation: he 'made beautiful speech, whether it was the delivery of dialect or the lyrical speaking of verse his goal'. Máire recalled 'long, not very comfortable sessions' with Frank Fay; Joseph Holloway, chronicler of Dublin's theatre world, was more forthright about the brothers' methods: 'it is mighty hard to pull with them, their tempers are vile and they treat those under them like dogs'.[11]

Their first play – a production of Alice Milligan's *The Deliverance of Red Hugh* in the Antient Concert Rooms in August 1901 – sufficiently impressed Yeats, one of a handful of observers, for him to allow his new play, *Cathleen ni Houlihan* (much of it, in fact, written by Lady Gregory), to be performed by Inghinidhe na hÉireann's players.[12] It was this collaboration which resulted in the formation of the Irish National Dramatic Society. According to Máire, the decision to form the Society was taken in her home in the Liberties, where Willie Fay boarded.[13] Their enterprise was characterised by a strongly collective ethos: 'we worked very hard, W. G. Fay making the scenery and, mind you, there was very little money, it was just gathered up between the Fays and a few friends'. Despite the humble setting – Máire recalled how the tiny stage of St Theresa's Temperance Hall in Clarendon Street 'wobbled dangerously' as the actors moved about – their first production had an extraordinary impact. Staged on 2 April 1902 as a fund-raiser for Inghinidhe na hÉireann, their performance of *Cathleen ni Houlihan* and George Russell's *Deirdre* brought together two distinct audiences: Dublin's literary set, for whom Yeats was a figure of stature, and the working-class nationalists from whom Inghinidhe na hÉireann drew its support. 'Gleaming shirt-fronts mingled with the less resplendent garb of the Dublin worker, in the tiny auditorium'. Máire, who played a small role, recalled the effect of Maud Gonne's performance as Cathleen:

> Watching her, one could readily understand the reputation she enjoyed as the most beautiful woman in Ireland, the inspiration of the whole revolutionary movement. She was the most exquisitely fashioned creature I have ever seen. Her beauty was startling. In her, the youth of the country saw all that was magnificent in Ireland.[14]

Her recollection may have been shaped by the event's retrospective significance – others recalled Gonne's appearance and histrionic acting in less flattering terms – but there is little doubt that her 'stage presence and her fiery reputation elevated the part of Cathleen from polemic to dramatic grandeur'.[15] Her performance, Stephen Gwynn believed, 'stirred the audience as I have never seen another audience stirred'.[16] The play also owed its influence to Yeats's powerful evocation of the Fenian spirit, which, in contrast to his more mystical offerings, appealed emotionally to Inghinidhe na hÉireann's followers: Máire recalled an 'audience vibrating with enthusiasm and quick to seize every point'.[17] After the performance she met for the first time the 'pleasant if at times rather condescending' Lady Gregory as she congratulated the cast backstage:

Máire Nic Shiubhlaigh models a costume from *Deirdre* (1902), George Russell's dramatic retelling of the story of Deirdre of the Sorrows from the Ulster Cycle mythology (NLI, PD 2159/TX/40/2).

We saw her talking earnestly with the Fays and Æ, pointing at parts of the stage, apparently suggesting improvements and renovations. Although we did not know it, we were witnessing the conception of the Irish National Theatre Society and the real beginning of the movement that was to bring us into the Abbey Theatre.[18]

The Irish National Theatre Society was a merger of the Fay brothers' Irish National Dramatic Company and the Irish Literary Theatre. Founded by Yeats, Gregory and Edward Martyn in 1899, the latter had collapsed because of a lack of funding and its limited appeal. In some respects, the collaboration seemed ideal. Yeats and Gregory provided artistic credibility, prestige and access to patronage, while Fay's company supplied the actors and commitment required for creating a national theatre movement with few resources.[19] The use of amateur performers, acting naturalistically in their own accents, lent a vitality missing from the Irish Literary Theatre's productions, which had relied on professional English actors. As Máire observed, 'English voices, no matter how well trained, could never lend themselves effectively to the expression of Irish idiom'. The two groups had similar objectives: to create a national theatre for the reflection of Irish thought, to provide an alternative to the popular British entertainment that dominated Dublin's cultural life, and to consign stage-Irishness to the past. The literary ambitions of Yeats and Gregory aligned, if uneasily, with the moral and political aspirations of the Irish-Ireland movement from which Inghinidhe na hÉireann emerged. The desire of both groups to establish a national theatre, as Máire noted, also reflected a wider European 'revolt against the commercialism and artificiality of the professional theatre'.

But the merger was far from a meeting of minds. The most obvious fault-line was political. From the outset, there was a discernible gap between Yeats's artistic aspirations and the radical nationalism of the Fays' players. Although Yeats adopted nationalist positions on certain issues, including the recent royal visit, he advocated a theatre movement 'which has no propaganda but that of good art'.[20] In contrast, Frank Fay – who in his capacity as theatre critic for Arthur Griffith's *United Irishman* had denounced Yeats's preoccupation with fairies as being of little use to the nation – had a more instrumental conception of the role of theatre:

all played behind a green
gauze which gave a very
weird effect. we, behind it
could n't see anyone in front
which was an advantage
for we were all very nervous
coming up to the show we
had to rehearse nearly
every night. and we were
all working in the daytime
so I need hardly tell you
it was a real labour of
love for all of us, we did
not know what would come
out of it but we were
working for something. Then
W B Yeats came along with
"Kathleen ni Houlihan" which
he had written for Miss Maud
Gonne, she brought it down
to our rehearsal and

and suggested that it could
go on with "Deirdre" on
Easter Monday & Tuesday 1902
everyone was delighted with
the play and Maud Gonne
was a perfect Kathleen
I played a small part in
it. After hard work
they were produced in St
Teresas Hall Clarendon St
Dublin under the auspices
of "Inghinidhe na hEireann" they
were a huge success, of a
crowded house, and an audience
vibrating with enthusiasm
and quick to seize every point
and to grasp every situation
be an augury for the success
of W G Fays experiment in
the production of Irish plays
by Irish players then the
future of Irish National

Dramatic Company should
be a bright one, However after
this first performance, "The
National Theatre Society" was
formed (W B Yeats President
Vice presidents Maud Gonne.
Douglas Hyde, George Russell.
Stage manager W G Fay and
Fred Ryan Secretary) to continue
if possible on a more permanent
basis – the work begun by
the Irish Literary Theatre.
and it has grown out of the
movement which the Literary
Theatre inaugurated – its
objects are to create an
Irish National Theatre by
producing plays in English
and Irish written by Irish
writers on Irish subjects, a
such, dramatic works of
foreign authors as would

Máire Nic Shiubhlaigh recalls, in later life,
how the Fay brothers' first production
of *Cathleen ni Houlihan* in 1902 led
to the founding of the Irish National
Theatre Society (NLI, MS 49,752).

The interior of the Irish National Theatre Society's first theatre, a shabby hall at 34 Lower Camden Street (NPA, PC 97/Lot 50/24).

Scene-painter, comedian, actor, producer and strict disciplinarian Willie Fay (1872–1947) at work at the INTS's Camden Street theatre (NPA, PC 97/Lot 50/25).

> Let Mr Yeats give us plays in verse or prose that will rouse
> this sleeping land. There is a herd of Saxon and other swine
> fattening on us. They must be swept into the sea with the
> pestilent breed of West Britons with which we are troubled,
> or they will sweep us there.[21]

Notwithstanding such rhetorical flourishes, the Fays were committed more to theatrical enterprise than to nationalist propaganda; the more pressing source of conflict within the Irish National Theatre Society stemmed from the political commitment of Inghinidhe na hÉireann actors like Máire. Viewing theatre as a means to an end, they saw the Society 'as a part of the broader nationalist movement'.[22] These tensions overlapped with less explicitly articulated class and sectarian distinctions. While the triumvirate who came to control the Society were middle-class or upper-class Protestants, its members were overwhelmingly Catholic and working class. Yeats's awareness of these differences was reflected in his description of the actors as 'shop-girls' (which Máire was), and his observation to Synge that women of Máire's class did not have 'sensitive bodies'.[23]

Although these tensions would ultimately split the Society, and lead to recurring crises over many years, all would later recall with nostalgia how in these early years, as Yeats observed, they strove together 'in little halls, generally in some shabby, out-of-the-way street' to create a national theatre movement.[24] In 1903 they acquired a semi-derelict hall, accessed through a door between a butcher's shop and a grocery in Camden Street. For Máire, it was the first Irish theatre:

> Though, as we later discovered, it was completely unsuitable
> for public performances, it became our first headquarters,
> not merely a rehearsal room, but a meeting-place, where,
> with complete freedom, we discussed our ambitions with
> each other and the many outsiders who became interested
> in our work. Here, more than anywhere else, were the
> foundations of the theatre laid. It was here that we gathered
> around us that homogenous collection of politicians, artists,
> poets and dramatists who formed the core of the movement
> … It was here, too, that we received our first touring offer;
> that we discussed the opening of the Abbey.

Chapter 3

Máire

1904–16

JOHN MILLINGTON SYNGE.

J. M. Synge (1871–1909). Although Yeats lauded Synge for his ability to 'go to the Aran islands and express a life that has never found expression', many nationalists were appalled by the playwright's unheroic depiction of the western peasant. Drawing by Ben Bay (NLI, PD 2159/TX/3/67).

The little halls where we performed could not hold a couple of hundred people at the utmost and our audience was often not more than twenty or thirty, and we performed but two or three times a month and during our periods of quarrelling not even that. But there was no lack of leading articles, we were from the first a recognised public danger. Two events brought us victory, a friend gave us a theatre, and we found a strange man of genius, John Synge.

—W. B. Yeats, 1923[1]

Amateur theatre offered Máire Nic Shiubhlaigh a means of self-expression and political engagement. Central to this was the egalitarian nature of the Irish National Theatre Society, which met as a group to decide which plays to stage, and how to perform them. In an era when there were few opportunities for women to interact with men as equals, this was a liberating experience. During the same period, Máire became a part of another cultural initiative that brought her into closer contact with the Yeats family. Run by W. B. Yeats's sisters, Susan ('Lily') and Elizabeth ('Lollie'), Dun Emer

Industries was a craft enterprise specialising in embroidery, fabrics and printing. Máire was treading a well-worn path: 'Dun Emer became a way-station, almost a rite of passage, for many young women involved in nationalist cultural enterprises: future writers, painters, Sinn Féin activists and Abbey actresses served their time there.'[2] She became friendly with the poet's sisters and his father, John B. Yeats, whose abilities as a portrait painter outweighed his business acumen. According to Nic Shiubhlaigh family lore, John, although more than four decades older than her, fell in love with Máire; he certainly made her the subject of two striking portraits.[3]

Máire's relations with W. B Yeats – fast becoming the dominant power within the Irish National Theatre Society – were less warm. She recalled him as 'always in the shadows' in the company's early days, when they rehearsed in the homes of such supporters as George Russell or in the Coffee Palace (when Willie Fay was flush). Yeats 'looked strangely out of place with his flowing cravat, loose clothes and unruly poet's hair beside us in our work-a-day clothes'. She considered him a poseur, although one capable of

EMBROIDERY . . LILY YEATS.
HAND PRESS . . ELIZABETH C. YEATS.

DUN EMER INDUSTRIES. LTD.,
DUNDRUM. CO. DUBLIN, IRELAND.

DUBLIN DEPOT, 28 CLARE STREET.

Hely's, Limited, Dame Street, Dublin.

Established by W. B. Yeats's sisters, Lily and Elizabeth, Dun Emer specialised in printing and crafts such as embroidery. Máire Nic Shiubhlaigh can be seen at work third from right (NPA, PC 97/Lot 50/35).

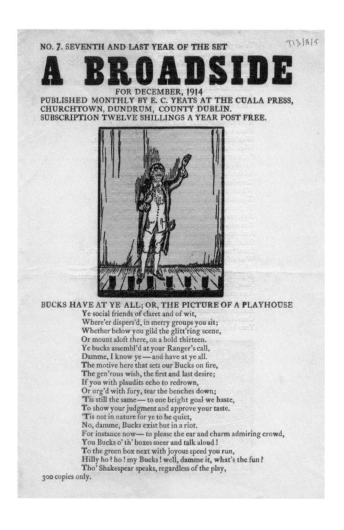

NO. 7. SEVENTH AND LAST YEAR OF THE SET   T13/A/5

A BROADSIDE
FOR DECEMBER, 1914
PUBLISHED MONTHLY BY E. C. YEATS AT THE CUALA PRESS,
CHURCHTOWN, DUNDRUM, COUNTY DUBLIN.
SUBSCRIPTION TWELVE SHILLINGS A YEAR POST FREE.

BUCKS HAVE AT YE ALL; OR, THE PICTURE OF A PLAYHOUSE
Ye social friends of claret and of wit,
Where'er dispers'd, in merry groups you sit;
Whether below you gild the glitt'ring scene,
Or mount aloft there, on a bold thirteen.
Ye bucks assembl'd at your Ranger's call,
Damme, I know ye — and have at ye all.
The motive here that sets our Bucks on fire,
The gen'rous wish, the first and last desire;
If you with plaudits echo to redrown,
Or urg'd with fury, tear the benches down;
'Tis still the same — to one bright goal we haste,
To show your judgment and approve your taste.
'Tis not in nature for ye to be quiet,
No, damme, Bucks exist but in a riot.
For instance now — to please the ear and charm admiring crowd,
You Bucks o' th' boxes sneer and talk aloud !
To the green box next with joyous speed you run,
Hilly ho ! ho ! my Bucks ! well, damme it, what's the fun ?
Tho' Shakespear speaks, regardless of the play,
300 copies only.

Published by Elizabeth Yeats,
Cuala Press's broadsides combined
W.B. Yeats's poetry and ballads
with Jack B. Yeats's illustrations.
Imitating the cheap ballad sheets
sold at nineteenth-century fairs, they
featured patriotic or, as in this case,
boisterous themes (HL, T13/A/5).

transforming himself from a haughty mysticism – 'one got the impression that he looked through and beyond you towards another world' – to a 'vigour almost terrifying in its finality'. She witnessed at first hand his intimidating ability to 'crush all who opposed him with the sheer force of his personality'.

Although their audiences in the dank Camden Street Hall declined, and the critical responses became less effusive, an offer by the Irish Literary Society for the company to tour England in 1903 – where their performances (and aims) were warmly received – extended an important lifeline. Moving to Molesworth Hall, the Irish National Theatre Society embarked on its 'most electric season yet' that autumn.⁴ Yeats's *The King's Threshold* was followed by a new play, *In the Shadow of the Glen,* by an unknown journalist, John Millington Synge. The plot Máire judged not original, but the treatment was. It was completely different to anything we had known before; the play itself was a masterpiece of dramatic construction. It was, in fact, the first of the Irish 'realist' dramas, and the quiet young man who sat unobtrusively in the background while Lady Gregory read aloud his words was to take his place among the greatest dramatists the Irish theatre produced.

The story of Nora Burke – a young woman who deceives her older husband, and abandons her lover, to wander the roads with a tramp – also caused public outrage. Synge's unsentimental depiction of the rural peasantry so idealised by urban nationalists led to denunciations of his play as 'un-Irish'. Many of the political controversies that followed would centre on the same tension between romantic and realist depictions of Irishness.

The decision to stage Synge's play brought to a head tensions within the Irish National Theatre Society. Several leading actors departed, while nationalist patrons of stature, notably Maud Gonne and Douglas Hyde, broke with the Society over what they perceived as its abandonment of its propagandistic imperatives.[5] Regarding Synge's portrait of rural society as 'unpleasant if realistic', Máire seems not to have shared these reservations. Although she described the press furore as 'stupid and ridiculous', she found the criticism of such advanced nationalists as Arthur Griffith, whose politics

W. B. Yeats, c. 1905. Photograph by Alvin Langdon Coburn. Photogravure (GI, 90764732).

Journalist, writer, artist and pioneer of co-operativism, George Russell played a leading role in the early years of the Irish National Theatre Society. Portrait by Casimir Markievicz, husband of Constance (HLG).

she shared, 'the saddest aspect of the whole unnecessary controversy'. The resulting rift between the Society and Inghinidhe na hÉireann (who demanded their props back) placed Máire in a difficult position.[6] However, the play offered Máire her first major role. Drawing from the lyrical dialect of the Aran Islands (where Yeats had sent Synge for inspiration), the play's dialogue – 'neither verse nor prose' – posed challenges. 'At first I found Synge's lines almost impossible to learn and deliver,' Máire recalled. 'Every passage brought some new difficulty and we would all stumble through the speeches until the tempo in which they were written was finally discovered.' Her 'erotically charged' performance as Nora won critical acclaim. Praised as a 'tragedienne of power and intensity', with a 'strange, wan, disquieting beauty', Máire was reputed to possess 'one of the most beautiful speaking voices which the young Irish theatre produced.'[7]

With Synge's arrival, the reputation of the Irish National Theatre Society soared. Máire played a small role in its next play, Synge's *Riders to the Sea*, which was hailed as a masterpiece. Its success intensified the pressures within the Society, which increasingly focused on the intertwined issues of creeping professionalisation and the tension between propaganda and art. The appointment of a reading committee (headed by Yeats) had undermined the Society's collective ethos, prompting suspicions about political bias in the selection of its plays. The rejection of Padraic Colum's anti-recruitment play *The Saxon Shillin'* led to the formation of a rival Cumann na nGaedheal theatre company, staffed by disgruntled Irish National Theatre Society players.[8]

Against this background, the role of Annie Horniman would prove crucial in both the establishment of the Abbey Theatre and the disintegration of the society that founded it. An heiress born in London, Horniman devoted much of her wealth (earned by her grandfather, a Quaker tea-merchant) to the arts. She was a patron of the Irish National Theatre Society, and her offer to provide £1,000 allowed Yeats to secure the disused Mechanics' Institute in Lower Abbey Street as a permanent home for the Society. Although acknowledging that Horniman's patronage 'placed the Irish National Theatre Society on its feet', Máire also believed it was responsible for 'the death of the original National Theatre Society'. Horniman, she observed, was not interested in their company 'as an Irish national-co-operative movement but as a society with a fresh approach to drama'.[9] Their new patron, who objected even to the retention of the word

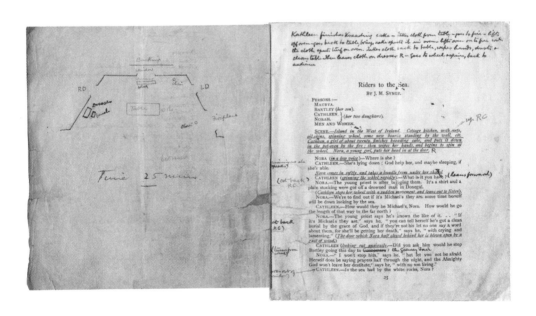

Excerpt from the prompt script for J. M. Synge's *Riders to the Sea* (1902), first performed at Dublin's Molesworth Hall in 1904. One of the great one-act plays, it depicts the harsh lives of Aran Island fishermen (AT).

'national' in its title, would not have disagreed. As Horniman told Synge, 'If anyone thinks that "Irish" or "National" are anything to me beyond empty words used to distinguish a society, merely a trifle for convenience, they are much mistaken.'[10]

On 27 December 1904 the Abbey Theatre opened to the public. From the beginning, Máire felt that the small theatre had an 'atmosphere which led to a feeling of intimacy between player and auditor.' Her status as one of the theatre's leading ladies was confirmed by the displaying of her portrait – alongside those of W. B. Yeats, the Fays and Annie Horniman – in the vestibule.

> That night I played Kathleen Ni Houlihan for the first time. This made the occasion doubly memorable for me. I suppose every player has a favourite part. This was mine.

Although the opening attracted the great and the good, the collective ethos of the Irish National Theatre Society was demonstrated by the presence on stage of Máire's brother Frank, while two of her sisters, Annie and Gypsy, sold programmes. Backstage, her mother worked as wardrobe mistress, while her father was responsible for much of the Society's printing. Máire recalled this period with nostalgia:

> For a long time we only played 3 nights a month, Saturday, Mon. & Tue., and indeed at times you could count the audience. We often looked out between the curtains to see who was in. It was a real joy to work in the Abbey in the early days. Everyone was so friendly. The actors were real pals. J. M. Synge, a very charming man, would sit among us making cigarettes for us.[11]

These were bittersweet memories. In retrospect, the founding of the Abbey marked the end of the co-operativist era:

Featuring Queen Maeve, an Irish wolfhound and a rising sun, the Irish National Theatre Society's emblem was designed by Elinor Monsell (1871–1954), an illustrator at Dun Emer press. This is an early working proof of the pear woodcut print (NLI, PD/2159/TX/28/1).

Less than six months after our opening, there was dissention within the group. Before the year was fully ended, the original Irish National Theatre Society was dead, and most of its members had left the Abbey.

By the following year, the Irish National Theatre Society had been restructured as a limited company controlled by an executive of three (Yeats, Gregory and Synge), an initiative described by Yeats as putting 'an end to democracy in the theatre'. The consequences were predictable. Noting the 'increasingly mutinous' spirit of the actors, Roy Foster later observed that 'people like the Walkers had come into the theatre for political self-realization as much as for stage-struck dazzlement.'[12] For Máire, professionalisation was incompatible with the Society's ethos:

> Some of the friendliness, the comradeship, vanished soon after the new arrangement came into force. When the directorate began to make decisions on certain matters without notifying the organisation as a whole, more and more of the players began to refer regretfully to the abandonment of the old policy of co-operation; the fears of others that the national ideals of the movement were in danger of being shelved were intensified.[13]

secured a hall in Camden St
at No 34 at the back of an egg
and Butter Shop, you know the
kind of shop that had boxes of
eggs outside in front of the
window and after six oc they
were put into the hall, well we
had to pass along the narrow
hall to our work room at
the back where all our work
was done making scenery and
Costumes rehearsing plays at
one end where there was a
pealform erected hammering
Going on at the other end for
everyone took a hand in the
work of course the poets I am
sure could hardly hold a
hammer however they had
other things to do for we had
Padraic Colum Seumas o'sullivan
George Roberts James Cousins and
Sometimes James Joyce would tir
in with Oliver Gogarty about this
time. Lady Gregory would come

Máire Nic Shiubhlaigh recalls the
egalitarian spirit that characterised
the early days of the Irish National
Theatre Society (NLI, MS 49,752).

& our rehearsals she had written
her play Twenty five which was
to go on with our next performance
which we were working for. The
held in the Molesworth Hall in
Molesworth St. where nearly all
our shows were held till we
went to the Abbey, well the Lady
Gregory would bring up a huge
Barm Brack all the way from
Gort from her Bakers there &
it would come twice a year &
we loved it for our cup of Tea
at 9 oc every evening I can
tell you no matter how busy
one of us would make the Tea
and sit round on boxes &
enjoy Lady Gregorys cake. we
were rehearsing ~~the~~
Padraic Colums Broken Soil for
our next performance. and while
we were in London Mrs Horniman
was very impressed with our work
she was at the time very keen on
Repertory Theatres in England she
had I think one in Manchester

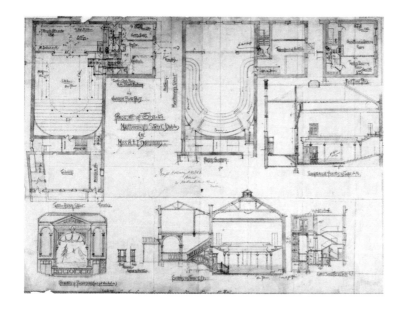

Architect and theatre-buff
Joseph Holloway's plans for the
Abbey Theatre (NLI, AD2193).

She attributed her decision to abandon the Abbey to these changes:

> Relations became rather strained. Commercialism was
> about to creep in and spoil the friendly atmosphere
> which was the whole charm about our acting.[14]

Yeats, unsurprisingly, remembered it all differently. He recalled that the theatre had been paralysed by its 'preposterous' organisation, as 'players and authors all sat together and settled by vote what play should be performed and who should play it' until order was restored when 'Lady Gregory and John Synge and I were put in control'.[15]

Máire's memoir does not record some of the other factors that deepened her disenchantment. In December 1905 she had plunged the Abbey into crisis by rejecting as insulting Yeats's conciliatory offer of an additional post as wardrobe-mistress to supplement her salary, and she resisted prolonged pressure to sign a new contract. Although Yeats, who relished conflict, threatened to sue her, he was forced to back down when Gregory and Synge (who chided Yeats for his bullying attitude) refused to support him. Describing his son as a 'mad poet' in the 'hands of vulgar intriguers', John B. Yeats also took Máire's side.[16] Seeking refuge from W. B. Yeats – she recalled

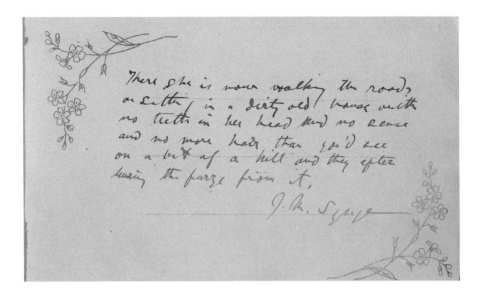

Entry by J. M. Synge in Máire
Nic Shiubhlaigh's autograph
book (NLI, MS 34,235).

him 'being shaken by fits of the most uncontrollable rage' – Máire fled to Lily and Lollie, who complained to Lady Gregory about their brother's 'sneery and offensive' treatment of Máire. The messy circumstances of Máire's departure were summarised by Adrian Frazier, who noted that she was

> upset because her brother [Frank] was upset, because
> Sara Allgood was paid more, because Yeats attacked
> her vanity, because he tried to make her think little
> of herself, because it was immodest for a woman to
> examine the wardrobes of the male actors (especially,
> Lady Gregory remarked in sympathy, the wardrobes
> of new employees 'we know not of what class'),
> because it seemed that both Yeats and Fay – the whole
> management – had turned against her.

Joseph Holloway described the resulting chain reaction: 'Frank Walker left "in a hump" at being offered fifteen shillings a week, taking his sister, his sister taking her lover [George] Starkey'.[17]

Programme for *The Well of the Saints* (1905). An influential dark comedy, Synge's first three-act play tells the story of two blind beggars who become disenchanted with the seeing world after their vision is restored by a wandering saint (NLI, EPH C822).

Máire Nic Shiubhlaigh was lauded for her performance as Queen Gormleith in Lady Gregory's *Kincora* (1905). A heroic, sexually charged Celt, Gormleith's love of conflict leads her to betray Brian Boru in favour of the foreign invaders (NPA, PC 97/Lot 50/05).

Máire may have remained at the Abbey had she been better treated, but the underlying issues that led to her departure were those that had divided the Irish National Theatre Society from the outset. She felt Horniman's offer of an annual subsidy of £500 to pay for full-time actors and a producer was inimical to the Society's co-operative ethos. Although two-thirds of the Society's remaining membership opposed the initiative, on the grounds that it would compromise the Abbey's 'independence as a national movement', the ruling triumvirate's support for the measure had been sufficient to implement it. The disputes that followed, Frazier notes, resulted from members of an idealistic enterprise being treated as paid employees of a commercial business. Horniman's generosity ended Máire's prospects of a career on the stage: 'I gave up what might have been a wonderful career for me,' she recalled, 'but it was not going to be a National Theatre. It never has been.'[18]

While Máire remained at the Abbey to serve out her contract – and later returned for a short period – her subsequent stage career reflected her commitment to her vision of theatre 'as an integral part of the national movement'. Along with other Abbey refugees, she found a more congenial environment in amateur companies such as Edward Martyn's Theatre of Ireland (which she helped to establish in 1906). Their political legacy would prove greater than their artistic impact.

Although her portrait remained prominently displayed at the Abbey, Máire came to believe that her contribution to the founding of the theatre had been forgotten. The jockeying for ownership of the National Theatre's legacy had actually predated the Abbey's establishment. By 1903 Yeats saw himself as the guiding spirit of the Irish National Theatre Society – 'my little theatre' – whose origins he located firmly in his Irish Literary Theatre. He told the press that the latter experiment had led him to realise the need to educate 'our own countrymen' for the stage:

> 'Let us go to the clerks and the shop girls,' one of us said, 'and train them for the stage after their work hours.' Let us try. We found the task far easier than we expected … We formed a company and rehearsed at night.[19]

Portrait of Annie Horniman (1860–1937) by John Butler Yeats. Despite her generous patronage, Horniman's antipathy to the INTS's political idealism alienated nationalists, as did her refusal to allow the theatre to sell sixpenny seats for the pit (AT).

Willie Fay (1872–1947) by John Butler Yeats. Like most of its founding members, Fay left the Abbey after falling out with its directorate, but the Fay brothers were pivotal in transforming a literary experiment into a living theatre (AT).

Such claims infuriated the Fays and Inghinidhe na hÉireann's activists. As Maud Gonne raged to Yeats,

> you forget the existence of the National Theatre Society was originally due to Inginide na hEireann and Cumann na Gaedhal … who financed each of Fay's first attempts at National performances … all this because we wanted a NATIONAL Theatre Co. to help us combat the influence of the low English theatres & music halls.[20]

Wearied by these rows, George Russell (whom Máire regarded as 'the real leader of our movement' in its early days) told Yeats of his intention to leave the Abbey: 'Remember that this dramatic society started among these people who came together & invited you in as President and you will see the thing in their point of view.'[21]

In his foreword to Máire's memoir, Padraic Colum insisted that the Abbey was 'the product of more than one man's genius'. As far as posterity was concerned, as Roy Foster has noted, the theatre's other founders 'were irretrievably swept aside into subordinate roles' by Yeats's 'increasingly powerful sense of his own history'.[22] Máire's career highlights the Abbey's ambivalent relationship with nationalism. Indeed, some have questioned the idea of the Abbey as a nationalist theatre, arguing that it owed more to Yeats's and Gregory's maverick Irish unionist tradition than to 'any of the wide variety of political nationalisms'.[23] Máire's political activism prior to joining the Abbey, and the importance of family influences in shaping her outlook, demonstrate how her involvement with the Abbey was more a consequence than a cause of her commitment to separatism. Despite her love of theatre, she insisted that her commitment to revolutionary activism rather than to a career on the stage was freely chosen:

> My great desire was to work in every way I knew for the complete national independence of Ireland. That above all. It was my great aim in life. Anything that threatened to occupy me to its exclusion I considered a danger.[24]

Yeats's influence had sent her out of the Abbey Theatre, rather than into the GPO.

A sketch from Máire Nic Shiubhlaigh's autograph book (NLI, MS 34,235)

Chapter 4

Peadar Kearney

1883–1916

A youthful Peadar Kearney (AT).

Towards the end of the evening, when everybody
was more or less drunk, [Standish James] O'Grady
spoke. He was very drunk, but neither his voice
nor his manner showed it ... He stood between
two tables, touching one or the other for support,
and said in a low penetrating voice: 'We have now
a literary movement, it is not very important; it
will be followed by a political movement, that will
not be very important; then must come a military
movement, that will be important indeed.' [Robert
Yelverton] Tyrrell, Professor of Greek in Trinity
College, known to scholars for his share in the
Tyrrell-Purser edition of Cicero's Letters, a Unionist,
but very drunk, led the applause. —W. B. Yeats's recollection of
a dinner in Dublin in 1899 given in his honour by T. P. Gill [1]

The first person to enter the derelict Mechanics' Institute in 1904 was Peadar Kearney. He was there to help his friend Seán Barlow, stage carpenter (and later stage manager) for the Irish National Theatre Society. The venue's association with theatre, cultural nationalism and the cultivation of disaffection preceded the founding of the Abbey Theatre. Originally established in 1820 by the cultured, handsome and ill-fated magistrate and theatre impresario Frederick 'Buck' Jones, the Royal Theatre Opera House was replaced, following a fire, by the Princess Theatre. In 1849 the building became the temporary home of the Dublin Mechanics' Institute, which, in characteristic Victorian pursuit of self-improvement, established a library and reading rooms. There, Young Irelanders, such as John Mitchel, met to consult periodicals, contemplate revolution and lecture on their vision of Ireland. In the 1850s the institute was racked by several years of infighting between Catholics and socialists following the library's accession of two questionable books, Count von Born's *Monachologia, or, Handbook of the Natural History of Monks* and William Sanger's *The History of Prostitution*.[2] By 1861, however, it had recovered sufficiently to host one of the most notable acts of revolutionary theatre in nineteenth-century Ireland, the lying in state of the Young Ireland revolutionary and escaper from Van Diemen's Land (Tasmania) Terence Bellew MacManus, whom the Fenians had enterprisingly exhumed from his grave in San Francisco. Although Archbishop Paul Cullen refused to allow the Pro-Cathedral to be used for his funeral, the Irish Republican Brotherhood orchestrated one of the largest funerals witnessed in Ireland.[3] Several years later, Frederick Engels – accompanied by his Manchester-Irish partner, Lizzie Burns, and Karl Marx's daughter Eleanor – spoke at the Mechanics' Institute. Thereafter, the venue reverted to its original theatrical function, specialising in 'blood-curdling and hair-raising' dramas.[4]

In the years before the Irish National Theatre Society moved in, the premises had witnessed a sharp decline, becoming a penny gaff for 'the submerged tenth where, amid the reek of cheap tobacco and ribald jokes, a lady in tawdry tinsel pathetically appealed to her grimy and not very attentive audience to join the chorus'.[5] Even less auspiciously, the site paid for by Annie Horniman's donation encompassed part of the old city morgue. When Peadar Kearney stepped through the door of the library (which would become the Peacock Theatre), 'the old newspapers and periodicals were lying on the table exactly as they had been left when the key was turned in the lock some years previously.' He later recalled how Barlow conscientiously

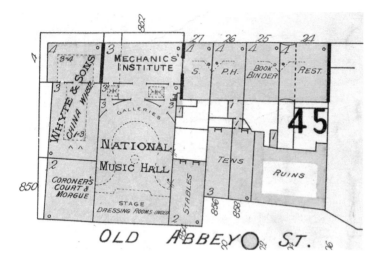

The site on which the Abbey Theatre was established was previously occupied by the Mechanics' Institute. Detail from Fire Insurance Map of Dublin by Charles E. Goad, 1893 (TCD).

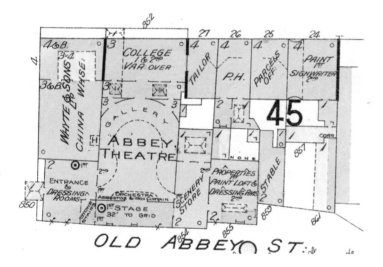

The layout of the Abbey Theatre's stage and auditorium differed little from its predecessor, but the site expanded beyond the Mechanics' Institute to include the Coroner's Court and Morgue and other surrounding premises. Detail from Fire Insurance Map of Dublin by Charles E. Goad, 1926 (TCD).

prevented him from helping himself to the books.[6] Although Peadar's role at the Abbey, where he would work for over a decade, was behind rather than on the stage, he chose to remain there because 'his heart was in the theatre'.[7]

Peter Paul Kearney was born in Dorset Street, Dublin, on 12 December 1883, the eldest of the three sons and three daughters of John Kearney and Katie McGuinness. John was previously a prosperous grocer, but the failure of his business reduced his family to a precarious livelihood. Peadar, like Máire Nic Shiubhlaigh, was the product of a radical family background. An early memory was the punishment meted out at the Model School in Schoolhouse Lane when he was wrongly blamed for his father's having torn a jingoistic British poem from his textbook. John routinely brought Peadar to visit historic locations associated with Dublin's insurrections, a formative experience shared by many revolutionaries. One such spot, as chance would have it, was the High Street house of his father's friend Matthew Walker, where 'father and son often sat chatting in the drawing-room where had been waked in 1798 the body of the Father of Irish Republicanism – Theobald Wolfe Tone'. Presumably, they were sometimes joined by Matthew's daughter Máire, who was the same age as Peadar.[8] Among the locations father and son also visited was the Mechanics' Institute library. Years later, Peadar vividly recalled learning there for the first time the horrific fate of the Manchester Martyrs, hanged for love of country on a grey November morning: 'As Willie Rooney reached the climax, his voice had almost fallen to a whisper, but so quiet was the room that every syllable was clearly audible.'

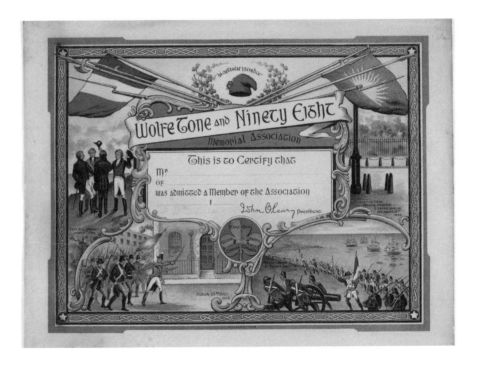

A membership card for the Wolfe Tone and Ninety Eight Memorial Association featuring Irish and French republican motifs. Many of the revolutionary generation were politicised by the 1798 centenary (NMI HH/1940/44/35).

According to Peadar's nephew and biographer, the writer and theatre costumier Séamus de Búrca (Jimmy Bourke), he applied himself neither to education nor to work, coasting by on a series of 'blind-alley jobs', including a well-paid position in a Sackville Street billiard-room, where he marked for John Redmond, leader of the Irish Party. Peadar was short, wiry and terse, and his intelligence, lack of deference (a Fenian trait) and commitment to trade union principles led to clashes with employers and authority figures throughout his life. Although aware of the 1798 centenary, Peadar recalled that the revival had left him unmoved until a moment of transformation, triggered by the death of William Rooney, founder of the Celtic Literary Society and a leading ideologue of the cultural revival, in March 1901. According to de Búrca,

> Peadar bought a halfpenny paper and read about the early, nationally tragic death of the man he had heard and seen in the Mechanics' Institute, and then he remembered all his father had taught him about Robert Emmet and Wolfe Tone and John Mitchel; and from that day Peadar Kearney never looked back. What was dormant inside awoke. He joined the Willie Rooney Branch of the Gaelic League.[9]

Some caution is required with this account. In crafting their narratives of rebellion, many separatists felt the need to identify such an epiphany. Clearly, as for countless separatists, the Gaelic League facilitated Kearney's radicalisation. De Búrca's biography, based on conversations with Peadar, describes his commitment to the Irish language in unusually utilitarian terms:

> Kearney's first reason for learning Irish was political. Separation from England at the time being impracticable, he resolved to be separate in language. But gradually a love of the language and all that it stood for superseded the first reason.[10]

Peadar regarded the Irish classes he gave from 1907 as a form of political activism. So did many of his students, including one of his first, Seán O'Casey, with whom he became friendly. The Gaelic League also enabled Peadar's radicalisation in a more direct form. The Rooney Branch he joined – where he first met Seán Barlow – was affiliated to Cumann na nGaedheal, founded in 1900 by Rooney and Arthur Griffith. With Peadar moving in these circles, and holding the right outlook, it was only a matter of time before he was sounded out about joining the IRB. In July 1903, on a busy Dublin street, he was sworn in by the prominent GAA official Dan McCarthy, 'the transaction being carried out as we picked our way through the shopping crowds'.[11] One of the first Fenian events he participated in was the Robert Emmet centenary, when several thousand men marched quietly through Dublin – a demonstration Peadar regarded as marking a new, more determined phase of the movement. John O'Leary, a veteran Fenian (and *de jure* president of the Irish Republic), delivered the short oration at the site of Emmet's execution in Thomas Street: 'My friends, until Emmet's epitaph be written, you and I have little to say, but we have much to do.'

Despite the frisson generated by such incidents, the swearing of a secret oath to the IRB was a considerably less portentous undertaking than it would later seem. Widely regarded as moribund, the republican ideology and physical-force methods the Fenians advocated had seldom been weaker or had less popular support. Although its clandestine nature and its historical association with insurrection ensured an aura of menace, 'the Organisation' was little more than an elaborate structure of fund-raising committees. The insurrectionary tradition the IRB embodied was sometimes eulogised by constitutional nationalist politicians but only as a romantic vestige of Irish history long consigned to the past by the Irish Party's more prosaic but effective methods. The elderly profile of the IRB's membership and the enjoyable social side to its activities (which included picnics, choral singing and drinking), combined with its uncompromising revolutionary rhetoric, also ensured that the Fenians were viciously mocked as 'prating mock rebels' by influential nationalists like D. P. Moran.[12]

Peadar's circle, masquerading as the Wolfe Tone Memorial Association, met monthly at 41 Parnell Square. The main business conducted was collecting subscriptions, organising commemorative events and initiating – often from a demoralisingly small pool of qualified candidates – those considered 'all right'. One of the IRB's great difficulties, Peadar conceded, was keeping 'the morale of the members up to par during a period

Wolfe Tone Memorial Committee

EMMET ANNIVERSARY CELEBRATION
(UNDER THE MANAGEMENT OF Messrs. J. T. JAMESON & SON).
IN
ROUND ROOM, ROTUNDA
ON
Thursday, 4th March, 1915,
AT 8 O'CLOCK.

Concert, Drama, Pictures

The Commemoration Address
(ILLUSTRATED)
WILL BE DELIVERED BY
MR. ARTHUR GRIFFITH.

The Production of " The Stranger"
(By SEAMUS O'KELLY)
IS IN THE CAPABLE HANDS OF
Miss Maire Nic Shiubhlaigh.
OTHER ARTISTES INCLUDE

MISS JOAN BURKE.	MR. WM. SHEEHAN,
MISS MOLLY O'BYRNE,	MR. SEAMUS O hAODHA.
MR. GERARD CROFTS.	MR. SEAN CONNOLLY,
THE WHEATLEY TRIO, &c.	

Prices 6d., 1s., 1s. 6d., 2s.
P. Mason, Printer

Among those performing at the Emmet concert organised by the Wolfe Tone Memorial Committee (a Fenian front whose membership included Peadar Kearney) were the future Abbey rebels Máire Nic Shiubhlaigh and Seán Connolly (NLI, EPH B538).

of inactivity. The best of spirits are apt to chafe under the monotony of monthly meeting, with the same dreary routine year in and year out.'[13] Although he believed that the IRB, despite its numerical weakness, had been re-established on a firm basis by 1905, most observers date its revival to Tom Clarke's return from America in 1908, and to the influx of a younger generation of radicals, such as Bulmer Hobson, founder of Na Fianna.[14] Tom Slater recalled how he was recruited by Peadar, whom he met through the Croke Hurling Club, following 'a conversation about nationality'.[15] Peadar further contributed to building support for the organisation during these fallow years by periodically embarking on long cycling tours to organise IRB circles in Leinster. Inevitably, he met his wife as a result of their shared interest in 'national affairs'. In 1914 Peadar married Eva Flanagan, a seventeen-year-old shirt-maker from a poor northside background, despite her family's objections: 'He worshipped her and she thought the world of him.'[16]

To a large extent, it was events beyond the Fenians' control that provided the long-awaited opportunity for insurrection. The Ulster crisis of 1912–14, when Ulster's unionists used the threat of physical force to oppose the Liberal government's efforts to introduce Home Rule (a limited measure of self-government that would have established a devolved assembly in

Dublin), was an important turning-point. The British government's failure to prevent the formation of the Ulster Volunteers in 1913 enabled the IRB to establish the rival Irish Volunteers, which drew on a wide spectrum of nationalist support, including many Redmondites. Infiltrating and controlling such a body was meat and drink to the Fenians, particularly given the polarisation that occurred as the Ulster Volunteer Force – and Irish Volunteers – armed themselves, and the British authorities struggled to maintain control of its Irish policy in the wake of the Curragh Mutiny of March 1914. The outbreak of the First World War weakened the republicans, as Redmond's pro-war position was backed by an overwhelming majority of Volunteers. In the longer run, however, 'England's difficulty' made an insurrection by a radical minority almost inevitable, particularly as popular fears about conscription, and scepticism about Britain's commitment to implementing Home Rule (suspended for the duration), gained ground.

Having risen to a senior level in the Brotherhood – as centre (or head) of his IRB circle he sat on the Dublin centres' board – Peadar Kearney was well informed about the drift to rebellion.[17] Tom Pugh related how Peadar, an assiduous networker ('a great man for getting into all those things'), had urged Tom Clarke to recruit the previously black-balled Patrick Pearse to the IRB once he became aware of his militancy: 'You'll have to get hold of this fellow.'[18] Peadar was present at the major revolutionary set-pieces that preceded 1916: the first meeting of Fianna Éireann in 1909, the IRB's decision to form the Irish Volunteers, the Volunteers' inaugural meeting at the Rotunda, and the gun-running at Howth in July 1914 (when he

A Fianna button badge featuring familiar symbols of 1798, a pike and sunburst (NMI, HE/EW/252h).

narrowly avoided being bayoneted by Scottish Borderers). Given this Zelig-like capacity, it was no surprise that he made it back to Dublin in time for the rebellion. He had been in Liverpool, completing preparations for a performance of St John Ervine's *John Ferguson* at the Royal Court Theatre, when he learnt that the insurrection was imminent. Like the Abbey's other rebels, he had no hesitation in giving priority to revolution over his commitments to the stage. Despite the threat of the manager, Ervine, that he would never work again in theatre, Peadar deserted the tour.[19]

His revolutionary activism notwithstanding, Peadar's life and legacy point more to the importance of culture as a means of political expression. Culture and politics were as intertwined for him as for Máire Nic Shiubhlaigh. A poet, songwriter, painter, dramatist and working-class autodidact, Peadar was a deeply cultured individual, but the principal drive behind his cultural activism was his belief in its importance as a means of political expression. With Seán Barlow he had worked for the Fays since before the establishment of the Irish National Theatre Society. Like Máire, he was present at the Irish National Dramatic Company's first performance of *Cathleen ni Houlihan*. Regarding Yeats's most patriotic play as having done more than any other literary work to influence 'the national resurgence', Peadar liked to recall the climactic moment when Maud Gonne, as Cathleen, predicted the return of her four green fields: 'You simply thought the woman was rising from the dead.'[20] After he joined the Abbey he alternated his work as a stage hand with occasional walk-on parts; playing a drunken insurrectionary in Lennox Robinson's play *The Dreamers*, for example, he was pleased to see 'the servant girls and shop girls in the gallery weeping' at Emmet's plight.[21] As with the Abbey's other radical actors, his political outlook was more clearly expressed on the amateur stage, through the patriotic melodramas he helped his brother-in-law P. J. Bourke (an actor and, later, theatre manager) produce at such venues as the Molesworth Street Hall.

Peadar was also a playwright, albeit from an older, more populist tradition than Yeats. He collaborated with Bourke (whose family he lived with in Dominick Street) on the latter's 1798 plays, such as *When Wexford Rose* (1910). Inevitably, Peadar also wrote his own (unperformed) 1798 plays. Both men drew on a vibrant popular theatrical tradition that encompassed such nationalist playwrights as J. W. Whitbread of the Queen's Theatre in Dublin and Dion Boucicault, who wrote enormously successful melodramas.

Fianna boys at Howth pier strain to land rifles from the *Asgard*, 26 July 1914 (NMI, HE/EW/1548/14/1).

Considered seditious by Dublin Castle (which ordered the removal of their posters from public display), Bourke's more politically charged plays had been barred from the stage of the Abbey.[22] In 1902 the *Freeman's Journal* contrasted the two dramatic milieus in which Peadar operated:

> The Irish Literary Theatre appealed to a limited audience because it was literary. At the other end of the Irish theatrical world we have had for many years an Irish drama that was not literary in either the modern or the Elizabethan acceptation of the term but which – as we know it in the Queen's Theatre – appealed very powerfully to the mind of the average man in Dublin, and especially the average working man. Superior people sneer at what they consider the crude and melodramatic pictures of '98 and other periods of Irish history which from time to time are presented in the oldest and most historic theatre in Dublin. For the most part they are critics who have never witnessed the wonderful influence which even a very plainly-told story of Irish patriotism has on the minds of the honest working-men and working-women of Dublin.[23]

Peadar Kearney's most important literary contribution to politicising his generation derived not from the stage but from his ballad 'A Soldier's Song', which would become the anthem of the Irish revolution. In 1907 he set the words to music composed by Patrick Heeney, 'a quiet, inoffensive man with tender eyes and a passion for music'.[24] They had collaborated since 1903, mostly on marching songs, which they tried out on other members of their hurling club as they hiked across the Dublin Mountains in 'preparation for soldierly duties in the not too distant future'.[25] 'The Soldier's Song', as it became known, was not an overnight success: concert singers found it difficult to sing, and Arthur Griffith declined to print its lyrics in the *United Irishman*.[26] In 1912, in response to its growing popularity among Na Fianna, Bulmer Hobson published the song in *Irish Freedom*. It became better known in 1913, its popularity growing alongside that of the Irish Volunteers. Two of the Abbey's other rebels were tangentially involved in its genesis. Although the place where it was composed is disputed, Ellen Bushell claimed possession of the first manuscript copy of its lyrics, 'which she took down from the lips of the author on the very night the words and music were wedded'. The song was first distributed by Séamus Whelan, a partner in Matthew Walker's Gaelic Press, which printed many of the seditious song-sheets and newspapers that circulated through Dublin.[27] Roy Foster has drawn attention to the importance of this popular print culture – which 'wrote the revolution into the hearts and minds of young radicals far more potently than the poems of Yeats or the fictions of George Moore' – in preparing the way for the violence that followed; equally striking is how such figures as Peadar Kearney and Máire Nic Shiubhlaigh bridged these worlds of high and low nationalist culture.[28]

Although it is undeniably rousing, it is difficult to know why this song in particular came to represent the aspirations of the revolutionary movement. Peadar wrote many similar ballads, such as 'Michael Dwyer', 'The Three-Coloured Ribbon' and 'Whack Fol the Diddle', none of which differs greatly from the banal ballads churned out in vast quantities by the

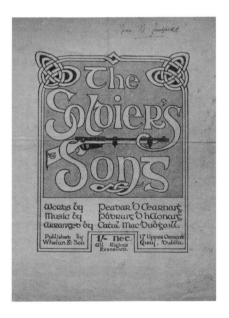

The first printed edition of 'The Soldier's Song' was published by Séamus Whelan in late 1916. The design, incorporating a rifle within a Celtic motif, effectively conveys the song's martial and patriotic appeal (ITMA/16902-SM).

Gaelic Press and its rivals. Like 'God Save Ireland' – its principal rival as the unofficial national anthem – and 'A Nation Once Again', its archaic language and sentiments drew on the early nineteenth-century *Moore's Melodies*.[29] Indeed its generic quality sometimes led to Peadar's authorship being overlooked, as many assumed that the song was a revived traditional ballad. Even its advocates tend to concede its hackneyed lyrics – 'We're children of a fighting race | That never yet has known disgrace' – and awkward rhymes (such as 'sireland' with 'Ireland'). One reason for its emergence was the need for a song to represent that particular generation's experience: the song it displaced, 'God Save Ireland', dated from 1867. 'The Soldier's Song' was also more martial and optimistic than the earlier ballad, which commemorated the Manchester Martyrs as the most recent in a centuries-long tradition of glorious failure:

> Whether on the scaffold high
> Or the battlefield we die,
> Oh, what matter when for Erin dear we fall!

The martial appeal of 'The Soldier's Song' even transcended ideological boundaries. Daniel Kelly was one of several 1916 internees who testified to the enemy's interest in the rebel song:

> We had an escort of four companies of soldiers of the Scottish Highlanders when we left Wakefield Jail. All the prisoners sang 'The Soldier's Song'. That was really the first time I had heard that air. We sang it on the platform while waiting for the train. The officers of the Scottish Highlanders were delighted with it and said it was the best marching air they ever heard. They brought Billy Denn into their carriage. He was a Kilkenny man and a grand singer. He had to sing 'The Soldier's Song' a few times and write it out for them.[30]

In Co. Tipperary, where the local Volunteers conspicuously failed to turn out in 1916, British soldiers enjoyed singing, 'Soldiers are we, who nearly fought for Ireland', when they encountered republicans.[31] In Cork, the same lines were sung defiantly by local girls 'who kept company with British soldiers'.[32]

Whatever its musical qualities, it is difficult to overstate the significance of 'The Soldier's Song' for ordinary revolutionaries. Charles Townshend cites its popularity as a revealing example of the psychological processes that contributed to the 'new collective self-definition' wrought by revolution. He also notes how, after the Rising, Sinn Féin concerts, where such ballads were sung, replaced the pre-war craze for theatrical drama.[33] This may have been due to the more dynamic nature of song: despite its powerful immediacy, theatre was a performance that was observed; singing 'The Soldier's Song' was usually a communal act requiring participation. Many Volunteers who recorded nothing about the ideological appeal of republicanism in their Bureau of Military History witness statements recall vividly when and where they first heard Peadar Kearney's song. 'Going down the hill after the meeting, the crowd fell in behind the band which struck up the air of "A Soldier's Song"', one Limerick Volunteer characteristically remembered, 'and as we marched along I could see in this procession the natural succession of all the Irish forces that had marched along the same route throughout our history.'[34] Although popular before 1916, the song became a phenomenon only after the Easter Rising. As with Yeats's *Cathleen ni Houlihan*, the Rising radically altered how it was received. Its militaristic, Gaelicist, Anglophobic sentiments embodied the emotional appeal of Irish separatism after 1916, when the Easter rebels had proved their valour through blood sacrifice. The Sinn Féin movement, whose popularity rose in tandem with Peadar's song, represented less a rational appeal to republican ideology than an emotional one centred on martial values, national identity and the idea of a heroic, ancient struggle between 'the sons of the Gael' and 'the Saxon foe' so powerfully conveyed in the popular historical narratives that Peadar's generation was raised on.

The politics of militarism. Framed
by Kearney's potent lyrics, Éamon
de Valera, in Irish Volunteer uniform,
addresses a republican rally in Ennis,
Co. Clare, c. 1917 (GI/3247099).

From 1917 its meme-like progress across the country can be traced through countless references in the Bureau of Military History. It is only really through this source – which describes the vast range of contexts in which the song was performed, and the diverse emotions with which it was associated – that its extraordinary appeal can now be appreciated. Volunteers sang 'The Soldier's Song' as they paraded to and from rallies; they sang it at fund-raising events; they sang it as they drilled for battle; they sang it as they waited for besieged barracks to surrender and as they endured trial, transportation and imprisonment. Volunteers were tried for sedition for singing it; they hummed it in custody to enrage the police; and they sang it in prison as they rioted. It was used to express camaraderie, pride, defiance and bravery – to restore spirits after defeat, to avert fear, to intimidate opponents and to express contempt for the enemy. In Dublin, republicans sang it to drown out 'God Save the King' at unionist gatherings; in west Cork an IRA court sentenced an insufficiently patriotic Skibbereen councillor to stand on a porter barrel to sing it; everywhere, children sang it on the streets to annoy the police. At the hospital where his sister lay dying in a coma, one republican learnt from a nun 'that she rallied a bit before she died and, sitting up in the bed, sang "The Soldier's Song" right through in a clear and musical voice, after which she lay back and died.'[35]

As with the centrality of theatre to pre-war separatist activism, the popularity of Peadar's song indicates the extraordinary power of culture – rather than political discourse – to express the emotions and aspirations that motivated his generation to fight and die for Ireland. An insight into the importance of Peadar's contribution to the struggle for independence is provided by Seán Moylan's account of the first time he heard the song that would soon echo through 'every parish in Ireland':

> I arrived in Kiskeam to be greeted by the resonant reveille of Tim [Kiely]'s cornet blaring forth in the notes of 'The Soldiers Song' his belief in a resurgent nationality. I still see him marching from the corner of the lane, towel on shoulder, his huge hairy chest thrusting through his unbuttoned shirt, placing particular emphasis on 'the despot and the slave' as he passed the doorway of a crony, John Daly, who had dared to argue the merits of constitutionalism ...

We cheer ironically as we pass the R.I.C. Barracks, and 'The Soldier's Song', as a cornet solo, once again assails our ears. As we progress the procession swells, each mountain and bog road yields its quota. Each new contingent is greeted with the brazen 'Soldier's Song' and finally we arrived in Kanturk, the meeting place … Strand Street was filled with people. It looked like Croke Park when the whistle goes after the hurling final; but this crowd was silent and expectant. A local singer got on the platform and opened the proceedings with the 'Soldier's Song'. There was a rustle in the crowd betokening the uneasiness felt by rural folk when one of their number makes a public exhibition of himself. Then Tim Kiely, emerging from an inn, a giant refreshed, chimed in with his cornet, his notes echoed off the walls of the houses; the singer faltered and went on, and then, drowning the music, came a defiant joyous full-throated roar from the crowd. No longer could there be any doubt of the success and enthusiasm of the meeting. The speeches did not really matter that day. Instinctively the people knew the terms of the message. They were concerned merely with the sincerity of those who brought it; accepted as a guarantee of that sincerity the story of their participation in the Easter Week Rising; knew now the lesson of Easter Week that a country unfree must be a nation in arms and that there was a place for each one in the Bearna Baoighill.[36]

Chapter 5

Helena Molony

1883–1916

Inghinidhe na hÉireann, c. 1905.
Maud Gonne is centre (behind
the banner, a sunburst on a blue
background), with Helena Molony to
her immediate right (wearing white-
frilled top) (KG, 13PO/1B54/14).

I am separate still!
I am I and not you!
And my mind and my will,
As in secret they grew,
Still are secret; unreached, and
untouched, and not subject to you.

—James Stephens, 'The Red-Haired Man's Wife'[1]

We believe in Ireland there is too much preaching
and too little practice. The chief fault we find
with men is that they talk very big and do
very little and we would like to foster among
Irish women a desire to work rather than talk
about it in the columns of newspapers.

—*Bean na hÉireann*, January 1909

Born on 15 January 1883 in Cole's Lane, near Henry Street in Dublin, Helena
Molony was the second child of the grocer Michael Moloney and his wife,
Catherine Mooney. Orphaned at a young age, she experienced a difficult
childhood because of her poor relationship with her stepmother.[2] Although she
remained close to her brother Frank, she rarely discussed her Catholic lower
middle-class upbringing in Rathgar in later life. Like many of her generation, she
attributed her political radicalisation to the cultural revival and the impact of the
1798 centenary, 'the starting point of the resurgence of real National idealism'.[3]
Like Peadar Kearney, she could recall a particular moment of awakening:

> I was a young girl dreaming about Ireland … when I saw
> and heard Maud Gonne speaking by the Custom House in
> Dublin one August evening in 1903. She was a most
> lovely figure, and she inspired me – as she did many
> others – with a love of Ireland … I had been reading
> Douglas Hyde – his history and legends. She gathered all
> this up and made it real for me. She electrified me and
> filled me with some of her own spirit … I went to join
> Inghinidhe na hÉireann.[4]

Almost immediately, Helena became embroiled in one of Inghinidhe na hÉireann's most celebrated protests. Calling at its offices, she was directed to Maud Gonne's house in Rathgar, where she found dozens of men, armed with sticks, 'spoiling for a fight' with the police who were gathered outside in large numbers. The cause of this confrontation was a black petticoat flying from a window of Gonne's house. Ostensibly a tribute to the recently deceased Pope Leo XIII, this provocative gesture was intended as a protest against King Edward VII's visit to Ireland. Many other houses in the prosperous suburb were displaying Union Jacks.[5] Widely reported by the press, the 'Battle of Coulson Avenue' exemplified Inghinidhe na hÉireann's flamboyant efforts to exploit popular nationalist sentiment to promote its radical objectives. Following this 'baptism of fire', Helena considered herself a committed republican: 'After eleven o'clock that night I walked home on air, really believing that I was a member of the mystical Army of Ireland. I was at once given work to do, and plunged into it with the greatest enthusiasm.'[6]

The campaign against the royal visit generated popular support, embarrassing the more acquiescent Irish Party and enabling a show of strength by militant separatists. Observing how the children at Inghinidhe's picnic swore undying enmity towards England, Yeats glumly wondered how many would 'carry a bomb or rifle when a little under or a little over thirty'.[17] Inghinidhe na hÉireann's radicalism usually confined it to the margins of nationalism. So did its status as a women's organisation at a time when women were denied the vote and largely excluded from cultural and political life. Inghinidhe na hÉireann's feminism was for the most part, however, firmly subordinated to its nationalist goals. In contrast to many suffragists, Helena, like most radical republican women, regarded the demand for a vote at Westminster as 'humiliating': Irish rights, she argued, 'must be won in

Ireland, not England or any foreign country'.[8] Originally formed to organise a 'patriotic children's treat' for those who had not participated in 'the orgy of flunkeyism' that marked Queen Victoria's visit to Ireland in 1900, Inghinidhe na hÉireann campaigned on material issues, such as the provision of school meals and the education of poor Dublin children, to whom they taught Irish, Irish history, Gaelic games and Irish dancing and music.[9]

This cultural agenda demonstrated the revival's impact on radical nationalism. Despite not speaking Irish, Helena, like many of her revolutionary generation, adopted a name of Irish origin ('Emer') to signify her personal commitment to an Irish identity. A central aim of Inghinidhe na hÉireann was to discourage 'the reading and circulation of low English literature, the singing of English songs, the attending of vulgar English entertainments at theatres and music halls, and to combat in every way English influence.'[10] Although in some respects at odds with its feminism, Inghinidhe na hÉireann's propaganda was stridently moralistic. Railing against 'the sad sight of Irish girls walking through the streets with men wearing the uniform of Ireland's oppressor', it warned of the danger to women's 'purity and honour'.[11] Although republican political culture was more egalitarian than constitutional nationalism, its moralism and idealisation of violence reinforced conservative notions of gender roles.

Against this, the central, deeply radical purpose of Inghinidhe na hÉireann was to give women a political voice. Its street politics also challenged prevailing ideas about women. Handing out leaflets to women who consorted with British soldiers was 'dangerous work', Helena insisted. 'Soldiers at that time had the habit of taking off their belts and attacking civilians with them'. Many of her friends disapproved of her activism: 'it was not thought "becoming"', she recalled; 'women and girls were still living in a semi-sheltered Victorianism'.[12] Helena, in contrast, delighted in Inghinidhe na hÉireann's theatrical pranks. Asked by a police sergeant to restrain youths from distributing seditious leaflets, Helena, 'pretending to sympathise with his difficulties, clapped him on the back as she was leaving him, at the same time sticking on a notice which appealed to young Irishmen not to join the British armed forces'. On another occasion, she plastered the Lord Lieutenant's official car with anti-recruitment leaflets.[13]

A committed agitator and an effective public speaker, Helena became a prominent activist, although she tended to play second fiddle to more dominant mentors. As secretary of Inghinidhe na hÉireann, she deputised for Maud Gonne, who was frequently absent from Ireland; later she worked closely with Constance Markievicz and James Connolly. In 1908 she established the ground-breaking journal *Bean na hÉireann*:

Helena Molony

Inġiniḋe na hÉireann.

IRISH GIRLS!

Ireland has need of the loving service of all her children. Irishwomen do not sufficiently realise the power they have to help or hinder the cause of Ireland's freedom.

If they did we should not see the sad sight of Irish girls walking through the streets with men wearing the uniform of Ireland's oppressor.

No man can serve two masters; no man can honestly serve Ireland and serve England. The Irishman who has chosen to wear the English uniform has chosen to serve the enemy of Ireland, and it is the duty of every Irishwoman, who believes in the freedom of Ireland, to show her disapproval of his conduct by shunning his company.

Irish girls who walk with Irishmen wearing England's uniform, remember you are walking with traitors. Irish girls who walk with English soldiers, remember you are walking with your country's enemies, and with men who are unfit to be the companions of any girl, for it is well known that the English army is the most degraded and immoral army in Europe, chiefly recruited in the slums of English cities, among men of the lowest and most depraved characters. You endanger your purity and honour by associating with such men and you insult your Motherland. Hearken to the words of Father Kavanagh, the Irish Franciscan Patriot Priest, who pronounces it a heinous crime against Ireland, for Irishmen to join the forces of robber England. Do you think it is less a crime for Irish girls to honour these men with their company. Remember the history of your country. Remember the womem of Limerick and the glorious patriot women of the great rebellion of '98, and let us, who are their descendants try to be worthy of them. What would those noble women think if they knew their daughters were associating with men belonging to that army, which has so often wrought ruin and havoc in Ireland, and murdered in cold blood thousands of Irishwomen and children. What English soldiers have done in Ireland in the past they would do again if ordered to do so. They would slaughter our kith and kin and murder women and children again as unhesitatingly as they hemmed in the helpless Boer women and children in those horrible concentration camps, where ten thousand little Boer children died from want and suffering.

Irish girls make a vow, not only that you will yourselves refuse to associate with any man who wears an English uniform, but that you will also try and induce your girl companions to do the same.

Women's influence is strong. Let us see, fellow-countrywomen, that we use it to the fullest for the Glory of God and for the honour and freedom of Ireland.

Inġiniḋe na hÉireann.

C.D. 119/3/1

'Irish Girls': Inghinidhe na hÉireann was much involved in anti-enlistment activism on Dublin's streets. This handbill employed a moralistic gendered language to reinforce traditional nationalist opposition to British army service (MAI, CD119/3/1).

It was a mixture of guns and chiffon. The national
position and international politics was front page news.
But we also had fashion notes (written in the interest of
Irish manufactured fabrics), gardening notes, written
by Countess Markievicz, and a Children's Corner, with
a serial fairy story, anti-recruiting articles (some from
Arthur Griffith) and good original poems from Pearse,
J. Plunkett, MacDonagh … It was a funny hotch-potch
of blood and thunder, high thinking, and home-made
bread. We were the object of much good-natured chaff.
Friendly newsagents would say 'Bean na hÉireann?
That's the woman's paper that all the young men buy.'[14]

Viewing Sinn Féin's social conservatism and non-violent strategy
as 'dull, and a little bit vulgar', *Bean na hÉireann* was the only newspaper to
openly advocate violence at that time. Whereas most nationalists in this
era regarded insurrectionary struggle as a romantic tradition belonging to
the past (or the stage), Helena's paper relentlessly advocated its utility in
the present: 'If the men really mean what they say let them act. If not let
them give up talking of still holding the principles of Tone and Emmet'.[15]
Praising revolutionary violence in other parts of the British Empire, *Bean na
hÉireann* published features with such titles as 'The art of street-fighting' and
'Physical force'. The striking militancy of such articles, with their impatient
discussion of the need for bloodshed, should 'be read as a deliberate response
to Griffith's arguments in *Sinn Féin* that the militarist option was irrelevant,
as it would simply be crushed by the might of the British Empire'.[16]

Through her role as editor of *Bean na hÉireann*, and her friendship
with such iconic figures as Anna Parnell and Maud Gonne, Helena became
'something of a keeper of the flame of women's nationalist activity'.[17]
Constance Markievicz 'came into national things through our paper',
Helena recalled. 'I was more or less political mentor to the Countess'. The
suffragist Dr Kathleen Lynn attributed her politicisation to Helena, who had
convalesced at her house in Belgrave Road: 'she converted me to the national
movement. She was a very clever and attractive girl with a tremendous
power of making friends.'[18] As Lynn's account suggests, Helena's personality
equipped her well for activism: she was modest and selfless and a generous

Edited by Helena Molony, *Bean na hÉireann* featured an appealing combination of 'guns and chiffon' (MAI).

bean na h-éireann. 5

The Ethics of Anti-Enlisting.

So many of our young men have such a vague idea of the British army. They know that their father was a Fenian, a patriot and a hero, and that he was in the army, sent there to do national work. Other men they hear mentioned with respect and honour as having done the same thing, and as having suffered for doing so. They do not know that circumstances have changed, that with another generation of Nationalists a new policy has been evolved. They do not see how their enlisting can hurt their country, simply because they have never been told.

Then, too, Irishmen come of a fighting race, and it is a great temptation to our young men of strong vitality with their taste for roving and with the love of adventure in their hearts to join the Irish regiments, where they may even wear the shamrock on St. Patrick's Day and march to the tune of "A Nation Once Again," or "The Boys of Wexford." Can no one tell these young men that—putting aside the question of nationality—it is a low and ignoble thing to take money, to earn your living, by killing other men. England's army is the only army in the world where men are paid to kill—make a profession of killing. England's Empire has been built up by men paid to fight against weaker nations, to kill, torture, imprison, and carry on a policy of extermination till the weaker nation was reduced to a loyal British province.

Directly you join the English army you pledge yourself to kill for money any man or woman that your officers bid you kill. You are just as much a paid assassin as the hangman. You are a member of the one mercenary army that survived the dark ages, scorned and despised by the other nations, and though it is a fine and noble thing to fight for your country, though it is a man's duty to fight to free his country, to die to preserve her independence, yet the man who takes money to fight is but a paid assassin.

One can point to the miseries of the ex-soldier. One can say, who wants an army man in his employment? Who—even the bitterest Unionist—will not rather employ anyone else. The Government push some of them into the Post Offices and others into employment on railways, or into the police. But, as a rule, no one wants a man who has spent years of his life in the ranks of an army composed of the ne'er-do-weels and disreputables of the four countries. You find these ex-soldiers in the workhouse and on the road. Tramping the long roads from north to south, from east to west, begging a penny to get drunk and drown their misery and degradation as soon as they can.

But what is the good of talking like this to young people who are face to face with unemployment and misery. A hungry man, seeking employment day by day, will not look ahead ten years. He may know what will probably be his fate some years hence, but it seems so far away, and after all he may have luck, or he may be dead. Anyhow the future may take care of itself. The nights are getting longer and colder, the wind and rain more piercing. He watches his clothes growing shabbier, he feels them growing thinner. With holes in his boots, his coat dirty and torn what chance has he of getting a job? From the day he gave up his clean collar he looked lower for work—every day that went by he would have been content with a poorer job. He thinks of America, but he has no money for a ticket—work is not to be had, misery and starvation go with him. Every day they show him men of his own nation and of his own class, well dressed and well fed, swaggering through the streets. Vaguely, in the bottom of his own heart he has the instinct that this is not right, but too often in the end starvation and misery—England's ready allies—win, and he joins the ranks of the enemy.

The choice is no new one; it is but the old, old struggle between the needs of the body and the soul. It is not only to-day, or even in Ireland that men have had to decide between comfort and security, with a traitor's heart and perjured soul to keep you company along life's road, or the fate of a starved and homeless wanderer, despised and rejected. It is only a great love of country, a high sense of duty, and a great feeling of national responsibility that will make a man choose starvation and the workhouse to enlisting. But the man who, knowing what he does deliberately chooses hardship, starvation and he workhouse, to the comfort and security of

6   bean na h-éiReann.

the British army has the soul of a hero, a spirit of renunciation and patriotism as great as a Tone or an Emmet.

But to look for a moment at the cheerful side of the question, I think that, considering the miserable economic conditions of the country, the love of battle that is in every Irishman's soul, and the de-nationalising education of our children, the proportion of Irishmen serving in the British army is small, and yearly diminishing. But we must not content ourselves with talking, writing, and bill sticking alone if we wish to really check the supply of men driven into the British army. We must study the economic questions of the country with a determination to help the workers all we can.

Undoubtedly many a man would not have enlisted, if his life had been a little less poverty stricken—a little brighter.

Men with decent jobs and understanding what nationality means will never enlist. Why should they?

It is very difficult to know how to help, especially if we have not much money. Perhaps the workers would show us? But we can all make up our minds to do one thing, and that is to spend what little money we have in Ireland, on Irish things, and to employ as many Irish people as we possibly can.

On the propoganda side of the movement, everyone can do a little, and workers are badly wanted.

Even if you can do no more than think of the English army as the army, and treat it as the army of our enemy, you have done something. Remember each time one of us tacitly accepts the army without protest, we are failing in our duty to our country.

It must be that we are ignorant of our country's history that we can take pleasure in seeing them march through our streets, or dance to the music of their bands. To a true Irishman the sound of their music should bring no thought but the memory of murders and assassinations, visions of smoking homesteads, of children tossed into the flames; of all the torture and misery that our race has suffered from them.

We who feel this a little, must teach our people what we know, and never tire of teaching, and of telling the truth about these

soldiers till doors are shut and blinds are drawn down when a regiment passes.

Till the people realise that the gaudy coats and gold lace, the blare of trumpets and the rattle of drums flaunting through our streets, are but the symbol of England's triumph, and our degradation and slavery.

Till every man and boy amongst us realises that if he swears loyalty to the King and the Empire, he is binding himself by oath to fight against Ireland—that he is pledging himself to fire on crowds of his own countrymen . . . to shoot down women and children, when England commands him.

Till our women realise the nameless torture, the undescribable horrors other Irishwomen have suffered at their hands. Till they feel that as well as the nation's wrongs, the woman's wrongs lie between them and the men in the British army. And that they, by associating themselves with soldiers that are betraying their country and their sex. All this we have to teach and much besides. Much we have to learn. We must grapple with the problems of the past, present, and future. We must try and understand the moral and physical, ethical and practical needs of our nation. Above all, we must learn self-sacrifice, for it is only by pain and self-sacrifice that a soul or a nation can rise great and immortal. Pain is the price we must pay for freedom, and it is only the petty, the selfish, the small-minded, who will stop to haggle over the price.

Nowadays there are many temptations. Nationality has grown such a safe and such a popular thing and so pleasant that it is easy to forget the really desperate struggle for existence that our nation is engaged in.

We are all National. We grow tearful and sentimental over the sufferings of our heroes, sung or told to us at concerts or lectures. We attend our classes, organise industrial exhibitions or sports. We dress beautifully in Irish-made stuffs, and eat heartily of Irish foods. But where does the sacrifice come in? Where is the risk, and why are we giving so little of our time, so little of our energy to the one item in our programme that involves a little risk? Is the old fire that has kept Nationality alive dying in the hearts of this generation? This question of the British army must be tackled.

beAn nA h-éiReAnn. 7

They first and formost stand between us and liberty. The men of '98 faced them without fear or shrinking on the open field; the Fenians, just as fearless, just as self-sacrificing, faced death or a felon's cell in their vain efforts to glean an Irish army from its ranks. The utmost we have to brave to-day is a few months in an English jail. I don't think that for very shame we ought to consider this, when we are asking men to face unemployment and starvation for the same principle. If they can face the workhouse—we can face the jail.

~~~~~~

SGéAL AOÙ RUAÙ.

Innir an rgéal ro vo na páiroib an mí reo.

Di buaCaill ann raro ó vár v'ainm Aoù Ruaù agur bí raitcior an vomá n ar na Saranaib roime. Mar rin cuir riaù long mór aг criall go Dun-na-nSall, aгur vubairt caiptín na luinge le Aoù go mberbeaù greann aгur rport mór aca, inr an luing. Annrin cuaiù Aoù ar borò, aгur cuir caiptín an long raoi reol ar a bruinte boire aгur reolaòar leo go Baile-Áta-Cliat.

Cuireaù Aoù irteac i bpriorún, ra reompa beat vorca, aгur níor tugaù vo act arán cruaiù aгur gac cuile rort mar rin. Dí Art aгur Hanraoi Ua Néill, i n-aonreact leir. Aгur raoi Novlag ruair riaù pópa, aгur v'eeluig riaù tríù an bruinneóг. Rit riaù go tarraig tuairim ré mile gur troiceaòar Sliab Ruaù. Dí an oiòce an-ruar aгur ní raib mórán eaвaig ar na buaCaillib aгur iav amuig rá rioc aгur rá rneacta aгur cuaiù ré com vian roin orta gur caill Aoù Ruaù órvóга na gcor aгur ruair Art Ó Neill bár.

Act táing Fiac Mac Aoòa aгur cuir ré Aoù Ruaù aг marcuiгeact ar capall mór breaг lairir, aгur Hanraoi ar capall eile aгur bí riaù ar roòar aгur ar corínáiòve gur rroic riaù an baile.

Adapted from StAiR-ceActA.

NOTAI

raitcioг an vomán—The fear of the world, i.e., very much afraid.
AR A bpuinte boisc—At once.
cuaiù sé com vian sin orta—It went so hard with them.

Sursum Corda, Mother Eire!

" I will strengthen that which was weak, and that which was driven away I will bring again," saith the Lord.

AH, the days are long departed
  When our Eire was a Queen,
Fairest princess 'mong the Nations
  In her robes of emerald sheen,
And her days in peace and gladness
  Sped as if by magic art,
And the laughter of her children
  Was the music of her heart.
But, alas! sweet Mother Eire,
  Where has all thy glory flown?
Why like Niobe thou wailest
  Childless, desolate, alone?
And that brow that in its beauty
  Thy fair diadem outshone—
Why should it be crowned with sorrow—
  Where have thy loved children gone?
The cruel fiends of Greed and Might
  Have chained thy beauteous hands,
Have seized by blood and treachery
  Thy fair and fertile lands,
Have driven from their happy homes
  Thy children far away,
But, oh, those weeping exiled ones
  Have hope for you to-day!
For there's something in the atmosphere
  One cannot yet define
Like the hovering of a spirit
  From some fair and mystic clime!
As of old when prophet breathed
  On the bones upon the plain,
There's the stir of life resurgent
  In our Nation's blood again.
Strong and patient God of armies,
  Retribution is at hand!
And the exile ones of Eire
  Thou wilt bring unto their land!
Yes, our cruel nightmare's ending,
  And the bondage we have seen.
Sursum Corda! Mother Eire
  Thou shalt be what thou hast been!
Soon those sunbursts on the hill top
  Will illume thy golden crown!
And 'mid ringing harps and cymbals!
  Will the foeman's flag go down!!

<div align="right">Una Ni Conĉubaiṙ.</div>

---

collaborator (on stage as well as in politics), albeit a campaigner rather than a theorist.[19] Helena helped Markievicz to plan the formation of Fianna Éireann in the house of her brother Frank in Sherrard Street: 'A good deal of things were hatched there'.[20] She helped to drill the boys (although, like Markievicz, she had to contend with their ungrateful efforts to expel them on the grounds that 'a physical force organization is no place for women').[21] Na Fianna was a significant initiative. As one of the boys who attended the first meeting reflected, 'it was there that things actually started'.[22] Although the IRB-infiltrated movement reflected prevailing republican and Irish-Ireland ideals – as well as mimicking the militaristic ethos of Baden-Powell's boy scouts, which had inspired its formation – Na Fianna was the first separatist movement of that period to adopt an explicitly military identity and structure. As Peadar Kearney observed, it also marked 'the starting of military drill on a systematic basis', foreshadowing the Irish Volunteers (which Na Fianna would drill and officer).[23] For Helena, as for Patrick Pearse, its purpose was as practical as it was propagandist: it was intended to form the nucleus of the army that would emerge to fight for Irish freedom.

It was not merely as a woman in the man's world of physical-force separatism that Helena challenged conventions. She participated in Maud Gonne's mystical 'Celtic' ceremonies at remote locations like Island's Eye. With Constance Markievicz and the determined young Fenian militant Bulmer Hobson she established a commune at Belcamp Park in north Co. Dublin in 1909. It was a large wreck of a house with seven acres, stables and a walled garden, and the profits from its produce were intended to finance the coming

Members of Inghinidhe na hÉireann in 'Celtic' costume. Maud Gonne's circle combined revolutionary republicanism and feminist politics with more mystical influences. Máire Nic Shiubhlaigh is third from left (NPA, PC 97/Lot 50/06).

revolution. Despite the involvement of a graduate of Albert Agricultural College (Donnchadh Ó hAnnagáin, who later led the IRA in east Limerick), it collapsed because of lack of expertise. Although she was *Bean na hÉireann's* gardening correspondent, Markievicz in her column tended towards the metaphorical: 'root out weeds, as you want to root out British domination'.

The unconventional living arrangements at Belcamp Park gave rise to scandal, with Helena's alleged love affair with Hobson and her heavy drinking – as well as Markievicz's estrangement from her husband – prompting scurrilous rumours. Hobson quickly jumped ship, landing Markievicz with the debts.[24] Helena and Markievicz moved to an unkempt Mount Street flat: 'no carpets, lovely oil sketches by both Markieviczes leaning negligently against the walls, an old skull beside a bronze bust of the nationalist martyr Robert Emmet on a table, portraits of patriots tacked up beside Russian icons, meals eaten casually in the kitchen.'[25] Life at their next residence, Surrey House, in leafy, unionist Rathmines, was equally unorthodox. The Fianna boys who overran Belcamp Park moved back in, holding meetings and sleeping overnight. Despite attention from the police, guns were tested in the back garden and seditious propaganda printed on a small press.

Like many visitors, the feminist Rosamond Jacob was intrigued by the bohemianism of life at Surrey House, recording the pair's fondness for smoking and their liberated sexual attitudes: Helena 'seems to regard men, as men, more as the relaxation of an idle hour than in any more serious light, does not appear to believe much in the one love of a lifetime, but rather in one minor flame after another. She prefers women and Madame prefers men.'[26] When Marie Perolz allowed Helena to move in with her some time

A Belfast-born Fenian from a Quaker background, Bulmer Hobson (1883–1969) was one of the most prominent of the younger generation of activists which revitalised the pre-war Irish Republican Brotherhood. His reputation was subsequently tarnished by his opposition to the Easter Rising (NLI, MS 13,174).

Making hay: Fianna boys at Belcamp.
Front row: Gussy Finlay with rifle, Leo
Walpole (holding Markievicz's dog
Rex), Joe Robinson (OC, Glasgow
Brigade), young boy, and Thomas
Fitzgerald. Second row: unknown man,
James Fitzgerald, Theobald Fitzgerald,
Donnchadh Ó hAnnagáin and (the first
known photograph of) Con Colbert.
On top is William Fitzgerald, with
pitchfork (NMI, HE/EW/2369).

later, she claimed that Helena appeared only 'for her letters and sleeps God knows where'.[27] This was a more exciting milieu than the chaste world of Gaelic League classes and Volunteer drilling recalled in many revolutionary memoirs. For Helena, it was less a lifestyle choice than it was for the more privileged Markievicz. One reason she often lived with her friends was her poverty; another was her depressive nature. She subsequently moved in with Kathleen Lynn after suffering a nervous breakdown.

By now Helena had begun to practise – as well as preach – revolution, which led some Inghinidhe na hÉireann members to complain that she was 'attracted more by violence than editorial work'.[28] The final issue of *Bean na hÉireann* appeared in 1911; with the publication of the IRB's *Irish Freedom* there was less demand for a women's journal advocating violence. During the same year, Helena became the first woman political prisoner of her generation after smashing an illuminated portrait of King George V ('smug and benign, looking down on us') during his royal visit.[29] Although ashamed – 'no one but rowdies went to the police station' – she was also dismayed to find herself released from Mountjoy Prison when Anna Parnell paid her fine. As Áine Ceannt noted of this brief incarceration, 'she was let out – as a matter of fact she was put out.'[30] Fortunately, Helena secured re-arrest by denouncing the King as 'a scoundrel' at the demonstration to mark her release: 'That was marvellous; I felt myself in the same company as Wolfe Tone'.[31] Although she and Markievicz (who had assaulted the police as they tried to arrest Helena) were convicted for breaching the peace, no sentence was imposed, 'on account of their sex'.[32]

Socialist Party in Ireland
(DUBLIN BRANCH).

THE ROYAL VISIT.

" The great appear great to us, only because we are on our knees:
LET US RISE."

FELLOW-WORKERS—As you are aware from reading the daily and weekly newspapers, we are about to be blessed with a visit from King George V. Knowing from previous experience of Royal Visits, as well as from the Coronation orgies of the past few weeks, that the occasion will be utilised to make propaganda on behalf of royalty and aristocracy against the oncoming forces of democracy and National freedom, we desire to place before you some few reasons why you should unanimously refuse to countenance this visit, or to recognise it by your presence at its attendant processions or demonstrations. We appeal to you as workers, speaking to workers, whether your work be that of the brain or of the hand—manual or mental toil—it is of you and your children we are thinking ; it is your cause we wish to safeguard and foster.

The future of the working class requires that all political and social positions should be open to all men and women ; that all privileges of birth or wealth be abolished, and that every man or woman born into this land should have an equal opportunity to attain to the proudest position in the land. The Socialist demands that the only birthright necessary to qualify for public office should be the birthright of our common humanity. Believing as we do that there is nothing on earth more sacred than humanity, we deny all allegiance to this institution of royalty, and hence can only regard the visit of the King as adding fresh fuel to the fire of hatred with which we regard the plundering institutions of which he is the representative. Let the capitalist and landlord class flock to exalt him ; he is theirs ; in him they see embodied the idea of caste and class ; they glorify him and exalt his importance that they might familiarise the public mind with the conception of political inequality, knowing well that a people mentally poisoned by the adulation of royalty can never attain to that spirit of self-reliant democracy necessary for the attainment of social freedom. The mind accustomed to political kings can easily be reconciled to social kings—capitalist kings of the workshop, the mill, the railway, the ships and the docks. Thus coronation and king's visits are by our astute, never-sleeping masters made into huge Imperialist propagandist campaigns in favour of political and social schemes against democracy. But if our masters and rulers are sleepless in their schemes against us, so we, rebels against their rule, must never sleep in our appeal to our fellows to maintain publicly our belief in the dignity of our class—in the ultimate sovereignty of those who labour.

P.T.O.

Helena Molony was arrested
after smashing a portrait of King
George V during the royal visit
of 1911 (NLI, MS 33,627)

Not all Irish people resented the royal family's visit. Spectators observing the military review at the Fifteen Acres in the Phoenix Park, 11 July 1911 (GI, 113210551).

In 1912 Helena began acting with the Abbey Theatre. Like that of Máire Nic Shiubhlaigh, her career on the stage was more a consequence than a cause of her political engagement. She first became interested in drama through Inghinidhe na hÉireann's acting classes; Dudley Digges, a founding member of the Irish National Theatre Society, was a particular influence. Helena acted with the Cumann na nGaedheal Theatre Company in the 1903 Samhain Festival, performing her first role, as many did, in *Cathleen ni Houlihan*. Like Máire, Helena did not agonise over the competing demands of art and politics. The purpose of her involvement in amateur theatre 'was to give dramatic expression to national political propaganda, as distinct from the "art for art's sake" school'.[33] With the Fianna players she performed in such propagandistic plays as *The Saxon Shillin'* by Padraic Colum, alongside youths such as Con Colbert, who would play a prominent role in the Rising. She was a talented actor, winning praise for her performance (and improvised dialogue) in the Markieviczes' production of George Birmingham's *Eleanor's Enterprise* (in which she played Mrs Finnegan, opposite Seán Connolly's Mr Finnegan).[34]

Establishing herself in amateur theatre circles, Helena progressed to the Abbey through the usual route, beginning with roles for the Abbey School of Acting. Her first professional appearance on the Abbey's stage, in January 1912, was as Second Hag in Lady Gregory's *Macdaragh's Wife*. By March she had made the Abbey's second company, and she graduated to the main company the following year. Despite the prestige and pay that came with employment at the Abbey, she maintained that 'the political situation had a bigger attraction for me than a theatrical career'. As it did for Máire Nic Shiubhlaigh, Helena's political commitment brought her into conflict with the Abbey, when its manager sought to prevent her from returning to the stage after she had taken advantage of a lengthy break between scenes in William Boyle's play *The Mineral Workers* to address a strike meeting at nearby Liberty Hall: 'with the backing of the company and her own insistence, she went on and finished her part'.[35]

By now, Helena was increasingly drawn to socialist politics: 'I knew little of Labour ideas. But I was always on the side of the underdog.'[36] Her *Bean na hÉireann* column on labour issues had brought her to the attention of James Connolly, then in the United States, who tried to persuade her to organise mill girls in Belfast. Helena's writings had sometimes evinced a narrow nationalism: 'love of Ireland and of everything great and small that belongs to Ireland because it belongs to Ireland', she claimed, should provide 'the great driving force' of cultural and political activism.[37] In contrast, Connolly criticised Inghinidhe na hÉireann for shedding 'bucketfuls of tears over the sorrowful fate of the Children of Lir' while supporting a capitalist 'system condemning thousands of the children of Irish workers to miseries'.[38] His return to Ireland reinforced Helena's social radicalism: 'I was fumbling at the idea of a junction between labour and nationalism – which Connolly worked out clearly.' Like many radical women, she was attracted to his egalitarian nature: 'Connolly – staunch feminist that he was – was more anxious to include women into the ranks on equal terms with men'.[39]

The impact of the 1913 Lockout – which highlighted the appalling deprivation and disease of Dublin's slums, among the worst in Europe – deepened her social radicalism. With Markievicz, Helena helped to run

Motley crew. L–R: Constance Markievicz (in leprechaun outfit), science student Konrad Peterson (as a woman), the rarely photographed Helena Molony (in mob cap), Michael O'Gorman (in eighteenth-century costume), and, standing at rear, George Doran, in RIC uniform (NMI, HE/EWP/199).

the soup-kitchen at the ITGWU's head office in Liberty Hall.[40] She put
her theatrical expertise to use in one of the most celebrated incidents of
the Lockout, disguising Jim Larkin as an elderly clergyman to facilitate
his dramatic appearance on the Imperial Hotel's balcony to address a
public meeting in defiance of the police.[41] Despite this, she had little
time for Larkin, describing him as 'a blatherskite ... who was all froth'.
Notwithstanding her support for the strikers, Helena recalled that 'not all
of us were in sympathy with James Larkin, or his outlook, which was that
of a British Socialist'. Rosamond Jacob also recorded Helena's complaints
'about the revolting unwholesome Englishness of Larkin & the strike'.[42]
Such comments demonstrate how the tensions between socialism and
nationalism were less easily reconciled than is suggested by Helena's
Connollyite assertion that 'Labour and the Nation were really one'.

The Lockout, Helena stated, 'profoundly affected the whole country',
producing 'a sort of social and intellectual revolution' that encompassed
the formation of the Irish Citizen Army, which was established to protect
workers from the police and employers' heavies during the final phase of the
violent dispute. Her view is debatable: many experienced the Lockout as a
demoralising defeat. Her experience of the Lockout probably contributed to
her breakdown, although she had previously struggled with depression and
alcoholism. She spent much of the next year convalescing with Maud Gonne
in France.

On her return to Ireland in 1915, which had been delayed by
uncertainty over her employment at the Abbey and the outbreak of the war,
she moved closer to James Connolly. She succeeded Delia Larkin as general
secretary of the Irish Women Workers' Union and became the proprietor
of Connolly's *Workers' Republic* (and, as a result, legally responsible for its
seditious content). Performing at the Abbey by night, she spent her days
running the workers' co-operative shop on Eden Quay.

Swept up in the militarism of the era, Helena organised 'the girls
as a unit of the Citizen Army'.[43] Although she refused to join Cumann na
mBan, which was permitted only a non-combatant auxiliary role by the
Irish Volunteers, she opposed the radical feminist argument that women
should only support movements that gave priority to women's rights: 'it
seems to me sound citizenship to put the welfare of the whole nation before
any section of it'.[44] Her insistence, however, that women in the Citizen
Army 'were an integral part of the army and not in any sense a "Ladies'
Auxiliary"' was misleading.[45] They were segregated into a women's section,

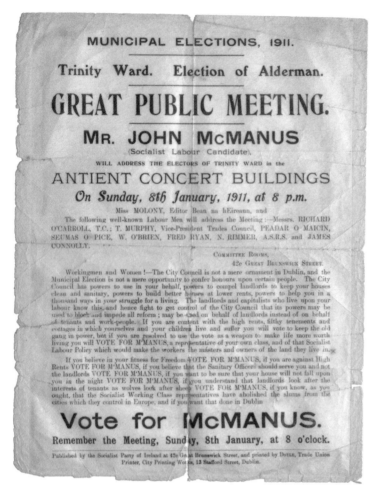

By 1911 Helena Molony was becoming prominent in socialist circles in Dublin. Other speakers at this Socialist Party of Ireland meeting include James Connolly and William O'Brien (NMI, HE/EW/5223).

which undertook gendered work, such as first aid, although they did learn to drill and shoot. For Helena, who trained the women's section in Liberty Hall's miniature rifle-range, her possession of a gun was an important mark of her radicalism and equality: 'I always carried a revolver'. She regarded the Citizen Army as a far more radical organisation than the Volunteers (dubbed by her the 'Fan go fóills', because of their reluctance to commit themselves to insurrectionary methods) and the Fenians, whom she dismissed as 'old maids'. She modified her attitude to both organisations when Connolly learnt in late 1915 that a radical faction within them, led by Tom Clarke and Seán Mac Diarmada, was set on rebellion.

With sections of Liberty Hall converted into workshops for producing armaments, it was obvious to many in the Citizen Army that their activism would have a practical outcome. At the workers' co-op, Helena oversaw

Tenement room, 38 Francis Street. Pre-war Dublin had the worst housing conditions in the United Kingdom. 26,000 families lived in inner-city tenements, about 20,000 of them in single-room dwellings such as this (RSAI, Lantern Slide Collection, Box 07/055).

the manufacture of ammunition cartridges and military equipment. Although Connolly's embrace of physical-force republicanism tends to be attributed to the crushing defeat of syndicalism in the Lockout, and to the collapse of international working-class solidarity in the First World War, this ideological shift must have been less of a problem for Helena, who had consistently venerated the insurrectionary tradition. The IWWU's premises at Eden Quay, which adjoined Liberty Hall, provided a discreet meeting place for the military council. She recalled that 'Volunteer leaders dropped in to discuss plans two or three times a week. It was the hub of the movement'.[46] The warren of rooms in Liberty Hall provided another place conveniently shielded from prying eyes. Helena recalled that

> the whole building was admirably suited for secrecy, rapid movement or defence. In a little office at the back of the shop, and leading to the printing works, Connolly, after hours, could be free of union business, but available for private visitors. As secretary to the co-op, I was always on hand to identify such callers. Pearse called many times, also Joe Plunkett and Tom MacDonagh. These men were all intimate friends of mine, so it seemed quite natural for me to encourage them to buy socks and ties from us.

James Connolly (1868-1916)

Possession of a gun marked out
the most committed separatists.
This was Patrick Pearse's pistol
(NPA, Pearse folder/box 6).

Trade-union leader, socialist
and republican, James Connolly
(1868–1916) helped to form the Irish
Citizen Army in 1913. Woodcut by
Harry Kernoff (NLI, EPH F312).

One of a small circle of trusted conspirators, Helena was sent by Seán
Mac Diarmada to England to repatriate the Volunteer organiser (and future
managing director of the Abbey) Ernest Blythe, who had been deported for
subversive activities. She evaded suspicion by residing in the theatrical lodgings
where she had toured with the Abbey. Although she failed to secure Blythe's
return, her efforts were not entirely wasted. She recalled how, at Euston Station
in London, 'a nice young lad – an Army recruit – carried my suitcase filled with
revolvers and gun parts to the boat train. The perfect gentleman!'

Helena's willingness to use violence is illustrated by her role in foiling
a police raid on her workers' co-operative shop. From an adjoining room the
printer Christopher Brady watched 'through a little door with two spy holes' as
she prevented the police from seizing copies of a proscribed newspaper:

> Connolly came down quickly, walked quietly to the counter
> with drawn gun in his hand. A few feet away Miss Molony
> was already covering the police with her automatic.
> Connolly looked sternly at the police and gave his command
> to them: 'Drop these papers or I will drop you.' At this
> moment Madame Markievicz ... appeared at the entrance
> to the co-op behind the raiding police ... She too had them

covered and they realised they were surrounded. At once
they changed their tune and said, 'Of course we are only
doing our duty and we have no warrant for this raid.'
With this they beat a quick retreat.[47]

Following the raid, Liberty Hall was placed under permanent guard
until the mobilisation at Easter. 'The atmosphere', Helena recalled, 'was like
a simmering pot.' Unwilling to risk missing the rebellion which Connolly
had hinted was imminent, she slept at Liberty Hall 'on a pile of men's
coats in the back of the shop'. She was closely involved in the last-minute
preparations, as Brady's account makes clear:

> When the printing of the Proclamation was completed I
> made up two parcels of the printed copies, 1,250 in each,
> and brought them to Miss Helena Molony who was lying
> on a couch in the co-op shop room in Liberty Hall. She
> told me to put them under her pillow. She was armed
> with a revolver.[48]

She would soon get an opportunity to use it.

Chapter 6

Barney Murphy

1887-1916

The elusive Barney Murphy,
with fellow Abbey rebel Arthur
Shields, 1927 (HL T13/B/339).

Stephen said one day to Madden:
– I suppose these hurley-matches and walking tours
are preparations for the great event.
– There is more going on in Ireland at present than
you are aware of.
– But what use are camáns?

—James Joyce, *Stephen Hero* (1944)

Until recently, little was known about Barney Murphy, the most elusive
of the Abbey Theatre's seven commemorated rebels. Despite extensive
enquiries, the local historian Séamus Scully was unable to ascertain a single
significant detail about his life, including where he had fought in 1916, in
an otherwise detailed account of each of the Abbey's 1916 rebels.[1] Other than
his limitations as a prompter, remarkably little is known about Barney's
career at the Abbey, where he worked for over thirty years as a stage hand.

In his witness statement for the Bureau of Military History, however, Séamus Kavanagh could recall where he first met Barney. Kavanagh had decided to attend the inaugural meeting of a new scouting organisation, following an unusual encounter in the Camden Street drapery shop where he worked. He recalled that

> it was the first time I had ever seen a lady smoking a cigarette. I was employed as apprentice cash-boy, and the milliner, who was serving her, called me to take the cash for the purchase to the cash office. When I came back with the change, the lady addressed me. 'Little boy', she asked, 'What is your name?'. I told her it was James Kavanagh, and she asked me would not 'Seamus' sound nicer. I said I thought it would. I thought to myself that it was peculiar for a person with an English accent to be asking me a question like that, at that time. She said, 'Will you promise me that you will never answer to any other name but Seamus in future?'. She followed that by asking me did I ever hear of Wolfe Tone, Robert Emmet, the Manchester Martyrs and '98. I said 'I did'. She asked would I not like to be like one of them. I said, 'I think I would'. Then she asked me would I join the Irish National Boy Scouts movement ...

Notwithstanding his suspicion 'that a titled lady should interest herself in a matter of this nature', he agreed to Constance Markievicz's suggestion. He had been reassured of her credentials by his employer, Joe McGuinness, who would later achieve notoriety as the first 1916 prisoner elected to Westminster.[2]

Kavanagh met Barney on 16 August 1909 at the inaugural meeting of Fianna Éireann, which took place in a dingy hall at the rear of 34 Camden Street. He also recognised Helena Molony, Peadar Kearney and Brian Callender at the meeting:

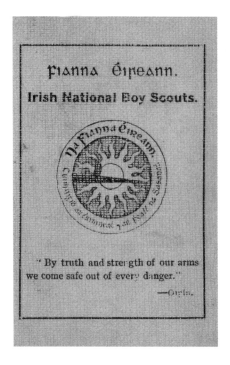

Membership card for Fianna
Éireann (NMI, EW/297bb).

The premises were lit by gas and oil lamps. Bulmer
Hobson gave a lecture on Wolfe Tone. I remember one
thing he said that struck me rather forcibly, and that
was about Tone being a Presbyterian and a person of
standing in the country, yet he became a member of
the United Irishmen, took the oath of allegiance to
the Republic, and was prepared to break away from
everything for the sake of his country.

Suitably impressed by the end of the meeting, about a hundred boys –
'mostly adventurers from the Coombe' – left their names with Con Colbert and,
later that week, began drilling in preparation for the fight for Irish freedom.[3]

Kavanagh remembered another detail about Barney. Along with
Peadar Kearney and Brian Callender, Barney had formed 'a Fianna pipers'
band', and he became an enthusiastic and accomplished piper. The following
year Barney joined the St Laurence O'Toole Pipe Band, which regularly
performed at republican commemorations, such as Bodenstown.[4] Piping,
in the right circles, could be a subversive pastime. With a body of patrons
comprising Seán Mac Diarmada, Patrick Pearse and Arthur Griffith – and with

Tom Clarke and Seán O'Casey as its founding president and secretary – the band's interests almost certainly extended beyond music appreciation.

The St Laurence O'Toole Pipe Band was an offshoot of the Gaelic League branch of the same name, founded in 1901 at Seville Place. One of its founding members was Edward Keegan, one of the Abbey's forgotten revolutionaries. Although Keegan had performed on the Abbey's opening night and was a player-member of the original Irish National Theatre Society, his name was omitted from the 1966 commemorative plaque.[5] A clerk, he was a noted hurler, elocutionist and actor. After breaking with the Abbey, he joined the more militant National Players, which was patronised by Maud Gonne and Arthur Griffith.

Barney Murphy attended the inaugural meeting of the Irish Volunteers at the Rotunda in 1913. Like many other members of Na Fianna, he had automatically transferred to that organisation, joining B Company, 1st Battalion, of the Dublin Brigade. He had a fair idea what was coming at

Constance Markievicz with the Fianna Éireann pipers at a festival in the Rotunda Gardens, 1910. Barney Murphy (not in photo) was a founder-member of the band (NMI, HE/EW/1773/1).

As a member of the St Laurence O'Toole Pipe Band, Barney Murphy (not in photo) performed regularly at republican commemorations, such as this one at Wolfe Tone's grave at Bodenstown in 1912. The band's founding president, Tom Clarke, can be seen standing at the back (NLI).

Easter, 1916. He spent the three weeks leading up to the Rising 'watching barracks' and 'taking messages to Ned Daly, Tom Clarke and things like that'. He spent Good Friday moving rifles from his house to Liberty Hall.[6]

As was the case with the Abbey's other rebels, Barney's career demonstrates the importance of a network of overlapping sports and cultural organisations, invariably honeycombed by IRB activists, in the cultivation of a militant sense of Irish identity and in the subsequent emergence of an armed revolutionary movement. Barney's radicalism may have been reinforced by his association with the St Laurence O'Toole Gaelic Athletic Club. Formed on 8 October 1901, when Edward Keegan persuaded his pals to form a hurling club after their Irish class had ended, it was one of many such clubs to emerge during the wave of enthusiasm resulting from the 1798 centenary and the Anglo-Boer War. If Barney's road to rebellion began here, he was far from alone: over seventy members of the Laurence O'Toole club would fight by his side at Easter, 1916.[7]

To the Boys of Ireland

WE of Na Fianna Eireann, at the beginning of this year 1914, a year which is likely to be momentous in the history of our country, address ourselves to the boys of Ireland and invite them to band themselves with us in a knightly service. We believe that the highest thing anyone can do is to SERVE well and truly, and we purpose to serve Ireland with all our fealty and with all our strength. Two occasions are spoken of in ancient Irish story upon which Irish boys marched to the rescue of their country when it was sore beset— once when Cuchulainn and the boy-troop of Ulster held the frontier until the Ulster heroes rose, and again when the boys of Ireland kept the foreign invaders in check on the shores of Ventry until Fionn had rallied the Fianna : it may be that a similar tale shall be told of us, and that when men come to write the history of the freeing of Ireland they shall have to record that the boys of Na Fianna Eireann stood in the battle-gap until the Volunteers armed.

We believe, as every Irish boy whose heart has not been corrupted by foreign influence must believe, that our country ought to be free. We do not see why Ireland should allow England to govern her, either through Englishmen, as at present, or through Irishmen under an appearance of self-government. We believe that England has no business in this country at all,—that Ireland, from the centre to the zenith, belongs to the Irish. Our fore-fathers believed this and fought for it: Hugh O'Donnell and Hugh O'Neill and Rory O'More and Owen Roe O'Neill; Tone and Emmet and Davis and Mitchel. What was true in their time is still true. Nothing that has happened or that can ever happen can alter the truth of it. Ireland belongs to the Irish. We believe, then, that it is the duty of Irishmen to struggle always, never giving in or growing weary, until they have won back their country again.

The object of Na Fianna Eireann is to train the boys of Ireland to fight Ireland's battle when they are men. In the past the Irish, heroically though they have struggled, have always lost, for want of discipline, for want of military knowledge, for want of plans, for want of leaders. The brave Irish who rose in '98, in '48, and in '67, went down because they were not SOLDIERS: we hope to train Irish boys from their earliest years to be soldiers, not only to know the trade of a soldier—drilling, marching, camping, signalling, scouting, and (when they are old enough) shooting—but also, what is far more important, to under-stand and prize military discipline and to have a MILITARY SPIRIT. Centuries of oppression and of unsuccessful effort have almost extinguished the military spirit of Ireland : if that were once gone—if Ireland were to become a land of contented slaves—it would be very hard, perhaps impossible, ever to arouse her again. We believe that Na Fianna Eireann have kept the military spirit alive in Ireland during the past four years, and that if the Fianna had not been founded in 1909, the Volunteers of 1913 would never have arisen. In a sense, then, the Fianna have been the pioneers of the Volunteers; and it is from the ranks of the Fianna that the Volunteers must be recruited. This is a special reason why we should be active during 1914. The Fianna will constitute what the old Irish called the MACRADH, or boy-troop, of the Volunteers, and will correspond to what is called in France an Ecole Polytechnique or Military School. As the man who was to lead the armies of France to such glorious victories came forth from the Military School of Brienne, so may the man who shall lead the Irish Volunteers to victory come forth from Na Fianna Eireann.

Our programme includes every element of a military training. We are not mere "Boy Scouts," although we teach and practice the art of scouting. Physical culture, infantry drill, marching, the routine of camp life, semaphore and Morse signalling, scouting in all its branches, elementary tactics, ambulance and first aid, swimming, hurling, and football, are all included in our scheme of training; and opportunity is given to the older boys for bayonet and rifle practice. This does not exhaust our programme, for we believe that mental culture should go hand in hand with physical culture, and we provide instruction in Irish and in Irish History, lectures on historical and literary subjects, and musical and social entertainments as opportunities permit.

Finally, we believe with Thomas Davis that "RIGHTEOUS men" must "make our land a Nation Once Again." Hence we endeavour to train our boys to be pure, truthful, honest, sober, kindly; clean in heart as well as in body; generous in their service to their parents and companions now as we would have them generous in their service to their country here-after. We bear a very noble name and inherit very noble traditions, for we are called after the Fianna of Fionn, that heroic companionship which, according to legend, flourished in Ireland in the second and third centuries of the Christian era.

"We, the Fianna, never told a lie,
Falsehood was never imputed to us,"

said Oisín to Saint Patrick; and again when Patrick asked Caoilte Mac Ronain how it came that the Fianna won all their battles, Caoilte replied: "Strength that was in our hands, truth that was on our lips, and purity that was in our hearts."

Is it too much to hope that after so many centuries the old ideals are still quick in the heart of Irish youth, and that this year we shall get many hundred Irish boys to come forward and help us to build up a brotherhood of young Irishmen strong of limb, true and pure in tongue and heart, chivalrous, cultured in a really Irish sense, and ready to spend themselves in the service of their country?

sinne

na fianna éireann.

(All communications regarding the formation of companies should be forwarded to the Hon. General

'To the boys of Ireland', 1914.
Patrick Pearse fuses history, myth,
masculinity and militarism in a potent
call to arms (NMI, HE/EW/991/21).

Chapter 7

Ellen Bushell

1884–1916

Ellen Bushell (1884–1948), the Abbey
Theatre's long-serving usher (AT).

'What is the use? It will only be a massacre'. This
was the comment of a patriotic Irish girl to whom I
remarked during a performance of *The Dreamers* – a play
dealing with Robert Emmet's Rising – in the Abbey
Theatre, some time before Easter Week, that another
rising was in the offing. 'What matter', I said, 'it will
keep up the old spirit'. During Easter Week my words
were recalled one night I chanced to have tea with
Mr J. J. McElligott … He asked me 'How do you think
things will turn out?' I replied, rather pessimistically,
'Of course we shall all be wiped out'. 'What matter',
he said, 'it will keep up the old spirit'. His remarks,
recalling to my mind my conversation in the Abbey
Theatre, were a source of satisfaction to me.[1]

— Michael Knightly, F Company, 1st Battalion, Dublin Brigade

Few individuals had as lengthy an association with the Abbey Theatre as
Ellen Bushell, who worked there from its opening night until shortly before
her death, in 1948. Although unknown to the public, she was a familiar
presence at the Abbey. The local historian Séamus Scully was snared into a
lifelong theatre habit after receiving a pass from Ellen for the cheap seats in
the parterre:

> I always called her Miss Bushell, to all her friends she
> was known as Nellie. She was but a slip of a girl of 16
> when as usherette she was at the opening of the Abbey
> in 1904 ... Daintily clad in black frock and skirt, fronted
> by white-laced apron, dark stockings and shoes, which
> Lady Gregory had asserted was the most graceful attire
> for the Abbey usherettes, she was a dignified figure as
> she guided patrons down the few parterre steps to their
> seats, and courteously presented them with the buff-
> grey coloured programme.[2]

Born in 1884, Ellen was the daughter of Edward and Sarah Bushell.[3] She was associated with the Fay brothers' theatre, and her involvement with the Irish National Theatre Society had predated the Abbey. According to Séamus de Búrca,

> she had been with the company as a young girl, with
> hair down to her waist, when they played in the
> Clarendon Street, Molesworth Street and York Street
> halls. She had acted as cashier, checked the tickets
> before the patrons entered the hall, and
> sold programmes.[4]

She typified the amateur ethos of the Irish National Theatre Society, working without pay until after the establishment of the Abbey Theatre, when part-time staff members were recruited from the Society's non-acting associate membership: 'I had been in the Abbey from '04 but I used to be at the poplin-weaving in the day-time for some years. Box-office in the Abbey.' Although Ellen did not perform on the stage, she was devoted to theatre: her 'deep-rooted love of the drama world could be expressed as intelligently as any astute critic'.[5] Her home in the Coombe became a popular meeting-place for Abbey staff members after performances, where, Peadar Kearney recalled, they would talk into the small hours, feasting on sausages, pudding and stout.[6]

Before the recent publication of the records of the Military Service Pensions Board, almost no details of Ellen's secret life as a revolutionary were known. She was one of many women republican activists who worked in the background. The biography of Peadar Kearney, for example, asserted that 'she was never attached to any political organisation'.[7] In this period, however, women were discouraged from formal membership of political organisations and were expected to play a subordinate role. Ellen's entry into advanced nationalist circles originated from her work as a poplin-weaver: she made cloaks and other supposedly traditional Irish garments which had recently become fashionable in Irish-Ireland circles. She was drawn into 'the Movement', however, when she was invited to join Na Fianna: 'a man named Callander brought me the letter telling me to come that night to this meeting, I had been appointed'.

This was Brian Callender. As secretary of the Celtic Literary Society, whose members included Arthur Griffith and Willie Rooney, Callender organised such activities as Irish classes, history lectures, choir-singing and céilithe: 'we had dancing and singing and any amount of tea and cakes', one member recalled fondly. Political activists, such as James Connolly, and writers, actors and poets, including Padraic Colum, Edward Martyn, the Fay brothers and Dudley Digges, frequented its rooms at 32 Lower Abbey Street, just a few doors from the Abbey Theatre. So did Yeats, 'although most of the boys disliked him'. Maud Gonne used the Society's rooms for her pro-Boer Irish Transvaal Committee, and founded Inghinidhe na hÉireann there. Máire Nic Shiubhlaigh rehearsed her *tableaux vivants* at the same venue.

Callender was a founding member of the Irish National Dramatic Company, and he had played a bit part as a messenger in the original production of *Cathleen ni Houlihan* in 1902.[8] A founding member of Na Fianna, he formed the Fianna Pipers, which counted Peadar Kearney and Barney Murphy among its small membership. He helped also to set up the Fianna Players, whose actors included Helena Molony, Seán Connolly, Constance Markievicz and Con Colbert.[9] This was the world into which Ellen Bushell had been invited by Callender.

Ellen was active, but not prominent, in Inghinidhe na hÉireann and Fianna Éireann: she allowed the boys to use her house in Newmarket Street for their activities.[10] As she informed the Pensions Board: 'I was attached to Fianna, on the Committee, making their kilts & general equipment from early 1910 till Volunteers started then I helped them also as I'd known many of the Leaders for many years & was much trusted by them.' She was particularly close to the IRB and Fianna leader Con Colbert. Young, disciplined, pious and abstemious, Colbert – a clerk educated by the Christian Brothers – represented a different revolutionary sensibility from that of figures like Molony and Markievicz. Through Colbert, who drilled the boys at St Enda's, Ellen was friendly with Patrick Pearse, for whose pupils she made kilts. Roger Casement's money paid for the kilts, Colbert provided the material, and Ellen voluntarily supplied her labour. She also made bandoliers out of mail-bags to hold the schoolchildren's .303 ammunition.

Pearse's boys are drilled at St Enda's school, probably by Con Colbert. Their kilts were made by Ellen Bushell (PM).

In 1913, during the Home Rule crisis, Ellen 'automatically went on with Con to work for the Volunteers'. Some of the rifles landed at Howth were hidden in her house. She described herself as 'an auxiliary member of F Coy, 4th Battn', but she did not join Cumann na mBan: 'both Con Colbert and Comdt. McDonagh kept me out of it, they said I was more use.' She spent the months before the Easter Rising making equipment for the Volunteers in her house, where their arms and ammunition were stored: 'they would be just left there and taken away again, parcels.' Having spent much of Holy Week running messages for Con Colbert, what followed came as no surprise: 'I knew it was the Rising we were working for and I knew it was coming off. I was in their confidence.'[11]

Seán Connolly

1882–1916

Seán Connolly (1882–1916),
Gaelic League activist, actor and
revolutionary (NPA, PC 97/Lot 50/04).

To enlist for Caitlin Ni Houlihan may mean a dark
and narrow cell for your body, but think of the great
joy it will bring to your soul.

—James Larkin, shouted to the crowd as he departed for the United States, 1914.[1]

What led you to those castle walls?
We mourn you Sean Connolly.

—Lady Gregory, scribbled on the back of a letter on the train to Galway, July 1921[2]

Born in Sandymount, Dublin, on 12 April 1882, John Connolly was the third
of the sixteen children of Michael Connolly and his wife, Mary Ellis.[3] John's
family moved to Gloucester Street when his father swapped a job on the seas
for one on the docks. His mother worked as a midwife and ran a shop from
the family home. Educated at North William Street National School and at St
Joseph's Christian Brothers' School in Fairview, Seán (as he became known)
found work as a despatch clerk at Eason's stationery shop. Seán O'Casey,
who briefly worked alongside him (before, characteristically, being fired for
insubordination), lyrically recalled his first meeting with Connolly, with
whom he chatted in Irish:

> A musical voice, a dark tenor, is calling out in the mist
> now, calling the papers to be placed together to form a
> parcel for some country newsagent ... He has a pale face,
> very gentle, very handsome, with firm lines round the
> delicately-formed mouth. He is gently but strongly built ...
> In the lapel of the coat he wore a button badge, having on
> it a Celtic cross with the words The Gaelic League over it.[4]

On that first meeting, O'Casey admired Connolly's defiant separatism and the calm manner in which he conversed in Irish, despite the sniggers of some of their workmates.

This radicalism owed something to his family background, the children being reared in the customary 'Irish national atmosphere'.[5] As a Christian Brothers' boy, Seán would have been further exposed to a staunchly patriotic 'faith and fatherland' interpretation of Irish history and Irish-Ireland values. As with most of his revolutionary generation, the Gaelic League and GAA provided a gateway to more militant endeavours. So too did Dublin's amateur dramatic scene, particularly the breeding-ground of revolution that was Inghinidhe na hÉireann's acting class. Seán performed in the Gaelic League's plays, debuting in Tomás Ó hAodha's *An Scrabhadóir* at the 1909 Oireachtas. He moved in the same circles as Máire Nic Shiubhlaigh and Helena Molony, appearing in productions by the Theatre of Ireland, the National Players (which recruited from Na Fianna and Inghinidhe na hÉireann), the Markieviczes' Independent Theatre Company and their Dublin Repertory Theatre.

In 1910 he married Mary Christine Swanzy, with whom he had two sons and a daughter. Despite his modest demeanour, Seán was a charming, talented actor with a fine singing voice. He 'might have been | A famous, a brilliant figure | Before the painted scene', Yeats later reflected.[6] Joining the Abbey in 1913, while the main company was touring America, he impressed Lady Gregory with 'his beautiful and distinguished work' in her *Kincora* and Edward McNulty's *The Lord Mayor*.[7] His first appearance on the stage of the Abbey was as the Miser in an English-language adaptation of Douglas Hyde's *An Pósadh* (The Marriage). He performed regularly for the Abbey from 1913, often playing alongside Helena Molony and Arthur Shields.

Seán Connolly (far left), Constance
Markievicz, George Miskell (?),
and the Abbey rebel Eddie Keegan
(far right) in a scene from Casimir
Markievicz's *The Memory of the Dead:
A Romantic Drama of '98*. The play
was produced by the Independent
Theatre Company at the Abbey in
1910 (AL, IE/AL/KL/5/1 1912).

Seán Connolly played opposite
Helena Molony (as Mrs Finnegan)
in George Birmingham's *Eleanor's
Enterprise*, 1911 (NLI PD 2159/
TX/3/8). The English-born artist
'Ben Bay' (Benjamin Talbot Bailey,
1887–c. 1922) worked primarily as
a journal illustrator. Wounded at
the Battle of Loos, he returned to
England, where he was arrested for
bigamy, c. 1920. He appears to have
died penniless in Egypt (information
by courtesy of Mary Broderick).

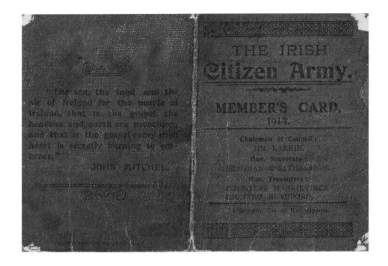

**Membership card for the Irish Citizen
Army, 1914 (NMI, HE/EW/499b).**

A political radical committed to an austere lifestyle, Seán Connolly
was deeply idealistic: 'young and maybe dangerous', O'Casey considered, 'for
like Robespierre, he believes everything he says'.[8] He combined class politics
– opting for the Citizen Army over the more popular Irish Volunteers – with
a strict Catholicism. The republican journalist T. F. O'Sullivan recalled Seán
as 'almost a Daily Communicant' who 'never touched intoxicating liquors
or smoked'.[9] After independence, this combination of class politics and
Catholicism would become more unusual, as socialism was increasingly
conflated with atheism. The tension between Catholicism and republicanism
may have presented greater difficulties for Seán: his refusal, on religious
grounds, to join the oath-bound IRB initially aroused suspicion.[10]

As a member of the ITGWU, Seán participated in the 1913 Lockout, a
more radicalising event than the Home Rule crisis for many Dublin workers.
Family influences may again have played some part here: his brother Matthew
(Mattie) recalled joining the Citizen Army at 'the request of my father'.

O'Casey ran into Seán Connolly the following year, during the
Howth gun-running, as they headed towards the Citizen Army's training
centre at Croydon Park for news: 'He was full of the gun-running'. O'Casey
watched as Seán organised groups of men to salvage the guns that panicked
Volunteers had jettisoned when they were confronted by the Scottish
Borderers. O'Casey was struck by Seán's defiance when he later refused to
return the rifles to the Volunteer leaders who called at Croydon Park.[11]

Connolly was relatively prominent in the Citizen Army. When it marched to the Mansion House in September 1914 to disrupt an enlistment meeting addressed by John Redmond and the British Prime Minster, H. H. Asquith, it was Seán who led the protesters in a rousing rendition of 'A Nation Once Again'. A handsome, much-admired figure, he reportedly inspired the character of Jack Clitheroe, the weak protagonist of *The Plough and the Stars*, whose commitment to the Citizen Army was based on vanity rather than idealism. Although he was reputedly 'the best-dressed man at ICA mobilisations',[12] too much should not be read into this characterisation in the light of O'Casey's stated admiration for Seán.

Seán's radicalism found expression in amateur theatre circles rather than on the Abbey stage. With his sister Katie (Barrett), whom he would fight alongside in 1916, he was prominent in the Liberty Players and the Irish Workers' Dramatic Company, which was managed by Helena Molony.[13] A fan of the Abbey, if not the of 'so-called cultural folk' who patronised it, Delia Larkin established the company at Liberty Hall, where 'the newer drama can be played and where the working classes can assemble without fear of being snubbed'.[14] As with the musical performances of the Workers' Orchestra, the company's political satire, grim urban realist plays and patriotic drama formed part of a broader cultural front at Liberty Hall. Offended by the popularity of British music-hall shows at the union's head office, James Connolly had insisted on more ideological fare. Citizen Army members, including Seán, subsequently came to the fore at Liberty Hall's Sunday-night revues, as one activist recalled: 'this little group had a complete social life of its own, with songs, poetry, dancing and plays, no less than military exercises, building up the rebel front.'[15]

Like many of the nationalist dramatic companies, they performed some of the Abbey's repertoire, while also positioning themselves against that theatre's suspect ethos. James Connolly's play *Under Which Flag?* is believed to have been written to counter George Bernard Shaw's pro-recruitment *O'Flaherty VC*, which the Abbey planned to stage in late 1915. Involved in the rehearsals for the (subsequently cancelled) performance, Seán and Helena may have provided James Connolly with details of Shaw's play.[16] In *Under Which Flag?* Seán played Dan McMahon, an 1848 veteran who – despite having been blinded by the English – encourages young men to fight in the 1867 insurrection. A (topically) anti-enlistment as well as pro-insurrectionary play, it centres on young Frank O'Donnell, who wins Mary's love by refusing to fight for the cause of 'bloody Empire'. Paraphrasing

REASONS WHY

YOU SHOULD JOIN

The Irish Citizen Army.

BECAUSE It pledges its members to work for, organise for, drill for and fight for **an Independent Ireland.**

BECAUSE It places its reliance upon the only class that never betrayed Ireland—the Irish Working Class.

BECAUSE Having a definite aim to work for there is no fear of it being paralysed in the moment of action by divisions in its Executive Body.

BECAUSE It teaches that "the sole right of ownership of Ireland is vested in the people of Ireland, and that that full right of ownership may, and ought to be, enforced by any and all means that God hath put within the power of man."

BECAUSE It works in harmony with the Labour and true National Movements and thus embraces all that makes for Social Welfare and National Dignity.

Companies Wanted in Every District.

RECRUITS WANTED EVERY HOUR.

Apply for further information, Secretary, Citizen Army, Liberty Hall, Dublin.

Irish Paper.] *City Printing Works, 13 Stafford Street, Dublin.*

Irish Citizen Army leaflet (NMI, EW/325/1).

'Neither King nor Kaiser'. The Irish Citizen Army outside Liberty Hall (NPA, KE 198).

Robert Emmet's celebrated speech from the dock, Blind Dan urges Frank to give his 'heart's blood' so 'that poor Mother Erin might be a nation among the nations of the earth'.[17]

Admiring the play's 'true spirit of patriotism', Francis Sheehy Skeffington believed that Seán's performance exerted 'a profound impression on the audience'.[18] In contrast, Seán O'Casey – who considered James Connolly's embrace of Fenian elitism a betrayal of socialism – wrote that the play 'blundered a sentimental way over a stage in the Hall in a green limelight, shot with tinsel stars'. In the light of its author's revolutionary socialism, what is most striking about this unsubtle play, which conforms to a well-established genre whereby the protagonist regains his manhood by resolving to serve the nation, is the conventional nature of its theme of 'public duty over private concerns', which echoed plays like *Cathleen ni Houlihan*.[19] In this respect, it illustrates the extent of James Connolly's shift from class struggle to insurrectionary violence prior to the Rising: 'His fine eyes saw red no longer', O'Casey wrote, 'but stared into the sky for a green dawn'.[20]

Seán Connolly's last performances at the Abbey occurred in two of the theatre's most significant insurrectionary plays. *The Dreamers* by Lennox Robinson offered a characteristically ambivalent take on Emmet's rebellion, but Seán's final appearance at the Abbey was in the more unambiguously patriotic *Cathleen ni Houlihan*. He played the part of Michael Gillane who sacrifices a life of promise to redeem his country. It is difficult to think of a more appropriate role given Seán's dedication to mounting the insurrection, which he knew was only weeks away: 'Often before the Rising took place we were speaking,' Seán's wife recalled: 'The love he had for Ireland burned him

IRISH CITIZEN ARMY.

HEADQUARTERS : LIBERTY HALL, DUBLIN.
COMMANDANT : JAMES CONNOLLY.

DATE ___22nd April, 1916.___

By warrant of the Army Council I hereby appoint

___Seán Connolly___

to take the rank of ___Captain___
with full power to exercise all the rights and perform
all the duties belonging to that rank.

(SIGNED)

James Connolly

COMMANDANT.

Seán Connolly was promoted to
the rank of captain (and, later that
same day, acting commandant)
shortly before the Easter Rising
(NMI, HE/EW/163/1).

like a fire, as the days and weeks went on it increased and he wished that he
could instil it into the heart of all Irish men.'[21]

His final appearance on stage was at Liberty Hall, less than a
fortnight before the Rising. *The Workers' Republic* mischievously advertised
Under Which Flag? as 'Next to the Revolution the Greatest Event of 1916'.[22]
The final line is spoken by Seán's character, Dan, after young Frank has
abandoned his lover to fight for Ireland:

> Mary (*turning to Blind Dan*): Now, Dan, the boys are all
> gone – and my boy with them.
> Dan (*kneeling, in which he is followed by all the Company*): And
> God's blessing go with him and them, and with the
> brave girls that sent them out to battle, and God's
> blessing be with the cause of the land that bore them.
> All: Amen.[23]

The Green Flag carried by Seán onto the stage at Liberty Hall is
thought to be the same one he carried into battle on Easter Monday, a prop
in a more powerful work of performance art.[24]

Chapter 9

Arthur Shields

1896–1916

Arthur Shields, c. 1920 (HL, T13/B/5).

I have just left Stephen Gwynn, we lunched together
and I send you his gloomy prophecy as much in his
own words as I can. Churchill and Grey have won
Asquith over to a postponement of the Home Rule
question ... The position will become very difficult but
if there is a cataclysm of some kind and a Conservative
Government is elected it will become desperate. The
Conservatives are pledged against Home Rule. Should
that happen, Ireland will have been betrayed by the
Liberals; and the Irish Party ... will cease to exist. It
will leave all political power to the Volunteers and let
them make what terms they can.

—W. B. Yeats to Lady Gregory, 28 August 1914.[1]

> Are they still going on with the old parliamentary
> methods – haven't they seen yet the utter futility
> of constitutional agitation? *Great applause*. Arms
> – arms is what we want, arms and then freedom.
> *Immense applause*. Think, think of Ireland, Ireland,
> the English banished from the country – (*subdued but
> determined applause*) & Ireland a free nation again!
>
> —Cesca Trench, recounting the response to Lennox Robinson's *Patriots* at the
> Abbey Theatre[2]

Although Yeats's concern about his responsibility for sending out men to die seems unwarranted in the case of the Abbey's other rebels, Arthur Shields was unambiguous about the literary revival's effect on his political consciousness: 'It was the plays of the Abbey Theatre that made me increasingly aware that I was an Irishman, even before I was a member of the [Abbey] Company'.[3] Intriguingly, the only rebel too young to have lived through the cultural revival was the one most clear about its political impact. However, as with the other rebels, a much broader range of influences – including family, the Home Rule crisis and the appeal of Volunteering – shaped his evolution from cultural nationalist to revolutionary.

Arthur's radicalism owed much to his father's influence. Adolphus Shields was no ordinary man, as is evident from the lessons he carefully imparted to his children during the family's Sunday-morning walks:

> Whenever they chanced on private fencing that cut
> off what Papa knew to be public domain, to the great
> delight of the children, he would kick it down, pull
> it apart and set them to scattering the pieces. He
> was careful though to make the distinction between
> wanton destruction and concerned action to protect
> public rights.[4]

A Protestant socialist, Adolphus Shields had a distinguished lineage as a radical, which he traced, through his mother's family, to William Orr, the Presbyterian United Irishman executed in 1797. Although his older brother was a Fenian, Adolphus – who lived through the 1867 rebellion – became a committed pacifist. Working as a printer's apprentice, an occupation often identified with radicalism, he progressed – as did many socialists in the United Kingdom – from teaching Sunday school to preaching Fabian socialism.[5] As district secretary of the National Union of Gasworkers and General Labourers, he led a strike against the city's coal merchants in 1890, the same year in which he chaired Ireland's first May Day celebration, in the Phoenix Park.

In 1896 Adolphus inadvertently altered the course of Irish history and, as it turned out, his son's destiny by inviting James Connolly to move from Edinburgh to Dublin to work as an organiser for the Dublin Socialist Club.[6] Formed by Fabians and Independent Labour Party supporters, this organisation had devoted itself to left-wing activism in the face of a hostile political climate. After Connolly's arrival, Adolphus helped him to found the Irish Socialist Republican Party. Although unsuccessful, the party proved influential in the longer term by bringing together republicanism and socialism, which had been largely antagonistic political traditions in Ireland. A reformist rather than a revolutionary, Adolphus soon left the party, but he remained friendly with Connolly. Although Arthur took a different political path, he was shaped by his father's idealism: 'He had a beautiful vision of society'.[7]

Born on 15 February 1896 in North Great George's Street, Lewis Arthur Shields – known as 'Boss' to family and close friends – was the sixth of the seven children born to Adolphus and his wife, Fanny, another rebellious soul. Resenting the restrictions placed on young women of her privileged background, Fanny Ungerland left Hamburg to find work as a governess, eventually making her way to Ireland, where she met Adolphus.[8] Arthur recalled the family's poverty, particularly the weekly chore of redeeming his father's suit from the pawnbroker's: 'We were always having to move because nothing could be paid. There never was enough money in those days, and the family was big.' This movement, however, also reflected Adolphus's improving social status. As he progressed from printer's apprentice to press reader, the family moved from the impoverished tenements of the inner city to the semi-rural villages of Clontarf and Howth, where Arthur spent his adolescent years.

Although his early education was patchy, he was a voracious reader, favouring non-fiction and poetry, including Yeats's work.[9] Like his siblings, who were also drawn to artistic pursuits and the cause of labour, Arthur was shaped by his parents' progressive ideals. He recalled how family and friends gathered round the kitchen table to discuss inequality and social questions: 'Every child was encouraged to develop natural talents, especially those dealing with arts or service to others'.[10] Grievances and disputes were formally considered at family tribunals. Along with a sceptical world view, and a liberal commitment to intellectual freedom, his father imparted to Arthur a secular outlook in an age of religious belief. The census returns for the eight members of the Shields household enumerated in 1911 list four Anglicans (including Arthur and his father), two agnostics, one atheist and a spiritualist (his widowed sister).[11]

Although intense, earnest and rather reserved, Arthur was drawn to the stage from a young age. When he was fifteen he set up the Kincora Amateur Dramatic Club, recruiting family, friends and neighbours to stage plays (mainly by Synge and T. C. Murray) in his dining-room. Its first production was Lady Gregory's rebel play *The Rising of the Moon*.[12] A regular attender at the Abbey despite his youth, Arthur left Merchant Taylors' School at fourteen, finding work as a clerk at Maunsel's publishing house. Remembered for its rejection of Joyce's *Dubliners*, Maunsel was a product of the Irish-Ireland revival, specialising in literature by Irish writers. It had strong links to the theatre, publishing the work of Yeats, Gregory and Synge.[13] After picking up a small part in a film on the life of St Patrick, Arthur persuaded his father to pay for him to study at the Abbey School of Acting. Making his first appearance on the Abbey stage in a walk-on part in December 1913, he got his first credited part as Major Butterfield in *The Lord Mayor* by Edward McNulty in March 1914. He appeared alongside Seán Connolly in the play, which was directed by another left-wing radical, Pat Wilson. A talented performer, Arthur had a commitment to the theatre, demonstrated by his regular presence at the back of the auditorium, where he studied the techniques of both actors and directors. He was offered a contract the following year.

By then, Arthur's interest in politics was evident. He told the Military Pensions Board that he joined the 2nd Battalion of the Dublin Brigade of the Irish Volunteers in July 1915.[14] Elsewhere, though, Arthur recalled joining in July 1914: 'one of my schoolmates at the Green Lane in Clontarf was a convinced republican, and I had got a great deal of feeling for the national movement from the theatre, so I joined F Company of the Volunteers'.[15] The earlier date may be accurate, as this is when Arthur's pal Charlie Saurin joined up. His decision was a response to the Bachelor's

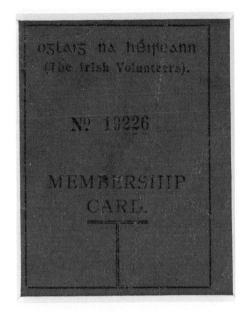

Leaflet advertising the inaugural
meeting of the Irish Volunteers, 25
November 1913 (NMI, EW/561). It was
attended by Arthur Shields, Barney
Murphy and Peadar Kearney.

Irish Volunteers membership card (NMI,
HE/EW/828a). Like many young men,
Arthur Shields joined the Volunteers
in the wake of the Howth gun-running
and Bachelor's Walk shootings when
the movement's popularity surged.

Walk shootings, when British soldiers – frustrated by the failure to prevent
the Howth gun-running (which Seán Connolly and Peadar Kearney had
participated in) – had opened fire on a jeering crowd, killing three. Their
actions prompted a nationwide surge in Volunteer numbers, although most
of those who flooded in were moderate nationalists rather than separatist
revolutionaries. Explaining his decision to join the movement, Arthur cited
a broad range of radical influences:

> The big strike of 1913 had just taken place; I can remember
> standing in Beresford Place listening to James Larkin
> speaking. He was a most dynamic speaker. My father was
> friendly with James Connolly. Dublin then was exciting,
> as far as the labour movement was concerned, as far
> as the national movement was concerned, as far as the
> literary movement was concerned.[16]

Despite his radicalism, Adolphus was saddened by Arthur's decision to join a nationalistic armed movement. Abetted by Seán Connolly, Arthur kept his rifle hidden at work, under the stage of the Abbey. He combined the pleasures of drilling – Sunday route marches across the Wicklow Mountains, mastering drill in St Matthew's Park, acquiring the accoutrements of soldiering – with the demands of work and his commitments at the Abbey.[17]

Only a tiny minority of the 150,000 nationalists who belonged to the Irish Volunteers in the summer of 1914 remained with that organisation after the split triggered by John Redmond's support for the war in September, and only a small minority of this radical faction turned out at Easter, 1916. What led Arthur to the GPO? His wife's biography, based closely on Arthur's reminiscences, described his visit to the Abbey Theatre to see *Cathleen ni Houlihan* in 1913 as the turning-point of his young life.[18] Although the passage of time, and the reinforcing of that play's incendiary reputation after 1916, may have accentuated his memory of the play's effect, an American academic who interviewed Arthur many years after the Rising recorded a similar account:

> He remembers the first time he ever saw the play – when
> he was perhaps thirteen or fourteen, a Saturday night
> at the Abbey – how it burst upon him, the incredible
> impact changing his life, the walk home as if on air,
> feeling the intense patriotic joy of being Irish. 'There
> were other plays, too, that influenced us, many of them,
> but that was the great one.'[19]

Chapter 10

Theatre of nation:

Radical networks and revolutionary spaces

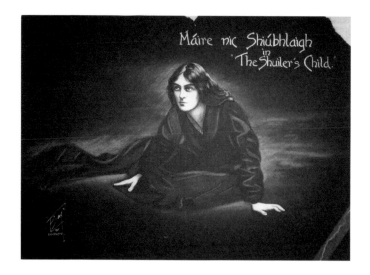

Máire Nic Shiubhlaigh won acclaim for her performance as Moll Wood in Seumas O'Kelly's *The Shuiler's Child* (1909). Illustration by Ben Bay (NLI, PD 2159/TX/3/44).

Victor Hugo said somewhere: 'It is in the Theatre that the mob becomes a people'.

—W. B. Yeats[1]

I am going to live the things that I have before imagined.

—Thomas MacDonagh, 1916[2]

How did theatre shape the coming revolution? Did the amateur companies that competed against the Abbey have a better claim than Yeats to have sent out those the English shot? Or was theatre merely one medium among many giving expression to separatist aspirations? Did its importance lie principally in providing a physical space for otherwise marginal activists? Or was there something particular to drama that invested it with revolutionary potential? Did theatre, as one playwright suggested, provide 'the place where a nation thinks in public in front of itself'?[3] The experiences of the Abbey rebels shed some light on these questions.

The radical companies Máire Nic Shiubhlaigh helped to found after leaving the Abbey were not only more in tune with the Irish National Theatre Society's self-sufficient ethos: they were explicitly committed to the promotion of the Irish language and political nationalism. The more sophisticated of them, such as the Irish Theatre Company, also 'appropriated the Abbey's original idea of cosmopolitan theatre', modelling themselves on

the 'theatres of revolt' emerging elsewhere in Europe.[4] Companies like the
Theatre of Ireland were admired by advanced nationalists, while the Abbey
(although assiduously attended by them) attracted their hostility.[5] However,
the features of these companies that radical nationalists most admired –
their amateur status and propagandist function – constrained their artistic
and commercial appeal.[6] Although *The Shuiler's Child*, Seumas O'Kelly's play of
1909 about a woman of the road who encounters her previously abandoned
child, offered Máire her most famous role, it was one of the Theatre of
Ireland's few commercial successes. Part of the reason it was so celebrated
was that Máire's 'success provided a useful stick to beat the Abbey with'.
Yeats was 'a fool', *Sinn Féin* informed its readers, for allowing Máire to leave
the Abbey.[7] To her credit, Nic Shiubhlaigh acknowledged both sides of the
argument about art and politics:

> Although for most of us who took the course of
> secession, the action meant the finish of any progress
> we might have been making individually towards
> international distinction as Irish players – in my own
> case it virtually meant the end of a career on the stage
> which might or might not have taken me away from
> Dublin altogether in the years that followed – I doubt
> if many of us had any regrets at the time ... I never
> thought of the National Theatre Society as a purely
> theatrical enterprise. It was merely a part of the larger
> national movement in which most of us were then
> participating ... But perhaps that was not a practicable
> idea. If the Abbey had remained subordinate to
> nationalism, political as well as cultural, in those years,
> it might never have achieved the success which it did. It
> had to stand outside the nationalist movement in order
> to make its mark on the theatre of the world.[8]

An important function of these small, overlapping and often short-
lived dramatic companies was to provide a network for like-minded activists
committed as much to politics as to theatre. After 1916, the cast of plays
staged by such companies as the Irish Theatre would read like a roll-call

The poet and revolutionary Joseph Plunkett (1887–1916): his neck scar resulted from an operation on his tubercular glands. Plunkett and his fellow-signatory of the Proclamation, Thomas MacDonagh were directors of the Irish Theatre (NPA, P2/338).

Máire Nic Shiubhlaigh often acted alongside William Pearse in the Leinster Stage Society's productions, which included the plays of William's brother, Patrick Pearse (NLI, EPH A752).

of revolutionaries. In helping to found the latter company (with Edward Martyn's financial backing) in 1914, following the collapse of the Theatre of Ireland, Máire was joined by two signatories of the Proclamation, the melodramatic dreamer Thomas MacDonagh and the flamboyant bohemian Joseph Plunkett. Through the involvement of William Pearse, the company was linked to the Proclamation's best-known signatory. Máire recalled that she 'used to go to St Enda's at Ranelagh to help now and then with the plays which were given there'. William was 'deeply interested in the stage'. Máire was initially less taken with his otherworldly older brother, Patrick, who was shy, physically unimposing and 'a bit of a poseur'. He was 'very neat', she noted disapprovingly: 'a lot of people said he was finicky about his clothes'. She came to admire him, however, and regarded his passion play, performed at the Abbey in 1911, as 'probably the first really serious piece of Gaelic dramatic writing produced'.[9]

Much of the political significance of theatre stemmed from its popularity as a medium. This ensured that, like the press or other cultural nationalist pastimes, it provided an important medium for connecting people and communicating ideas. As Máire noted:

> At that time, in 1912, no less than at any other time during the early years of the century, Dublin was drama-mad in every sense of the word. Almost everyone in the city was a playgoer, for there were not many other kinds of entertainment available, and although the kinematograph had more or less arrived at one Dublin hall, the Rotunda, about 1910, it was not then sufficiently developed to divert attention from the legitimate stage ... The most unexpected people in Dublin, poets, writers, artists, revolutionists, were interested in the theatre; everyone was ready to discuss a new play or the work of a player.

The importance of theatre for political organisations in Dublin is also conveyed in Máire's memoir:

> Almost all the national clubs, literary, political or otherwise, were associated with theatrical groups in the young years of the dramatic movement. Many young nationalists appeared as players with amateur companies, and a lot of the political clubs, led by Arthur Griffith's Cumann na nGaedheal, had dramatic societies attached, either as a means of gathering funds or of disseminating propaganda.[10]

One practical reason for theatre's appeal for such organisations was that it offered small groups with few resources a focus for collective activism, its members' commitment being the most important requirement. Staging a play, as Sydney Gifford noted, 'meant that boys and girls, who had worked hard all day, gave up their evenings through the winter months to rehearsing in ice-cold basements, so that they might give one or two performances in a tiny hall.'[11] Requiring not just a dramatist with a vision but also a company, an audience and a public venue, drama was particularly suited to political activism. It allowed otherwise marginal groups – including republicans, feminists and socialists – a public space denied them in conventional politics, creating 'a broader terrain for battles within nationalism to be fought upon'.[12]

In this sense, theatre should be seen as part of a much broader network of overlapping associational bodies that met in pubs, church halls and the back rooms of shops. Irish-Irelanders, Sinn Féiners, republicans, advanced nationalists, intellectuals, socialists, academics, professionals, artists and ordinary workers made up this vibrant if

Advertisements from the Irish National Dramatic Company's programme for *Cathleen ni Houlihan*, April 1902. As these notices (including one in Irish for Matthew Walker's tobacco shop) illustrate, amateur theatre lay at the heart of a broader web of cultural, economic and political enterprise (NLI, EPH C821).

THE GAELIC LEAGUE

ESTABLISHED 1893.

President: DOUGLAS HYDE, LL.D.   Vice-Presidents: REV. M. P. HICKEY, D.D., M.R.I.A.; REV. PETER O'LEARY, P.P.

OBJECTS:

1. The preservation of Irish as the National Language of Ireland, and the extension of its use as a spoken tongue.
2. The study and publication of existing Irish Litertaure, and the cultivation of a modern literature in Irish.

Upwards of 350 affiliated Branches.

The Gaelic League is strictly non-political and non-sectarian.

Support the movement by contributing to The Irish Language National Fund.

For all information regarding the work of the Gaelic League, Rules for the formation of Branches, Pamphlets, Leaflets, &c., write to—

THE GENERAL SECRETARY, GAELIC LEAGUE,
24 UPPER O'CONNELL STREET, DUBLIN.

CYCLES!

BUY FROM

KEATING,

3 LOWER ⅓ ABBEY STREET, DUBLIN.

inʒiniðe na h-éireann.

On Wednesday, Thursday, and Friday Evenings,

2nd, 3rd, and 4th April, 1902,

MR. W. G. FAY'S IRISH NATIONAL DRAMATIC COMPANY

WILL PRODUCE AT

THE HALL OF ST. TERESA'S

Total Abstinence Association, Clarendon St.,

For the First Time on any Stage,

"DEIRDRE,"

A Play in Three Acts by "A.E."

KATHLEEN NI HOULIHAN,

A Play in One Act by W. B. YEATS.

Scenery by A.E. and W. G. FAY.

DRESSES MADE BY inʒiniðe na héireann FROM DESIGNS BY A.E.

Orchestra: String Band of the Workmen's Club, 41 York St.

PROGRAMME, ONE PENNY.

PIM BROTHERS, Limited,

STH. GT. GEORGE'S ST., DUBLIN.

WHOLESALE ONLY FROM

IRISH MANUFACTURE,

SPECIAL VALUE IN

Penny Packet of Note and Envelopes,

[12]

ceannuiʒ ðeaʒ-ruð ⁊ tá aʒat saor-ruð.

Keep on Smiling and write for Patterns

OF

Irish Tweeds, Serges, &c,

TO

DUBLIN WOOLLEN CO.,

15 BACHELOR'S WALK.

CUT LENGTHS.   SPLENDID GOODS.

Cash Only.

sinn féin, sinn féin, amáin.

DUBLIN WORKMEN'S INDUSTRIAL
ASSOCIATION,
47 YORK STREET, DUBLIN.

Clothing, Boots, Furniture, Bicycles, supplied on Weekly Payment System, all of Irish Material and Workmanship Guaranteed.

Office Hours, 7 to 9 each Evening.

Irish-made Paper.   Abbey Printing Works, 9 Great Strand Street, Dublin.

fragmented oppositional culture whose significance is overlooked by a more conventional focus on the political dominance of constitutional nationalism and the electoral weakness of its radical opponents. As P. J. Mathews has argued, the extent to which the progressive impulses generated by this movement – rather than Yeats's literary revival – contributed to the subsequent revolution has yet to be fully recognised: 'The closest thing to a unified movement within Irish life at that time was not to be found in the meeting rooms of parliamentary politics but within the branch organisations and societies of the broad self-help alliance.'[13] The intense sociability of this world, and its concentration in inner-city Dublin, enhanced its dynamism. The Wexford journalist Robert Brennan recalled how a 'visit to Dublin in those dark days was like a tonic. Every person one met seemed to be a rebel of some sort and one felt it was only a matter of time until all Ireland would follow Dublin's lead.' Nor was 'this stimulating atmosphere' confined to the political sphere: 'There were poets, essayists and artists galore and one met them everywhere.'[14]

Even allowing for nostalgia, accounts of pre-war separatist Dublin convey its energetic and egalitarian atmosphere. P. S. Doyle recalled how his revolutionary circles drew from all strata of society:

> Connolly, the foremost figure in the labour movement, could be the friend and confidant of Tomás MacDonagh, who was a professor in the National University. Pádraig Pearse, one of the foremost figures in the language and educational movements in the country, could associate and work and plan with the most ordinary worker on the Dublin quays. There were soccer and football and rugby men. They came from the staff of the Abbey Theatre, as well as from the ranks of the Trades Union.[15]

At céilithe, Ernie O'Malley noted, one only met people who were 'all right'. Uniting separatists of 'different classes, outlooks and creeds', the armed movements that emerged from this milieu preserved much of this spirit, O'Malley believed. 'On my right was a newsboy, on my left an out of work, covering me in the rear rank was a Master of Arts, since Professor of Romance Languages, next to him a final medical.'[16]

What is less apparent from such accounts is that relatively few people within these circles became revolutionaries. Whether performing on the stage, learning Irish with the Gaelic League or playing sports with the GAA, most nationalists were not radicalised by cultural nationalism. This is not to discount the importance of Irish-Ireland circles for the radical minority that was, or their role in preparing the way for the subsequent popularity of separatist politics. The importance of cultural nationalism also lay in its ability to bring together people from diverse backgrounds. It provided, for example, a space for women that mainstream politics did not. Compared with class struggle or separatist ideology, it appealed to many people who did not come from a Catholic nationalist background.[17] In addition, as Seán T. O'Kelly recalled, even relatively unpromising cultural organisations were routinely established, patronised or infiltrated by the Irish Republican Brotherhood. 'The IRB element was most assiduous in urging support of organisations like the Abbey Theatre, and there would seldom be a night of the Abbey Theatre when many members of the IRB would not be present.'[18] As well as facilitating the dissemination of republican values, cultural organisations provided a cover for the Fenians' subversive activity.

A wealth of sources allow us to map revolutionary Dublin in remarkable detail. Some networks were clearly more influential than others. The extent to which Inghinidhe na hÉireann influenced the Abbey's rebels is evident. The intersection between feminism and nationalism that it represented was particularly influential for those outside separatism's natural constituency: 'For Protestant women the key introduction to rebel politics was the feminist movement and the demand for equal suffrage rights.'[19] When the history of the independence movement was written in a more conservative era following the revolution, the importance of this radical organisation was underestimated. Fianna Éireann proved similarly influential, bridging the turn-of-the-century cultural revival and the later Volunteering phenomenon. Drama played an important role within both organisations. It was Constance Markievicz's interest in drama that first brought her into contact with Inghinidhe na hÉireann: 'it was there that I first met her,' Máire recalled. 'Madame attended all the first nights, discussed plays, acted in them, later she produced some too when she began a dramatic company of her own in the city. She wrote a lot for the stage too'.[20]

Some meeting-places proved more significant sites of activity than others. The draughty hall behind the egg-and-butter shop at 34 Lower Camden Street that provided such an unsuitable venue for the Irish National Dramatic Company's first plays also hosted Fianna Éireann's inaugural meeting, which four of the Abbey's rebels – Barney Murphy, Helena Molony, Peadar Kearney and Ellen Bushell – attended. Count Plunkett's ramshackle eighteenth-century building in Hardwicke Street housed the militant Irish Theatre's productions but also, from 1912, Dun Emer's co-operative workshop. Among its accomplished designers was Elinor Monsell, who created the Abbey Theatre's striking emblem of Maeve with a bloodhound. The boys of Na Fianna also used the Hardwicke Hall, as did the Irish Volunteers, who held officers' classes, military lectures, drilling and musketry instruction there. Cumann na mBan hosted fund-raising concerts, céilithe, plays and lectures in the hall. In the days before the Easter Rising, the IRB stored 'a considerable dump of ammunition' under its stage.[21]

Matthew Walker's tobacconist's shop, where as a young girl Máire helped her father behind the counter, provided another such site, connecting a diverse range of people from obscure backgrounds. His 'shop became the rendezvous for all the Gaels of the city', James Kavanagh recalled: 'He placed a large room at the back of the shop at our disposal without any charge. He didn't even suggest nor expect us to be customers.'[22] Among those whom Harry Phibbs (a member of the Celtic Literary Society) recollected as frequenting this nondescript shop were the socialist revolutionary Liam Mellows ('a quiet, fair-haired young fellow') who led the insurrection in Galway; the Citizen Army activist Michael Mullen (the inspiration for Seamus Shields in *The Shadow of a Gunman*); Peadar Kearney ('one of the young fellows with a talent for verse'); his friend, the Abbey stage manager Seán Barlow; a 'red-haired school-teacher named Jinny O'Flanagan' (who married Éamon de Valera); and the 1916 martyr Michael O'Hanrahan ('it was understood he was ... with one of the secret organizations').[23]

Amateur theatre clearly fulfilled a similar function, providing a conducive milieu for people from diverse backgrounds to engage in sociable patriotic endeavour. But to what extent did the nature of theatre – its ability to engage the emotions and intellect of a public audience – prove a politicising force? It has been argued that the nature of drama ensured that it played a distinctive role in the process of nation-invention and radicalisation. 'Though it seemed to conspire with carnivalesque disorder,'

Amateur theatre was arguably a more influential breeding ground for revolutionaries than the Gaelic League or GAA. The cast of this 1904 production of *An Pósadh* (The Marriage, 1902) at the Gaiety included (L–R) Seán T. O'Kelly (revolutionary and future Irish president), Peadar Macken (killed in 1916), Sinéad O'Flanagan (wife of Éamon de Valera), Michael O'Hanrahan (executed in 1916), and the play's writer, Douglas Hyde, first president of Ireland (KG, 12PC/1A45/02).

Declan Kiberd suggests, 'the playhouse also provided the necessary antidote, for it encouraged a randomly gathered crowd to sense its growing, cohesive power.'[24] Roy Foster has similarly observed: 'What happened on the fringes of the Abbey, in [Alice] Milligan's portentous *tableaux vivants*, within the Theatre of Ireland, on the fit-up stages of Na hAisteoirí, at the Hardwicke Street Hall, in the Cork Dramatic Society or in St Enda's productions, was an intense and potent form of national-consciousness raising.'[25] A striking example of this is provided by Terence MacSwiney's plays, which have been read as 'an exercise in self-fashioning, presenting the heroic self-image to which he aspired'.[26] In *The Revolutionist* (1914) the resonantly named Hugh O'Neill, who models himself on Robert Emmet, comes to realise that self-sacrifice offers the most effective means of uniting the people, who disapprove of his militancy, to fight for Ireland. After 1916, revolutionary theatre gave way to theatrical acts of revolution. Press accounts of MacSwiney's hunger strike, for example, used 'theatrical metaphors to portray his long ordeal, conveying the idea that it was a role anyone could perform if they possessed the inner strength to do so'.[27]

Revolutionary plays also offered a means of addressing some of the central problems involved in staging a rebellion. The autobiographical scenarios they enacted can be read as self-indulgent wish-fulfilment, or as genuine attempts to resolve inner tensions. Set fifty years in the future, Thomas MacDonagh's *When the Dawn Is Come* (1908) imagines a revolutionary military council dominated by a leader whose extreme secrecy sees him mistaken for a traitor by his more fanatical comrades. The hero is vindicated only by his death in battle. Produced by the Irish Theatre in 1915, MacDonagh's subsequent play, *Pagans*, dramatised the tension between bohemian individualism and bourgeois respectability, culminating in its protagonist's commitment to serving the Irish nation.[28] MacDonagh's plays, which featured strong roles for women, have also been read as an argument for more equal gender relations in the new Ireland.[29]

Revolutionaries also dramatised some of the key debates within political nationalism. In MacSwiney's *The Revolutionist*, Hugh O'Neill articulates the central dilemma facing a revolutionary vanguard seeking to mount an insurrection:

> HUGH: We acted in the belief the country would gradually be won over. I have come to feel it will not be so. The people will receive a shock and come over together.
> CONN: The time is too tame.
> HUGH: The time will always be – as dangerous as we make it.[30]

The play also presents a strong argument in favour of open political organisation over conspiratorial methods. Hugh aligns himself against revolutionary secret societies on the grounds that their divisive methods will prevent republican unity, a prescient concern given that MacSwiney ended up among the anti-insurrectionary majority who failed to obey the military council's orders in 1916 – a regret he carried to his deathbed. Notoriously ill-informed about the rebels' intentions, owing to a lack of informers, the British authorities could have done worse than attend some of these productions. Tactical differences over the form an insurrection might take were role-played by the Irish Theatre in Hardwicke Street. Although some of its plays suggested

CLuiceoo iri·na·h·Ourcann

SECOND PERFORMANCES OF THE SEASON	The Cast includes Maire Nic Shiubhlaigh,
THE ROTUNDA (Large Concert Hall),	Honor Lavelle, Eibhlin O'Doherty, Joseph
Thursday, Friday & Saturday, March 21, 22 & 23,	Goggin, Proinsias Mac Siubhlaigh, E. Keegan,
At 8.15 p.m. Admission 2/-, 1/- & 6d.	Thomas R. Madden, Fred A. Macdonald, etc.

Postcard advertising two productions by the Theatre of Ireland, Padraic Colum's *The Fiddler's House* (1907) and Alice Milligan's *The Last Feast of the Fianna* (1900). The cast included Máire Nic Shiubhlaigh, her sister, 'Eileen O'Doherty', her brother Proinsias, and the Abbey rebel Edward Keegan (NLI, PD 2159/TX/52/12.

– as most Irish Volunteers believed – that separatists should not rise until public opinion supported them, others argued (as did the IRB's radicals) in favour of the transformative impact of insurrectionary violence. As James Moran notes: 'A secret society like the IRB could hardly conduct an explicit public debate about their rebellion, and so the playhouse provided an alternative meeting place for ideological and tactical discussion.'[31]

Patrick Pearse used theatre to convey his understanding of the messianic power of sacrificial violence. MacDara, the hero of *The Singer* (1915), sacrifices his life to lead his people, who are too frightened to fight, to freedom. He understands that with his death in battle he has ensured his immortality. His final speech is often seen as evidence of Pearse's mind-set on the eve of the Rising:

> One man can save a people, as one man redeemed the world. I will take no pike. I will go into battle with bare hands. I will stand up before the Gall as Christ hung naked before men on the tree![32]

Prudently, Pearse abandoned his plan to perform the play the week before the Rising, concerned that he might alert the authorities to his intentions. In much the same way as the IRB exploited traditional public spectacles, such as the funeral of O'Donovan Rossa, the revolutionary generation used the 'catalysing, inspirational, and insurrectionary' power of the stage to rehearse rebellion.[33]

Although the idealistic young activists who devoted their energies to drama and other cultural nationalist pursuits would have shaped Irish politics and society under Home Rule, few could have foreseen how a destabilising series of events from 1913 would transform a vibrant, disparate counter-culture into a revolutionary movement capable of confronting British rule. Máire Nic Shiubhlaigh noted how the militarisation of politics that followed affected the Irish Theatre as such figures as Plunkett and MacDonagh devoted their leisure time to practising revolution on the streets rather than performing it on the stage.[34] A similar process occurred elsewhere. The staging of MacSwiney's play *The Revolutionist* 'marked the demise of the Cork Dramatic Society, which dissolved with the establishment of a Cork branch of the Volunteers in December 1913'. Its theatre, An Dún, was converted into a drill hall.[35] In the period leading up to the Rising, Máire described this transition from drama to drilling:

> I formed Cumann na mBan and I became an active member of it, drilling and learning first-aid and going around the country with concert parties doing propaganda work and that led me to St Enda's and Padraig Pearse and his plays with his pupils. He was very much influenced by the Abbey Theatre and W. B. Yeats. He wrote some beautiful little plays and it was such a wonderful training for the boys. Thomas MacDonagh and Padraic Colum taught there and in the end we know how it ended. When the call came at Easter 1916 we all answered it and took part in the greatest drama of all. Plays and theatres were all forgotten for what has proved to be our salvation. I am proud today I was in Jacob's garrison under Thomas MacDonagh and Major [John] MacBride and I am glad I left the Abbey Theatre when I did for if I had remained there I might have missed the greatest part of my life's work.[36]

Part II

Easter, 1916

I have met them at close of day
Coming with vivid faces
From counter or desk among grey
Eighteenth-century houses.
I have passed with a nod of the head
Or polite meaningless words,
Or have lingered awhile and said
Polite meaningless words,
And thought before I had done
Of a mocking tale or a gibe
To please a companion
Around the fire at the club,
Being certain that they and I
But lived where motley is worn:
All changed, changed utterly:
A terrible beauty is born.

—W. B. Yeats, 'Easter 1916'

The General Post Office after Easter Week
(NMI, 984S0739/1). The building had been
lavishly refurbished before the insurrection.

Chapter 11

Easter

1916

No matter what's the odds, no matter though
Your death may come of it, ride out and fight,
The scene is set and you must out and fight.

—W. B. Yeats, *The Death of Cuchulain* (1939)

The war has hit our Irish theatre ... On Easter
Monday several hours after the Rebellion had broken
out & firing began the usual audience turned up
at the Abbey Theatre, also one of our actors, who
explained that he had been given two hours leave
of absence by his rebel captain to play his part – he
was then to return to the ranks. It was to be an
afternoon performance but our manager fearing
to have himself & the audience killed by shell fire
closed the theatre ... We lost one actor killed & two
imprisoned, but none of our well known players
were drawn into the wild business, which business
however has swept off many of the best of our young
men – a sort of vertigo of self-sacrifice.

—W. B. Yeats to Edward Gordon Craig, 1 August 1916[1]

The Easter Rising began as it would end: in confusion and acrimony. A
series of disasters – the British navy's interception on Good Friday of the
German arms shipment bound for Co. Kerry, the capture of Roger Casement,
and Eoin MacNeill's bitterly resented 'countermanding order', which
instructed the Irish Volunteers not to turn out on Easter Sunday – forced
the last-minute postponement of the insurrection. It also ensured that a
rebellion initially planned as a nationwide revolt of ten to fifteen thousand
Volunteers, mobilising in Cork, Limerick, Galway and other separatist
strongholds, became an essentially symbolic protest centred on Dublin. The
military council adopted a defensive strategy, as just over a thousand rebels
occupied a ring of buildings across the centre of the city. Despite the Rising's
strategic limitations, the scale of the violence and destruction that occurred
over the next six days was sufficient to achieve the organisers' desired
outcome: devastating much of the city centre, the impact of the rebellion
and its ruthless repression destroyed the credibility of the Irish Party and
created popular support for the demand for an Irish Republic.

Máire Nic Shiubhlaigh assumed that MacNeill's countermanding order, which she read to her father over breakfast at her home in Glasthule, meant that the manoeuvres were cancelled. Matthew Walker, who had recently come out of retirement to return to the family business of printing subversion, was better informed: 'Get the next tram in to [Éamonn] Ceannt's,' he said. 'See Lily O'Brennan yourself and ask her if this is genuine. Make sure you see her and don't ask anyone else.' Máire spent Sunday at Ceannt's house:

> Instinctively I felt that something important was taking place, but I could not guess, of course, that Ceannt, as one of the seven who were trying to lead the fighting the next day, was trying to straighten out the upset which the countermanding order ... had wrought.[2]

The following morning, when a telegram from Lily summoned her to town, 'the possibility of a rising never struck me.'[3] Leaving ten o'clock Mass, where her father had found her, she slipped into uniform and caught the tram into Dublin. She passed large numbers of Volunteers outside the College of Surgeons: 'Some wore slouch-hats, trench-coats, criss-crossed with bandoliers; a few of them had picks and shovels; most of them carried rifles.' She spotted Joseph Plunkett at the top of Grafton Street, and Thomas MacDonagh and John MacBride waiting at York Street. Although she failed to find Ceannt's Volunteers, it was clear, from the rattle of gunfire and the excitement sweeping town, what was happening. On learning that the rebels had taken Jacob's factory in Bishop Street, Máire made her way there, arriving just as the Volunteers smashed their way into the building.

Irish War News, 25 April 1915. Working with Joe Stanley, Máire Nic Shiubhlaigh's father, Matthew, and her brother Charles published republican propaganda during Easter week (NMI, HE/EW/812b).

IRISH WAR NEWS

THE IRISH REPUBLIC.

VOL. 1. No. 1   DUBLIN, TUESDAY, APRIL 25, 1916.   ONE PENNY

"IF THE GERMANS CONQUERED ENGLAND."

In the London "New Statesman" for *April 1st*, an article is published—"If the Germans Conquered England," which has the appearance of a very clever piece of satire written by an Irishman. The writer draws a picture of England under German rule, almost every detail of which exactly fits the case of Ireland at the present day. Some of the sentences are so exquisitely appropriate that it is impossible to believe that the writer had not Ireland in his mind when he wrote them. For instance :—

"England would be constantly irritated by the lofty moral utterances of German statesmen who would assert—quite sincerely, no doubt—that England was free, freer indeed than she had ever been before. Prussian freedom, they would explain, was the only real freedom, and therefore England was free. They would point to the flourishing railways and farms and colleges. They would possibly point to the contingent of M.P's, which was permitted, in spite of its deplorable disorderliness, to sit in a permanent minority in the Reich-stag. And not only would the Englishman have to listen to a constant flow of speeches of this sort ; he would find a respectable official Press secret bought over by the Government to say the same kind of things over and over, every day of the week. He would find, too, that his children were coming home from school with new ideas of history. . . . They would ask him if it was true that until the Germans came England had been an unruly country, constantly engaged in civil war. . . . The object of every schoolbook would be to make the English child grow up in the notion that the history of his country was a thing to forget, and that the one bright spot in it was the fact that it had been conquered by cultured Germ ny."

"If there was a revolt, German statesmen would deliver grave speeches about "disloyalty," "ingratitude," "reckless agitators who would ruin their country's prosperity. . . . Prussian soldiers would be encamped in every barracks—the English conscripts having been sent out of the country to be trained in Germany, or to fight the Chinese—in order to come to the aid of German morality, should English sedition come to blows with it."

"England would be exhorted to abandon her own genius in order to imitate the genius of her conquerors, to forget her own history for a larger history, to give up her own language for a "universal" language—in other words, to destroy her household gods one by one, and put in their p'ace

E.W. 812.
8

For Máire, as for many rebels, the revolution was a family affair. Working under James Connolly's directions, Máire's father, Matthew, and her brother Charles commandeered a printing press to publish *Irish War News* during Easter Week.[4] An elderly, well-dressed man, Matthew walked from Glasthule into town each morning, passing through the military's cordons, making his way to the GPO, where he collected Pearse's despatches. Máire's sister Gypsy also turned out: unable to get into a garrison, she carried despatches for Cathal Brugha. Other Abbey rebels also fought alongside family members. Seán Connolly was joined at City Hall by his sister Katie and three of his brothers, Eddie, George and Mattie; a fourth brother, Joe, who worked as a fireman at Tara Street Station, fought at the GPO.[5] Even women who did not participate could play an important supporting role. Initially sceptical of the rebels' determination to fight, Peadar Kearney was persuaded to mobilise by his wife, Eva.

Despite the military council's efforts to ensure secrecy, many rebels were better informed than Máire, particularly in the Citizen Army, where security was more lax. Seán Connolly and Helena Molony had been caught up in the dramatic crises of Easter Weekend as one disaster followed the next. Seán first shed his blood on Holy Thursday, losing part of his thumb to a bread-slicing machine as the Citizen Army made sandwiches for the rebellion: 'he was afraid it would impair his use of the rifle'. It was Seán who brought the despatch announcing Roger Casement's capture to Seán Mac Diarmada's safe house in Mountjoy Street in the early hours of Easter Saturday.[6] On Sunday morning Seán stood guard outside the small room in Liberty Hall where the military council agonised over their response to MacNeill's countermand. A comrade described his reaction to the decision to postpone the Rising: 'In a terrific state of excitement he burst into a room where a number of us were; off came hat, belt and coat, and he cried in vexation. The whole thing was off!'[7] Helena was also present at Liberty Hall: 'They were all heartbroken, and when they were not crying they were cursing,' she recalled. 'Many of us thought we would go out single-handed, if necessary'.[8]

Seán – who had a wife and three young children – understood the consequences of his actions: 'I am going to a regular death trap, but the risk has to be taken.'[9] According to William Oman, James Connolly was also pessimistic: 'As we were about to march off, Commandant Connolly approached Captain Sean Connolly, shook his hand and said: "Good luck, Sean! We won't meet again".'[10] If Seán was fatalistic as he led his contingent off, he did not let it show: it was not only Pearse who understood that he was performing a role for posterity. 'He was great looking in full uniform,' Jim O'Shea remembered. 'He was as brave looking as if he was Robert Emmet, and I believe looking back as if he was imbued with the ... spirit of the dead patriot. He seemed to stand out in posture and speech as such.'[11] Helena was in a similarly euphoric state of mind: 'When we walked out that Easter Monday morning we felt in a very real sense that we were walking with Ireland into the sun'.[12]

Although he had just returned from England on Easter Sunday, Arthur Shields must have had a fair idea what was planned, as his friend (and future brother-in-law) Charlie Saurin knew that the Volunteer mobilisation was 'only a cover for the "real thing"'.[13] Arthur's presence among the considerably smaller number of rebels who turned out at Father Mathew Park on Easter Monday is evidence of his commitment. This did not, however, entail ignoring his responsibilities to the Abbey. Arthur received permission from his commanding officer to make his way to the Abbey 'for a matinee'.[14] From there, he went directly to the GPO, where he was greeted by James Connolly: 'I hope you will prove as good a man as your father.'[15]

Although he had been working on the same tour as Arthur Shields, Peadar Kearney had made greater efforts to ensure that he did not miss the rebellion. He was back in Dublin by Spy Wednesday, when Thomas MacDonagh delivered a remarkably indiscreet speech to B Company of the 2nd Battalion: 'What is death?' Peadar recalled the commandant of the Dublin Brigade asking. 'Most of us have nothing to lose. Personally I will be of more pecuniary value to my relatives dead than I am alive.' MacDonagh's dispiriting pessimism, Peadar felt, contributed to his company's poor turn-out.

Alerted to the interception of the *Aud* through his IRB contacts, Peadar assumed that any rebellion would be futile. Disillusioned by the countermanding order, and sceptical that an insurrection would proceed, he mobilised only with great reluctance. He was further disheartened to discover that only one other member of his company had made it to the Stephen's Green rendezvous: 'Watching the number of men and boys moving about puzzled and doubtful,' he wrote, 'one could laugh or cry according to individual temperament.' Announcing that he was off to the Grafton Bar for a consoling pint, Peadar was warned that Volunteers under the influence of alcohol would be shot:

I simply grinned and said 'The way things are going you'll all be shot, order or no order, before the night is out'. I crossed the road and called for the usual: the gentleman behind the bar ... who had a very poor opinion of Volunteers, passed some sarcastic remarks when he saw the rifles etc. and wondered how men could go around making fools of themselves. About one hour after, his adventures in trying to find some place which he considered bullet-proof, were anything but pleasant.[16]

Peadar's account leaves no doubt about the lack of support for the rebels from many ordinary Dubliners. Manning a barricade at Blackpitts, an inner-city area of terraced houses and artisans' workshops, he was confronted by a mob of women, some apparently drunk, who sang pro-British songs, danced and hurled stones at them.[17] Describing this 'heart-breaking' scene, he recalled how they tried 'to take the rifles from them' and that 'one actually spat in my face'.[18] Like most rebels, he attributed this hostility to their reliance on the separation allowances they received as a result of their husband's or sons' military service, although there were other potential explanations for their anger, not least the danger to life and livelihood posed by the rebels' actions. Peadar did not record that the men on his barricade fired on these civilians, although he may have been thinking of this when he described the encounter as 'a painful experience ... and easily the worst part' of Easter Week.[19] He may have agreed with this ruthlessness. Infuriated by the sight of several policemen giving 'a lead to the crowd in insulting and degrading our men', he had sought permission to arrest them: 'It was bad enough to put up with the women and it would be possible to find an excuse for them, but to allow men in enemy uniform to hurl insults was a different thing altogether.' That he was prevented from doing so on the grounds that they were unarmed 'showed how meek and mild the revolutionaries of Easter Week were'.[20] Further civilian attacks forced an ignominious withdrawal from their outpost. As they forced their way through the hostile picket that had formed outside Jacob's, each received 'a parting salute from a hand or foot, whichever was most convenient for the ladies'.[21] Later, the crowd would attempt to set the building alight by stuffing burning rags under the door.

As they hastily filed up Dame Street, Seán Connolly and Helena Molony were also mocked by Dubliners who were gathered throughout the city to enjoy the fine bank-holiday weather: 'Here's the Citizen Army, with their pop-guns!'[22] Helena was one of about thirty Citizen Army rebels, under Seán's command, sent to attack Dublin Castle, centre of the British administration in Ireland. The extraordinary ease with which this small band, armed with pistols, rifles, shotguns and pikes, penetrated the Castle's defences would come to symbolise the humiliating unpreparedness of Augustine Birrell's administration.

Finding his entry to the Castle blocked by a solitary, unarmed policeman, Seán fired one of the first shots of the rebellion, instantly killing Constable James O'Brien. After hesitating briefly – whether due to shock or confusion – they advanced into the Castle grounds, overwhelming the guardroom and briefly occupying the Upper Castle Yard. They then fled the Castle. Helena, and the few British officials present, agreed that the Castle would have fallen had the rebels made any effort to take it. Remarkably, its sentries had not been equipped with live ammunition, and the nearest reinforcements consisted of no more than twenty-five soldiers at the Ship Street Barracks on the far side of the Castle buildings.[23] For a rebellion whose impact was primarily symbolic, the failure to seize the seat of British power was a missed opportunity (albeit one that was consistent with Robert Emmet's 1803 Rising). As Helena recalled: 'It breaks my heart – and all our hearts – that we did not get in'. The failure was due to the military council, rather than to Seán Connolly, who had received orders to occupy City Hall. Attacked merely for 'psychological effect', the Castle was considered too large and well defended to secure.[24]

Quickly occupying City Hall – for which they had a key, as Seán worked there as a clerk in the motor-tax office – they took up positions on the roof. Overlooked by Dublin Castle's clock tower, its attractive open balustrade provided little cover. It wasn't long before Seán was shot. His fifteen-year-old brother Mattie saw him 'coming towards me, with one sleeve of his tunic rolled up to the elbow. He had what, at first, appeared to be a red handkerchief bound round his forearm. I asked what it was for, and, holding out his arm, he said, "Look at the blood I'm shedding for Ireland!"'[25] At about 2 p.m. he shed more blood for Ireland. 'It was a beautiful day, the sun was hot', Kathleen Lynn recalled, when they noticed Seán 'coming towards us, walking upright, although we had been advised to crouch and take cover as much as possible. We suddenly saw him fall mortally wounded

-32-

The Countermanding Order.

What happened on Easter Sunday overshadowed everything else. At last we had definite knowledge. If there was talk I either did not hear it or pay attention to it. My mind was preoccupied with the one thought, "I can't believe this will really happen. I know we can depend on the Citizen Army, but what about the rest?".

I saw Eoin MacNeill's countermanding order in the paper and heard the discussion in Liberty Hall. Connolly was there. They were all heartbroken, and when they were not crying they were cursing. I kept thinking, "Does this mean that we are not going out?" There were thousands like us. It was foolish of MacNeill and those to think they could call it off. They could not. Many of us thought we would go out single-handed, if necessary.

That Easter Sunday was a day of confusion, excitement and disappointment in Liberty Hall. I stayed there all day and all night. There was a lot of work to be done preparing food upstairs for the men who came from different parts of the city and had brought no rations. As a result of the calling-off of the fight, there was plenty of food. Large joints were cooked and all the Co-operative girls were busy cutting up bread, butter and cooked meat. They were killed working. One of them that I remember was Brigid Davis. Dr. Lynn went home, but Jinny Shanahan and I slept again on the overcoats in the room behind the shop.

The Rising on Easter Monday.

On Easter Monday morning twelve o'clock was the hour for mobilisation. The women had no uniform, in the ordinary sense - nor the men either. Some of the men had green coats. They wore an ordinary slouch hat, like the Boer hat.

Helena Molony recalled the attack on Dublin Castle in her witness statement to the Bureau of Military History, written in 1950 (MAI, BMH WS 391).

-33-

and mostly a belt. They insisted that they were citizen
soldiers, not military soldiers - at the same time regimented
and disciplined. I had an Irish tweed costume, with a Sam
Browne. I had my own revolver and ammunition. At the
last minute, when we were going off at twelve o'clock,
Connolly gave out revolvers to our girls, saying: "Don't
use them except in the last resort". There were nine girls
in our party, going to the Castle. We were instructed to
go to Dublin Castle, under Captain Seán Connolly. We were
to attack the Castle. It was a very wise move. It was
expected that the psychological effect of attacking Dublin
Castle, the citadel of foreign rule for seven hundred years,
would be considerable when the news spread through the
country. By the way, it was at the Castle that the first
shot was fired.

I did not know beforehand what was to take place. I
did not know to which place I was going. I remember being
rather surprised at not going to the G.P.O. with James
Connolly. Winnie Carney acted as his secretary all through.
She was a good shorthand-typist. I remember I wondered at
his saying to me: "You go with Seán". As I said already,
Seán was an old friend of mine, and acted in the Abbey
Theatre along with me. He was a very good actor. He was
a Citizen Army Captain - and Dr. Lynn's Captain too. She
came with us on Easter Monday to Dublin Castle and the City
Hall.

On Easter Monday we advanced up Dame Street towards
Dublin Castle. I could not say how many there were
altogether. We went out in detachments. Seán Connolly
and, I think, about twenty men perhaps, walked up Dame
Street; and I, walking at the head of my nine girls, was,
I believe, perhaps two or three ranks behind Seán. We

-34-

simply followed the men. I can only remember the names of
a few of the girls, the two Norgroves, Jinny Shanahan and,
I think, Brigid Davis. Seán turned left and went towards.
the Castle Gate. I think there may have been other
detachments behind us. I will check this up with some of
the Citizen Army men. Some of the men drifted into Henry
& James, Tailors, at the opposite corner of the City Hall.
Others went to the "Evening Mail" premises. One party went
to attack the front gate of the Castle. The orders were, I
presume, to each Sergeant: "Take your men to the "Mail"
office". "Take your men to Henry & James". Perhaps
someone got orders to go to the City Hall.

Failure of attack on the Castle.

I, with my girls, followed Seán Connolly and his party.
We went right up to the Castle Gate, up the narrow street.
Just then, a police Sergeant came out and, seeing our
determination, he thought it was a parade, and that it
probably would be going up Ship Street. When Connolly went
to go past him, the Sergeant put out his arm; and Connolly
shot him dead. When the military guard saw that it was
serious, he pulled the gates to. It may be an interesting
point, in connection with the secrecy of the arrangements
for the Rising, that it appeared that the men behind Connolly
did not really know they were to go through. Connolly said:
"Get in, get in" - as if they already did not know they were
to go in. That guarded secrecy, not to let it look like
anything other than the manoeuvres which were taking place
for weeks before, may have been the reason; but certainly
there was hesitation on the part of the followers. Seán
Connolly shouted: "Get in, get in". On the flash, the
gates were closed. The sentry went into his box, and began
firing. I thought no one had succeeded in getting in.

-35-

It breaks my heart - and all our hearts - that we did not get in. We would have captured the Under Secretary, who was having lunch in the Castle. We went into the City Hall, and at once manned it. Probably, if all the men in the party at the Castle Gate had known they were really to get through the gate, they would have rushed. I would conclude from that, that they did not know what the action was to be. I would say that the men were not certain that they were not to pull up Ship Street. Connolly said, in an excited voice, "Get in, get in". He was excited because he had shot the policeman dead. We were all in excitement. When I saw Connolly draw his revolver, I drew my own. Across the road, there was a policeman with papers. He got away, thank God. I did not like to think of the policeman dead., I think there were a couple of soldiers killed later. I think the policeman at the gate was killed instantly, because they were quite close. The police did not think the Citizen Army were serious. Seán Connolly veered round his gun, and said, "Get into the City Hall".

Occupation of City Hall

We met with no opposition at the City Hall, because it was a Bank Holiday, and the place was empty. Some of the men must have broken in the door. I have no recollection of having any difficulty except walking in with the girls. There was not much delay. It is possible that Seán Connolly might have had a key, because he was a clerk in the City Hall. I cannot remember any smashing in of windows or doors. I remember we climbed over the railings; but I don't remember any difficulty at the doors. Of course, they might have had to do something about it before we arrived.

We took up various positions when we got in to the City

by a sniper's bullet from the Castle.'[26] Seán died in Helena's arms: 'He was bleeding very much from the stomach. I said the Act of Contrition into his ear.' His slow and painful death was witnessed – from a heart-breaking distance, on the other side of the roof of City Hall – by his brother Mattie, who 'cried bitterly' but did not abandon his position.[27]

Like many rebel positions, the outpost at City Hall was poorly chosen: unable to prevent British reinforcements from streaming into the Castle, they soon came under continuous heavy fire. Alluding to their lacklustre efforts to engage the military, Kathleen Lynn suggested that Seán's death 'had a demoralising effect on the City Hall men'. Helena's account is similarly downbeat. There 'was nothing to do, only sit', she recalled. 'The men fired desultory shots all day.' Helena was fortunate not to share Seán's fate: a British officer later told her that 'he very nearly "got me" on the roof once or twice'.[28]

Later that day, peering out of a window to ascertain whether a withdrawal from City Hall might be feasible, Helena observed what she initially mistook for sleet but quickly realised was a hail of bullets.[29] The fire intensified as the day progressed. 'On the roof level, on which were glass windows, and through the windows on the ground floor of the City Hall, there were machine-gun bullets pouring in,' she recalled. 'From the ceiling the plaster began to fall.'[30] The outpost was soon overwhelmed: 'A window was smashed at the back, and then we knew they were pouring in'.[31] Helena's rebellion was over.

Her experiences highlight the active role played by some Citizen Army women. With the exception of such unusual individuals as Constance Markievicz, who is thought to have killed a policeman at Stephen's Green, most women in the Citizen Army were confined to cooking and first aid.[32] Popular accounts, however, often suggest that they fought as combatants, presenting James Connolly's egalitarian conception of freedom as the road not taken after 1916.

In comparison with women in the Citizen Army, members of Cumann na mBan encountered greater obstacles to their participation in the rebellion. When Ned Daly, commandant of the 1st Battalion, told the women assigned to the Four Courts that their 'services would not be required', they simply ignored him. Éamon de Valera, the commandant at Boland's bakery, refused to allow women to enter his garrison.[33] After forcing her way through the same hostile mob faced by Peadar Kearney, Máire Nic Shiubhlaigh had to persuade Thomas MacDonagh to allow her

Death certificate for Seán Connolly, written from Mountjoy jail by Kathleen Lynn, a medical doctor who had fought with the Irish Citizen Army at City Hall (NMI, HE/EW/2359).

in: 'We haven't made any provisions for girls here,' he told her.[34] Máire's experiences demonstrate how the role played by women who secured a place among the combatants was carefully demarcated. Like most of the women who participated in the rebellion, she did so as a result of her own determination. Those who did get through the door were, like Máire, confined to cooking, nursing or carrying messages. Many women did not object to these gendered roles. Máire upset one rebel on the roof of Jacob's by grabbing his gun and firing a scarce bullet into the air. She had always wanted to fight for Ireland's freedom, she explained, but not at the cost of hurting someone.[35]

Ellen Bushell also struggled to gain entry to a garrison. This was partly a result of the confusion of the countermand, and also because it was felt that she could provide assistance on the outside; but it was mainly due to the rebels' reluctance to allow women in. 'I was rambling round trying to get in somewhere', she recalled. 'It was all confusion and sorrow'.[36] Despite being turned away from several outposts, she persisted in her efforts: 'I went into town and tried to get in at various places. It was an upset day. We did not know what to do. I brought some whiskey and first aid round with me in my pocket.' Although Ellen resented her treatment, she did play a useful role, carrying despatches, ammunition and food between the garrisons. Scouting out the surrounding streets, for example, she evacuated Con Colbert and his men from Watkins' brewery to safety.[37] At the end of the week, it was Ellen who brought MacDonagh's order of surrender to Marrowbone Lane.

4.

when I went back to Marrowbone Lane.

Q. How did you get into Jacobs? You say you got into Jacobs?
A. Yes. I was in Jacob's every day by the Peter St. door.

Q. This was Wednesday when you brought Kavanagh's guns. Did you get a message then?
A. It was then I got it. I was there for quite a long time with McDonagh discussing the situation in general.

Q. What message did you get from him?
A. For Colbert - to ask him how things were there and to tell him they were all right. A general message to that effect.

Q. You were a kind of telephone line?
A. Yes. It was not a written message. It was verbal.

Q. Did you go back on Wednesday to Marrowbone Lane?
A. Yes.

Q. Was it then Christy Byrne asked you to get some ammunition?
A. I think so. I was sent back again by the Sergt. of the Guard. Ned Neill was his name. I was sent back to buy rashers and butter. It was impossible to get butter. I had to get margarine.

Q. You got food?
A. I was not allowed in up to that. He wanted me to throw the stuff over the gate. I insisted on getting in. I said I had a message.

Q. You got into Marrowbone Lane. Did you got into any other post later on?
A. I was sent by McDonough with a letter to Mick Mallin.

Q. You went back to Jacob's again?
A. I don't think it was that evening. I did not go back to Jacob's. I remained in Marrowbone Lane for some time and there was nothing else to be done.

Q. Was it that day you went to Christy Byrne's?
A I don't think so. I think it was the next day.

Q. Thursday?
A. It was pretty hot. I was caught between cross fire but there might have been cross fire on the Wednesday. I think it was Thursday.

Q. You did not stay in Marrowbone Lane any night?
A. They would not let me stay.

Q. Did you get home on Wednesday?
A. Yes, home every night - home or in a friend's place. It depended on the time I got home from the post.

Q. On Thursday were you out again?
A. Yes.

Q. What were you doing? Going between Marrowbone Lane and Jacobs?
A. Yes, backwards and forwards. I think it was on the Thursday also I brought the note to the College of Surgeons. I cannot place the days very well in detail.

Q. Were you out every day?
A. Yes, every day.

Nellie Bushell testified about
her Easter Week service to the
Military Service Pensions Board
in 1939 (MAI, MSP Bushell).

5.

Q. Who gave you the message for the College of Surgeons?
A. Tom McDonagh to Mick Mallin.

Q. You got there?
A. Yes.

Q. Were you out again on Friday?
A. Friday, yes, backwards and forwards between the two places.

Q. One of these days you say you were caught in a cross fire?
A. Yes. It was when going along the canal. I was going the back
   way to try and get on to Basin St. There was firing and the
   soldier at this bridge was shouting to stop and I did not let on
   it was me he was talking to. He went down with his bayonet and
   very forcibly stopped me. I did not get the ammunition.

Q. Was it then you were caught in the cross fire, when you were
   going for the ammunition for Christy Byrne?
A. Yes. The bullets were not near me but they were scrapping from
   one side of the canal over.

Q. When did that garrison surrender?
A. On Sunday evening - Marrowbone Lane garrison after Jacob's. It
   was I was sent with the message to surrender. It was an unconditional surrender.

Q. Had you been doing messages all the time?
A. Yes.

Q. Saturday?
A. Yes. In the early part of Sunday I could not get into Jacob's.
   There was heavy sniping going on and I was advised not to go up by
   one of the garrison that was knocking around outside.

Q. Did you take a message from Jacob's to Marrowbone Lane,
A. In the evening when I went back I met one of the Kavanagh brothers
   and he was rushing. I was coming back from Marrowbone Lane.
   He said I was to go back and take the message - an unconditional
   surrender and any man that could escape to get away.

Q. When was this?
A. On Sunday evening. Jacob's had surrendered in the meantime while
   I was away at Marrowbone Lane.

Q. And you met Kavanagh getting away from Jacob's?
A. Yes, he was leaving. He was the first of the men leaving that I
   met.

Q. That was more news than a message. It was not an instruction?
A. He was being sent with the message. He seemingly had been sent to
   get in to Marrowbone Lane and he met me and he sent me to let
   him be free to go on some other messages.

Q. You got home yourself after that?
A. I went to Marrowbone Lane and remained there till the surrender.

Q. Whom did you give the message to?
A. Two boys named Walsh. When I got in there was a Council meeting
   and there was a priest in. He just came out as I got there. The
   officers were a while talking so the message was sent up to Seamus
   Murphy by Ned Neill. He sent a Vol. up to the room where they
   were debating.

Q. When the surrender took place you went home?
AQ.Yes, just got a chance and rushed through.

Ironically, Ellen probably faced greater danger traversing the increasingly chaotic battleground than did the rebels inside their garrisons: 'It was pretty hot. I was caught between cross fire'. An additional threat was posed by the mobs that surrounded the outposts, seeking rebels to attack, particularly as several garrisons refused to allow her in when she arrived with despatches: 'The Sergt. of the Guard told me to show in my message. There was a big crowd outside.' Returning later to the same outpost, she was told to 'throw the stuff over the gate. I insisted on getting in. I said I had a message.'

Women enjoyed some advantages in performing these duties. They were less likely to be shot, and could talk their way through the cordons closing around the rebel garrisons by the middle of the week. Marie Perolz, who was subsequently incarcerated with Helena at Aylesbury Prison in Buckinghamshire, borrowed her young niece, 'dressed in a blue velvet coat and bonnet', to accompany her as she dropped revolvers off throughout the city. She did, at least, inform her niece of the purpose of their mission: '"O Mamma, can I come too to drive out the English?" said she to her mother'.[38]

However, as Ellen Bushell recounted, it was not always possible to talk one's way through a dangerous situation: 'There was firing and the soldier at this bridge was shouting to stop and I did not let on it was me he was talking to. He went down with his bayonet and very forcibly stopped me.' That the women of 1916 were largely confined to non-combatant roles should not detract from their contribution. Although the contradiction between the egalitarianism of the Proclamation and the attitudes of many rebels is striking, so too is the willingness of many women to challenge these attitudes.

In contrast to Seán Connolly and Helena Molony, most rebels spent Easter Week isolated within well-fortified garrisons, an often frustrating experience. Some of the outlying outposts in the narrow streets around North King Street and Church Street witnessed ferocious battles, but the main Four Courts garrison achieved little, as is indicated by Barney Murphy's sparse summary of his activities: 'Strengthening barricades. Cooking. Doing Sentry on Roof.'[39] Rebels positioned outside the garrisons – such as Arthur Shields, who spent the week in a series of small outposts around the GPO – often saw more action. Arthur was one of a party of men who broke into the Atlantic School of Wireless in Reis's Chambers. There, they reassembled the transmitter, erected an aerial on the roof under sniper fire and attempted to transmit the Proclamation.[40] By Thursday, Arthur had withdrawn to the relative security of the GPO, which – like the other

On Easter Monday 1916 whilst proceeding to place of Mobilisation I was met by Comdt Edward Daly O.C. Four Courts Area. He at once dispatched me with Volunteer Seán Byrne + 2 others whoom I have never met before nor since to Cut off communication with West of Ireland at Liffey junction. Having done So I returned to report to. O.C. Ed Daly. he told me Verbally to take arms from. W. L. Coles Establishment at Little green St, + take them to Four Court. Having failed to enter "Coles". I reported to Lieutenant Joe McGuinness at Four Courts. who Kept me in Four Courts to Strengthen. garrison. I remained in Four Courts. Strengthening barricades. cooking. doing Sentry on Roof, Church St Bridge, along quay. under Peadar Clancy. on Saturday I noticed garrison becoming Strong, on making inquiries I learned they were being driven in while erecting a barricade in Hammond. I was ordered to cease on going to Church St Bridge I met Comdt E. Daly. he allowed me to See order of Surrender. I told him I would not Surrender but I would make a bid to escape or Die in the attempt. I disregarded Peadar Clancy's order to fall in. snatched an automatic pistol from another Volunteer named Joseph Brabason + got Clear into my own home. I got Clear away from my home on Monday + never returned—Bernard Murphy. B. Coy. I Batt. I. V. 1916 20. S. Nicholas St (Late 7 inns quay) Dublin P.T.O

Barney Murphy's account of Easter week
at the Four Courts (MAI, MSP Murphy).

garrisons – exerted little influence on the fighting. The British decision to use artillery, rather than to directly engage the rebels, denied them the possibility of a heroic denouement.

Jacob's factory, where Máire Nic Shiubhlaigh and Peadar Kearney fought, was the most ineffectual garrison, its impregnability offset by its strategic irrelevance. Despite the occasional feint – Peadar described how British troops who tried to set up a machine-gun post in Digges Street 'were literally blown out of it' by a dozen Howth Mausers – it was the only garrison sufficiently unimportant to escape artillery bombardment.[41] It was easily cordoned off, allowing the British forces to advance on the GPO. Peadar makes no great claims as to the rebels' strategy, observing that their original plans – such as manning barricades in order to maintain communications between garrisons – had relied on a much larger turnout of four thousand rebels that had failed to materialise: 'the surprise was, that under the circumstances there was any fight at all'.[42]

Máire's account conveys the unsettling atmosphere inside Jacob's, a gloomy, cavernous, candle-lit building where rebels 'covered with flour from head to toe' moved slowly about, like ghostly apparitions.[43] 'No one knew what was happening elsewhere,' she recalled. 'There was a constant feeling of isolation.'[44] Its small contingent of fewer than two hundred rebels was 'swallowed up into the vastness of the place. Though calls could be heard from the upstairs rooms, the sound of footsteps, an occasional clatter as a rifle fell, there was an eeriness about the place; a feeling of being cut off from the outside world.'[45] Time weighed heavily. 'Inside the building and on the street', Máire noted, 'everyone seemed to be waiting for something to happen'.[46] Wild rumours swept the building:

Advertisement for Jacob's factory, Bishop Street, 1908. Although well fortified, the garrison at Jacob's exerted little influence on the fighting (DCLA).

We heard that German troops had landed at Wexford …
the Volunteers were fighting bitterly along the coastline
to Cork where the city was supposed to be out like Dublin;
British troops were being rushed from the Curragh
… Dublin Castle was on fire; the British were using
explosive bullets and shooting prisoners; buildings all
over the city were being burned indiscriminately; Dublin
was almost in ruins … there were rumours of civil riots;
irresponsible civilians looting, and stories of outrages by
hysterical British soldiers.

Peadar recalled a similar stream of fantastic rumours, alternately
heartening and demoralising: Kynoch's explosives factory had been taken
by the Wexford men, who were marching on Dublin; the south lay in rebel
hands; Dublin Bay was swarming with German submarines; the British
were placing mines under Jacob's factory.[47]

Boredom presented an unanticipated challenge. Máire found
inactivity the most unpleasant feature of the week. The rebels did their
best to pass the time, telling jokes and singing songs. The 'men reclined,
smoked, read and chatted, some wrote diaries', Seosamh de Brún recalled.
'A piano was strummed occasionally in an upper portion of the building in
contrast with the rifle fire. The book-case in the library was broken open and
pillaged. I can distinctly remember the interest evoked by quotations from
Julius Caesar'. Peadar formed a study circle: 'It reminded one of a school
rather than a war camp.'[48]

They also spent a lot of time praying. For some, Easter Week was more
religious revival than revolution. Peadar described the reaction when the
Republic – destined not to be a secular one – was proclaimed as they gathered in
Ussher's malt-house in Fumbally Lane: 'A cheer of pent-up relief and gladness
greeted his words and instinctively we went down on one knee and said a short
prayer.'[49] The Rosary was recited daily at Jacob's. Recounting how John MacBride
(who, like many Fenians, had been estranged from the Catholic Church)
returned to the sacraments, Máire described remarkable scenes:

When darkness settled, a group of Volunteers entered the
bakeroom with candles which they set about the room
in empty biscuit boxes ... There was a murmur of voices
from the doorway, and men started to shuffle into the
light. The whole garrison, with the exception of those
on sentry-duty, gathered inside the circle and knelt.
Someone started the rosary. As those in the bakeroom
responded to the prayer, the men on the stairs took it
up, the sound passing slowly from room to room until
the whole building vibrated with the rise and fall of the
mumbled voices. The candles threw an uncertain light
on the faces of the Volunteers; caught the glint of the
rifles they had laid beside them. Now and then you could
hear the noise of firing, through the prayers; a strange
background sound you could never, never forget.[50]

Such scenes highlighted a potential tension between the secularism
associated with republican ideology before 1916 and the Catholicism with
which the Rising would afterwards become identified. Like many Fenians,
Peadar Kearney had little difficulty reconciling his religious beliefs with
membership of an oath-bound organisation condemned by the Catholic
Church. A similar pragmatism prevailed during Easter Week: Peadar
observed how one priest, who took advantage of an invitation to minister
to the rebels 'by haranguing us on the guilt of our actions', was expelled
from Jacob's, while a more accommodating Carmelite priest was allowed to
remain to 'prepare men for death'.[51]

For most rebels, such piety strengthened their resolve. Charlie
Saurin described a remarkable scene following the arrival of a young curate
at Father Mathew Park, where he and Arthur Shields had mobilised:

We all knelt down and were given conditional
absolution. He held up a crucifix before us all and
spoke directly on the sacrifice we might have to make
before long and the need to be prepared for it. He also
heard confessions of men who wished to make their
confession direct to him in the hall. It was while he was

speaking to us all as we knelt each on one knee before
him clasping our rifles in both hands that Peter Traynor
came round the corner and halted suddenly at the scene
before him … I caught the look in his eyes and could
see that he was struck by the drama and by something
deeper than just drama in the young priest holding up
the crucifix and exhorting the kneeling armed men
before him to think on what it represented and of our
brief mortal life.[52]

As a Protestant, Arthur Shields found himself among a tiny
minority that literally stood out. After one of their comrades was killed in
the Hibernian Hotel, one rebel remembered: 'we all knelt down to say a
prayer and Arthur Shields stood in a corner because he was not a Catholic'.[53]
Revealingly, it had become a smaller minority by the end of the week, as
some of Arthur's Protestant comrades, such as Cathal MacDowell (organist
at St John's Church, Sandymount), succumbed to the religious fervour:
'He laid down his Howth rifle beside him and the priest baptised him'.[54]
Experiencing an epiphany during the Rising, Constance Markievicz also
converted. 'The lads in her command in the College of Surgeons frequently
said the Rosary,' she explained. 'I must be of the same religion as my
splendid boys'.[55] Roger Casement followed suit before he was hanged at
Pentonville Prison in London, explicitly conflating faith and nation in his
resolve to die 'in the religion of Cathleen ni Houlihan'.[56]

As Markievicz's experiences suggest, some within the Citizen
Army proved as devout as any Volunteer, despite the Catholic Church's
condemnation of its socialism. Seán Connolly's brother Mattie went into
battle armed with a Rosary, a small brass crucifix and a prayer written on a
scrap of paper: 'Who fights for Ireland, God guide his blows home | Who dies
for Ireland, God give him peace.' He described the bemused reaction of the
British soldier who searched him after the surrender at City Hall: 'He looked
into my face, and then back at the paper, as if I were mad.'[57] Did such piety
foreshadow the Catholic state that emerged from the revolution? Although
the Rising's religiosity – which played an important role in retrospectively
legitimising the rebels' actions among wider nationalist opinion – was
subsequently exaggerated by republican and Catholic propagandists, and
despite the fact that the leaders' use of religious language as a convenient

way of conveying the depth of their political commitment was sometimes misinterpreted, the suggestion that the rebels' ostentatious devotion was intended to repudiate 'those ecclesiastics who said that the rebels were no longer Catholics' is unconvincing.[58] Some of the Rising's leaders did misleadingly claim a spurious endorsement from the Pope for their actions, but there is no indication that the fervour of the rank and file reflected anything other than the profound spirituality they experienced at Easter Week. After 1916, the depiction of the rebels as Catholic martyrs also formed part of a more deliberate process that subsumed the radicalism of the Proclamation's aspirations within a socially conservative Catholic nationalism. To the disappointment of a secular minority, which included Arthur Shields, the legacy of 1916 would be embodied by such figures as Éamon de Valera who, like most Irish Volunteers, conceived of their country as a Catholic, Gaelic nation rather than as a secular republic.[59]

As the week progressed, practical matters assumed greater importance. Máire Nic Shiubhlaigh was responsible for the catering at Jacob's: 'We had six women – well, I could not call them women. I was 33 years of age – they were all under 20, we were there to cook for the men.'[60] As the rebels had disconnected the gas and electricity in order to prevent fires, two enormous copper boilers served as makeshift urns for boiling stew and drinks in the small forge that served as the garrison's kitchen. They melted vast quantities of cooking chocolate into a dark-brown, syrupy stew: 'It looked horrible, but at least it was sustaining'. There was an abundance of figs (the principal ingredient of Jacob's celebrated fig rolls), 'slabs of rich fruit-cake', 'plain and fancy' biscuits, shortbread and tons of cream crackers; but savoury food such as vegetables, bread and meat was scarce. Confinement in a biscuit factory proved less congenial than some had anticipated: 'a couple of hearty meals of Jacob's best gave the sweet-toothed members of the section a feeling of nausea when they saw an Oxford Lunch.'[61] One of the garrison's first casualties was the young Fianna boy who downed a cake with such 'remarkable speed' that he was incapacitated by the 'dire results'.[62] Inadequate rations and exhaustion posed more difficulties than the enemy.

> For the first 48 hours sniping and spasmodic volleys
> were the order of the day, but by Wednesday the
> pandemonium of noise grew into a crescendo and at

night the skies gave a vivid picture of a huge inferno. One never knew whether the flames were in the neighbouring street or a mile away and, according as the wind changed, the ear-splitting crash of all sorts of arms gave the impression that the building was being attacked front and rear. All this meant that nerves were as taut as a violin at pitch, in addition to which physical exhaustion and lack of sleep had the men in such a condition that rows of houses marching solemnly away was a usual occurrence.[63]

Self-inflicted wounds became more frequent as exhausted or paranoid rebels accidentally discharged their guns, which they were required to carry at all times.

Máire recalled 'great excitement' rather than exhaustion: 'the whole week seemed to pass like one long day', blending 'into one long disjointed picture'. Although they were cut off from the other garrisons, the scale of what they had achieved was becoming apparent. On Thursday evening Máire ascended one of the factory's towers to view the devastation:

Over in the north the GPO was blazing fiercely; it seemed as though the flames had spread the length of O'Connell Street. There were huge columns of smoke. Around us, in the turret, the Volunteers were still keeping up a steady fire on British outposts nearby. In the distance the crackle of gunfire was accompanied by sudden little flashes. All around, through the darkness, bombed-out buildings burned. From where we stood, the whole city seemed to be on fire. The noise of artillery, machine-gun and rifle fire was deafening.[64]

By Friday, Peadar thought that 'every man of common sense realized that the end was in sight', but he felt they were resolved 'to make the inevitable success of the British as costly as possible'. Máire, in contrast, had believed Thomas MacDonagh's intentionally misleading accounts: 'He never tired of repeating that we might be in Jacob's for months, that the position was so well in hand, nothing could stop a republican victory.'[65] Like Peadar, though, she was resigned to her fate:

> What might happen if we lost meant nothing, life or death, freedom or imprisonment, these things did not enter into it at all. The great thing was that what you had always hoped for had happened at last. An insurrection had taken place, and you were actually participating in it.[66]

At the GPO, its upper storeys an inferno, it was more obvious that the end was near. Burning debris tumbled onto the rebels, who sought to move their explosives out of the path of the fire as it descended, floor by floor, filling the building with fumes. Their position gradually became untenable: 'the floors began to give way. Debris crashed in. Thick columns of smoke and flame rose steadily', Desmond Ryan recorded. 'Walls of flame seem to surround the yard. Sheets of flame seem to cover the top of the

Although it had not been occupied by the rebels, Liberty Hall was the first building shelled by the *Helga* as it sailed up the Liffey on the Wednesday of Easter Week (NPA, KE 120).

ground floor and the floor above. Cracks begin to show in the outer walls.'[67] With the ceiling in danger of collapsing, officers sought to avert panic. Puffing on a cigar, Liam Tannam strolled 'up and down trying to appear as nonchalant as possible' and led his men in a rousing rendition of 'The Soldier's Song' as the fire raged about them.[68]

Arthur Shields participated in the inevitable evacuation, as several hundred rebels fought their way from the GPO, along a series of narrow lanes, to the relative safety of Moore Street. There they advanced in the darkness, as quietly as possible, using crowbars and sledgehammers to bore through the walls of the terraced houses. Most were now in terrible shape, weakened by stress, hunger and exhaustion. As men passed out, they were carried along from house to house as they progressed along Moore Street. They witnessed, for the first time, the horrors inflicted on the civilian population in the besieged streets around the GPO, which remained under artillery and machine-gun fire. An attempt to blast through a locked door at Henry Place killed fifteen-year-old Bridget McKane; in Moore Street a rebel groped in the darkness to help a girl wounded under similar circumstances: 'He thought he put his fingers into her mouth as he thought he felt her teeth, but when he struck a match he found that it was through a hole in her skull he had put his fingers'.[69] Remarkably, the rebels received encouragement from some they encountered. An elderly woman rounded on her feckless son as the Volunteers knocked through their living-room wall: 'It's out helping these men you should be,' she told him, 'instead of sitting here as you are.'[70]

On the first floor of an overcrowded Moore Street shop, Charlie Saurin was reunited with Arthur Shields, whom he had not seen since they parted on Easter Monday. He found Arthur kneeling by the window, rifle in hand:

> The din was most terrific outside as there was an intensive fire down the street from British forces at the Great Britain Street end, in addition to the roaring of the flames from the GPO and other burning buildings in Henry Street and the shooting by our fellows from places all around. It was, of course, night time now and the room was practically in darkness, yet I could dimly make out men sitting all around the walls and lying on the floor. In the corner quite near to me sat Tom Clarke

with his hands clasped around his knees. A Volunteer
beside him was irritably taxing him with taking
his place. Even making allowances for the state of
nerves everyone might have been in, I thought this
was going too far and leaned across and told him who
he was attacking, at the same time placing a hand
upon his knee. He ceased complaining and clung to
my hand as if it was a sheet anchor. Arthur Shields
and I were now and then peering out of the window
wondering could we get in a shot at the forces at the
top of the Street but it was a risky business because
bullets were scoring along the sides of the houses and
ringing off the side of the window opening.

They eventually moved on, joining an 'exhausted crowd, dirty
and dusty, some wounded and bandaged, some carrying a miscellaneous
assortment of provisions but everyone clinging to his weapons' as the
crowd followed the tunnellers' slow progress through the terraced
houses.[71] The procession finally came to a halt at Hanlon's fish shop, the
last headquarters of the Provisional Government, in the early hours of
Saturday morning.

Arthur and Charlie were stationed with five other men behind
the shop in a small loft with a delivery hatch that overlooked the heavily
manned army barricade at the top of Moore Lane. At one point, they were
joined by Patrick Pearse. Saurin recalled that he was

calm and self-possessed and looked long and
searchingly at each of us in turn as if he was gauging
the amount of resistance we had left in us. Pearse
stood upright in the opening and looked long and
coolly up the lane. He was certainly taking a chance
of getting a bullet through the head. He drew back
then and without a word descended the steps.[72]

Some hours later, Arthur and Charlie learnt that they had been chosen to form part of an attempt to break through British lines to allow the rebels to link up with the Four Courts garrison. A previous charge led by the O'Rahilly had ended in disaster. They were understandably sceptical: 'Apparently the seven of us in the loft at the back of Hanlon's were on a given word to jump out through the open doorway down on to the lane below, fire a volley and charge the barricade'.[73]

Wiser counsels prevailed, and a ceasefire was agreed in order to allow negotiations to proceed. From their vantage point, using a pair of binoculars Arthur had commandeered, they could observe the changing mood of the British soldiers: 'They were standing up, moving about, smoking and chatting, and an officer leant negligently over the top gazing down in our direction'. A trickle of civilians were permitted to pass through the barricade. The final hours of the Republic were not heroic: exhausted men sat around, depressed, sleeping or bickering about food.

Sitting in a yard, bathed in brilliant sunshine, Arthur and Charlie shared a meal of tinned salmon, raisins and biscuits. 'There was no shooting near us but we could hear rifle fire afar off and yet occasionally there was the sound of a shell burst quite close,' Charlie recalled. 'The sky was intensely blue and peaceful-looking but disgust was spreading amongst us.'[74] Nearby lay dead comrades, their upper bodies covered by blankets. The bodies of civilians, some still grasping the white sheets with which they had approached the army's barricades, lay scattered in Moore Street. Finally, at 3:30 on Saturday afternoon, Major-General William Lowe met Pearse to accept his surrender.

The Starry Plough. The bullet-riddled flag of the Irish Citizen Army was flown over the Imperial Hotel. Perhaps not coincidentally, the hotel was owned by Connolly's nemesis, William Martin Murphy, who had led the employers during the 1913 Lockout (NMI, HE/EW/2362).

In the chaotic twenty-four hours that followed, the remaining garrisons surrendered. The only other garrison to capitulate on Saturday was the Four Courts, although the surrounding outposts refused to surrender until the following day. Most within the Four Courts agreed to surrender, marching behind Ned Daly in an impressively disciplined formation, but Barney Murphy refused: 'I met Daly and he showed me the surrender,' he told the Military Pensions Board. 'He wasn't able to read it to us he was in such a state. He told us to fall in. Seán Flood gave the order to fall in; I wouldn't. I took an automatic and went home.'[75] His personal statement is fairly consistent. 'I would make a bid to escape or die in the attempt', he recalled telling Daly, whom he described as a good friend. 'Snatched an automatic pistol from another Volunteer named Brabason & got clear into my own home.'[76]

At Jacob's factory, the garrison's inaction and isolation ensured that the surrender order came as a shock. Peadar Kearney was reinforcing the building's defences with sacks of flour.

> When on Sunday morning Tom Hunter came down from headquarters and drawing his sword smashed the blade in two, announced with broken voice and tears in his eyes that surrender had been decided on, the scene that followed was beyond word painting. Fierce anger predominated, while the best of men collapsed and became temporary imbeciles. Torn between loyalty to their officers and the confused feeling that something had been done behind their backs, the situation, for a while, looked ugly.[77]

Máire Nic Shiubhlaigh was equally devastated: 'I fainted at the news, it nearly broke my heart.'[78] She remembered desperate scenes as distraught rebels broke down: 'Everyone was talking at once. The noise was deafening. I saw a man throw down his rifle and put his hands over his face. Another was smashing the butt of a gun against a wall.'[79]

Thomas MacDonagh, 'care-worn and dishevelled', summoned the rebels, informing them 'that the surrender was none of his making, and that he was carrying out orders'.[80] Earlier that day, he had refused to obey

Pearse's surrender order until Major-General Lowe personally explained the consequences for both the rebels and the surrounding civilians. As men shouted that they would not allow themselves to be shot like dogs, MacDonagh declared, 'They can't shoot us all.'[81] Father Augustine, who had accompanied MacDonagh to negotiate with Lowe, restored order by assuring the rebels that none would be shot, and warning that 'the man who fires another shot in the building will incur a terrible responsibility.'[82]

Peadar Kearney, like Barney Murphy, had resolved to avoid arrest, believing that the G men (members of the detective division of the Dublin Metropolitan Police) would single him out for attention because of his Fenian background. He was unable to persuade any of his comrades to accompany him until the intervention of John MacBride, the Anglo-Boer War veteran (and estranged husband of Maud Gonne), who had spontaneously joined the rebels on Easter Monday: 'Liberty is a precious thing,' MacBride told them, 'and any one of you that sees a chance, take it … Many of you may live to fight some other day, take my advice, never allow yourselves to be cooped up inside the walls of a building again.'[83] Peadar recalled how MacBride's authority was reinforced by his impressive demeanour:

> That Sunday morning the majority, from Commandant MacDonagh down, were unkempt, unwashed, unshaven and covered with the debris of the week, but not so with MacBride: wearing a speckless serge suit, well-groomed, and smoking a cheroot, he had all the appearance of having walked out of a drawing room.[84]

Along with six others, Peadar slipped quietly out of Jacob's into a 'hostile and fear-stricken city'.

Concerned that the sight of captive women would further demoralise his men, MacDonagh ordered the remaining women to leave the garrison before the formal surrender. 'I started to protest,' Máire recalled, 'but he turned away. One could never imagine him looking so sad.'[85] Although Máire had resolved to stay, when Louise Gavan Duffy and Min Ryan entered Jacob's they found her in a bad state:

We made Máire come with us as she was on the verge of being hysterical. When we came to the door, a high-ranking officer and a young officer were arriving to take the surrender. They came in a small two-seater car. I suppose the high-ranking officer was General Lowe. The young officer stood, and we stood too. Louise stood up with great dignity. One of the officers said: 'We are not taking women, are we?' The other said: 'No'. We went off. Louise said: 'The cheek of him anyway – not taking women'. When we got home to 19 Ranelagh Road, we put Máire Nic Shiubhlaigh to bed. She was worn out completely. We sat again, and sat and sat.[86]

'Ypres by the Liffey': Fire and shelling destroyed much of Abbey St and Sackville St during Easter Week (NPA, KE 119).

Chapter 12

Punishment

O but we talked at large before
The sixteen men were shot,
But who can talk of give and take,
What should be and what not
While those dead men are loitering there
To stir the boiling pot?

—W. B. Yeats, 'Sixteen Dead Men'

An Irishman knows well how those who met
their deaths will be regarded. 'They shall be
remembered for ever; they shall be speaking
for ever; the people shall hear them for ever.'

—Padraic Colum, 1916[1]

Many rebels understood that, through their actions in Easter Week, they 'were living out history and in history'.[2] The British authorities demonstrated less awareness about the likely impact of their actions, which conformed to the rebel leaders' expectations. Irish nationalist opinion, in contrast, was shocked by the ruthlessness of the executions and the nationwide repression that followed, as some three thousand suspects, many innocent of any involvement in the Rising, were imprisoned. Accountable to British – rather than Irish – public opinion, and understandably giving priority to the war effort over Irish political considerations, the British government had no hesitation in implementing a punitive response. Before the executions had ended, the consequences of their actions were made clear to the British government. 'It is absolutely impossible to slaughter a man in this position without making him a martyr and a hero, even though the day before the rising he may have been only a minor poet', warned George Bernard Shaw in an open letter to the English press. 'The shot Irishmen will now take their place beside Emmet and the Manchester martyrs in Ireland.'[3] Although an increasingly nervous Downing Street impressed on General John Maxwell, the first military governor of Ireland since Cromwell, the necessity of a measured response, the tally of 'sixteen dead men' proved sufficient to transform public opinion in Ireland.

Although of the Abbey rebels only Helena Molony and Arthur Shields were arrested, the others did not return to normal life. 'I got clear away from my home on Monday & never returned', Barney Murphy recorded. Ellen

Bushell, returning to Marrowbone Lane on Sunday, bearing a message from Jacob's factory urging 'any man that could escape to get away', also managed to evade capture: 'just got a chance and rushed through.' Over the weeks that followed, she sheltered numerous rebels at her house in the Coombe, where republicans knew to look for a key on her window ledge: 'On and off they would stay the night and come in, country fellows.' As G men trawled the city, Peadar Kearney went on the run, finding many doors closed to him. One of the few people willing to shelter him was Ellen, who found some old clothes to replace his suspicious military-style Norfolk jacket. She also helped to hide weapons and documents, including, curiously, the minute books of the Celtic Literary Society, which she buried. During this period, Ellen's house was repeatedly raided – 'I think that was only spite of the police who saw me in Jacob's' – and she was eventually forced to move to Inchicore, as 'the police were giving me a bad time'.[4]

Arthur Shields, with the rest of the GPO garrison (including his friend Charlie Saurin, who left a detailed account of their experiences), was brought under armed guard to Sackville Street, where they were disarmed and lined up for inspection. Although some rebels had hoped to be treated as combatants rather than criminals, the British officers' attitude made it clear, as Charlie observed, that 'there was not going to be so much of the prisoner-of-war business for us'.[5] About four hundred rebels were confined to a small lawn in front of the Rotunda Hospital where they lay huddled together overnight, without food, water, shelter or – humiliatingly – sanitary provision. Drunken soldiers abused them, while some (Irish) soldiers defended them, prompting altercations between different units. Most soldiers did not behave vindictively, regarding the rebels with more curiosity than hostility. A Royal Irish Regiment soldier brought them hot tea. According to Charlie, 'Arthur Shields, Seán Russell and myself and a couple of others on the edge of the grass were grateful to him for this'.

The DMP constables who replaced the military guard the next morning were also sympathetic. Charlie noted that 'they could not or would not look straight at us and I think I can give them the credit of stating that I felt they were ashamed of the part they had to play.'

Others were clearly less sympathetic. Plain-clothes policemen from G Division walked among them, pulling out the ringleaders, including Tom Clarke, who was stripped and beaten. Although some of the G men were merely doing their job, others deliberately sought to humiliate the prisoners, many of whom they knew.

As Johnny Barton stopped in front of Joseph Connolly he opened his conversation by saying, 'What is your name?' though he knew perfectly well beforehand that he was a brother of Seán Connolly's. The next observation was 'Seán is dead'. Joe replied, 'He died for his country', to which Johnny retorted, 'He was a disgrace to his country'. For resenting this insult, Joe was separated from us.[6]

Barton, judged to have done 'more than his duty', and his colleague Daniel Hoey, who 'appeared to be relishing the job', were subsequently assassinated by the IRA.[7]

Retaining a soldierly bearing despite their exhaustion, Arthur Shields's contingent were led off by the South Staffordshire Regiment. They marched past dead civilians, overwhelmed by the scale of the destruction they had brought about: 'Buildings were just empty shells with smouldering fires still burning in them'. Outside the GPO an old 'shawlie' taunted them: 'Look at what was trying to keep out the government. You might as well try and keep out the ocean with a fork.' Charlie recorded that, in Francis Street, a British soldier used the butt of his rifle to protect them from

The remains of the rebel-held Dublin Bread Company at 6–7 Lower Sackville Street. It was only after the general surrender that the extent of the destruction in the city centre became clear to the rebels (NLI, INDH14).

a mass of howling, shrieking women from the back streets who called us filthy names and hurled curses at us. The mounted officer in charge of us showed faint amusement at all these women's hatred and excitement; the Staffords marched stolidly on.[8]

Public opinion, while still generally hostile, clearly varied throughout the city. In Thomas Street, Charlie detected sympathetic expressions from silent observers. Outside the Guinness brewery in James's Street, which employed many Protestants and servicemen, shirt-sleeved officials leant 'out of the windows looking at us with superior, contemptuous smiles'.

Their journey ended at Richmond Barracks, where about three thousand suspects were processed. Hearing shots as they entered the barracks, Charlie panicked. Arthur appeared more composed:

The Staffords stood at ease on each side of us, but when Arthur Shields with a cigarette in his mouth, attempted to smoke, a sallow-faced corporal came up and rudely told him to stop, and asked him sarcastically did he know where he was. This corporal was joined by a lanky foxy-haired young sergeant who proceeded to cast aspersions on our morals by saying with an air of disgust that we had women with us in the Post Office. He then told the corporal that he had been digging graves all day yesterday. 'I hope', he added, 'I'll be on a firing party tomorrow'. In contrast to him a very fine white moustached old N.C.O. of the Royal Irish Regiment pushed his way through the escort with a dixie [metal pot] full of water ... It was a bold thing for him to do in the circumstances and we thanked him fervently each time he came back with a full dixie.

The rebels were led to the gymnasium, where the G men again continued to comb through them. Because the police lacked reliable intelligence on the organisers, rebels were often singled out on arbitrary grounds. Uniforms, for example, were mistakenly considered evidence of seniority.

> Arthur Shields who wore glasses and who, consequently, in the eyes of the 'G' men, may have looked an intellectual and, therefore, important, was asked his name by the individual who picked out Willie Pearse, and also where he worked.

Charlie was surprised by Arthur's treatment:

> The Abbey Theatre should have been suspect as one of the birthplaces of twentieth-century Irish nationalism, but this did not seem to dawn on the 'G' man and Shields was left beside me, after a final question as to whether he knew Philip Guiry, another Abbey Player.

Later that evening they were marched back into the city. According to Charlie, 'Arthur Shields and I contrived to get side by side going down the stairs and thereafter we were not separated'. Outside the barracks, they were led past 'another party of screeching, cursing women', although this time they felt that the demonstration had been staged for their benefit. Individual soldiers abused them, but most demonstrated little animosity: 'it seemed to be all part of their day's work and their relations with us were quite impersonal'. As they marched along the quays, flames could still be seen rising above Sackville Street. While they waited to embark on a cargo ship, two soldiers fought about their treatment of the rebels. On board, Charlie recognised an army officer, an old school pal whose father's pub the rebels had occupied.

Very soon we heard the engines starting, the ship
began to shudder all over and we moved away from
the quayside. The curly-haired little officer who had
conducted Pádraig Pearse up to the loft we were in at
the back of Moore Street, called out 'Slán agat, a Éirinn'.
After that all the prisoners said the Rosary and when
it was over were not long about falling into a sleep of
utter exhaustion from which the majority of us did not
awaken until we reached Holyhead.[9]

Arthur Shields was held at Knutsford Detention Barracks in
Cheshire, where conditions, initially at least, were harsh. Republican
prisoners were mistreated, poorly fed and deprived of beds and blankets.
One rebel described the effect of two weeks in solitary confinement: 'I
thought a hundred times I would go mad – then I would wish to be mad,
anything to replace the hunger and loneliness and darkness.'[10] By late May,
however, conditions had improved: 'Things here have changed a great deal,'
Arthur told his family. 'We can talk, read, smoke, receive newspapers and
parcels.'[11] He was more concerned with his family's welfare than with his
own: 'Papa, I was worried as to what you were doing. I saw, the day we
left Dublin, that there was a great deal of damage done to the Freeman
office, I hoped that it wasn't properly destroyed.'[12] Conditions at Knutsford
continued to improve over the next weeks. Charlie Saurin wrote to Arthur's
brother Will, describing how they were allowed visitors and other privileges:
'Books – that's what we missed most. Now we're alright.'[13]

As it became apparent that the civilian prison system could not cope
with a vast influx of disciplined internees, the prisoners were moved to a
military camp (formerly housing German prisoners of war) near the town of
Bala, in the picturesque Welsh mountains. The remote location of Fron Goch,
an abandoned whiskey distillery with its own railway siding, surrounded
by desolate moorland, made it an ideal internment camp. Although
administratively convenient, the decision to centralise the detention of
about two thousand political prisoners proved dubious. The internees at Fron
Goch, subsequently dubbed the 'university of revolution', fell under the sway
of such energetic organisers as Michael Collins, keen to assert themselves
by challenging the relatively liberal regime. A Sandhurst-style 'military
academy' was established to study guerrilla tactics, while an inner circle

Arthur Shields writes home from
Knutsford detention barracks,
30 May 1916 (HL, T13/A/8).

He received 2 loaves some butter & cheese & you know what you sent me; we were able to exchange. C. giving me a loaf etc. & he getting half my things.

That chocolate was delicious. Don't bother sending me any more things it costs too much & I can get along well enough with what I get here.

Lfa I was very worried as to what your were doing. I saw, the day we left Dublin, that there was a good deal of damage done to the "Freeman" office, I hoped that it wasn't properly destroyed.

Its great to hear Mick. that you are getting on well Will you give each of the kids a kiss from me.

Paper as you can imagine is rather scarce so I can't write as much as I want. It was grand to see the handwriting of Mama. Bid. Nell. I always keep these letters. Yesterday I was given a piece of an old "Herald" It had an adv. for "The Playboy" It made me very sad. It also contained a notice of the death of Sean Connolly (God rest him) He was a grand man, I'll not forget him.

Its well for Will going out camping. C & I were remembering one another yesterday, when it was very hot, of the run from the tent across the sandhills to Portmarnock strand. I have invented a grand hand-shout.

There is a library here & we each were given a book & as soon as we are finished we exchange, so don't send any. Thanks all the same

Love to you all   Boss (Arthur Shields)

South Camp, Fronʒoch. 1

Arthur and most of the 1916 internees ended up at the abandoned whiskey distillery at Fron Goch in Wales (KG, 2012/0179).

began rebuilding the IRB. Clashes with the authorities over prisoners' rights culminated in hunger strikes and mass disobedience, although this was a result more of the battle of wills between militants and the regime than of conditions at the camp. Some prisoners found the discipline imposed by their own officers more onerous than that of their warders.[14]

A phalanx of committees, sub-committees and councils, together with an executive, was established, with an elected civilian council jostling for influence with a self-appointed military staff. Gradually, the prisoners' democratic structures were subordinated to the camp's military hierarchy. Appointed to the amusements sub-committee, Arthur devoted his energies to Fron Goch's dramatic society, which he helped to establish. 'Mostly, he read novels (there was a prison library), smoked cigarettes and lay in bed.'[15] Music also provided a welcome distraction for the men: the internees defiantly sang 'The Soldier's Song' when they arrived, and bands were formed, open-air performances organised and Sunday-night concerts staged in the canteen. Sports, including the Wolfe Tone Tournament, organised by the All-Ireland champion Dick Fitzgerald, proved popular, although hurling was banned, because the camán was considered a lethal weapon. Garrison games were banned by the prisoners' executive, although baseball, skittles, weight-lifting and shot-putting were permitted. Educational classes of every variety were formed: poetry, art and writing were pursued, and crafts, such as macramé, bone-carving and jewellery production, were mastered. The internees – who included many journalists and printers – produced their own newspapers, such as the *Daily Wire* and the *Frongoch Favourite*. They were

THE FRONGOCH FAVOURITE.

(Read by everybody in Frongoch, except the Censor)

No. 2   Saturday 19th August 1916.

To the numerous readers who have sent us letters, wires, boquets &c. in appreciation of our first issue, we tender our hearty thanks.

They, one and all, realize that we have filled a long-felt want. We can assure them that, like the Frongoch prisoners, we have come to stay.

ANOTHER FIRE !

Our peaceful district was much disturbed on Wednesday by the outbreak of a fire in Room 3. The Fire Brigade was quickly on the scene and with much expedition had the various Rooms emptied in double-quick time. From a window of Room 2 Capt Colgan assured the crowd that the fire was well in hand by the Brigade. Shortly afterwards not a flame could be seen.

Interviewed yesterday by one of our reporters, Captain Colgan said the only damage done was the almost total destruction of a valuable copy of the "G-man's Journal." However, a resolution of confidence in John Redmond had been saved from the conflagration. He wished to deny the Rumour that it was through his fault he was last out of Room 2. This he said was only drawing a red-herring across the track.

MOTTOES OF THE MOMENT.

For the Tailors' Shop — "As you sew, so shall you rip." "A stitch in time saves nine"
For the Shoemakers' Shop: — "Its never too late to mend."
For the Barbers' Shop: — "Cleanliness is next to Godliness."
For the Ne-uld: — "The games of children satisfy the child." "Men are but children of a larger growth."

HELD OVER,

Several interesting articles are held over till next issue.

The *Frongoch Favourite*, one of several humorous newssheets compiled by internees (NLI, MS 46,074).

A sketch of the internees'
accommodation at Fron Goch
recorded in John Toomey's
autograph book (NLI, MS 41,662).

even allowed to leave the camp for route marches. Security could be lax; fit
young internees helping the more elderly prison guards to carry their heavy
rifles across the Welsh mountains. Despite all this, most prisoners found
life at Fron Goch pretty miserable. The camp was cold, wet, dreary and rat-
infested; Arthur suffered a chest infection that may have been responsible
for his subsequent health problems.[16]

Although the British authorities' penal experiment at Fron Goch
helped create the nucleus of the Irish Republican Army that resumed the
struggle in 1919, Arthur would not find a place among it. In contrast to
many internees, including some unjustly swept up in the repression that
followed the Rising, he did not find imprisonment a radicalising experience.
One reason for this was that he proved impervious to the two cultural
influences that proved so cohesive within the prisons, and to which many
were devoted: the Irish language and Catholicism. For the revolutionary
generation, Irish – as the writer and revolutionary Sean O'Faolain observed
– 'acted both as a matrix to the tissues of our political faith and as its sign
and password; our zeal to speak Irish bound us into a community, a new,
glowing, persecuted, or about-to-be persecuted political sect'.[17] Arthur
felt differently: 'I wasn't terribly interested in it. I thought we could be
an Irish Nation with a foreign language. It wasn't foreign to me, and it
wasn't foreign to the vast majority of the people.'[18] Catholicism was less
explicitly identified with the republican ideology that developed after 1916.

However, because of its emotional appeal and its association with Irish national identity, it exercised a similar function in practice. At Fron Goch, where Arthur was one of only five Protestant internees, the Rosary was recited daily in Irish. He may have been recalling this experience when he attributed his subsequent decision to leave Ireland to his unwillingness to say his 'prayers in Gaelic'.[19]

The authorities quickly recognised the counter-productive nature of indiscriminate repression. In late June 1916 an advisory committee, chaired by Mr Justice Sankey, was appointed to identify prisoners whose circumstances did not justify continued imprisonment. Its decision to release all but 579 of the detainees indicated the government's conciliatory intentions. Internees often found the resulting judicial process farcical. Clearly a theatre buff, Mr Justice Pim commenced Arthur's hearing at Wormwood Scrubs Prison in London by congratulating him on his performance in St John Ervine's *Mixed Marriage* at the Abbey.[20] Ordering his release, Mr Justice Pim advised Shields 'to go home, stick to the theatre and forget about all this revolutionary nonsense'.[21] Arthur did just that. Released in August 1916, he was back on the Abbey stage – performing in Shaw's *Widowers' Houses* – by October.

Captured on Easter Monday, Helena Molony spent the week confined to a filthy room in the Ship Street Barracks in Dublin Castle: 'before a day had passed we were all covered with vermin', she recalled, although the 'soldiers were decent enough to us'.[22] Recounting the same experience, Kathleen Lynn, like many women prisoners, dwelt on the inadequate sanitary arrangements.[23] Despite these conditions, they remained defiant, rejoicing when the supply of food to the soldiers (and themselves) was cut off towards the end of the week. After the general surrender, Helena was moved to Richmond Barracks in Inchicore, where most rebels were processed, and then on to a disused wing in Kilmainham Jail, which had been reopened to accommodate the large influx of prisoners. Conditions there were poor: the women were jeered by soldiers, some reportedly drunk, as they used toilets without privacy. Helena was devastated by the executions: 'I heard the shots every morning at dawn and knew that that meant they were executing our men'.[24] Following a spirited effort to tunnel out of Kilmainham Jail with a spoon, Helena was moved, with the remaining women prisoners, to Mountjoy Prison, where they were 'hailed with joy by the warders', who regarded them as 'interesting prisoners' rather than 'ordinary criminals'.[25] Under the more congenial regime, they were allowed parcels, visitors,

Venus: an image of the goddess drawn by a female anti-Treaty republican prisoner on her Kilmainham cell. Among the activists' names recorded on the cells is that of Helena Molony (following the fighters project).

exercise and free association, leading one rebel to inform her mother, with a touch of regret, that 'we are almost too well off now and do not feel a bit like martyrs'.[26]

Although many of the women refused their captors' pleas to disavow their actions, 73 out of the 79 women prisoners were quickly released. This reflected condescension rather than kindness. They were freed on the assumption that they had been misled by the men into taking part, or that they had participated out of a desire for 'excitement' rather than out of conviction. General Maxwell was relieved to find himself rid of 'all those silly little girls'.[27] British sensitivities about the treatment of women were also illustrated by the decision not to execute Constance Markievicz, 'solely & only on account of her sex'.[28] The authorities were influenced by public relations as well as by patriarchy: British propagandists had made much of Germany's barbarism following the execution of Edith Cavell, an English nurse found guilty of treason in German-occupied Belgium.

One of only half a dozen women interned in England (compared with over 2,500 men), Helena received exceptional treatment. This was partly because she was armed when she was captured. One of her comrades admiringly recalled the British officer who arrested Helena describing her as a 'walking arsenal', while her Special Branch file recorded that her revolver had been discharged. But it was also because Helena was regarded as a dangerous extremist. She would have been delighted to learn that a senior Dublin Castle official described her as 'the most dangerous woman in

Ireland'.[29] Despite the small number of women internees, and their known history of militancy, General Maxwell, the commander-in-chief in Ireland, had faced resistance from Downing Street in his efforts to incarcerate the handful of women he considered 'older, better educated and real believers in a free Ireland'.[30]

Helena was initially held at Lewes Prison in Sussex, where such prominent republicans as Éamon de Valera and Harry Boland were also held, but was then transferred to Aylesbury Prison, a gloomy Victorian prison in Buckinghamshire. As internees rather than convicts, Helena Molony, Nell Ryan and Winifred Carney were isolated – along with suspected German spies – on their own wing. They sought, unsuccessfully, to renounce their internee status (which permitted them letters, visits and food parcels) in order to join Constance Markievicz among the convicts. Helena continued to cause problems for the authorities, taking advantage of the visit of the wife of an Irish MP to have an article (exposing the conditions in which internees were held) smuggled to Sylvia Pankhurst's Workers' Suffrage Federation. She also remained involved in trade union affairs, persuading Louie Bennett to take over the IWWU in her absence.[31]

Helena stayed in touch with events at the Abbey, corresponding with Ellen Bushell: 'I wish you could write me a long gossipy letter about Abbey affairs. I am lost for insider news.' She revelled in the news of St John Ervine's acrimonious departure from the Abbey following a players' revolt:

> Sometime I shall give way to a temptation I have long resisted – in public anyhow – and take to play-writing. I shall begin with a farce called 'The Passing of the Managers'. It should play to packed houses (entirely composed of past managers and unappreciated Great Actors).

Urging Ellen to visit, in a letter composed with the prison censor in mind, Helena described the Home Office's policy of refusing visits from 'objectionable persons'. Even 'a bowing acquaintance with the cousin of a friend of a person suspected of Sinn Féin views', she complained to Ellen, 'would cause grave doubts & long delays'. She added: 'Luckily, you have always been a good loyal subject, and far removed from such indiscretions.'[32]

Imprisoned republicans were aware of the potential for propaganda arising from their treatment, which aroused far greater public sympathy than their actions during Easter Week. Helena's internment was raised in the House of Commons by the Irish Party MP T. M. Healy, who enquired indignantly about the arrest of 'women in Ireland, the offence of one being that she had played at the Abbey Theatre'.[33] The Dublin Trades Council characterised Helena's detention as a vindictive response to her devotion to the labour movement. An experienced propagandist, Helena was aware of the capital to be mined from their incarceration at Lewes Prison: Marie Perolz recalled that 'Helena Molony said that we should not admit we were well treated'.[34] Keen to draw a line under the insurrection's toxic fall-out, the new Prime Minister, David Lloyd George, announced a general amnesty for internees in December 1916. By then, Helena and Winifred Carney had won over their women warders at Aylesbury Prison, as Helena informed Nell Ryan:

> I really believe that whole household loved the three Irish ... If I had my choice I would rather have stayed over Christmas. They were all so overwrought that we both hated leaving them. Mrs Herbert played from 11 o clock and it was like a country pub to see them singing and shaking hands with us and their eyes flooded with tears the whole time you'd think we were their nearest relation. Miss Carney collapsed on the table sobbing and even I felt a bit damp. It was sad, leaving them on Christmas Eve.[35]

Helena regarded her imprisonment as a sign of her commitment to the cause; her friends joked that its short duration was especially 'hard on her', as 'she had looked forward to it all her life'.[36] She sought to pick up the threads of her old life, despite straitened circumstances. 'Marie Perolz and Helena Molony came to us after their release', an activist for the Irish National Aid Association recalled. 'We did what we could for them'.[37] Helena continued to survive 'from hand to mouth and spent a good deal of time in the homes of friends'.[38] By February 1917 she had returned to the stage, appearing in *Uncle Vanya* for the Irish Theatre in Hardwicke Street.

She had returned to a new Ireland. The impact of the executions and repression had been intensified by the revelation of such atrocities as the murder of Francis Sheehy Skeffington and a botched attempt to cover up the murder of civilians in North King Street. Popular support for the Irish Party had begun to collapse, although it was not yet clear what would fill the vacuum left in its wake. Peadar Kearney realised that public opinion had shifted when he saw the crowds flocking to the Pro-Cathedral for the month's mind requiem Masses held for the executed rebels. When Helena and the other internees arrived back home at Christmas, they were greeted as heroes: 'Failure was greater than triumph and victory less than defeat'.[39] Despite this, the emergence of a popular republican movement did not appear predestined to Helena: 'we were defeated; nobody thought we would rise up again.'[40] In contrast to Arthur, she threw herself back into revolutionary agitation. Her militancy, however, would see her increasingly out of step with the wider revolutionary movement, as well as with organised labour, which, following the death of James Connolly, no longer sought a place in the vanguard of separatism.

Heroes: released prisoners at Westland Row, 1917 (NPA, Keogh 127). Jeered by many Dubliners when they were deported, the rebels were lauded on their return.

Part III

After

Come gather round me players all:
Come praise Nineteen-Sixteen,
Those from the pit and gallery
Or from the painted scene
That fought in the Post Office
Or round the City Hall,
Praise every man that came again,
Praise every man that fell.

From mountain to mountain ride the fierce horsemen.

Who was the first man shot that day?
The player Connolly,
Close to the City Hall he died;
Carriage and voice had he;
He lacked those years that go with skill,
But later might have been
A famous, brilliant figure
Before the painted scene.

From mountain to mountain ride the fierce horsemen.

Some had no thought of victory
But had gone out to die
That Ireland's mind be greater,
Her heart mount up on high;
And no man knows what's yet to come
But Patrick Pearse has said
In every generation
Must Ireland's blood be shed.

From mountain to mountain ride the fierce horsemen.

—W. B. Yeats, 'Three Songs to the One Burden'

Chapter 13

Terrible Beauty:

Yeats and 1916

The Irish are essentially a dramatic people as the French are, as the English and Germans are not. When Mr. W. B. Yeats created the Irish Theatre it was with an almost uncanny knowledge of the needs and capacities of the Irish.

—*Daily Chronicle* report on the Easter Rising, 9 May 1916[1]

On this day I tried to tell her something of my generation's sense of loss by Yeats's death. I was genuinely moved, a little pompous, discussing a great literary event with my aunt, a well-read woman who loved poetry.

Her large, blue eyes became increasingly blank almost to the polar expression they took on in controversy. Then she relaxed a little: I was young and meant no harm. She almost audibly did not say several things that occurred to her. She wished, I know, to say something kind; she could not say anything she did not believe to be true. After a pause she spoke:

'Yes,' she said, 'he was a Link with the Past'.

—Conor Cruise O'Brien's recollection of Hanna Sheehy Skeffington's response to Yeats's death, 1939[2]

So close was the Abbey to the heart of the rebellion that the fire that raged throughout Easter Week scorched the edge of the theatre: 'bricks from burning buildings fell even on the steps'.[3] By the end of the rebellion, forty-eight businesses in Lower and Middle Abbey Street had been destroyed, but the theatre remained intact. The only damage reported by the Abbey's manager, St John Ervine, was 'a broken lamp outside the Stage Door, and a few panes of glass outside the Pit Door'.[4] Although it evaded the inferno, the theatre did not escape the rebellion's impact. With the surrounding area devastated, and much of the city's infrastructure wrecked, Ervine predicted an uncertain future:

I am afraid this business has brought the Abbey much
nearer disaster than even the European war, as, of
course, it is impossible to open while Martial Law
prevails. In any event, I do not think the desire for
theatrical entertainment is particularly strong at the
moment, and as the area around the Abbey is either
demolished or tottering, it is highly improbable that
anybody would venture near us.[5]

Yeats was no less shaken by the rebellion. He confided to Ervine
his sense of 'a world one has worked with or against for years suddenly
overwhelmed.'[6] The Rising's transformative effect is clear from the rapidly
changing tone of the correspondence between Lady Gregory, Yeats and
his sister Lily over the next weeks. Living in rural Co. Galway, one of the
few areas where the rebels had taken to the field, Gregory was isolated
during Easter Week, as rumours of arrests, attacks and besieged policemen
circulated. She was sympathetic to the 'foolish young lads' caught up in
the rebellion, and to the intellectuals among its leadership with whom
she was acquainted, but opposed to the insurrection: 'One has no pity for
those who know what the Germans have done in Belgium and want to bring
them into Ireland, and who have taken German money.'[7] Lily, writing from
Dublin, was scathing, ridiculing the leaders' pretensions, and denouncing
the Citizen Army as unemployed 'drunken dock workers'.[8] One week later,
though, Lily's rage was directed against the government. Infuriated by its
decision to execute the 'foolish idealists', she predicted, accurately, that the
government's actions would prove 'the beginning of Ireland'.[9] Gregory was
undergoing a similar change of heart, stating that

my mind is filled with sorrow at the Dublin tragedy,
the death of Pearse & McDonough, who ought to have
been on our side, the side of intellectual freedom – &
I keep wondering whether we could not have brought
them into that intellectual movement ... I have a more
personal grief for Sean Connolly who I had not only
admiration but affection for – He was shot on the roof of
the City Hall – there is no one to blame but one grieves

there are barricades across the roads, and at a village, Clare-
bridge (near that Raftery Fais you were at) there are at this moment
five policemen besieged. There have been a few arrests, but there are not
enough police in the district to go out and fight, and we have no military.
We doubt these will soon be sent, and then there will be punishment, for
the country has been put under martial law. One has no pity for those
who know what the Germans have done in Belgium and want to bring them
into Ireland, and who have taken German money. But I'm afraid a great
many foolish young lads have been drawn in, believing they were doing
something for the country. ..There is a chance, the first, of sending
some letters by motor, and I am writing this to let you know how we are
faring, so far.
May 9, 1916. We have just got back into communication with the outer
world. We are in the centre of a disturbed district, and with rails piled *pulled*
up at one side and roads barricaded on the other we were absolutely
without certain news of anything, or any news of friends. Some prisoners
are still being taken, but all is quiet. I knew and liked both Pearse and
McDonough, and wish they could have taken some other way of showing love
of country...I dont know how Dublin can ever recover. Ervine writes that
we may have to disband the Abbey Company but I think we may get on, we
have some English music Hall engagements before us. The Abbey building
escaped by miracle, bricks from burning buildings fell even on the steps. I
am thankful the Modern and National galleries escaped. Had Hugh's first
wish been carried out and the Gallery been built in Stephens Green it
would have suffered.

The war seemed very far away while we were isolated, and it is painful coming back to it, the papers full killings and wrangles and the re-
criminations of nations that seem mere spiteful gossip. I am thankful the
children dont know anything about it but vaguely...

'I don't know how Dublin can ever recover'. Lady Gregory describes her experiences during Easter Week to W. B. Yeats, 8–9 May 1916 (NYPL, Gregory papers).

> all the same – It seems as if the leaders were what is
> wanted in Ireland – & will be even more
> wanted in the future – a fearless & imaginative
> opposition to the conventional & opportunistic
> parliamentarians, who have never helped our work even
> by intelligent opposition ...[10]

Despite his dislike of her shrill nationalism, Yeats was struck by the response of Maud Gonne, whose estranged husband, John MacBride, had been executed. 'The deaths of those leaders', she told Yeats, 'are full of beauty & romance & "They will be speaking forever, the people will hear them forever".'[11] Several days later, Yeats remained preoccupied with Gonne's assertion that 'tragic dignity has returned to Ireland'. He confided to Lady Gregory: 'I am trying to write a poem on the men executed – "terrible beauty has been born".'[12] The power of this poem, 'Easter 1916', completed in September but not published until the autumn of 1920, stems from Yeats's ambivalence about the Easter Rising – from his doubts about its necessity and the motives of its leaders, and about their fanaticism – and from his final, reluctant re-evaluation of their status, as he concedes their transformation from subjects of his mockery to figures whose sacrifice compels him to inscribe their names in Irish history.[13]

By transforming Ireland's future, the Rising also changed its past. The relationship between the Abbey Theatre and political nationalism was recast as myth began to displace history. Maud Gonne's reference to *Cathleen ni Houlihan* in her letter to Yeats was one of countless examples of how the Rising was interpreted in Yeatsian language. Writing on 9 May, as the executions continued, the *Daily Chronicle's* correspondent wondered what the Rising's leaders –'these university professors, these fledgling poets' – really had in common with Tone and Emmet: 'Nothing, except the dreams and ideals.'[14] For the *Chronicle's* correspondent, Yeats's theatre provided the link between 1798 and 1916:

> Has not this revolution in some sense a genesis in the
> Irish Theatre? Where out of Paris would you find the
> Countess Markievicz? That kissing of the revolver now
> before she handed it up! The terms in which the main

body of the insurgents surrendered, 'the members of the
Provisional Government', 'the units of the Republican
Forces', the sounding titles of such men as P.H. Pearse
and James Connolly, it is all of the stuff
of drama ...

The Rising altered how Yeats's previous work was interpreted. Prior
to 1916, plays such as *Cathleen ni Houlihan* were read as a lament for the death
of romantic Ireland, a critique of the soulless present. After 1916, they were
interpreted as prophecy, even incitement. The recollections of the Chief
Secretary for Ireland, Augustine Birrell, provide a revealing example of
this shift. His comment (in his memoir of 1937) that 'the programme of the
Abbey Theatre became to me of far more real significance than the monthly
reports of the R.I.C.' has been cited as evidence of the cultural revival's
role in precipitating revolution.[15] Testifying to the Royal Commission of
Inquiry on the rebellion on 19 May 1916, however, Birrell provided a far more
nuanced assessment of the revival's impact:

This period was also marked by a genuine literary
revival, in prose, poetry and the drama, which
has produced remarkable books and plays, and a
school of acting, all characterised by originality and
independence of thought and expression, quite divorced
from any political party, and all tending towards and
feeding latent desires for some kind of separate Irish
national existence. It was a curious situation to watch,
but there was nothing in it suggestive of revolt or
rebellion, except in the realm of thought. Indeed it was
quite the other way. The Abbey Theatre made merciless
fun of mad political enterprise, and lashed with savage
satire some historical aspects of the revolutionary. I was
often amazed at the literary detachment and courage
of the playwright, the relentless audacity of the actors
and actresses, and the patience and comprehension
of the audience. This new critical tone and temper,
noticeable everywhere, penetrating everything, and

influencing many minds in all ranks, whilst having its disintegrating effects upon old fashioned political beliefs and worn-out controversial phrases, was the deadly foe of that wild sentimental passion which has once more led so many brave young fellows to a certain doom, in the belief that in Ireland any revolution is better than none. A little more time, and, but for the outbreak of the war, this new critical temper would, in my belief, have finally prevailed, not indeed to destroy national sentiment (for that is immortal), but to kill by ridicule insensate revolt. But that was not to be.[16]

Birrell does, admittedly, rather gloss over the significance of 'the realm of thought'. As an early historian of the Abbey observed, 'revolutions are born in the mind and the Abbey Theatre helped to develop the thought of the nation'.[17] It is clear that *Cathleen ni Houlihan* influenced many individuals (including future revolutionaries) by crystallising the emotional force of a romantic interpretation of Irish history. Recalling Willie Fay's intention that his staging of Yeats's play would send 'men away filled with the desire for deeds', Nicholas Grene has observed how 'again and again the testimony was to the extraordinary kinetic impact of the play.'[18] That a substantial part of the Chief Secretary's testimony to a commission into the causes of the rebellion concerned the role of the national theatre is in itself revealing. But if it was based on the content of such Abbey plays as *The Dreamer* by Lennox Robinson – which juxtaposed the impractical world view of revolutionary idealists with the banal self-interest of the masses – the British administration's fear of their incendiary potential was 'an understandable but misdirected anxiety'.[19]

Despite this, the idea that the Rising occurred as a consequence of the emotions stirred by plays like *Cathleen ni Houlihan* became an article of faith, not least because such republicans as Constance Markievicz testified from their prison cells to that play's status as 'a sort of gospel'.[20] More revealing, though, was the response of Patrick Pearse, who clearly had Yeats's play on his mind as he planned the Rising:

When I was a child I believed that there was actually a
woman called Erin and had Mr Yeats' *Kathleen ni Houlihan*
been then written and had I seen it, I should have taken it,
not as an allegory, but as a representation of a thing that
might happen any day in any house. This I no longer believe
as a physical possibility ... But I believe that there is really a
spiritual tradition which is the soul of Ireland.[21]

It was this tradition that gave *Cathleen ni Houlihan* its tremendous power,
but it was a tradition more powerfully conveyed for most revolutionaries by the
Abbey's competitors – by popular historical narratives and by commemoration of
1798 – than by Yeats's literary theatre. Forced to choose between the complexity
of the Abbey Theatre's 'ambiguous and thorny' relationship with revolutionary
nationalism and the appealing simplicity of the retrospective myth, most – like
Birrell – would eventually plump for the latter. Although the Rising ensured the
status of *Cathleen ni Houlihan* as one of the 'sacred works' of republicanism, William
Thompson has provided a more accurate assessment of the play's relationship to
the Rising: 'Art helps to create a historical consciousness, but once that historical
consciousness exists, it is history itself that becomes the work of art.'[22]

Lady Gregory, performing as Cathleen
ni Houlihan, opposite Arthur Shields's
Michael Gillane (HL, T13/B/240).
Máire Nic Shiubhlaigh, whose failure
to appear in this 1919 production led
to Gregory's rare stage performance,
cattily observed that the latter's
appearance, 'oddly reminiscent of an
elderly Queen Victoria, can hardly have
been in keeping with the character Yeats
had in mind when he wrote the play'.

Chapter 14

Barney

1916–38

Barney Murphy (1887–1938):
the prompter with no belief
in actors' pauses (AT).

The heavy-hearted expression of Mrs Sheehy-
Skeffington about 'The Ireland that remembers with
tear-dimmed eyes all that Easter Week stands for'
makes me sick. Some of the men can't even get a
job. Mrs. Skeffington is certainly not dumb but she
appears to be both blind and deaf to all the things
that are happening around her ... Tears may be in the
eyes of the navvies working on the Shannon scheme,
but they are not for Ireland.

—Seán O'Casey, replying to criticism of *The Plough and the Stars*, 20 February 1926 [1]

Until recently, as little was known about Barney Murphy's fate after
the Easter Rising as about his life prior to it. In contrast to middle-class
revolutionaries – more likely to generate for posterity diaries, letters and
memoirs, and whose careers often brought them to public attention – few
sources exist for the working-class rebels who returned to obscurity after
1916. Since 2014, however, an extraordinary new archive, the Military
Service Pensions collection, is transforming our understanding of how the
rank and file experienced the revolution and its afterlife.

In June 1923 the Free State government introduced a pension scheme to recognise and compensate wounded individuals and the dependants of deceased revolutionaries. In the coming decades the scheme was gradually widened to include individuals with 'active service' in the rebellion and in the political conflicts that followed. From the government's point of view the scheme, introduced just weeks after the end of the Civil War, offered a means of reintegrating veterans in society, as well as a potential source of political patronage.[2] It also recognised the physical and economic hardship endured by many revolutionaries.

The experience of Edward Keegan, who, like Barney Murphy, belonged to St Laurence O'Toole Gaelic Athletic Club, provides one example of the high price paid by some as a result of their service in 1916. On the evening of Easter Monday, as he repelled a British attack at the South Dublin Union (a garrison that witnessed sharp and brutal fighting), Keegan was shot through the lung. After the Rising he was fired from his position as a clerk in the advertising manager's office of the *Irish Times* as a result of his 'disloyalty'. He died in 1938, just a week before Barney passed away, having endured a life of ill-health.[3]

While the Military Service Pensions collection attests to the courage and selflessness of many of the revolutionary generation, the light it sheds on the administration of the scheme, and on the poverty and inequality of post-independence Ireland, is less edifying.[4] With 66,300 of its 82,000 applicants rejected, the scheme engendered considerable resentment. Although many of the best-known applicants received the relatively generous higher grades of payment, many recipients were unhappy about the level of award they received. However, even the lowest grade of pension – the equivalent today of about £1,500 – prevented some veterans from sliding into destitution.[5] There was a determination that there should be no 'soft pensions', so the vetting process was onerous and slow.[6] Containing 'many voices of desperation and urgent pleas', the Military Service Pensions collection's vast archive of 300,000 files constitutes, as Diarmaid Ferriter has observed, a chronicle of disappointment.[7]

Barney Murphy testifies to the Military Service Pensions Board about his 1916 service, July 1937 (MAI, MSP Murphy).

SWORN STATEMENT MADE BY BERNARD MURPHY (21471)

BEFORE ADVISORY COMMITTEE ON 7. 7. 1937

Q. When did you join?
A. In 1913 at the Rotunda.
1st Period:
Q. Were you out in Easter Week?
A. Yes.

Q. What did you do on Easter Sunday?
    Were you mobilised?
A. No. I was mobilised for Sunday, but it was broken off.

Q. When were you mobilised ?
A. I was practically holding myself in reserve for a week
    beforehand.

Q. You didn't parade anywhere on Sunday?
A. I was stopped going on parade.

Q. You spent Sunday at home then?
A. Yes, and Sunday night.

Q. Standing-to ?
A. Yes, all the time.

Q. Were you mobilised on the Monday?
A. Going to the place of mobilisation Commdt. Daly stopped me
    and told me to get my men and go with a man named Sean
    Boylan(?) and cut the wires at Liffey Junction.

Q. Did you go there?
A. Yes.

Q. How long were you away on that job?
A. 1½ hours.

Q. Where did you go then?
A. Came back to North King St, met Commdt. Dalu, reported.
    He sent me to Coles(?) to the market.

Q. You got into the Four Courts Garrison area?
A. Yes.

Q. Some time on Monday evening?
A. No, early in the day. I was sent to Coles of Little
    Green St. We were trying to break into it to get some stuff
    that was inside - we failed. Went down and reported to Joe
    Maginnis who was in charge of a certain area in the Four
    Courts. He told me to go inside and take charge of prisoners

Q. How long were you in charge of prisoners?
A. Half an hour.

Q. Where were you on Monday night?
A. In the Four Courts.

Q. Tuesday?
A. Four Courts.

Q. Wednesday?

-2-

A. On top of the roof.

Q. Thursday?
A. Church St. Bridge.

Q. And Friday?
A. In the Four Courts, Church St. Bridge and round by Green Street.

Q. Saturday?
A. Four Courts and Church St. Bridge

Q. Were you continuously in the Four Courts area?
A. Yes, from the time I went in I never left it.

Q. Were you in the surrender?
A. I was at it but didn't surrender.

Q. When? Saturday
A. On the Sunday. I met Daly and he showed me the surrender. He wasn't able to read it to us he was in such a state. He told us to fall in . Seán Flood gave the order to fall in; I wouldn't. I took an automatic and went home. I was living beside it.

Q. What time did you get home?
A. I'd say it was about 7 o'clock in the evening.

Q. You weren't arrested?
A. No.

2nd Period:

Q. For the 3 wks. before Easter Week were you able to do any special work?
A. Watching barracks and taking messages back and forward.

Q. You were working at your own job in the day time?
A. Yes. I was conveying ammunition to various places.

Q. How often did you do that?
A. About 4 times during the week before Easter - particularly Good Friday.

Q. How much stuff did you convey on Good Friday?
A. Rifles from my own place to Liberty Hall.

Q. On how many other occasions in Holy Week were you doing work like that?
A. That was the only one I think. I was back and forward taking messages to Ned Daly, Tom Clarke, and things like that. We were three personal friends and Seán McDermott. There was another chap named J.H. Doyle too; he was active and was able to get around very quickly.

Q. Did you take messages very often between those men?
A. About 4 times.

Q. You dropped out after that?
A. I didn't exactly. I was engaged day and night working and I couldn't keep it up. I did convey ammunition here and there and took messages; but the two men, Peadar Clancy and another, are both dead.

Q. Is your name on the Roll of Honour?
A. Yes.
_____

NF

201

Barney Murphy was one of the 15,700 successful applicants, and his award of a pension generated an administrative record of his material circumstances from the date of his application in December 1935 to his death. Although Barney played some role in the War of Independence, he applied only on the basis of his Easter Week service, presumably because his subsequent involvement with the IRA would not have met the high bar set for active service: 'My service from 1916 was mostly unofficial as seldom free from work. I could not attend official parades. The persons I mostly worked with are deceased'.[8] Nor did he participate in the Civil War.

Barney's files reveal that he endured extreme poverty in the final years of his life. In October 1936 the Society of St Vincent de Paul asked the Department of Defence to give priority to his application on the grounds that 'the claimant who has a large family is unemployed and utterly destitute'. The disastrous effect of his sudden unemployment, presumably from the Abbey Theatre, was compounded by the cost of keeping his three sons and two daughters in education.[9] Although Barney's testimonials and sworn testimony, provided in July 1937, indicated 'a clear qualifying case for Easter Week', no decision had been made by the assessors by November 1937, when the Associated Easter Week Men (jointly founded by Edward Keegan) informed the Department of Defence that Barney was 'in straitened circumstances at present and badly in need of money'.[10] The assessors, however, felt they had insufficient evidence on which to base a decision.

In July 1938 his former comrades again appealed on his behalf, pointing out that Barney was now a patient in the Dublin Union Hospital. His presence at that institution, still known locally as the Workhouse, a term which conveyed the stigma with which it was associated, indicated the extent of his poverty. After a more urgent appeal the following month – 'This man is rapidly sinking' – Barney's case was adjourned for further investigation.[11]

By the time a more detailed reference from his former officer was received, in November 1938, Barney Murphy had died of heart disease.[12] Although his widow, Mary, wrote four months later to explain that she was also 'in a very bad way financially', the assessors remained unable to reach a decision. The following year, by which time Frank Fahy, the Ceann Comhairle of the Dáil, had written in support of Mary's case, and further evidence of Barney's 1916 service had been supplied, he was posthumously awarded a grade E pension (about £30 per annum).

SOCIETY OF ST. VINCENT DE PAUL.

CONFERENCE OF ST. NICHOLAS OF MYRA.

MYRA HOUSE,
100 FRANCIS STREET,
DUBLIN, W.1.

The Secretary,
Department of Defence,
Parkgate Street,
Dublin.

Monday,
12th October,
1936.

Military Service Pensions Act 1934
Claim Bernard Murphy, 20G. Nicholas
Street, Dublin. Your Ref: F.3

DEPT. OF DEFENCE,
RECEIVED
1 3 OCT 1936
PENSIONS BRANCH

Dear Sir,

We would be glad to know whether anything could be done to
give priority to the hearing of the above claim as the claimant who has
a large family is unemployed and utterly destitute.   His circumstances
are made more difficult by the fact that for some years preceding the
date of his becoming unemployed some months ago he was earning high
wages and had his children attending secondary schools in the City.
An effort is being made for the moment to continue the childrens education
but unless the claim can be heard or the claimant gets back into
employment, which is unlikely for the present, this can hardly be continued.
We expect that if the circumstances were brought to the notice of the
Board special priority would be given.

We would be glad to hear from you.

Yours faithfully,

J.P.L.Murphy

The Society of St Vincent de Paul
ask the Department of Defence to
expedite Barney Murphy's military
service pension application, 12
October 1936 (MAI, MSP Murphy).

Cumann Óglaiġ na Cásga

1916

ASSOCIATED EASTER WEEK MEN

7 EUSTACE STREET

DUBLIN

P.S.M.   1934

OIFIG AN RÉITEÓRA   21st July, 193....
FÁIGETE

A 22 IÚL 1938

DÚN Óí GAEDETHA

A Chara,

        We wrote you on several occasions recently with reference
to our member B. Murphy, who is still a patient in the Dublin
Union Hospital.

        Further to a call made at your office by our Vice-President,
we were in communication with Mr. P. Holohan who promised to do
whatever was necessary to have this matter cleared up.

        We would be glad to know what progress, if any, has been
made in the case.

                        Is mise,

                        Denis Reelo

                            Runaide

E. Burke,
    Secretary.

The Associated Easter Week Men
submitted an appeal on behalf of
their destitute former comrade after
he was admitted to the Dublin Union
Hospital in 1938 (MAI, MSP Murphy).

The back payment due to Barney up to the date of his death was only authorised, as was standard practice, once Mary agreed to accept the level of award proposed and to undertake not to make any further representations for payment. Following a further appeal by Robert Briscoe TD, because of continued delays, Mary received £79 later that year, allowing her to meet the costs of Barney's funeral and other debts resulting from his unemployment and illness.[13] Although this process – experienced by many veterans who lacked the right political connections – must have provoked humiliation and resentment, it was not particularly unusual: 'some applicants had to endure years of waiting, frustration and tortuous correspondence, often with no positive outcome'.[14]

Aged fifty-two, Barney Murphy had died on 29 September 1938. A large crowd attended the removal of his remains at St Audoën's Church, High Street, including members of the Old IRA, the Associated Easter Week Men and the Old Republican Soldiers of Ireland – some of the numerous bodies that had emerged to campaign for the welfare of revolutionary veterans. Draped in the Tricolour, his coffin was accompanied by a guard of honour of former comrades. Barney was buried in Glasnevin. The service prompted a short note in the *Irish Independent* under the heading '1916 man's death'.[15]

Chapter 15

Peadar

1916–42

oġLáiġ ná h-éiReánn.
(IRISH VOLUNTEERS.)

An All-Ireland Convention of the Irish Volunteers has been held recently, and a new Executive elected. The principal duty of this Executive will be to carry on the re-organisation of the Irish Volunteers throughout the country, and put them in a position to complete by force of arms the work begun by the men of Easter Week.

In order that we may not be hampered in our next effort by any misunderstanding such as occurred on the last occasion, as a result of conflicting orders, Volunteers are notified that the only orders they are to obey are those of their own Executive. [See note.]

They are at liberty, and are encouraged, to join any other movement that aims at making Ireland a separate and independent nation.

They are reminded, however, of what occurred when Parnell induced the Fenians to fall into line with him—a fusion that resulted in the almost complete abandonment of physical force as a policy. They are warned, therefore, against devoting too much time or energy to any movement other than their own, but to help them solely for the reason that they may enable them to spread the principles of their own organisation, which is the one to which they owe and must give first allegiance.

Each Volunteer is expected to do his own part under the present difficult circumstances towards making himself an efficient soldier in the National Army, and each county is expected to see to the training and arming of its own men. It must also see that well-defined lines of communication are kept with the surrounding counties. The Executive, of course, are in the last degree responsible for all this work, and they call with confidence on all officers and men to co-operate with them in carrying it out as speedily as possible. They guarantee, in return, that they will not issue an order to take the field until they consider that the force is in a position to wage war on the enemy with reasonable hopes of success. Volunteers as a whole may consequently rest assured that they will not be called upon to take part in any forlorn hope.

Let each one get to his work at once, and when the Executive are satisfied that the right moment has come—that is, when we are strongest and the enemy weakest—they will give the order to strike—*and then let it be done relentlessly.*

By Order,

EXECUTIVE IRISH VOLUNTEERS.

Dated 22nd May, 1917.

NOTE.—All orders of the Executive will be signed "For and on behalf of the Executive." This does not apply to matters of detail pertaining to organisation, training and communication, which will, of course, be signed by the respective directors.

Although this statement of May 1917 by the Irish Volunteer Executive emphasised the necessity of military means to achieve the Republic, it was careful not to commit the movement to the sacrificial tactics of 1916. The circle would later be squared by a campaign of guerrilla warfare and assassination (NLI, EPH C184).

> We made no mourning that night: we roared
> defiance instead, and found relief in the 'Soldier's
> Song' – the Dublin carpenter's song that had been
> sung in the Post Office in Dublin in a circle of fire.
> We were conscious that a new spirit of self-reliance
> and discipline and faith had come into Irish life.
>
> —Daniel Corkery, *The Hounds of Banba* (1920)

> It is a hard service they take that help me. Many that
> are red-cheeked now will be pale-cheeked; many that
> have been free to walk the hills and the bogs and
> the rushes will be sent to walk hard streets in far
> countries; many a good plan will be broken; many
> that have gathered money will not stay to spend it;
> many a child will be born and there will be no father
> at its christening to give it a name.
>
> —W. B. Yeats, *Cathleen ni Houlihan* (1902)

In contrast to Barney Murphy, Peadar Kearney remained a committed activist after the Easter Rising. He returned to B Company, 2nd Battalion, Dublin Brigade of the Irish Volunteers, which was commanded by Paddy Daly, who would later lead Collins's notorious Squad. Describing himself as 'sort of an organiser', Peadar was more of a fixer than a fighter. As the Volunteers revived in the wake of the release of the Fron Goch internees, he helped to set up and arm companies in Dublin and further afield. As with his earlier IRB activism, he combined his work as a painter with revolutionary activism, cycling throughout Leinster, for example, to support the campaign against conscription in the spring of 1918.

With the suppression of the Dáil in late 1919, violence began to replace politics. The same venues which previously hosted cultural nationalist activity – Gaelic League halls, trade union premises (including Liberty Hall), the workingmen's club in York Street – now provided the meeting-places for young men to learn how to drill and shoot:

Beneath a placid surface, there was an activity
unbelievable in its intensity. Through their streets, with
their sauntering couples, went a young lad here and there
who, at some unpretentious doorway, melted away from
the scene. That was usually around seven-thirty or eight
in the evening and these young men did not come back
on to the streets again until ten o'clock or after. Without
hurry or apparent secretiveness, they re-joined the
saunterers and went home on the late trams.[1]

It was the violence of the Volunteers, beginning with the Squad's ruthless
campaign against G Division of the DMP, and gradually extending to intelligence
agents and government officials, rather than the political agitation of Sinn Féin,
that spurred the revolution on in the capital. The struggle for independence
was conducted rather differently – if no less brutally – in inner-city Dublin than
in the villages and towns of rural Ireland. Death more often came as the result
of carefully planned executions than of ambushes, with the intelligence war
conducted with growing intensity by both sides. In the first year of the conflict
eleven policemen had been assassinated in the city, paralysing the force that
traditionally acted as the eyes and ears of Dublin Castle. In response, the British
authorities militarised policing in Ireland, raising new forces, such as the ill-
disciplined Black and Tans and the more effective Auxiliaries. By the middle of 1921
more than three hundred Dubliners – half of them civilians – had been killed as a
result of political violence.[2]

Even within this murky field of combat, Peadar Kearney occupied
a particularly uncertain role. The Sinn Féin solicitor Michael Noyk recalled
Peadar as one of a group of 'unknown soldiers' who operated out of Seán
Farrelly's public house at the corner of Stephen's Green and Grafton Street.[3]
Tom Pugh, whom Peadar recruited into his own IRB circle, described their
tight-knit group – which included Peadar's brother-in-law Mick Slater – as 'sort
of a Labour crowd' who were under orders 'not to do any drilling or marching
with the others'.[4] As well as their overlapping membership of the IRB and
the IRA, they were connected through their membership of craft unions,
whose expertise and contacts they drew on to provide logistical support to the
movement, allowing them to move people, arms and equipment throughout
the country.[5] Describing his unit as an unnamed department 'controlled by
D. [Diarmuid] O'Hegarty', Gregory Murphy recalled that 'we were engaged

TO ENGLAND.

SEPTEMBER 25th, 1917.

Hail ! Mother of Civilization,
    Hail ! strength of the lowly and weak
(*You sink of the earth's degradation*),
    Give ear while we speak :
Once more you have bade us remember
    That your thrice-accursed flag is blood red,
And Ashe, in his glory and vigour,
    Is strangled and dead.

He is dead, but his spirit triumphant
    Soars high over thraldom and death
(And he scorned your friendship, O England,
    With his last dying breath).
You may smile in the filth of your brothels,
    You may sneer in your arrogant might,
But lo ! even now you are reeling
    'Neath a withering blight.

And you stand in the market-place, England,
    With your leprous soul laid bare,
The scorn and contempt of the nations,
    Who spit on you there.
THEY know that your sentence is written,
    That Freedom and Right shall prevail,
But the Power that shall carve out that sentence
    Is the Power of the Gael.

And we call on the nations to witness,
    The sons of the Inde and the Gael,
Who have learned the truth of your teaching
    By gibbet and jail ;
And their blood in one sacrifice column
    In Heaven shall justice demand,
And when Heaven shall mete out its justice,
    YOUR hour is at hand.

Then hail ! to your mission, O England,
    To plunder and ravish and slay.
YOU give us red milestones to Freedom,
    WE follow alway.
We'll follow that red road to Glory
    (The white-livered traitors assail),
And you'll hear with your death-rattle, England,
    The Curse of the Gael.

                   Peaḋar Ó Cearnaiġ.

Kearney's embittered ballad, 'To England', was a response to the death of Thomas Ashe on 25 September 1917 as a result of force-feeding by prison officials (NLI, EPH A212).

procuring and distributing arms, collecting intelligence reports, etc.'[6] A senior IRB and IRA figure who worked closely with Michael Collins and Harry Boland, Diarmuid O'Hegarty was dubbed the 'civil servant of the revolution', being responsible for the administration of the revolutionary government and its underground departments.[7]

Much of the time, this network of activists operated out of the drawing-room over Shanahan's public house in Foley Street. The revolutionaries who gathered here – including the Tipperary IRA leaders Dan Breen, Seán Treacy, Seán Hogan and Séamus Robinson – were, as another member of Peadar's unit put it, 'the driving force in getting things done throughout the country'.[8] The clientele of the pub, situated in the heart of Monto (Montgomery Street, now Foley Street, and the surrounding area), a district to the north-east of the Custom House notorious for its concentration of Dublin's brothels and shebeens, included trenchcoat-wearing gunmen up from the country, sailors, brothel madams, crooks and chancers – the latter category exemplified by the enterprising Jimmy Walsh, responsible for operating Templemore's 'bleeding statue', which had brought thousands of pilgrims to Co. Tipperary in the summer of 1920, raising much-needed funds for the IRA in the process.[9] The prostitutes of Monto, then one of the largest red-light districts in Europe, continued to cater to the needs of British soldiers during the revolutionary period while often supporting the republican cause. 'The lady prostitutes used to pinch the guns and ammunition from the Auxiliaries or Tans at night, and then leave them for us at Phil Shanahan's public house,' Dan Breen recalled. 'I might add that there was no such thing as payment for these transactions, and any information they had they gave us.'[10]

A Co. Tipperary grocer and publican who was out in 1916, Phil Shanahan had been elected an MP for Sinn Féin in 1918. His premises, used as a meeting-place, arms dump and safe house by Michael Collins and Dick McKee, provided a venue both for planning military operations and for late-night revelry: 'Public houses then closed at eleven at night, but in the "room above" one never heard "Time, gentlemen, please".'[11] Within this revolutionary demi-monde, teetotal Tipperary flying-column men mixed with working-class Dubliners. 'We were a rough crowd,' recalled Peadar, 'but when Seán Treacy was present every man kept his tongue in check. He would not tolerate obscene language, and no man dare take the name of God in vain in his presence.'[12] Although Monto's vibrant, disreputable milieu has been vividly depicted in literature – most famously as 'nighttown' in James Joyce's *Ulysses* but also, for the revolutionary period, in *The Informer* by Liam O'Flaherty (who described it as a 'disgustingly sordid place' with 'great demonish charm') – its role in the conflict received scant attention from memoirs and histories of the War of Independence.[13] As Séamus de Búrca noted, this was largely due 'to feelings of delicacy because of its notorious reputation'.[14] In 1925 Monto was largely obliterated when the state's new police force combined with the Legion of Mary to close down its brothels in a revealing demonstration of the respectability of the new political order.

Peadar's involvement in the War of Independence came to an abrupt end at three in the morning on 25 November 1920, when his house in Richmond Parade, on the banks of the Royal Canal, was raided by a party of Auxiliaries; they were accompanied by a nervous member of the DMP whom Peadar took great satisfaction in recognising. The raiding party –which, Peadar conceded, refrained from smashing up his house, and treated his wife sympathetically – allowed him to say goodbye to his two young boys:

> He had taught them to recite a prayer, 'The Lord have mercy on the souls of the men who died for Ireland', to which had been added the names of Seán Treacy, Peadar Clancy and Dick McKee. The children saluted and the Auxiliary watching the performance remarked, 'Some training, Kierney'.[15]

Peadar was lifted only four days after Bloody Sunday, 21 November 1920, a day of horrific violence that had resulted in the death of thirty-five people in the capital, in three waves of killings that began with the IRA's co-ordinated attempt to wipe out British intelligence operatives in Dublin. Peadar's arrest formed part of the ensuing crackdown, which saw five hundred arrests within a week. Within hours of the shootings on Sunday, the decision had been taken to accelerate plans for interning a much larger number of republicans in order to intensify the pressure on the IRA. These aggressive counter-insurgency tactics would soon be accompanied by a more subtle effort to engage the republican movement in secret negotiations for a settlement.

Peadar was initially held in Collinstown Camp (now the site of Dublin Airport). Carrying their youngest infant in her arms, his wife, Eva, walked to the holding camp. According to de Búrca, 'she had the consolation of seeing Peadar at a distance, standing among a group, and he waved to her.'[16] From

Ballad of a Prisoner's Son

The soldiers came to our house on a dark December night
They came and took my father from his bed
With their helmets & their rifles & their bayonets shining bright
Oh they filled my mothers heart with fear & dread

But father didn't worry when he kissed us all good bye
For he often said some day I'd be a man
That he had a rifle hiding he would give me bye & bye
To finish off the work that he began

Some day the Khaki soldiers will not find us in our bed
Like a baby helpless on its mothers knee
When our 45's are spouting forth their blazing trail
of lead
Teaching Saxon swine a song of liberty

They may slaughter all the fathers they may clap them
into jail
They may ship them oer the sea to rot & die
But their sons will take their places in the Army
of the Gael
And the foe will pay the piper bye and bye

Peadar ó Cearnaig
Baile Comhal Ópia   Iúl 1921

In 'Ballad of a Prisoner's Son' (1921),
Peadar Kearney recalls the military
raid on his home from his son's point
of view (NMI, HE/EW/1726/003).

there, the prisoners were brought to Dublin Castle three weeks later, before embarking for Belfast from the North Wall. On 11 December, after a rough voyage, they were greeted on arrival at Belfast Lough with screams of 'Fenian bastards' and a shower of 'Belfast confetti', as the shipyard's loyalist work force hurled nuts, bolts and rivets at them.[17] They endured further attacks from hostile locals – along with encountering the occasional act of kindness – as they progressed through the city and on to Ballykinler, an isolated military camp on the coast of Co. Down exposed to a cutting sea-wind and flooding. By the following spring more than 3,500 Dubliners had been interned, with over 2,000 ending up, like Peadar, at Ballykinler.[18]

As at Fron Goch, the prisoners formed their own executive, led by Peadar's friend Joe McGrath. As camp librarian, Peadar devoted much of his time to reading, to discussing history, literature and politics, and to playing chess. He taught Irish classes, contributed to the prison newspaper, *Ná Bac Leis*, and learnt to play the violin, performing in the camp orchestra, for which he wrote the popular 'Ballykinlar March'. He also managed to sell the occasional song to publishers, including Joe Stanley. He formed an enduring friendship with Martin Walton, a young Volunteer who had also fought at Jacob's and who later went on to establish the successful music firm. In their more optimistic moments, Walton recalled, they dreamed about the future that awaited them after the war:

> We talked things over, inside out and upside down, about
> founding an Irish College of Music. Peadar told me that
> he had a pledge from Collins that he would send three
> of us away to the Continent. He didn't think we knew
> enough to found a proper college of music, and thought it
> was important that we study European methods.[19]

Peadar's correspondence with Eva provides a much bleaker record of his year-long confinement. He found the monotony and hardship of life in the camp increasingly difficult to bear: 'I'm sick and tired of this rotten hole'. As was the case for most prisoners, the food constituted his most pressing grievance. The inadequate rations provided by the authorities meant that the parcels they received from outside became an important source of sustenance.[20] Eva often bore the brunt of his frustration:

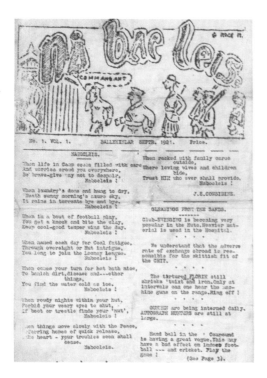

Peadar Kearney occasionally contributed to the camp newspaper, *Ná Bac Leis* – 'don't mind it' (KG, 2015/0129/01).

The Ballykinlar Orchestra: Peadar Kearney (bearded) is on the right in the third row from front. His friend Martin Walton, also bearded, stands at the extreme right (KG, 19PO 1A32-07).

Got letter on Tuesday Parcel yesterday (Wednesday) contained only ¼lb tea & ½lb butter first since Tuesday week. Do you think its worth a shilling postage? Do you know that the parcels I get are a joke? I call them parcels because they're not letters. If you happen to have my letters you'll probably find that I've asked time after time for better packing & lists of contents to be written in every possible space. Whats the use? I'm also sick & tired writing my opinion about the going home business ... Do you read my letters? Have you or Maire or Mick [Slater] tried to realise how hard it is for me to say what I want to say in letters like these & Im quite sure Im no fool at writing a letter. Not a word from you about the letter I addressed to lads or what they said about it. God help me. Im very foolish.

Dont stop writing anyhow as its the only link I have
with home.[21]

Conscious that their correspondence was read by censors, Peadar
refused to comply with Eva's repeated requests for an expression of his love:

Talking about ourselves I cant write all I feel in a letter
such as this suffice to say that you & the lads are never
never out of my mind morning, noon & night & the
only punishment that can be inflicted upon me is the
separation from you & them.[22]

The strain on his wife's mental health resulting from his
imprisonment is clear:

I am real sorry but quite helpless. I can only pray for you,
but I am always doing that for you all. If you are going
to let your nerves get control of you till I go home then I
fear there won't be much of you left.[23]

The strain on their relationship caused by their separation was
evident also from Peadar's frequent attempts to reassure Eva of her
importance to him:

My fancy never paints a picture of the future that does not
include you & the lads. The lads occupy a big space in my
dreams, but without you there would be no picture.[24]

Despite his constant complaints, the closeness of their relationship is clear:

> I'd like to write a good 'wicked' letter to you but as other
> people might be shocked you must only fancy that my
> arms are round you and that I'm whispering to you,
> rather poor satisfaction, but there's nothing else for it.[25]

Peadar's health, never strong, deteriorated with imprisonment (although, characteristically, he refused to see the prison doctor following a perceived slight):

> I use to buzz round a lot, but Ive given up & I hardly as much
> as read now … fits of energy dont come my way lately.[26]

The prisoners were crammed into poorly heated huts with damp bedding and inadequate sanitation; the camp's exposure to the elements ensured that bad weather brought miserable conditions, particularly for the older men, like Peadar. By June 1921 six internees had died, although two of these had been shot for disobeying an order to stop talking to internees across the barbed-wire barrier that partitioned the camp's two 'cages' (as the compounds were known). In November a third prisoner was shot as he celebrated the departure of a group of internees, and another prisoner was removed to be hanged after his conviction for involvement in the events of Bloody Sunday. The mental stress of life in the camp affected many, including Peadar: 'fits of depression are very hard to shake off and there are times when I can't go near anything even the violin.' Despite the cramped conditions, he was often lonely: 'I wish I was back on the Royal Canal; but wishing is foolish in Ballykinlar'.[27] Like the other married men, he found separation from his family among the most difficult aspects of incarceration to deal with. 'You must pray every day that it wont be long till we are together again,' he wrote to his sons. 'Anything you ask God for He will give it to you.'[28]

Despite the Truce agreed on 11 July 1921, the internees remained behind barbed wire while the Treaty negotiations in London dragged on, a source of growing tension and frustration:

> You'd get the horrors here listening to two subjects
> Football & release, morning noon & night. The stiffs in
> Dublin & London who fancy themselves as statesmen
> have a lot to answer for.

Liberty by Maurice MacGonigal (KG, 2010/0207). A Ballykinler internee, MacGonigal (1900–1979) later became a member of the Royal Hibernian Academy. He also worked with the Abbey, designing the set for Seán O'Casey's *The Silver Tassie*. His grandson Fiach Mac Conghail is the current director of the Abbey Theatre.

Holy war? A detail from the Book of Ballykinlar (MAI, Book of Ballykinlar, p. 122). Designed by Micheál Ó Riada and autographed by over a thousand internees, this richly illustrated volume incorporated art work and writing. It was presented to Fr Thomas Burbage, a Ballykinler internee, in 1921.

The prisoners' decision to smash every window in their huts as a protest against their treatment by the prison authorities – a decision Peadar considered ill advised – made conditions at the camp even more difficult as they faced into a second winter. Notwithstanding these discomforts, Peadar remained defiantly resolute, as he made clear to Eva shortly before his release:

At times you feel you would do anything on earth to get
home to those you love, but it is a temptation that is
put under foot. We internees are not much use to any
person or thing, we can at least be faithful until death.
One thing I wish and that wish will come true:– my sons
will honour and respect me. I know that & Im happy in
the knowledge. I care nothing about what anybody on
this earth thinks while they with your help will remain
fit representatives of a great name, to carry on. Swank?
but it's true, & mark my words they who live shall see.
Thank God. No matter what the immediate future may
hold this will be some country & there are tiny lads
toddling around who will be some men.[29]

On 25 November 1921, as the negotiations in London neared
conclusion, Peadar Kearney was finally released on parole. The signing of
the Anglo-Irish Treaty on 6 December ensured that he did not have to return
to Ballykinler. Imprisonment had taken a toll on both Peadar and his family,
as he subsequently informed the Military Pensions Board: 'I was in very bad
health, the wife had been receiving money from White Cross'.[30]

Influenced by Michael Collins, Peadar supported the Treaty, despite
his militant republicanism. He served as a prison censor during the Civil
War, but his motives were probably more economic than ideological.
Unemployed since his release from Ballykinler, his only income was the
revenue provided by royalties from 'The Soldier's Song'. He worked in prisons
in Maryborough (Port Laoise), Kilmainham and the North Dublin Union at
Grangegorman. A subsequent press report indicates that he was sympathetic
to the anti-Treaty prisoners: 'Peadar Kearney was reputed to be the not
unkindly censor of letters to and from the hundreds of women prisoners
in the North Dublin Union, but for all that the old songs retained much of
their favour among the prisoners.'[31] His prospects under the new regime,
and perhaps also his loyalty to it, were eroded by Collins's death in August
1922. Peadar later told the Military Pensions Board that Collins 'called here
on his way south he chatted to me & said my job was only temporary one but
I was to sit tight.' He resigned shortly afterwards, reportedly because of his
unwillingness to search the parcels of women prisoners.[32] Given his staunch

nationalism, Peadar is also likely to have been ill at ease to find himself part of an increasingly draconian Free State regime, particularly following the internment of anti-Treaty members of his own family, including his brother-in-law Stephen Behan.

Although a minority of pro-Treaty veterans secured well-paid jobs in the public service, and generous military pensions after the revolution, Peadar's experiences were more typical of the many veterans who 'paid a high price for their involvement, enduring humiliation, disability, poverty, obscurity and even death'.[33] For some veterans, political connections determined which of these categories one ended up in. By 1926 Peadar felt he had been let down by some of his more successful former comrades, as he made clear in a submission for support to the government:

Commandant Toomey was going down to Maryboro' to take charge of the Prison and asked me as a personal favour to go with him to take charge of the censoring, and I went. Michael Collins often assured me I would be all right … When out of employment Mr. J. [Joe] McGrath [a government minister] gave me the impression that he was very anxious to fix me up, and when *eventually* I asked him to get me fixed up he told me I would never have to work again, that he was looking after a small annuity and that as a matter of fact a cheque for a substantial sum (I heard £250) was actually drawn in my favour and was awaiting signature … I was employed in P.O. [Post Office] Factory about 18 months. It was very unsatisfactory employment for me as certainly the people in charge there made no secret of their hostility to me. On my being disemployed Mr. J. J. Walsh [a government minister] was getting me a job in Dockrells' but for me to start climbing ladders, etc. would be a physical impossibility … I believe I am entitled to some little consideration and my own friends can hardly credit I am penniless and go so far as to say that it serves me right for taking things so quietly but all my life I have detested publicity and sincerely hope this matter will be settled in peace and decency.[34]

When Peadar applied for a military pension in 1926, he was essentially
destitute, surviving on handouts from informal relief schemes for veterans
who had fallen on hard times: 'It would take at least £150 to entirely clear me
of debts which have accumulated since the beginning of my internment', he
informed the government. 'I have no personal means, the last small cheque
being badly wanted for rent, clothing etc. and still left portion of food bill
due'.[35] In contrast to Barney Murphy, Peadar did at least have the connections
to ensure that his application was promptly dealt with. His file contains a
poignant letter, written to his former comrade Diarmuid O'Hegarty, who
had risen to the powerful position of secretary of the Executive Council
(government), of which several of his former comrades were now members:

> I was told that I would not receive much but despite it
> being a pittance it is greatly and urgently needed. I am in
> poor health and my wife is bedridden. I am not happy to
> be disclosing my state of need but I have two boys to keep
> at school and they must be fed and clothed. If you can do
> anything at all to expedite my pension payment it would
> be the best thing you will have ever done.[36]

The Minister for Finance sanctioned a modest annual pension of £30
the following week. Although Peadar returned to his old trade as a painter,
he struggled to earn a living, partly because of his ill-health. Following
long periods of unemployment, he retired in 1933, as he was no longer able
to climb ladders without suffering dizzy spells. He lived a largely reclusive
existence thereafter, seldom venturing from his house in Inchicore.

Despite Peadar's growing disenchantment with the Free State, his most
famous song became an increasingly important symbol of the new regime. Like
the Tricolour, 'The Soldier's Song' was initially regarded as a divisive emblem of
party, rather than of nation, by Home Rulers, and also by unionists, many of
whom continued to sing 'God Save the King' at public ceremonies. Consequently,
the Free State government resisted pressure to formally adopt it as the national
anthem, a measure that would also have antagonised the British government.
At the same time, the song's identification with the struggle for the Republic
ensured that it was regarded as a valuable commodity by the new regime, as
Diarmuid O'Hegarty later reflected:

SP 3880

Peadar O'Cearnaigh 25 Donahue St Inchicore

I was one of the original organisers of Vols. I was a house painter. Mobilised Easter Monday out all the week & at the time of surrender I escaped from Jacobs. I had to lie low after 1916 for nearly 12 months, doing no work avoiding arrest reported on release of Frongoch men I was a sort of an organiser rejoined B. Coy. I helped in forming B. Coy. I was organising throughout the county & en Scotland in 1917 I formed 1st arms Committee. I got the first cheque for £50 from Gen Collins to pay for arms I travelled all round Ireland & Scotland on organising & arms armed patrols & getting arms arrested November 1920 the time of round up of 1916 men released in June 1921 When I came back on release was in very bad health My wife had been receiving money from White Cross. I had a small income from the soldiers song of which I wrote the words at the time of the Four courts beg a very intimate friend of Gen Collins,

Peadar Kearney describes his
post-Rising service in support
of his application for a pension
(MAI, MSP Kearney).

at the end of July or beginning of August
1922 I went to Maryboro as
Military Censor I belonged to an
organisation from release from
Ballykinlar I was absolutely unfit
during the time. In Maryboro
till Gen Collins called there on
his way south he chatted to
me & said that my job
was only temporary one but I
was to sit tight & I would
be all right. I was paid £4–4–
0 a week. I travelled with the
soldiers & officers in the
lorries I was not compelled
to do it but when I did
this I was armed. I might
have a .45 in my bed room
I messed with the officers
went from Maryboro to Kilmainham
then to U.D.U. about June
1924 there was a general demob
& release of prisoners

Evidence on 6/26 I went in the
last week of July to Maryboro
there were 2 other censors.

My position in Maryboro Goal I was
an old comrade of Brennan's & wherever he
travelled I travelled I was most in Brennan's confidence
I decoded messages from Irregulars backwards & forwards
& I discovered such messages going in & out. The result of
close connection with Journey Gilroy travelled with them
armed. One incident was a letter going through in code from people inside
that letter was brought to Jim Mahony he could not decode it
I decoded it it related to arms going through the 2 censors
were not in this decoding work

224

> As far as the Tri-colour and the 'Soldier's Song' are concerned
> – it was essential in 1922 to take these over as they would
> have been an incalculable asset to the Irregulars if they had
> been allowed to retain possession of them.[37]

The real contentiousness of the song in the early years of the state, like that of other republican symbols, was rooted in the Civil War's divisions. Anti-Treaty republicans monitored the state's use of Peadar's song closely. On the one hand, they denounced the playing of 'The Soldier's Song' by the Free State authorities as 'an insult to the memory of those who fought and died to rid Ireland of English Kings and Governor Generals', deriding its use as 'part of the Free State camouflage of its Crown-colony partitioned freedom'.[38] At the same time, they also condemned any reluctance by the government to play the song at formal occasions as evidence of its abandonment of the republican ideal.

The militaristic lyrics of 'The Soldier's Song', and its strong identification with acts of violence, reinforced its contested status. As James Dillon (son of the Irish Party leader John Dillon, and a future leader of Fine Gael) told the Dáil, 'I will not stand up when you play the "Soldier's Song" because I detest it, and it is associated, in my mind with horrors'.[39] Other TDs ridiculed it as 'a jaunty little piece of vulgarity' and 'an abomination to any one who knows anything about music'.[40] Such remarks, almost invariably made by those who did not come from a republican background, prompted a forthright response from T. F. O'Higgins:

> National Anthems come about not because of the
> suitability of the particular words or notes, but because
> they are adopted generally by the nation. That is exactly
> how the 'Soldiers' Song' became a National Anthem in
> this country. It happened to be the Anthem on the lips
> of the people when they came into their own and when
> the outsiders evacuated the country and left the insiders
> here to make the best or the worst of the country. It was
> adopted by the people here before ever it was adopted by
> the Executive Council.[41]

25 Donohoe St
Inchecore.
Oct 11th 1926.

[Handwritten letter in Irish, signed Peadar Ó Cearnaigh, SP 3880]

In this appeal to his former comrade Diarmuid O'Hegarty, Kearney outlines his dire circumstances: 'Dear Friend, I hope I am not disturbing you with this note but my situation is desperate and I am sure that you will do everything in your power on my behalf. I received notice recently from the Board of Assessors that my pension query had been sent to the Department of Defence. I was also told that I would not receive much but despite it being a pittance it is greatly and urgently needed. I am in poor health and my wife is bedridden. I am not happy to be disclosing my state of need but I have two boys to keep at school and they must be fed and clothed. If you can do anything at all to expedite my pension payment it would be the best thing you will have ever done. Your old friend, Peadar Ó Cearnaigh' (MAI, MSP Kearney). Translation by Éanna Ó Caollaí.

It was this latter view which ultimately prevailed, with several politicians drawing a comparison with 'La Marseillaise', written and composed by Claude-Joseph Rouget de Lisle in 1792, which eventually came to be considered an acceptable national anthem despite its xenophobic and questionable exhortations ('Let an impure blood | water our furrows'). In 1926 the Executive Council quietly resolved that 'The Soldier's Song' should represent the Irish state at home and abroad, and in 1929 an instrumental arrangement of the chorus by the director of the Army School of Music, Colonel Fritz Brase (who reportedly loathed the tune), became the *de facto* national anthem.[42] As leader of the opposition, de Valera repudiated the government's right to use either 'The Soldier's Song' or the Tricolour as emblems, although, characteristically, once in power he reinforced the state's identification with both republican symbols.[43]

Despite its fame, the song brought Peadar little material reward. Although a successful version had been arranged by Victor Herbert (then one of the world's most notable composers) in the United States, Peadar never succeeded in collecting more than a small share of the royalties due to him. The revenue stream from America, moreover, was diverted by Irish-American republicans after Peadar refused to publicly oppose the Treaty. Although Michael Collins had reportedly declared 'that nothing too good could be done for the man who gave Ireland the "Soldier's Song"', his more parsimonious political successors refused to pay Peadar royalties for its use by the state. In response, Peadar embarked on a seven-year campaign to embarrass the government into either paying him royalties or granting him a pension for life.[44] The government's reluctance to compensate him stemmed from its belief that he had not established his claim to copyright over the music (as opposed to the lyrics). However, Peadar strengthened his case by declaring that he had contributed to the composition of the music, a claim which won the support of the family of Patrick Heeney, who had written the tune. In 1932 Peadar – who had taken an action to prevent the Catholic Truth Society of Ireland from distributing the lyrics of his song – intensified the dispute by serving a writ against a prominent theatre company, forcing Dublin's cinemas and theatres to suspend the recently introduced tradition of playing the national anthem after performances. The change of government finally brought the dispute to a close. Regarding it as 'inadvisable and undignified that the National Anthem should be made the subject of legal wrangles', the Fianna Fáil government paid Peadar Kearney £1,300 in order to acquire the copyright.[45]

Ironically, by the time his song's status as the national anthem had been established beyond any doubt, Peadar had become an outspoken critic of the Irish state. In late 1933 he identified himself with republican opposition to the state by speaking at an anti-Poppy Day rally organised by the IRA in College Green, at which he urged the audience to 'tear up every emblem of the Empire'.[46] In 1935, by which time de Valera's government had decisively moved against its former IRA comrades by banning the organisation and reinstituting Cumann na nGaedheal's hated Military Tribunals, Peadar joined Helena Molony at a public meeting denouncing the government.[47] Two years later, Peadar penned a new verse of 'The Soldier's Song', which he offered as 'a present for the nation' and which made clear his disappointment at the failure to address partition:

> But Ulster wide, whate'er betide,
> No pirate brood shall nourish:
> While flames the faith of Conn and Eoghan,
> While Cave Hill guards the fame of Tone,
> From Gullion's slopes to Innishowen,
> We'll chant a Soldier's Song.[48]

Peadar Kearney's final years were spent in relative obscurity and poverty. On 24 November 1942 he died of cardiac failure. He was survived by his wife, Eva, and his two sons, Pearse and Colbert. The political disenchantment of his later life was less a result of his generation's failure to achieve the Republic than of what he saw as the self-serving hypocrisy of his former comrades whose unacknowledged compromises facilitated their acquisition of political power. The unfinished revolution affected Peadar's own family. Following his death, his nephew – who was serving a fourteen-year sentence in Dublin for shooting at a policeman – was denied permission to attend the funeral of his favourite uncle. 'I wouldn't let Brendan Behan out on a chain', the Minister for Justice, Gerry Boland, had reportedly declared.[49]

In death, at least, Peadar was accorded the status his prickly personality and uncompromising politics denied him in life. Buried in the Republican Plot in Glasnevin Cemetery, he shares an imposing memorial with the hunger-striker Thomas Ashe, one of the great icons of the revolutionary struggle. Ironically, considering Peadar's political militancy, his most famous song has become the accepted symbol of the established political order: when people hear 'The Soldier's Song' they no longer think of 'political ideals or historical events, but simply of their membership of the Irish nation.'[50] It is difficult to know what Peadar would have made of this, or of the fact that his grave has become the site of an annual pilgrimage by government minsters, whose political compromises he so despised.

Chapter 16

Ellen

1916–48

Ireland, Mother Ireland, with your freedom-loving sons,
Did your daughters run and hide at the sound of guns?
Or did they have some part in the fight?
And why does everybody try to keep them out
of sight?

—Brian Moore, 'Invisible Women'

Despite the unwelcome police attention that forced Ellen Bushell from
her home, she continued to support the republican movement. Although
Con Colbert, along with the Rising's other leaders, had been hastily court-
martialled, executed and buried in quicklime, Ellen retained her close
involvement in F Company, 4th Battalion of the Dublin Brigade as it sought
to regroup following the devastating effect of the rebellion. One of its
officers, Paddy O'Connor, recalled:

> It was in her house 2 New Rd Inchicore that the initial
> organisation meetings of F Company IV Battalion
> were held. From that time on she was recognised
> as an auxiliary member of the company, was fully
> cognizant of company affairs and in the confidence of
> the officers. She attended all demonstrations organized
> by the company: anti-conscription, anti-recruiting,
> reception for returning prisoners. Her house was used
> for conferences and as an assembly point until it came
> under notice.[1]

Ellen's patriotism was not always appreciated at the Abbey, where,
Máire Nic Shiubhlaigh recalled, she 'often turned the torn-ticket box into
a miniature arsenal'. Among the theatre-loving IRA men whose guns Ellen
checked at the door was Michael Collins, whom she smuggled out of the
Abbey during a Black and Tan raid. Peadar Kearney claimed that Ellen stored
sufficient explosives and gelignite in the theatre's library (for which she
possessed the sole key) to 'blow the Abbey sky high'. Ellen's testimony to the
Military Service Pensions Board confirms this. On one occasion she stored
a cart-load of 'guns, bombs and ammunition and a thing they called Irish

Cheese' in the cloakroom: 'The horrible part of it was I hid them all day [until] they came with an ass and cart that night when the performance was on – the rifles – we had a job to get these across the Abbey Hall and out through the door into the car.'[2] Because her house was constantly raided, Ellen often moved weapons from there to the Abbey: on one occasion she 'carried 2 boxes of ammunition, 2 rifles, 6 or 7 revolvers and hid them in the Abbey Theatre'.[3] She also helped plan an IRA raid on the Abbey, intended to seize the camera of a press photographer wrongly identified as a British spy.

Most often, the theatre provided a safe, convenient and central location for storing the weapons used by the Dublin Brigade IRA men who carried out Michael Collins's campaign of assassination on the streets of Dublin. Before these operations – which most often targeted G men, British army intelligence officers and Dublin Castle officials – IRA men would call to the Abbey to collect their weapons, or Ellen would meet them, the guns being returned to her after the operation. In her testimony she was unable to recall exactly how frequently this occurred: 'Pretty regularly'.[4] Initially paralysing G Division of the DMP, this brutal campaign paved the way for the militarisation of the police, leading to an equally ruthless campaign of counter-terror by the Black and Tans and the Auxiliaries.

Although Ellen's subversive tendencies were known to the Abbey's more radical staff, W. B. Yeats and Lady Gregory would presumably have been appalled by her behaviour, particularly given the potential consequences for the Abbey had it come to the attention of the authorities. As manager, Lennox Robinson appears to have adopted a prudent intermediate position between staff and directors, ineffectually discouraging Ellen's subversive activities, without actually acknowledging them.[5]

By early 1921 the Abbey was characteristically recalibrating its political orientation as the War of Independence approached its denouement: the play that had led to the IRA's raid on the theatre was *The Revolutionist* by Terence MacSwiney. The decision to stage it, and its public success, was a sign of the times. Yeats, like many people, had been moved by MacSwiney's death on hunger strike the previous year, which led him to rewrite *The King's Threshold*, his play of 1904 about a poet who undergoes a hunger strike against a king.[6]

Until now, the remarkable extent of Ellen's involvement in the War of Independence has remained hidden from view. As she told the Military Service Pensions Board assessors: 'I was at hand day & night to look after

(CONTINUATION).

1.

Sarah Ellen Bushell (22326).

HEARD ON: 8.6.'39.

A. I was under orders as many times as they would want to go
to Battn. Council meetings; at this time they were armed,
they were always carrying guns, I would often meet them,
take them to their own homes or until they came back to my
place.

Q. Did it happen ½ dozen times?
A. More I would say.

Q. A dozen times outside the Custom House and Bloody Sunday?
A. Yes.   That happened very often. You could easily say ½
dozen times or more.   You did not take note of the things
at the time.

Q. After this raid on your home which was in Nov. 1920, you
could not keep arms there subsequently, you kept some in the
Abbey did'nt you?
A. Even before that they were in the Abbey.

Q. The point I want to get at is after your raid in Inchicore
you could not take any?
A. There were. We chanced it now and again because we had
several places, they were never got locally.

Q. Did the Tans raid you after this 14 days period?
A. Yes. That was a big round up. I could not call it a raid
on my house. Previous to that there were a lot of raids,
that was 1919.

Q. The Tan raids.   Bloody Sunday was in 1920 were any arms kept
in your house after that?
A. Yes. Certainly they would to the very last, they would be
left in if it was only for an hour or two.

Q. But not to the same extent as before?
A. No.

Q. What did you do with the guns in the Abbey?
A. I had them hidden there, they would have to come and take them
when they wanted them or I would have to bring them.

Q. Did you ever bring them out of the Abbey?
A. Yes.

Q. For whom?
A. Dwyer and O'Connor. I would have to take these home to
Inchicore.

Q. Paddy O'Connor was it?
A. Yes. Paddy O'Connor and Dwyer, I took his gun also on Bloody
Sunday.

Q. Having used these guns would they leave them back in your
house in Inchicore, you would take them to town to the Abbey?
A. Of course, Dwyer was staying in my place. Sometimes he would
have his gun at home, in fact he always had it.

Q. Did you often have to take these guns from the Abbey to your
home and back again?
A. Yes. Whenever they would be wanted.

In her testimony to the Military
Service Pensions Board, Ellen
Bushell described her involvement
in the IRA's ruthless campaign of
assassination (MAI, MSP Bushell).

2.

Q. How often was that?
A. Pretty regularly. Of course it is hard to know how to answer you, I do not know exactly what you want.

Q. Did it often happen that you took guns from the Abbey?
A. Yes. Home to my place.

Q. Or hand them to men in the streets?
A. They would come in to me for them. One day a cab drove up to the theatre with guns, bombs and ammunition and a thing they called Irish Cheese, we had to pack them under the cloakroom counter until that evening. The horrible part of it was I hid them all day they came with an ass and cart that night when the performance was on - the rifles - we had a job to get these across the Abbey Hall and out through the door into the car. We got them into the car threw cabbage on top of them. That particular load was 3rd Battn. the boy's house was being raided, Byrne, he had to get his friendly cab man to take the stuff and take it up to the Abbey.

Q. It was there all day?
A. Yes. From about 11 or 12 in the morning until half eight or later that night. I know the people had gone in.

Q. Then you got it away in an ass and cart?
A. Yes.

Q. Did you ever go to any particular place where an ambush was being staged?
A. I was on duty in one ambush on the Quay, up past Adam and Eve's Chapel. One night a lorry should have only had straw or something and there was a fight developed and I had to take there was a man put in my charge whose name I do not know - I was watching him he did not know the area.

Q. Was he wounded?
A. No, not but I had to bring him away to safety. I brought him up to lanes that took us up there by Audeon's Church, around that lane, we got lost. The soldiers scattered, there was a fight, I could never recall his name, the only thing I always thought Seamus Kavanagh gave me instructions.

Q. You cannot recollect who he was?
A. Officer i/c. whatever happened him I do not know, I never saw him.

Q. Did you ever attend any ambush for the purpose of rendering First Aid?
A. No.

Q. Is there anything else in the period prior to the Truce which you would like to add?
A. I do not know. I would not like to start to say anything in case I would be telling nonsense. Anything you ask me.

Q. It is for yourself to make your case.

Q. Did you cease your connection at the Truce?
A. When the Treaty came. There was nothing much to be done in 1922, my health had broken down pretty badly I was not able for very much.

Q. There was nothing in the Truce you did - the Truce lasted 12 months?
A. No. There was not.

Volunteers'. Joe Larkin informed the board that he owed his life to Ellen, who sheltered and nursed him after he was badly burnt during a raid on a police barracks. Another IRA officer testified that

> it would be impossible to enumerate in detail the
> number of times she carried arms or messages for us,
> diverted suspicions … stored arms, verified or procured
> information on certain points or performed the hundred
> and one little services that were so important at that time.

Ellen also spied for the IRA, procuring intelligence and permits for prison visits through her contacts with an army officer at Dublin Castle.[7]

An extract from the board's summary of her testimony during the most intense period of the War of Independence demonstrates how her commitment placed her at some of the IRA's most dangerous operations:

> She was raided frequently by the Tans, as many as 8
> times in a fortnight. They smashed up her home and she
> was without shelter for 5 weeks. Up to then she had kept
> first-aid dressing at her home, on the understanding
> that it should be used as a field dressing station. In all
> 6 or 7 cases were dealt with there. Her home continued
> to be used as a dump … She frequently went up to meet
> men on ambushes … She relieved P. [Paddy] O'Connor of
> his gun at the Custom House Fire. On Bloody Sunday she
> took 2 guns and ammunition to a friendly house. She
> thinks she would have carried guns for men at least 6
> times after meetings … She was given the duty of acting
> as a guide to a Vol. who participated in an ambush at
> Merchant's Quay, who did not know the City. She went
> to the scene of the ambush, remained there during the
> fight and took charge of him after it.[8]

She was active on Bloody Sunday in November 1920. Following Paddy O'Connor's unsuccessful attempt to assassinate Lieutenant-Colonel Jennings in Leeson Street, Ellen, according to O'Connor's statement to the Military Service Pensions Board,

> assisted Dwyer & myself to escape giving warning of the operations in Mount St. She arranged to dump our arms and advised us to the route for get away. (We were not familiar with that part of the city). Late that same day she helped us to escape when surrounded by enemy at Inchicore.

Ellen's Military Service Pensions files record many similar incidents that testify to the importance of the hidden war fought by republican women, an aspect of the conflict that went largely unrecorded in the subsequent histories of the independence struggle. Ellen is not mentioned, for example, in the five-page essay devoted to 'How the women helped' in the revealingly titled anthology *Dublin's Fighting Story, 1913–1921: Told by the Men Who Made It*, published in 1949.[9] Her revolutionary career largely came to an end with the Treaty: 'There was nothing much to be done in 1922, my health had broken down pretty badly. I was not able for very much.'[10] Her sympathies lay with the anti-Treaty IRA. 'Personally I didn't take active part in Civil war. My house was used by some of the Volunteers and Lt. O'Dwyer resided there till his arrest'. The fine distinction reflected by this arrangement, perhaps understandably, was lost on the National Army, which raided her home '4 or 5 times'. Ellen's tolerance for the presence of gunmen in her house over such a long period gave rise to the following exchange during her testimony to the Military Service Pensions Board, although it is not clear from the minutes whether it was prompted by humour or concern about the IRA, which remained in business in the 1930s:

> Q. How long was your home used by these men …
> Cannot you put a time limit on it after Frongoch?
> A. … The house was being constantly used.
> Q. Are they using it still?
> A. No. I am speaking of the period.[11]

Few details of Ellen's life between the end of the Irish revolution and her death are known other than those recorded in her Military Service Pensions files. Like almost all women applicants, she was awarded the lowest level of military pension. Her records testify to the harsh realities of the social conditions endured by many working-class Dubliners. Ellen never married, spending the remainder of her working life at the Abbey; poor health forced her to give up work in March 1948. Séamus Scully, a friend who visited her during her final illness, described a neglected and lonely figure:

> Many of her old comrades, now in high places, were missing. She was but another of the now forgotten rank and file who had answered to the call of Cathleen ni Houlihan. [12]

Confined to bed with heart disease, and unable to get by on her military service pension, Ellen requested the special allowance that the Army Pension Act (1946) provided to veterans who were no longer capable of supporting themselves. But before her application was processed she had died at her home on 11 August 1948. She lived just long enough to see the Irish Republic proclaimed. Her large funeral, attended by republicans and her friends from the Abbey Theatre, took place at the Oblate Church in Inchicore. At Mount Jerome Cemetery, where she was buried, her former comrades draped a Tricolour over her coffin, sounded the Last Post and fired a salute over her grave. [13]

Chapter 17

Máire

1916–58

Although Máire Nic Shiubhlaigh
remained politically active,
1916 was the high point of her
involvement in the struggle for
independence (private collection).

When you are old and grey and full of sleep,
And nodding by the fire, take down this book,
And slowly read, and dream of the soft look
Your eyes had once, and of their shadows deep ...

—W. B. Yeats, 'When You Are Old' (1892)

Although she returned to Cumann na mBan after the rebellion, Máire
Nic Shiubhlaigh played only a minor role in the War of Independence.
In contrast to the pre-revolutionary years, when women – whether in
the radical press or in the theatre – played a prominent part in raising
nationalist consciousness, women activists were more firmly subordinated
to an auxiliary role in support of the Irish Volunteers. Máire's subsequent
dealings with the Military Service Pensions Board demonstrate that less
value was placed on women's political activism during these years than on
'service of a military nature', such as carrying despatches, sheltering men,
hiding arms and carrying out intelligence work.[1]

     After the Rising, Máire became treasurer of the Irish National Aid
Association, which supported the families and dependants of imprisoned
and deceased rebels.[2] Under Michael Collins's guidance, this organisation

CONSTITUTION, CORUGHADH.

Cumann na mBan is an independent body of Irishwomen pledged to maintain the Irish Republic established on January 21st, 1919, and to organise and train the women of Ireland to work unceasingly for its international recognition. All women of Irish birth or descent are eligible for membership, except that no woman who is a member of the enemy organisation or who does not recognise the Government of the Republic as the lawfully constituted Government of the people can become a member.

OBJECTS :   **(Cuspora)**

    I.   (*a*)   The complete separation of Ireland from all foreign powers.
         (*b*)   The Unity of Ireland.
         (*c*)   The Gaelicisation of Ireland.

II. **MEANS**:   **(Slighthe).**

    1. To maintain the Republic by every means in our power against all enemies, foreign and domestic.

    2. To assist Oglaigh na h-Eireann, the Irish Volunteers, in its fight to maintain the Republic.

    3. That at elections, Cumann na mBan, as such, give no assistance to any Organisation which does not give allegiance to the Government of the Republic.

    4. To become perfect citizens of a perfect Irish Nation by : —
        (*a*) Taking Honour, Truth, Courage and Temperance as the watchwords of Cumann na mBan ; (*b*) by fostering an Irish atmosphere, politically, economically and socially ; (*c*) discouraging Emigration by brightening the social life of the district ; (*d*) supporting Irish industries.

    5. At all times and in all places to uphold the spirit and the letter of the Cumann na mBan Constitution.

    6. The Constitution of Cumann na mBan may not be altered except by a two-third majority vote of a Convention.

Although asserting the organisation's independent status, Cumann na mBan's constitution makes it clear that its role was to assist the Irish Volunteers (KG, 2015/0483).

Cumann na mBan first-aid certificate awarded to Máire Nic Shiubhlaigh (NLI, MS 27,624). Designed by Máire, this certificate was printed by her family's company, the Gaelic Press. The militarisation of republicanism after 1916 entailed a greater emphasis on traditional gendered roles, such as nursing, within the movement.

became a formidable vehicle for rebuilding the shattered separatist movement. Máire was mostly involved in what she described as 'ordinary Cumann na mBan duties': fund-raising, distributing money to prisoners' dependants, canvassing for Sinn Féin at elections, parading at public meetings and, increasingly, at funerals, including those of Thomas Ashe and Richard Coleman.[3] Like many other Cumann na mBan activists, she attended to the sick and dying during the influenza epidemic that claimed over twenty thousand Irish victims in 1918. She also continued to perform on the stage, although rarely in amateur theatre, which took a back seat to the wider drama being played out across the country.

> I was doing a lot of concert work – Volunteer concerts.
> Most of my time was taken up down the country –
> Sunday Meetings. I looked on it as Volunteer work,
> assisting at Concerts, and then I was working in the
> Gaelic Press. It was raided, and closed up ... I was always
> there to do work – I could not say what I did, whatever I
> was asked to do when free to do it.[4]

In August 1918 Máire was caught up in the aftermath of a raid on the Art Depot in Mary Street. This was an outlet for republican propaganda – including song-sheets, pamphlets, pictures, speeches and postcards – owned by her brother-in-law Joe Stanley (who had purchased her father's struggling Gaelic Press in 1913).[5] Following the raid, Sinn Féin's barrister George Gavan Duffy obtained a writ against the police for unlawfully seizing the shop's goods, naming Máire as the plaintiff. The case was eventually thrown out of court; but, as the solicitor Michael Noyk explained, 'we had got our objective in the breathing space created and our literature was made available.'[6] Stanley, whose printing press and equipment had been smashed up by the G men, was put out of business by the raid. Although it was Máire's sister Annie (who gave her stage name, Eileen O'Doherty, to the police) who was present during the raid, Máire had presumably been named as the proprietor in order to keep Stanley (a 1916 internee) out of the proceedings, and because any costs awarded against her would not be recoverable. In 1918 Máire moved to Drogheda to work for Stanley, who was setting up a chain of cinemas. She set up a branch of Cumann na mBan there. Sent to Cavan by Stanley, she assisted local republicans there but felt 'there was not much to be done'. She appears to have had little involvement in the War of Independence after this point.

Máire married Éamon ('Bob') Price in 1929. Bob had reportedly vowed to marry Máire when he first saw her at Jacob's factory, where he was also stationed during the Rising; theirs was one of many romances to bloom amid the chaos of Easter Week.[7] Bob had been one of the IRA's most senior leaders during the War of Independence, a member of Michael

(*left*) Peadar Kearney wrote 'Dora' (an acronym for the Defence of the Realm Act) while interned at Ballykinler (NLI, MU/sb/1367). This music sheet was published by Joe Stanley's Art Depot (where Máire Nic Shiubhlaigh worked).

(*right*) Seized in the raid on the Art Depot, 'The Birth of the Irish Republic' illustrates how propagandistic depictions of 1916 presented women as inspirational but vulnerable emblems of nationhood, in contrast to the virile role ascribed to men. The depiction of the rebels in conventional military uniform reinforces the conservative nature of this representation of revolution (TCD, OLS/Samuels Box 4/112a).

Collins's inner circle at GHQ, where he served as director of training and director of organisation. A bright Christian Brothers' boy from a poor background, he was an officer in the 2nd Battalion of the Dublin Brigade of the Irish Volunteers before 1916 and had been centre of Collins's IRB circle.[8] Republicanism ran in the family: his sister Leslie, under whom Máire served, was Cumann na mBan's director of organisation. After his release from Fron Goch, Bob was one of a wave of young militants – led by Collins – who joined the revived Irish Volunteer executive.[9] He was a prominent organiser, and his mainly administrative (and distinctly thankless) job saw him travel the country, settling disputes and imposing GHQ's nominal authority on resentful provincial officers. Dapper and articulate, he was an effective operator: 'He could be both wittily and sarcastically polite, spoke very good English and other languages, and dearly loved a "half one".'[10]

By 1921, however, his drinking had spiralled out of control. A senior IRA officer recalled an occasion when Bob was found 'in the gutter', his pockets 'filled with papers'. The hard-drinking culture at GHQ, whose business was often transacted in pubs and hotels, together with the psychological pressures of years of conflict, had created a serious, if unacknowledged, problem within the IRA.[11] Despite his struggle with alcoholism, Bob retained his seniority in the Civil War, serving as a major-general in the National Army. The Prices, like many republican families, were divided by the conflict. Bob's sister Leslie had married the legendary West Cork flying-column leader Tom Barry, who became one of the most senior leaders in the anti-Treaty IRA. Bob became embroiled in the most sordid incident of the Civil War when he conducted the tribunal of inquiry that covered up the murder of seventeen anti-Treaty prisoners by former members of Collins's Squad in Co. Kerry. The inquiry encompassed the conflict's most notorious atrocity, which occurred when Free State soldiers murdered eight prisoners by tying them to a mine. For days afterwards, Dorothy Macardle wrote, 'the birds were eating the flesh off the trees at Ballyseedy Cross'.[12]

Whether these experiences contributed to Bob's troubled life is unclear. Many Treatyites attributed their post-revolutionary disillusionment to the Civil War, which shattered the idealism that had bound the revolutionary movement.[13] Like many veterans, Bob and Máire struggled to find their place in independent Ireland. Although Bob secured a highly paid job as a clerk in the civil service, he retired because of ill-health (presumably alcohol-related) in 1929, while only in his late thirties. They moved to Laytown, Co. Meath, where they helped Máire's sister Gypsy (whose husband had died) to raise her son Edward Kenny.

St Patrick's Day Greetings, c. 1918 (NMI, HE/EW/297q). The Cumann na mBan emblem (initials entwined with rife) is adorned with festive shamrock, green, white and orange ribbons, and Irish Volunteer uniform brass button.

Although they were surrounded by reminders of the splendid years – a George Russell portrait of Máire performing in *Deirdre of the Sorrows* dominated the living-room – their lives were tinged with regret, compounded by an awareness of Máire's decline from leading lady to provincial obscurity.[14] A letter written in 1950 to another isolated and neglected figure, the Ulster playwright Alice Milligan, conveys a sense of this:

> Any chance of any broadcasting? I never get anything
> to do if you can put anything in my way or if there is
> anything of yours going to be read, don't forget Máire
> Nic Shiubhlaigh.

If judged by her reply, Milligan, a leading figure in the cultural revival, was no better off:

> I am so glad to have your address at last. I wd have been
> sending you … tickets … only I have no cash at all for
> a couple of months … Of course I can get clothes and
> food on credit till then but not perhaps newspapers or
> washing done.[15]

It was not only her role in the revival that Máire felt had been forgotten. Although she was awarded a military pension, she felt slighted by the board's failure to acknowledge the value of her post-Rising activism. She wrote to the Department of Defence:

> I received an award in respect of Easter Week and a fraction of a year of the remainder, the other portion of my service not apparently coming within the category of 'Active Service'. I am not certain if this fraction entitles me to a medal but I wish to be sure and now make a claim for one in respect of my services which if not technically 'active service' were voluntary and of considerable advantage to the National Cause.[16]

Máire organised amateur drama festivals in Cos. Meath and Louth, and worked in broadcasting (producing and acting in plays associated with the Abbey Theatre on Radio Éireann); but her relationship with the Abbey remained distant. In 1937 she turned down an offer to appear as the Widow Quin in the Abbey's revival of *The Playboy of the Western World*. Aptly, given the influence of 1798 on her generation, her final public performance was in Lady Gregory's play *The Gaol Gate*, staged at the Olympia Theatre in 1948 to mark the 150th anniversary of Wolfe Tone's death.[17] She remained politically active, joining the Anti-Partition League in 1947, and she lectured to such organisations as the Irish Countrywomen's Association.

Bob Price died in 1951. Although he had been awarded the highest grade of pension, his death left Máire in a precarious financial position. She wrote to the Department of Defence requesting the outstanding portion of his final month's payment: 'I would be very glad to get it as I am not very well off'.[18] Suffering from ill-health, and surviving on her military and non-contributory pensions, she had her circumstances assessed as 'poor'. She found work as a temporary librarian at Meath County Library until her failing health necessitated her retirement in 1956.

Bob Price (seated), with friends
(private collection). A former GHQ
officer, Bob married Máire in 1929.

Remembering the past – discussed in a later chapter – remained
important for Máire and Bob, who died before he could complete his
memoirs.[19] With the assistance of her nephew Edward, Máire succeed
in publishing her memoirs in 1955, allowing her to place on record her
involvement in the Easter Rising and, just as importantly, in the founding
of the Abbey Theatre.

Máire died on 9 September 1958. Concerned about her declining
status in life, she would have been pleased to know that she was
remembered in death. The press extensively covered the death of 'one of
the great Abbey actresses of the early days'. She was buried in Glasnevin
Cemetery with military honours at a funeral attended by leading figures
from public and cultural life.[20]

Chapter 18

Helena

1916–67

Mrs Kelly: It seems to me that the whole strike has
been a very troublesome business, and that it would
have been better if it had never taken place.

Edward: Ah, now, don't say that, Mother. We
must try every means in our power to lift the toilers
from the slough of poverty.

Tom: Aye, and when we have tried every means
in our power, when we have exerted every tissue,
fibre and muscle in the lifting process, we'll see the
toilers wallowing, sinking, struggling, choking in
that slough!

—Pat Wilson, *The Slough* (1914)[1]

Here we are rapidly becoming a Catholic statelet
under Rome's grip – censorship and the like, with a
very narrow provincial outlook, plus a self-satisfied
smugness. Result of a failure of revolution really.
I have no belief in de Valera. Well-meaning of
course, better than Cosgrave, but really essentially
conservative and church-bound, anti-feminist,
bourgeois and the rest.

—Hanna Sheehy Skeffington to Esther Roper, early 1930s[2]

The election of Constance Markievicz in the general election of 1918 and the prominent role played by Cumann na mBan in the War of Independence are often seen as evidence of how women's involvement in the Easter Rising reaped political rewards. From the viewpoint of such radicals as Helena Molony, however, the popular movement that emerged after 1916 proved disappointing. The emergence of mass support for republicanism, and the militarisation of that movement during the conflict that followed, inevitably placed constraints on the role played by women activists. One early indication of this was provided by the status of women in Sinn Féin, the party that rapidly became the vehicle for republicanism after 1916.

As a member of Cumann na dTeachtairí (an association of women deputies), which represented Cumann na mBan and other women's organisations, Helena fought for women to be given a place among the leadership of the republican movement. In April 1917 she and Countess

Plunkett had been hastily added to the Mansion House Committee – the umbrella organisation representing the competing separatist factions that claimed the political legacy of the Rising – after Helena denounced its exclusion of women.[3] However, following the merger between Sinn Féin and its principal rival, Count Plunkett's Liberty Clubs, women were again excluded from the republican leadership. Despite pointing out 'the risk women took, equally with the men, to have the Republic established', Cumann na dTeachtairí's demands for female representation on Sinn Féin's executive were ignored. Helena and three other women were eventually co-opted, but on the condition that they represent Sinn Féin branches rather than their gender – a measure intended to prevent 'the formation of an organised feminist caucus'.[4] Only twelve women delegates attended the 1,700-strong Sinn Féin ard-fheis, which nonetheless passed a resolution affirming its commitment to the 'equality of men and women'.[5] Although four women were elected to the new executive, only two women candidates were nominated for the general election in 1918, one of them in a unionist constituency. It was clear that there would be little room for women in the politics of the new Ireland.

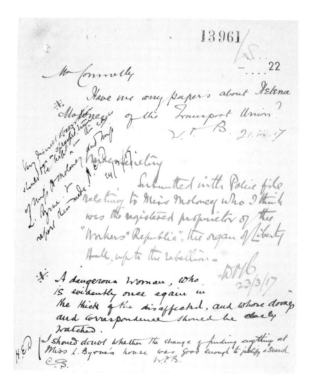

'A dangerous woman' (NAUK, CO 904/210/305). Helena Molony remained under surveillance after the Rising, and her correspondence was monitored by the British authorities.

26.9.18.

HELENA MOLONEY. — 3

Helena Moloney, aged 31 years, is the daughter of a Dublin Publican who at one time carried on business at Georges Quay. She studied for the stage in her youth. She first came under notice associating with the Countess Markievicz and other extremists early in 1911.

On 4th July, 1911, four days before the arrival of Their Majesties on a Royal Visit to this Country, she attended and spoke at meetings organised by extremists, which were held at Foster Place and Smithfield, protesting against the present-ation of a Loyal Address by the Dublin Corporation to Their Majesties, and to consider what action they would take in the event of the Corporation presenting such an Address to His Majesty. After the meeting and when on her way home in a brake she threw stones at the Police, was arrested, and on the following day was sentenced by Mr. Drury to 40/- fine or one months imprisonment.

On 6th August, 1911 after her release, she was arrested along with Countess Markievicz at a meeting at Beresford Place for using language calculated to provoke a breach of the peace by calling King George V "the greatest scoundrel in Europe." They were brought before Mr. Macinerney, who convicted both prisoners, but on account of their sex imposed no penalty.

She did not take a very active part in the Suffragette Movement in 1912 and '13, but she attended and spoke at meet-ings of the Irish Women's Franchise League, and the Women's Social and Political Union. She was at this time living with the Countess Markievicz at 49B Leinster Road, Rathmines.

In the Autumn of 1915 she succeeded Delia Larkin as Hon. Secretary of the Irish Women Workers' Union, Liberty Hall, and in this capacity she was closely associated with the late James Connolly and the Countess Markievicz in the activities of that Establishment up to the outbreak of the Rebellion

− 4
. . . .

in Easter Week of 1916.

On 16th January, 1916, "The Workers' Republic," the official organ of the Larkinite Party, was registered as a Newspaper, and in the particulars supplied Helena Moloney, Actress and Clerk, 70 Eccles Street, and 31 Eden Quay, is given as Owner, Printer, and Publisher.

She took part in the Rising, and was arrested by the Military in the City Hall on 24th April, 1916, having in her possession an auto pistol and ammunition. She then described herself as Secretary of the Women's Union and Commandant of the Women's Section of the Citizen Army. She was deported and interned at Lewes on 26.6.16, subsequently transferred to Aylesbury, whence she was released on 23rd December, 1916.

She returned to Dublin and resumed her position as Hon. Secretary of the Irish Women's Workers Union; Offices Eden Quay, to which she appears to be devoting most of her time since her release. She, however, has been occasionally observed associating with Dr. Kathleen Lynn, Marian Perolz, and Mrs. Joseph Plunkett.

P.T.O.

14251

S.4930

DUBLIN METROPOLITAN POLICE.

Detective Department, 11

Dublin, _____ 30th April ___ 191 7.

Telegrams: "DAMP, DUBLIN."
Telephone No. 22.

Subject, MISS HELENA MOLONEY, 9, BELGRAVE ROAD - IRISH WOMEN WORKERS'
UNION, and MISS LILLIE BYRNE, 615, N. C. ROAD.

With reference to attached, I beg to state that Miss
Helena Moloney, Secretary of the Irish Women Workers' Union,
35, Eden Quay, is now residing with Dr. Kathleen Lynn at 9,
Belgrave Road, Rathmines.

Discreet observation has been kept on this woman's
movements. She attends almost daily at the office of the
Irish Women Workers' Union in connection with her business
as secretary.

On 3rd inst. she was one of a deputation which consisted of a number of ladies who waited on Sir John Irwin in
reference to suggested Communal Kitchens for Dublin poor
(see cutting from newspaper attached).

On 9th inst. between 1 & 2 p.m. she was amongst the
spectators in Sackville Street opposite the ruins of the
G.P.O. from which the Republican Flag was hoisted and on the
occasion she was in company of Suspects Charles Shannon, Belfast; Miss M. Perolz, Miss Winifred Carney & Mrs. Joseph
Plunkett.

On the 19th inst. she attended at the Sinn Fein Confer-
ence held in the Mansion House, and was in company of Dr.
Kathleen Lynn and Miss M. Perolz, at which Count Plunkett
presided.

A Communal Kitchen has been established in Liberty Hall,

and

THE SUPERINTENDENT,
G DIVISION.

12

and Miss Moloney assists in directing operations, other lady workers being Miss Ffrench Mullen, Miss Perolz and Miss Bennett.

During the week ending 28th inst. she attended from 7-30 to 11 p.m. at the Irish Theatre, Hardwick Street.

Miss Lillie Byrne, resides at 615, North C. Road, with her brother and sister, and acts as the housekeeper.

She works at her home at the Dressmaking business for private customers and also sews children and ladies underwear for houses in the retail drapery trade.

Her movements, during past month, have been observed and she has not associated with any suspected person. Her brother is an electrical contractor in a small way trading as Fitzpatrick and Byrne, at 39, Thomas Street, Dublin, and her sister, Margaret, is engaged in a retail Coal office, at 3, Lord Edward Stret, employed by a man named Barton who retails coal in small quantities to persons of the working class.

P Smyth.

Detective Sergeant.

The Chief Commr
Submitted
Owen Brien
Smyth
30/4/17

"ARGUMENTS"

AGAINST THE TREATY

Cumann na nGaedheal general election
poster, 1923. Pro-Treaty propaganda
presented their opponents as destructive
and criminal (CCCA, MS. U271/K).

Although the Irish Citizen Army was by now a pale shadow of its pre-
1916 predecessor, Helena played a minor role within it during the revolution,
supporting the sporadic efforts by workers to occupy factories and establish
revolutionary 'soviets'. She acted as a district justice in the Ministry of
Labour's arbitration courts in Rathmines, 'settling disputes, wages and
that'. Although nominally enrolled as a member of Cumann na mBan,
she refused to wear the uniform. Much in demand as a public speaker, she
remained active in prisoners' campaigns. She was considered sufficiently
dangerous to be placed under police surveillance in 1917–18, partly because of
wartime concerns about her secret communications with her brother Frank,
who was active in Irish-American separatism.[6] She opposed the Treaty as an
abandonment of the Republic and supported the anti-Treatyites in the Civil
War. During that conflict she participated in the usual range of women's
activities: first aid, procuring and concealing weapons, work for prisoners'
dependants, and propaganda.[7] Her prominent profile ensured unwelcome
attention, although it now came from the Irish rather than British state
forces. She was kept under surveillance by the Free State authorities, as well
as receiving more overt attention: 'I was raided constantly. It would be easier
to record the times I was not raided.'[8]

Helena's commitment to revolutionary politics saw her prominence
in the Irish Women Workers' Union decline as less militant colleagues, such
as Louie Bennett and Helen Chenevix, with more time to devote to trade
union activities, came to play a greater role. Temperamentally, as well as
in relation to her abilities, Helena was more suited to radical activism than
administration, although she had a reputation as a skilled union negotiator.

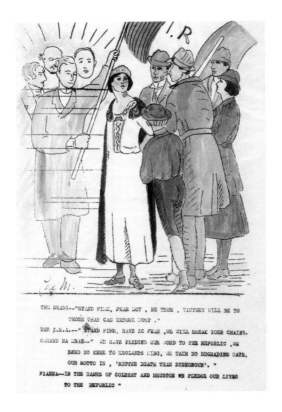

THE DEAD)--"STAND FIRM, FEAR NOT, BE TRUE, VICTORY WILL BE TO
    THOSE THAT CAN ENDURE MOST."
THE I.R.A.--"STAND FIRM, HAVE NO FEAR, WE WILL BREAK YOUR CHAINS.
CUMANN NA MBAN--" WE HAVE PLEDGED OUR WORD TO THE REPUBLIC, WE
    BEND NO KNEE TO ENGLANDS KING, WE TAKE NO DEGRADING OATH,
    OUR MOTTO IS, 'BETTER DEATH THAN DISHONOUR'."
FIANNA--IN THE NAMES OF COLBERT AND HEUSTON WE PLEDGE OUR LIVES
    TO THE REPUBLIC"

Constance Markievicz's cartoon from 1922 demonstrates how anti-Treatyites drew on the legacy of 1916 and the rhetoric of fallen comrades (such as Terence MacSwiney) to depict their cause as a continuation of the struggle for the Republic (NLI, PD 3068/TX/A).

In 1918 she took on a new, broadly defined role in the IWWU as an organiser, a position she held until her retirement. She was also active on the Dublin Trades Council and on Rathmines and Rathgar Urban District Council.[9] Despite her lauded performance in Lennox Robinson's *Crabbed Youth and Old Age* (in which she played Mrs Swan, a mother so attractive that the suitors of her three daughters fall for her), her career on the stage of the Abbey declined sharply from late 1922. Although praised for her comic abilities and adaptability – O'Casey wanted to cast her as Mrs Gogan in *The Plough and the Stars* – she appears to have decided to focus on her union work.[10]

   After the revolution, Helena resisted the erosion of the egalitarian principles of the Proclamation as a paternalistic ethos that valued women as wives and mothers rather than as citizens gained ground. Acknowledging that the feminist impulse was 'long spent', she complained that, despite helping to secure independence, women retained 'their inferior status, their lower pay for equal work, their exclusion from juries and certain branches of the civil service, their slum dwellings and crowded, cold and unsanitary schools for their children.'[11] Denouncing the hypocrisy of the Labour Party's efforts to identify itself with Connolly's revolutionary ideals while

HIS EASTER OFFERING.

(Left) Helena Molony
(NMI, HE/EW/612).

(Right) Faith and fatherland (NLI,
PD HP/1916/4). Religious-inspired
depictions of the Easter Rising
reinforced conservative ideas
about the role of women, who
were presented as passive victims
rather than active citizens capable
of shaping their own destinies.

advocating mild social-democratic reforms, she condemned the party's acceptance of the 'imperialist' Treaty settlement, viewing its deputies' willingness to swear an oath to the Crown as a betrayal of the Republic.[12] She also sought unsuccessfully to maintain the party's commitment to workers' control of industry.[13] She was scathing about the marginal status of women in the labour movement: railing against the party's 'sorry travesty of emancipation', she urged her colleagues to study Connolly's writings.[14] Against the background of an increasingly reactionary political climate, her moderate colleagues resented her efforts to commit the party – for which she was 'not prepared to go out and fight' – to utopian ideals.[15]

Despite their political differences, and the conservative climate, Helena Molony, Louie Bennett and Helen Chenevix formed 'a formidable triumvirate on behalf of women workers'.[16] Helena devoted much of her time to often unsuccessful efforts to organise women in such poorly paid occupations as laundry work and domestic service. She fought against patriarchal measures like the Conditions of Employment Act (1935), which permitted the state to exclude women from certain occupations. When de Valera told a delegation from the IWWU that he 'could not see that men and women could be equal', the union secured the blacklisting of the Irish Free State by the International Labour Organisation in Geneva. Believing that such discriminatory measures were prompted by reactionary impulses rather than concern for women's welfare, Helena helped to establish the short-lived Mná na hÉireann to campaign for the equality promised by the 1916 Proclamation.[17]

Described by the Catholic Archbishop of Galway, Michael Brown, as 'leisured ladies, philanthropists, & slumming do-gooders', advocates of gender equality provoked extraordinary hostility in this period. For example, when Helena argued that women deserved representation on the Commission on Vocational Organization because, as home-makers, they would be affected by its decisions, she was asked if she also thought that children should serve on state bodies. Such attitudes forced Helena to concede to what now appear to be conservative positions: 'We all believe that woman's place is in the home provided she has a home.'[18] The demand for gender equality won limited support among the Labour Party. Reflecting the interests of its overwhelmingly male membership, many trade union leaders also opposed the demand for equal pay and rights: 'Woman is the queen of our hearts and of our homes,' declared one delegate to the Irish Trades Union Congress faced by Helena's motion against the Conditions of Employment Bill, 'and, for God's sake, let us try to keep her there.'[19] Pointing to women's role in the revolution in order to justify the demand for equality, Helena took every opportunity to defend that legacy. For example, she chastised Sean O'Faolain for his unsympathetic portrayal of Constance Markievicz's motivations in his biography (for which she had been interviewed):

It is a curious thing that many men seem to be unable to believe that any woman can embrace an ideal – accept it intellectually, feel it as a profound emotion, and then calmly decide to make a vocation of working for its realisation. They give themselves endless pains to prove that every serious thing a woman does (outside nursing or washing pots) is the result of being in love with some man, or disappointed in love of some man, or looking for excitement, or limelight, or indulging their vanity. You do not seem to have escaped from the limitations of your sex.[20]

Ironically, O'Faolain was no less opposed to the Free State's narrow Catholic ethos. His novels, which were censored by the state, sympathetically explored the plight of those who had 'become misfits in a restrictive society'. Helena's comments, however, reflected her frustration at

THE ABBEY REBELS OF 1916

the relentless marginalisation of women's revolutionary role.[21]

Her disappointment should be seen in a broader context. Throughout inter-war Europe, women gained greater rights as more democratic – or, in some cases, revolutionary – states emerged from the chaos of the First World War. Although women were usually enfranchised by these states, feminists soon discovered that suffrage in itself did not lead to the more fundamental social changes they had expected. As Susan Pedersen has noted:

> Early campaigners were often radicals and visionaries, determined to make the world anew. Convinced of women's worth, and prone to ascribe virtually all evils to male dominance, they were certain that women's suffrage, once achieved, would protect children, end poverty, clean up politics and end war. When it didn't achieve those grand aims, they sometimes lost heart, retreating from politics entirely or turning to other, more extreme, causes.[22]

Helena did not lose heart – she worked on practical campaigns, such as affordable housing, and with charities, such as Save the Children – but she also turned to a host of extreme causes. She helped found the Friends of Soviet Russia, spoke at meetings of the League against Imperialism, campaigned for the Prisoners' Defence League and supported anti-fascist agitation. Although Helena was a Catholic who was not above quoting papal encyclicals in support of her political views, her criticism of the Vatican provoked two weeks of hostile press coverage after her comments were reported by the *Irish Independent* under the headline 'Attack on the Pope'.[23] Her radicalism saw her out of step not just with the state but with her own labour movement. She was forced by the IWWU to resign from the IRA's political front, Saor Éire, in 1931. She was a member of the communist-aligned Revolutionary Workers' Groups, a forerunner of the Communist Party of Ireland, and was regarded as a useful figure by Moscow. The Friends of Soviet Russia sought to counter anti-communist press reports, which reached hysterical levels in this period (in part because they allowed Catholic conservatives to suppress broader secular and progressive currents). Helena advised Moscow on its Irish propaganda and published rose-tinted eye-witness accounts of life under Stalin, whose regime, she asserted, was more popular than that of the Free State.[24] After her visit to the Soviet Union as part of a labour delegation sent to observe the October Revolution celebrations, her trade union refused to purchase copies of its largely positive report of the Soviet Union, instead passing a motion regretting that the principles of religion and liberty were not upheld in Russia. On this, as on other occasions, Helena's radicalism sharply divided the leadership of her union.

Helena was elected president of the Irish Trades Union Congress in 1937, only the second woman to hold the office. By 1941, however, she had been forced out of trade union office. Her retirement was attributed to her poor health, but her alcoholism and her compromising links to the wartime IRA also contributed to her early retirement. Her support for the pro-German IRA front Córas na Poblachta had brought her to the attention of military intelligence during the Second World War. Along with Maud Gonne's daughter, Iseult Stuart, she was one of a circle of republican women who sheltered the German spy Hermann Goertz in safe-houses, including her own. Despite close surveillance, the police were unable to discover anything more compromising than her heavy drinking, depression and indebtedness.[25] She had not qualified for a pension when she retired, although she was awarded a small disability allowance by the IWWU. As a result, her personal circumstances remained precarious. She continued to rely on appeals to her former trade union, and on the kindness of her friends, to make ends meet. In later life, however, she was rehabilitated within her trade union, becoming a life member.[26]

Helena's close relationship with the psychiatrist Evelyn O'Brien, with whom she reportedly lived happily from the 1930s until her death, has prompted speculation about her sexuality. Although she was also romantically linked (without firm evidence) to both Bulmer Hobson and Seán Connolly, Helena has been claimed by feminists as a member of an influential lesbian network prominent in overlapping feminist, labour and republican circles.[27] Others include the Irish Citizen Army rebels Kathleen Lynn and Madeleine ffrench-Mullen (who jointly founded St Ultan's Hospital); the Cumann na mBan activists Julia Grennan and Elizabeth O'Farrell (who conveyed Pearse's letter of surrender to the British military); and Helena's trade union colleagues Louie Bennett and Helen Chenevix. Although these women fought and lived together, and (in some cases) were buried together in the Republican Plot in Glasnevin Cemetery, this dimension of their lives has remained largely invisible. Whatever the precise nature of these relationships,[28] they are inadequately acknowledged in the numerous allusions in the Royal Irish Academy's *Dictionary of Irish Biography* to their unmarried status or to lifelong friendships with other women. Along with the suppression of their radical impulses, the sanitising of revolutionaries' sexual lives formed part of the post-revolutionary reconstruction of Irish society.[29]

When Helena Molony died at the age of eighty-four, in 1967, there remained sufficient surviving veterans from the ranks of the Irish Citizen Army, the Old IRA and Cumann na mBan to form a guard of honour to escort her coffin to the Republican Plot. 'Her death was front page news and the list of mourners at her funeral was a who's who of republicans, trade unionists and government'. The Defence Forces sounded the Last Post as 'a cluster of Helena's nearest friends wept quietly'. Describing her as 'one of the great patriotic women of the time', the president of the Irish Republic, Éamon de Valera, delivered a generous oration: 'With James Connolly and Countess Markievicz she worked for Irish freedom, for the Irish worker and for the poor. She stood firmly for the rights of women and their political equality with men in our society.'[30] The same could not have been said for de Valera himself, whose conservative vision of society proved so much more representative of his times.

Revolutions, like political lives, end in disappointment. Irish republicanism triumphed after 1916, but the state that emerged from Sinn Féin's revolution fell short of the radical vision for which Helena had struggled. This failure to transform society was partly a result of 'the contraction of political options that came with world war, revolution, and partition',[31] as the optimism and energy of the cultural and separatist revival gave way to a conservative state that gave priority to power over liberation. It reflected also the ideological incoherence of Irish republicanism and the limited appeal of the radical vision that inspired a tiny minority before 1916. Fitting 'uneasily in the well-established narratives that prescribe women as symbol, icon or emblem of the nation', the memory of activists like Helena Molony lingered on as a 'repressed memory' in the national story.[32]

COPY

3364

AN GARDA SIOCHANA,
(Division of Dublin and Wicklow)

Chief Superintendent's Office,
Bray.
2nd July, 1941.

SECRET
UIMHIR:
3C.257/39/41.

Coimisineir "3C".

Re: Mrs. Iseult Stuart, Laragh Castle, Glendalough, Co. Wicklow.

Submitted please. I beg to report that information has been received to the effect that Miss Helena Moloney is at present recovering from the after effects of heavy drinking and that she is under the care of Dr. Kathleen Lynn, 9 Belgrave Road, Rathmines, assisted by two nurses. It is feared by her friends, that Miss Moloney will lose her position as Official of the Women Workers Union to which she is attached as a result of her latest drinking bout. Dr. Lynn has requested Mrs. Stuart to accommodate Miss Moloney at Laragh Castle for a couple of weeks to permit of recuperation. Provided nothing unforeseen occurs, Miss Moloney, accompanied by a Mrs. Byrne who will act as escort to Laragh Castle and return to Dublin on same day, will travel by the Saint Kevin's 'Bus from St. Stephen's Green, Dublin, on Thursday 3rd July, 1941 at 11.30 a.m. to Laragh Castle. Miss Moloney who has hitherto been referred to as "Chick" is now known to Mrs. Stuart as "Emer".

Mrs. Stuart's son, Ian, intends to spend a holiday with a family named Finlay-Mulligan, believed to be Accountants with offices at 114, Grafton Street, Dublin. H was to have gone for a week on 1/7/41.

Madam Gonne McBride, Roebuck House, Dundrum, mother of Mrs. Stuart, who has been ill for some time past, is to visit Laragh Castle to recuperate her health as from Saturday 5/7/1941, if a car can be procured to convey her to Laragh Castle.

Mrs. Stuart will be alone at the Castle with Mrs. Clements, who returned there on 27/6/1941, from this date as her two children are now on holidays. It is not known yet whether the arrival of Miss Moloney and Madam McBride at the same time to "recuperate" is a mere coincidence or has another meaning. It is known that Miss Moloney and Madam McBride do not agree well together, so that their location at Laragh Castle at the same time may have some significance, however, supervision may reveal if there is anything strange taking place.

There is nothing so far to indicate the presence of a stranger at Laragh Castle, the food intake has not increased above the usual amount and enquiries do not support the suspicion that there is a stranger within the premises, although the daily maid has been warned not to speak of affairs at Laragh Castle. They may be a simple precaution as Mrs. Stuart knows that she is suspect.

A copy of this minute has been submitted to Leas Coimisineir D.M.D. for action on 3/7/1941. I will report developments.

(Signed) W. Quinn

Ard Cheannphort,
W.P.Quinn.

Garda report, 2 July 1941 (MAI, G2/3364). Helena Molony was placed under surveillance by G2 (military intelligence) during the Second World War because of her links with militant republicans who were known to be harbouring German spies.

AN GARDA SIOCHANA - ROINN NA CATHRACH.

CONFIDENTIAL.

3.C/725/40.
S. 404/40.

Detective Branch,
(Special Section),
Dublin Castle.
8th May, I942.

Ard Cheannphort,
Detective Branch,
(Special Section).

Re: Helena Maloney, Wexford St., Dublin.

I beg to refer to previous reports furnished concerning Helena Maloney, and to state that she is at present residing with Mrs. Austin Stack at 167, Strand Road, Merrion.

In report furnished on the 30th Jan. 1942, dealing with Mrs. Francis Stuart, it was stated that a rumour was then in circulation to the effect that Helena Maloney was suffering from a broken leg. It has now been confirmed that this rumour was correct as Miss Maloney is at present using a crutch, and is only able to move about with difficul -ty. This accounts for her not having been seen since the 6th Jan. I942.

As already reported, Miss Maloney resided in house known as St. Alban's, Dalkey, from Ist Aug. I940, to 3Ist March, I94I. This house had been let furnished for the period to a Miss Mary E. O'Brien who is also at present staying with Mrs. Stack. St. Alban's was used by Hermann Goertz and information is to the effect that members of the I. R. A. also frequented and stayed there. The rent was £8 per month.

Observation is now being maintained in the vicinity of Mrs. Stack's residence. Both Miss O'Brien & Miss Maloney have already been seen there.

In view of the fact that Miss Maloney purchased the hut at Brittas which was used by Goertz Summer, and her other known connection with that alien, is imperative that she should be interrogated, but she not at present in a fit state to be taken into custody and.

Something may be gained by keeping observ on the movements of Miss O'Brien and on Mrs. Stack's and it is suggested that consideration should be given course, to a search of the house used by the suspected persons.

It is suggested that Ard Cheannphort, informed of present whereabouts of Miss Maloney.

(M. J. WYMES.)

An Leas Choimisineir,
Roinn na Cathrach.

Garda report, 8 May 1942 (MAI, G2/3364). The authorities were unable to confirm their belief that Molony had sheltered Hermann Goertz, the most effective of the twelve spies smuggled into Ireland by Abwehr (German military intelligence).

Précis of Helena Molony's
correspondence intercepted by the
Garda Síochána (MAI, G2/3364).

Chapter 19

Arthur

1916–38

The Irish revolution, which began in Easter Week,
has also triumphed solely in externals. Our spiritual,
cultural, and intellectual life has not changed for
the better. If anything, it has retrograded. Nothing
beautiful in the mind has found freer development
... The mass of people in the country continue to
think as they did before the revolution ... Seven
years of sensation had dulled the heart and made it
insensitive. If a Republic were proclaimed in Ireland
next year or the year after, would there be any more
exultation? I think not.

—George Russell, 'Lessons of revolution', 1923[1]

You have disgraced yourselves again.

—W. B. Yeats to the audience of *The Plough and the Stars*, 11 February 1926

An aftershock of the Easter Rising was experienced at the Abbey Theatre in
the form of a players' revolt against its manager, St John Ervine. Ervine's
hostility to the rebels (including that 'damned dago de Valera'), and his
purported invitation to General Maxwell to visit the theatre, may have
sparked the revolt, but it was a long time coming.[2] Ervine's efforts to
position the Abbey as a regional British theatre were resented, as was his
domineering managerial style. The critic Joseph Holloway considered him
more fitted 'to run a tea shop than a theatre'. Ervine's disastrous decision
to dismiss the striking actors in the belief that they would beg for their jobs
back eventually prompted his removal by W. B. Yeats and Lady Gregory.
Meanwhile, the splitters had formed the Irish Players, which toured the
Abbey's repertoire abroad, confusing foreign audiences, who assumed that
they were watching the real thing. Although abrasive and arrogant, Ervine
had also inherited a precarious financial situation, an undisciplined staff
and a badly run theatre at a low artistic ebb.[3] Nor did his removal resolve
these crises: the unsettled political climate that followed the Rising,
particularly the curfews imposed during the most violent years of the
revolution, left the theatre close to collapse. Increasingly, its survival was
assumed to hinge on securing some form of government support.[4]

For Arthur Shields, the departure of the Abbey's senior players
brought opportunity and responsibility. As a result, both Arthur and his

brother Will (better known by his stage name, Barry Fitzgerald), who had joined the Abbey in 1917, won more substantial roles. In Ernest Blythe's view, Barry's 'touch of strangeness in appearance and speech' marked him out for character (and comic) parts, whereas Arthur's 'ability to give an absolutely smooth and convincing performance in a straight part' brought him more conventional leading roles.[5] In 1919 W. B. Yeats, whom Arthur revered, turned to him to produce Brinsley MacNamara's play *The Rebellion in Ballycullen*, inaugurating what would become an influential behind-the-scenes role for him at the theatre. Although Lennox Robinson credited the play's success with partially revitalising the Abbey, the theatre's survival remained contingent on fund-raising and overseas tours.[6] Speaking publicly in 1923, Yeats implicitly conceded an element of creative exhaustion:

> It is too soon yet to say what will come to us from the melodrama and tragedy of the last four years, but if we can pay our players and keep our theatre open, something will come. We are burdened with debt, for we have come through war and civil war and audiences grow thin when there is firing in the streets. We have, however, survived so much that I believe in our luck.[7]

Arthur spent much of the revolutionary period away from Ireland. In 1919 he found work in the London production of Lennox Robinson's most successful play, *The Whiteheaded Boy*, an intelligent, gentle comedy about family, set in rural Ireland.[8] While there, Arthur met his future wife, Bazie Magee, whom he described as a 'clever, talented, fascinating conversationalist, a woman who reasoned like a man, sharp-tongued and quick-tempered'.[9] An outspoken, vivacious Catholic from Lisburn, 'Mac' was working as a chauffeur for the British army when she saw Arthur on stage. They married in Chelsea in April 1920, spending much of the next year touring the United States and Australia. Adopting the stage name Joan Sullivan, Bazie performed alongside her husband.

Following his return to the Irish Free State in February 1923, Arthur joined F. J. McCormick, Eileen Crowe, Maureen Delany, Shelah Richards, Ria Mooney and his brother Barry in what became widely acknowledged as one of the theatre's greatest companies. Although Arthur was admired for his 'inimitable stagecraft, ascetic-looking presence and ringing musical voice', it was the breadth of his understanding of theatre that marked him out. One critic observed that he

> was an actor but was interested in the total effect
> of a production; he was a director but rejoiced that
> playwrights were in charge. He insisted on an ensemble
> style both austere and controlled but wanted to achieve
> it with actors possessed of a dangerous wildness ... He
> was unqualifiedly a product of the Abbey but also looked
> beyond Ireland for inspiration.[10]

Despite his prominence as an actor, he assumed an increasingly important role as a director and producer: 'I played in about 198 plays. And in those I played about 210 parts,' Arthur recalled. 'And then I directed a number of the plays. I was stage manager for a while, I helped to make scenery.'[11]

In later life Arthur regretted not focusing more on acting, but his versatility was partly a product of necessity. He recalled that

> the Abbey was so shockingly poor we were not able to
> build any new scenery for about four or five years. We just
> had to revamp other pieces, and many things were done
> with a minimum of staging, because there was no money
> to buy new stuff. We worked on miserable salaries, very,
> very miserable ... I got the equivalent of a dollar a week ...
> It just about paid my tram fare home and allowed me to
> get a sandwich in the daytime.

Although staff members – playwrights and players alike – were paid a pittance for their work, poverty brought one benefit:

> We had to concentrate on playing, rather than relying
> on the nice things that you have generally in a good
> production that you can lean on. We had nothing. But it
> didn't seem to bother the audience.

Although inclined to romanticise his early years at the Abbey in later life, Arthur believed that its vitality stemmed from its tradition as a writers' theatre, and from its engaged working-class audience, which included the workers from Liberty Hall, just around the corner from the theatre, who paid sixpence to sit in the pit.

> You did not play to the people, you didn't play for the
> people, you played as much for the playwright as for
> anyone else. They didn't come to see you particularly, or
> the play ... You got as much from the tradesman, who
> felt he had as much right to tell you what was wrong
> with your part, or O'Casey with his play, as you did from
> the professional critic.[12]

THE DVBLIN DRAMA LEAGVE

Programme cover for a 1928 production of Eugene O'Neill's *The Fountain* (1923), designed by Harry Clarke (1889–1931). Until the establishment of the Gate Theatre in 1928, the Dublin Drama League was the principal venue for modern international theatre (AT).

Arthur became the leading force in the Dublin Drama League, established in 1918 to expand the Abbey's repertoire beyond Irish writing. By 1924 he was producing most of its plays, which were staged at the Abbey on Sunday and Monday nights. Although commercially unsuccessful, it brought European and American drama to an insular theatre scene. Arthur's friend Mícheál Mac Liammóir considered the League's influence – which led indirectly to the establishment of his more experimental Gate Theatre in 1928 – to be almost as significant as that of the early Abbey: 'whereas the Abbey set out to show Ireland to itself and then to the world, we in the Gate began by attempting to show the world to Ireland.'[13] Many considered it to be the more successful theatre by the 1930s.

For Arthur it was the arrival of Seán O'Casey – the most admired Irish playwright since Synge – rather than the modest state subsidy, that ended the Abbey's malaise: 'before Mr O'Casey reached us our theatre nearly died'.[14] In fact, just one month before the first play in O'Casey's Dublin trilogy opened in 1923, the press had declared the Abbey dead. O'Casey was a combative, working-class, Protestant socialist, and his 'variety hall of poetic, melodramatic, and realist elements' revitalised the Abbey artistically and commercially. It also reignited the conflict between Yeats's theatre and Irish nationalism. The resulting clash was complicated by the annual subsidy, which, although ensuring the survival of the Abbey, reinforced its identification with the Irish Free State, as did Yeats's seat in the Senate. The only theatre to close in order to mark Arthur Griffith's funeral, it was also the only one to defy the anti-Treatyite ban on public entertainment in March 1923.[15] As well as undermining the theatre's independence, the subsidy created an enduring source of conflict by providing for government representation on the Abbey's board, ensuring that any disgruntled citizen or politician could seek to call the government to account for its objectionable productions.

Depicting the lives of the poor of Dublin's tenements rather than the rural peasantry (hitherto the Abbey's forte), O'Casey's trilogy – *The Shadow of a Gunman* (1923), *Juno and the Paycock* (1924) and *The Plough and the Stars* (1926) – savaged political violence and the romantic nationalism used to justify it. Set respectively in the War of Independence, the Civil War and the Easter Rising, O'Casey's plays presented patriots as self-aggrandising rather than selfless, caricaturing their flaws, and setting – unfairly, some would say – the virtues of domesticity against the posturing of revolutionaries.[16] If we consider when they were staged – *The Shadow of a*

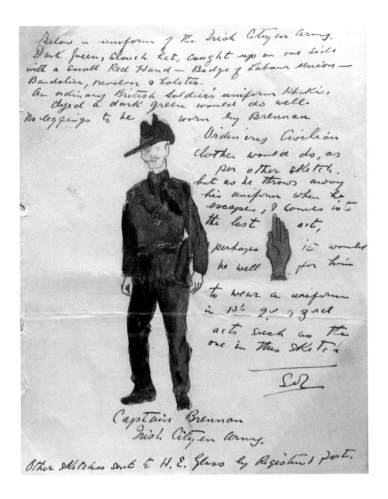

Seán O'Casey watercolour depicting
the uniform worn by 'Captain
Brennan' in *The Plough and the
Stars* (BIL, Robinson papers).

Gunman was performed under armed guard for an audience that had to be instructed that the gunfire they would hear was a sound effect – O'Casey's plays were remarkably audacious. Although the message of the first two works in the trilogy could be interpreted by the political establishment as a potentially useful critique of violence at a time when republican extremism threatened the survival of the state, the challenge to the new political order represented by the satirical treatment of the Easter Rising in *The Plough and the Stars* was more direct.

The *Plough and the Stars* depicts the plight of Nora Clitheroe, a pregnant young woman who begs her husband, Jack, not to abandon her to fight for the Irish Citizen Army. Motivated by vanity rather than patriotism, Jack spurns her pleas. Political ideology – both nationalism and socialism – is skewered by O'Casey (who himself had broken with both the IRB and the Citizen Army), particularly in a key scene where Pearse's lofty rhetoric is juxtaposed with the

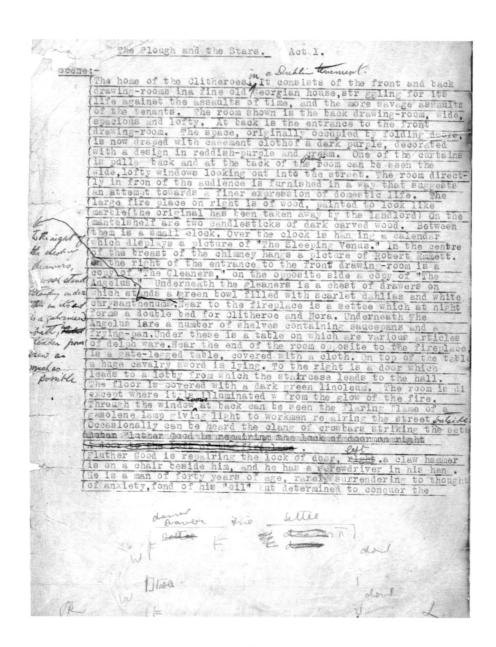

The Plough and the Stars.   Act 1.

Scene:-

The home of the Clitheroes. It consists of the front and back drawing-rooms in a fine old Georgian house, struggling for its life against the assaults of time, and the more savage assaults of the tenants. The room shown is the back drawing-room, wide, spacious and lofty. At back is the entrance to the front drawing-room. The space, originally occupied by folding doors, is now draped with casement cloth of a dark purple, decorated with a design in reddish-purple and green. One of the curtains is pulled back and at the back of the room can be seen the wide, lofty windows looking out into the street. The room direct-ly in fron of the audience is furnished in a way that suggests an attempt towards a finer expression of domestic life. The large fire place on right is of wood, painted to look like marble(the original has been taken away by the landlord) On the mantelshelf are two candlesticks of dark carved wood. Between them is a small clock. Over the clock is hanging a calendar which displays a picture of "The Sleeping Venus." In the centre of the breast of the chimney hangs a picture of Robert Emmett. On the right of the entrance to the front drawing-room is a copy of "The Gleaners," on the opposite side a copy of "The Angelus." Underneath the gleaners is a chest of drawers on which stands a green bowl filled with scarlet dahlias and white chrysanthenums. Near to the fireplace is a settee which at night forms a double bed for Clitheroe and Nora. Underneath The Angelus are a number of shelves containing saucepans and a frying-pan. Under these is a table on which are various articles of delph ware. Near the end of the room opposite to the fireplace, is a gate-legged table, covered with a cloth. On top of the table a huge cavalry sword is lying. To the right is a door which leads to a lobby from which the staircase leads to the hall. The floor is covered with a dark green linoleum. The room is di except where it is illuminated w from the glow of the fire. Through the window at back can be seen the flaring flame of a gasolene lamp giving light to workmen repairing the street. Occasionally can be heard the clang of crowbars striking the sets

Fluther Good is repairing the lock of door, left. a claw hammer is on a chair beside him, and he has a screwdriver in his hen. He is a man of forty years of age, rarely surrendering to thoughts of anxiety, fond of his "oil" but determined to conquer the

The prompt script for the original production of *The Plough and the Stars* (1926), handwritten amendments by Seán O'Casey (AT).

ABBEY THEATRE, DUBLIN.

"The Plough and the Stars."

CURTAIN CUES.

(ACT 1.   Time 33 minutes).

WARNING.   When band off stage plays "It's a long way to Tipperary"

CURTAIN.   ("Mollser") Is there nobody goin', Mrs. Clitheroe, with
a titther of sense?

(ACT 11.   Time 26 minutes).

WARNING.   (Clitheroe) Death for the independence of Ireland.

CURTAIN.   (Clitheroe) Dublin Battalion of the Irish Citizen Army, by
the left, quick march! Band plays "The Soldier's Song".
CURTAIN.

(ACT 111.   Time 25 minutes).

WARNING.   (Bessie) Fluther would go only.he's too drunk ... we'll
have to try to get a doctor somewhere.

CURTAIN.   (Bessie) God, be Thou my help in time of trouble, and
shelter me safely in the shadow of Thy wings. (MORE SHOTS)
CURTAIN.

(ACT 1V.   Time 30 minutes).

WARNING.   (Sergeant Tinley) Pour it out, Stoddart, pour it out. I
could scoff anything just now.

CURTAIN.   When "Sergeant Tinley" and "Corporal Stoddart" come to the
finish of the chorus of "Keep the home fires burning."
Curtain on second night

Curtain cues for the original 1926
production of *The Plough and the Stars*
(AT). Kearney's 'The Soldier's Song'
featured as part of the production, as well
as being sung by hecklers to disrupt it.

Poster for the Abbey Theatre's 1934 production of *The Plough and the Stars* (NLI, EPH F179). The Abbey staged a remarkable thirty runs of the play between its debut and 1939.

squalid realities of prostitution, poverty and drunkenness in an inner-city pub. By suggesting that it was ordinary Dubliners, rather than the rebels, who were sacrificed for Ireland in 1916, O'Casey anticipated 'revisionist' critiques of the rebellion that were not debated publicly until half a century later. Despite the play's popularity with the public, the decision to stage it cast the Abbey once again as an anti-nationalist institution, but in a rather different climate from that in which the previous controversy provoked by Synge's *Playboy of the Western World* occurred.

Characteristically unobtrusive, Arthur went largely unnoticed in the midst of the resulting storm. As assistant director, he helped to stage *The Plough and the Stars*, and he featured in one of its most controversial scenes, in which, as Lieutenant Langon, he carries a Tricolour into a pub. Other than a few hisses on the second night, the Abbey seemed to have 'got away with it', until, two nights later, a riot erupted, as audience members jeered the players, hurled stink-bombs and tried to set the curtains alight.[17] Arthur's appearance on stage may have triggered the orchestrated protest: one press report noted how the 'presence of a flag in one of the actor's hands caused excitement'.[18] In the ensuing melee, an attack on one actress was deflected by Arthur's short but burly brother Barry, who punched the assailant off the stage.[19] Yeats, not much one for emollience, ineffectually hectored the crowd: 'You have disgraced yourselves again'. Later, backstage, Yeats failed to restrain his delight: 'I am sending for the police, and *this time* it will be *their own* police.'[20] The protest continued with a rendition of 'The Soldier's Song', until order was restored by the police. As the revolutionary widows and mothers (including Kathleen Clarke, Margaret Pearse and Seán Connolly's sister Katie) walked out, Hanna Sheehy Skeffington (whose murdered husband, Francis, had not fought in the Rising) declared to the cast, 'I am one of the widows of Easter Week. It is no wonder that you do not remember the men of Easter Week, because none of you fought on either side.'[21]

In finest theatre tradition, the show went on, despite an attempt by armed republicans to kidnap Barry later in the week (they called to the wrong house). Yeats relished the controversy, seeing it as an opportunity for the Abbey to assert itself against a growing climate of intellectual conservatism. More astutely, Lady Gregory warned 'that the widows of 1916 could prove more formidable and embarrassing opponents than those who had naïvely defended Irish peasant virtues'.[22] The intervention of Hanna Sheehy Skeffington, who, pointedly, did not call for the play to be censored, proved Gregory's point:

> I am one of those who have gone for over 20 years to performances at the Abbey, and I admire the earlier ideals of the place that produced 'Kathleen Ni Houlihan', that sent Sean Connolly out on Easter Week; that was later the subject of a British 'Royal' Commission; the Abbey, in short that helped to make Easter Week, and that now in its subsidised sleek old age jeers at its former enthusiasms.[23]

Although many at the Abbey disliked both the play and O'Casey, and some actors refused to speak his dialogue, Arthur dismissively referred to the protesters as an 'ultra group'. He supported O'Casey in his disputes with the Abbey and regarded the dramatist's eventual break with the theatre, following its rejection of *The Silver Tassie* (1928), as a disaster for the Abbey.[24] In contrast, Barry's lack of support for their friend occasioned the only enduring row that Arthur could remember with his brother. What is crucial to an understanding both of the ferocity of the response to *The Plough and the Stars* and of Arthur's position on the play is that it was an attack not so much on the Rising as on its legacy. After 1916, as James Moran has noted, the 'Rising became a national triumph rather than a covert and risible debacle, but during the transformation it had lost some of its contradictions and

Krause v8.5, p- 165

LR/120

NL Box 21

422, North Circular Road,

10/1/26.

Lennox Robinson, Esq.

Dear Mr. Robinson —

     I have carefully and (I hope) impartially re-read
The Plough and the Stars, lingering thoughtfully over those passages that
have irritated or shocked some of the members of the Caste, and I cannot admit
into my mind any reason for either rejection or alteration.

     Miss Crowe's hesitation over part of the dialogue of Mrs.Gogan
seems to me to be inconsistent when I remember she was eager to play the central
figure in "Nannie's Night Out", which was as low (God help us) and, possibly
lower, than the part of Mrs. Gogan.

     Neither can I see any reason standing beside the objection
to such words as Snotty, Bum, Bastard or Lowsey. To me it isn't timidity but
cowardice that shades itself from them. Lowsey is in "Paul Twyning"; is it
to be allowed in that play and rejected in mine ?   Bastard in "The Devils
Disciple" is said with all the savagery of a callous bigot to a young child:
is the word to flourish in that play and wither in mine ?   Snotty is simply
an expression for sarcastic or jeering. The play itself is (in my opinion)
a deadly compromise with the actual ; it has been further modified by the
Directors, but I draw the line at a Vigilance Committee of the Actors.

     I am sorry, but I'm not Synge; not even, I'm afraid, a
reincarnation. Besides, things have happened since Synge; the war has shaken
some of the respectability out of the heart of man; we have had our own changes,
and the S.S.RR has fixed a new star in the sky. Were corrections of this
kind to be suffered the work would be one of fear, for everyone would start
a canonical pruning, (As a matter of fact Miss Mooney has complained to me
about the horror of her part) and impudent fear would dominate the place of
quiet courage.

     As I have said, these things have been deeply pondered, and
under the circumstances, and to avoid further trouble, I prefer to withdraw
the play altogether.

     Sincerely yours,

     Sean O Casey.

Pressured by the Abbey's directors
to modify *The Plough and the Stars*,
O'Casey threatened to withdraw his
play when the actors demanded further
changes (BIL, Robinson papers).

rough edges: the parts of the rebellion that had been socially radical were forgotten, and instead 1916 was commemorated as a straightforwardly Roman Catholic event.'[25] By caricaturing the rebellion as unheroic farce, O'Casey was attacking the founding myth of a state that had barely been established. Only in Ireland, Hanna Sheehy Skeffington complained, could a state-subsidised theatre mock 'a revolutionary movement on which the present structure claims to stand'. Although many were appalled by O'Casey's depiction of the rebels as hypocrites, cowards, drunks and deluded egomaniacs, what was really subversive about his play was its critique of the political establishment's construction of a conservative vision of the Easter Rising. As Roy Foster observes, *The Plough and the Stars* represented O'Casey's attack on 'the post-revolutionary dispensation that perpetuated an agreed lie about what had actually happened, creating a sterile culture'.[26] Arthur Shields had good reason for sympathising with this critique.

The fall-out resulting from O'Casey's eventual return to the Abbey a decade later would help to determine Arthur's future. In the meantime, financial problems remained a more pressing concern: despite Arthur's promotion to assistant producer in 1927, the birth of his son Adam brought home his financial insecurity. Struggling to support his family, and unable to persuade Lady Gregory to increase his salary, he left for revue work in London. Finding the work lucrative but artistically embarrassing, he returned to the Abbey, where, in Lennox Robinson's absence, he was promoted to producer.

On Robinson's return, Arthur agreed to lead a nine-month tour of the United States in 1931. With the subsidy and its box-office income insufficient to meet the Abbey's outgoings, overseas tours would become increasingly essential to the theatre's survival. Arthur's participation was also driven by financial considerations (although his role as company manager and tour director entailed a huge amount of work for an additional $200 per week). His difficulties were compounded by the organisational limitations of Robinson, a heavy drinker: there was, Arthur recalled, 'a great air of informality to the Abbey in those days'. The first American tour – 238 performances in seventy-four cities (with 47 one-night stands) – did not go smoothly. Sets had to be hastily set up and dismantled, often in unsuitable venues, such as hotels or cavernous, half-empty 5,000-seater halls. But the tour generated vital revenue.

The Abbey players returned to North America with Arthur in 1932 for 274 performances in twelve cities (including a more manageable 8

Arthur Shields in the Abbey's convivial Green Room, 1930. To his immediate left is his mentor, Lennox Robinson (HL, T13/B/340).

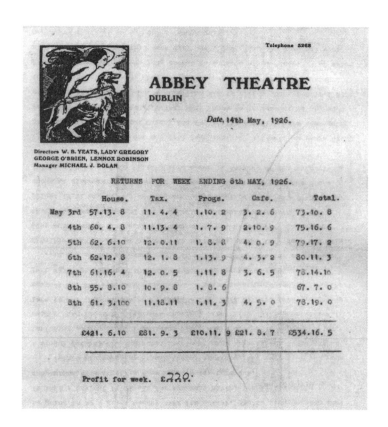

Box office returns for *The Plough and the Stars* (NYPL, Gregory papers). The commercial and critical success of O'Casey's Dublin trilogy contributed to the Abbey's survival during the lean 1920s and 1930s.

one-night stands). In 1934 Arthur led a third American tour, taking in 296 performances in twenty-seven cities. A fourth tour, led by the Abbey's producer, F. R. Higgins, with Arthur as company manager and director, followed in 1937.[27]

Crossing as many as twenty-five states, these extensive tours brought the players not just to the big cities but also to remote universities, obscure towns and even high schools. Arthur's letters home – mostly to his sister Lini – mainly record the difficulties of leading a coast-to-coast tour through Depression-era America on a shoestring budget. One low point was the collapse of a bank in Cincinnati, resulting in the loss of thousands of dollars: 'For the first time since we arrived here I was unnerved,' he wrote. 'I had to take – with a fight – 50% of the receipts in the theatre and just got out of the city on Sunday night with the co. half paid. It was all exciting and not at all pleasant'.[28] He was embarrassed by the shoddiness of the Abbey's sets and props: 'when I went round to the stage hands to show them what we had, oh, they were vary scathing'.[29] But he was also struck by the lack of vitality of the much better-funded American theatre scene, and by the absence of a dramatic tradition throughout much of the country. Characteristically modest, he seldom drew attention to the occasions when 'the plays were liked & the notices good',[30] but this was one of the Abbey's strongest companies, and its naturalistic, expressive performances were often rapturously received. 'We played Juno last night and the critics

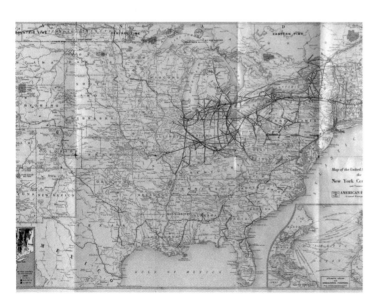

'I have all our journey marked in red on a map and it makes a long red line'. American railway network map with the route of the Abbey's 1931–32 transcontinental tour highlighted (HL, T13/A/58).

have gone just crazy in this morning's papers', wrote one actor from San Francisco.[31] Arthur's performance as Christy in Synge's *Playboy* was regarded by the leading American critic Ashton Stevens as among the ten greatest stage performances he had witnessed.[32]

Arthur's fascination with the diversity of North America is evident from his letters home. Vancouver had a 'Chinese quarter, a Japanese quarter, a Sikh quarter and lots of others', he marvelled. 'Crowds of interesting looking oriental people.'[33] Frozen Winnipeg had air 'so beautiful that it makes me happy to just cross the street.' Chicago 'was horrible', he wrote – 'damn glad to leave'.[34] Texas was filthy: 'Everywhere things are thrown about. Old motors, machinery, houses, pieces of paper, everything & anything just thrown into heaps. It's extraordinary. The people generally down here are rather uncouth.'[35] Detroit was no better: 'I hate Detroit, it's ugly & dirty.'

His correspondence often focused on the hardships of touring. Personal relationships, with the players spending nine months in close proximity to one another, presented a challenge. With two months to go on the first tour, Arthur was counting down the days:

Arthur Shields (as Christy Mahon), Barry Fitzgerald and Eileen Crowe in a 1932 production of Synge's *The Playboy of the Western World* (HL, T13/B/160). Arthur's conventional good looks ensured that he received larger parts than his brother Barry, who was often confined to comic roles.

A scene from a mid-1920s production of *The Playboy of the Western World* featuring Michael Dolan, Maureen Delaney, F. J. McCormick, Arthur Shields, P. J. Carolan, Barry Fitzgerald and Eileen Crowe. Drawing by Grace Gifford, widow of Joseph Plunkett (NLI, PD 2159/TX/16/54).

> Oh I'm longing for it. I'm going to have a great week's rest
> on the boat. And all the company can fight & squabble &
> backbite as much as they like & I don't give a damn.[36]

The 'company is not a very gay one to travel with', Barry reported glumly, on learning of a second tour, but 'the money will probably be good and it might be wiser not to refuse.'[37]

Although some of the younger actors relished the adventure and freedom from responsibility involved in touring, Arthur found life on the road stressful and lonely. He greatly missed his son Adam, who was being reared by his sister Lini and her husband, Charlie Saurin (Arthur's 1916 comrade).[38] As Arthur's marriage disintegrated, his personal life began to complicate his career. Although Bazie accompanied him on the 1933 tour, mental illness and alcoholism increasingly confined her to home.[39] In 1936 he began an affair with Aideen O'Connor.[40] A middle-class girl from Ranelagh, Aideen had joined the players in 1933, after graduating from the Abbey School of Acting. A New York journalist described Aideen, only twenty-one when she went on tour, as 'the prettiest and youngest member of the Abbey Players, and the darling of the troupe'.[41] While tolerated, their relationship was a source of scandal. After a confrontation between Aideen and Bazie at the Abbey made the affair more widely known, Aideen left the family home.

Arthur seldom recorded political opinions in his letters. A rare comment on domestic politics noted potential repercussions for the Abbey. On learning of de Valera's victory in the general election of 1932, he wondered

> what will happen. I'm sure we'll lose the grant. I really
> think though that a change of government – that is if it
> not too drastic a change – will be good for the country.
> C na G. have been in power too long & if FF don't make a
> mess of things the change should have a good effect on
> both parties.[42]

The Abbey players in Philadelphia, 1934. Arthur's troubled wife, Bazie Magee, is third from right, back row. Aideen O'Connor is second from left, front row. Barry, grumpy or mugging, perches on the edge of the couch, while Arthur, with arms folded, appears proprietorial (HL, T13/B/311).

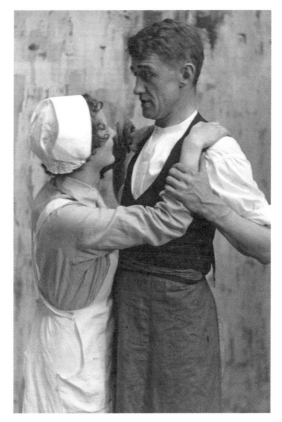

Aideen O'Connor (as Helen) and Arthur Shields (as Michael) on the Abbey stage in Lennox Robinson's *Drama at Inish*, 1934 (AT).

Aideen O'Connor, c. 1937. She began
an affair with Arthur shortly before this
photograph was taken (HL, T13/B/132).

Although he rarely mentioned American politics, the issue of race
does recur in his correspondence. He was struck by the response of the
audience at the Tuskegee Institute, the black university founded by Booker
T. Washington in Alabama in 1881: 'So quick in seeing the humour that
is so often lost on the white audiences here'.[43] It 'seemed as if they were
so with us that they almost anticipated each thing,' he marvelled. 'Never
saw Blacks [at performances] elsewhere'.[44] On another occasion, he sought
tickets for the civil rights activist James Weldon Johnson: 'Like a fool I told
the manager the colour of the Johnsons. He tried to put me off with tickets.
Finally he gave them two seats, but didn't sell seats next to them.' He was
struck both by the vitality of the Deep South's black churches and by its
blatant racism: 'The taxi driver bragging about being in on a lynching. The
train hits a car of blacks and no one, except men of Abbey helping. Had to
wait for a Negro ambulance.'[45]

The pressure of touring – 'We are all very tired; really too tired' – was
compounded by the company's *de facto* status as a cultural ambassador, a role
for which Arthur Shields was temperamentally ill equipped:

> The part that I particularly loath is the entertaining
> end of the job. I mean when these societies ask us
> out to a rotten lunch or tea and in return expect an
> address. The job usually falls on me. I hate it. I'm
> getting a little more used to it and soon I won't give

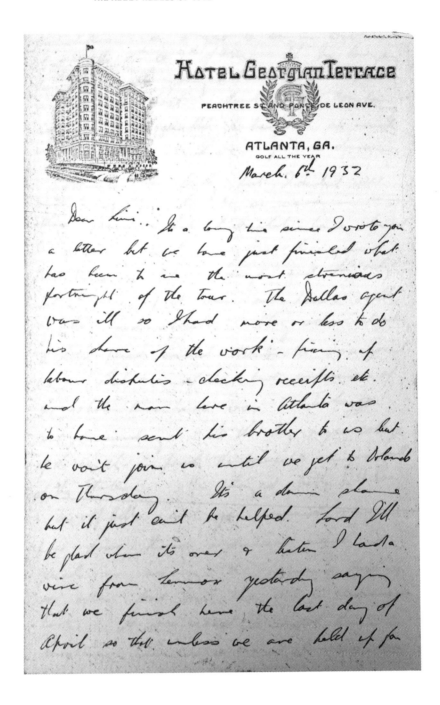

Arthur Shields writes to his sister, Lini Saurin, from Atlanta, 6 March 1932. As ever, he was feeling the strain of leading the tour, although he revelled in their reception at Tuskegee University (HL, T13/A/76).

formalities we ought to be in Dublin
about the 8th or 9th of May. Oh I'm longing
for it. I'm going to have a great week's
rest on the boat. And all the company
can fight & squabble & backbite as much
as they like & I won't give a damn.

Houston was lovely but I didn't see
much of it. Then too we were in some
other places that I would have loved
to see. Just imagine being in
New Orleans for 2 days and the only
bit I saw of it was an hours walk
in the back streets. They were interesting.
A little place called Montevallo was great
too. But one of the best experiences of
the whole time here was in Tuskegee
last Wednesday. Its the big negro college
of the south. in fact the principle negro coll.
of the States. We played both U.H. Boy
& "Far off Hills" and you cannot imagine
how fine those audiences were. So
quick in seeing the humour that is
so often lost on the white audiences
here. It was great to watch them
laughing. Laughter seemed to effect them

Hotel Georgian Terrace

PEACHTREE ST AND PONCE DE LEON AVE.

ATLANTA, GA.

GOLF ALL THE YEAR

much more than it does us. I saw your
men rolling about — throwing their arms
& legs up — getting on their feet & doing
a little dance. It was extraordinary
& they loved the plays. Every now
+ again we were held up because
bursts of laughter or applause lasted
so long. Ah it was great. I'll never
forget it.

I've seen nothing of Atlanta but
it seems to be a dull place. We have
had some very warm weather but today
has turned very cold & we are almost
regretting having put away our heavy
coats. Tomorrow we go to Tallahassee
We leave here tonight at 11.30 arrive there
at 1.25 P.M. matinée at 4 P.M. & night show
at 8. There's a day for you. But it just

on ordinary one.

I meant to get a cheque here yesterday to send you but I hadn't the time before the Express office closed. I hope you have enough to go on with. Did you get some I sent from Denver? Mac was a bit seedy for a few days but she seems to be all right again. I'm beginning to feel the strain & will be very glad of a rest. Anyway I have a definite date to look forward to. I wonder what boat will go by. & where will land.

Heard today for the first time the real results of the elections. I wonder what will happen. I'm sure we'll loose the grant. I really think though that a change of government – that is if it not too drastic a change – will be good for the country. C. na G. have been in power too long & if F.F. don't make a mess of things the change should have a good effect on both parties. I believe the Dail is to meet next Thursday. I'll be on the lookout for news.

I am enclosing a photo of the audience & stage at Tuskegee which

a damn. This town [Toronto] has been particularly
awful. With entertainments every day. Tomorrow
I have to make two addresses ... I don't know what
to say.[46]

There was a more troubling side to this ambassadorial role. Irish-
American discourse about the Abbey's tour was often framed by the politics
of ethnic identity. The paving contractor John McGarry, for example,
wrote to Arthur on behalf 'of the old race here in Chicago' to thank him for
'making a distinct contribution to a better understanding artistically of
our people in the home land'.[47] More representative of those who felt the
need to convey directly their opinions of the Abbey's productions was the
less satisfied Boston attorney William J. Sullivan. Any 'man, playwright,
or anybody else, who violates the law of God, as well as the law of the land
should be punished severely', he told Arthur. 'Never in my life have I been so
insulted or my sense of decency so offended'.[48]

Although they provoked less controversy than in 1911, when Irish-
American protests orchestrated by the leading Fenian Joe McGarrity had
led to the arrest of Máire Nic Shiubhlaigh and the other Abbey players in
Philadelphia for staging 'a sacrilegious and immoral performance', the

Arthur Shields performing in
O'Casey's *Juno and the Paycock* in
Chicago, c. 1935 (HL, T13/B/186).

political context in Ireland was now very different.[49] The subsidy, moreover, ensured that such protests could be considered a matter for official disapprobation. Writing from Philadelphia in 1938, Catherine Kelly asked de Valera if his government was paying for the Abbey's 'disgraceful' plays: 'it makes a decent Irishman or woman blush with shame why are they allowed to come here and degrade the Irish race'.[50] The Padraic Pearse Council of the American Association for the Recognition of the Irish Republic informed de Valera that *Juno and the Paycock* had left a very bad impression, 'especially so on the minds of the native-born Irish, who were humiliated to see this sordid picture of so-called Irish life'.[51] These views received a second wind from the Abbey's opponents at home, who expressed alarm about foreigners receiving such 'a grotesquely untrue impression of Irish life'. Writing in the *Irish Rosary*, the district justice and amateur dramatist Louis J. Walsh expressed his 'shame and horror' at the Abbey's 'defiance of Catholic and Irish sentiment'.[52] A Dominican priest lamented 'the stab in the back given to our unsuspecting exiles in the United States' by government support for plays which 'expose shamelessly before hostile and alien eyes the festering sores of our metropolitan slums'.[53] A minority voice in the wilderness, the *Irish Times* argued that such complaints reflected an unhealthy culture of self-delusion: 'In Ireland, at the moment, there are a dislike of blunt truths and a fear of criticism which are quite as bad as the excesses that are condemned.'[54]

The election of de Valera's populist government ensured that these complaints fell on receptive ears. In 1934 de Valera complained that the inclusion of O'Casey's plays in the Abbey's next tour would 'injure the reputation of the country and ... arouse feelings of shame and resentment among Irish exiles.'[55] Informing Lennox Robinson that the subsidy was to be reduced by a quarter (ostensibly because of 'the present financial position'), the Minister for Finance, Seán MacEntee, insisted that the Abbey change the wording of its programmes to make it clear that the government did not approve of its productions.[56] He also warned the Abbey that it would lose the subsidy if criticism from America continued. This crude attempt at censorship elicited a spirited response from Yeats, who suggested that the controversy was got up by Fianna Fáil's newspaper, the *Irish Press*: 'We refuse such a demand; your Minister may have it in his power to bring our Theatre to an end, but as long as it exists it will retain its freedom.'[57]

As the 1930s progressed, the consequences of de Valera's efforts to impose Catholic, Gaelic values became more apparent, particularly in the cultural sphere, where the government's efforts to redefine Irish

AMERICAN ASSOCIATION FOR THE RECOGNITION

OF THE IRISH REPUBLIC

PADRAIC PEARSE COUNCIL   HARTFORD. CONN.
                                          November 1, 1934.
Hon. Eamon De Valera:-

 Most respectfully the Padraic Pearse Council of
A. A. R. I. R. of Hartford wish to bring to your attention
the present Tour of the Abbey Players of Dublin who have
recently appeared in the Parsons Theatre, Hartford, in a
series of Dramas.

 Some were good and some were very bad. We wish especially
to draw attention to one of these Dramas - "Juno and the Peacock"
which was presented here and which was not very edifying, was
not Irish, and left a very bad impression of Ireland on the
minds of all classes and races that attended - especially so
on the minds of the native born Irish, who were humiliated
to see this sordid picture of so-called Irish life, holding
the race up to ridicule as presented at Hartford.

 We have been informed that this organization - which is
used in America by a syndicate of Foreigners as a box office
attraction for their own pecuniary gain and the disedification
of Ireland - is now seeking an appropriation from the National
Government in Ireland for the further dissemination of this
Anti-Irish and pernicious propaganda throughout the world.

 We would respectfully suggest that if this appropriation
is given them that the National Censor in Dublin censor all
Dramas played by this organization (The Abbey Players) for
foreign consumption, and only present to the world real
Irish Folk Plays, which was the purpose originally intended
for the founding of the Abbey Players by Lady Gregory Lynge
and the other founders.

     Respectfully yours,

     Andrew F. Sullivan

     Andrew F. Sullivan, Secretary,
     1164 Broad Street,
     Hartford, Conn.

Copy of Letter sent to   )
President De Valera by the) - Kindly Publish.
Padraic Pearse Council,   )
Hartford A. A. R. I. R.   )

'Sordid'. Andrew Sullivan of the
American Association for the
Recognition of the Irish Republic
urges de Valera to censor the
Abbey's overseas productions, 1
Nov. 1934 (NAI, D/Taois. S8208).

290

17th April, 1934.

Lennox Robinson, Esq.,
Director,
Abbey Theatre,
DUBLIN, C.8.

A Chara,

I am directed by the President to acknowledge
receipt of your letter of the 31st ultimo and the
accompanying list of plays from which it is proposed to
select the programme for the forthcoming American tour
of the Abbey Theatre Company.

The President observes that three plays by Mr.
Sean O'Casey are included in the list. All three touch
upon the struggle for national independence in a manner
which tends to create a false and unfavourable opinion of
the motives and character of men who during that struggle
risked their lives in the service of their country.
Whatever may be said to justify the production of these
plays in Ireland, where the audiences are sufficiently
familiar with the history of the independence movement
to be capable of making allowance for the element of
caricature and exaggeration in Mr. O'Casey's representation
of it, it appears to the President that their production
abroad is likely to injure the reputation of the country
and would certainly arouse feelings of shame and resentment among Irish exiles. The President is aware from
protests received by him at the time that the production
of these plays during last year's tour was bitterly
resented by many Americans of Irish origin.

While the selection of plays for production by the
Abbey Company is, of course, a matter for the Directors of
the National Theatre Society, the President has to keep
in mind the fact that many people believe that the Government
has some responsibility for the Company's repertoire. This
mistaken belief was unfortunately strengthened in the
United States by an announcement printed on the Company's
programmes during last year's tour which implied that the repertoire had obtained the approval of the Free State Government.
The President knows that the National Theatre Society
arranged for the deletion of this statement from the
programmes when attention was drawn to it. The mis-
apprehension created by it must, however, remain in many
American cities, and the President hopes that, if the
Society decides on the production of Mr. O'Casey's plays during
the coming tour, it will be made clear that the Government
is in no sense responsible for the selection of plays.

The President desires me also to refer to the
inaccurate account of his recent interview with the
Directors of the National Theatre Society which was
published in certain Irish and English newspapers. Statements
alleged to have been made by Dr. Yeats during the interview
were cited. The President regrets that Dr. Yeats appears
to have issued no denial or correction of the inaccuracies
contained in this report.

Is mise, le meas,

Rúnaidhe.

'Shame and resentment': de Valera's
disapproval of the decision to
stage O'Casey's plays in America
is made clear to the Abbey, 17
April 1934 (NAI, D/Taois. S8208).

DEPARTMENT OF FINANCE.

F. 161/1/26.   27th February, 1933.

A Dhuine Uasail,

    With reference to the letter addressed to you on the
10th September last on the subject of the Grant-in-Aid of the
expenses of the National Theatre Society, Limited, I am
directed by the Minister for Finance to inform you that
representations have been made to the Minister for External
Affairs by representative Irish Societies and influential
individuals in the United States to the effect that certain
plays produced by the Abbey Theatre Company on its American
tour were, in their opinion, open to serious objection on
various grounds.

    It will be understood that in considering the advisability
of continuing the Grant hitherto made the Minister could hardly
disregard representations of this kind. It might even happen
that if the representations were of sufficient weight and
substance he would be compelled to make the continuance of the
Grant conditional on an undertaking that, in the event of
another American Tour being contemplated in the future, the
repertoire of plays should be such as not to arouse criticism
of the nature indicated.

    The Minister's attention has also been drawn to the words
"By special arrangement with the Irish Free State Government"
which have been inserted in the programmes distributed in
America and he requests that you will be good enough to furnish
your observations on this misleading statement.

    With regard to the payment of a Grant during the current
year, I am to enquire whether you are in a position to furnish
the assurances indicated in the second paragraph of the letter
referred to above, namely that a competent company is being
maintained in the Abbey Theatre during the present season
and that no part of the Grant will be spent in contributing to
the expenses of the American Tour. It has been decided to
insert provision in the Estimate for Miscellaneous Expenses,
1933/34, for a Grant-in-Aid of the expenses of the Society but,
in view of the present financial position, the Minister has
reluctantly felt himself compelled to enforce a reduction in
the provision to £750. As previously intimated, however, the
inclusion of an item in the Estimate does not necessarily
imply that the Grant will, in fact, be made and in addition the
Minister desires me to emphasise that, before consideration is
given to the payment of the grant in 1933/34, he will require
to be assured that the stipulations mentioned above as attach-
ing to the current year's Grant continue to be observed.

    I am further to state that the Minister has consented
to the appointment of Professor W. Magennis of the National
University of Ireland, as a Government representative on
the Board of Directors of the Society in the place of
Dr. Walter Starkie who has resigned from acting in that
capacity.

                        Mise, le meas,

                    (Sgd.) J.J. McElligott.

J. J. McElligott, secretary of the
Department of Finance, threatens
to reduce the Abbey's subsidy if its
productions continue to provoke
Irish-American criticism, 27 Feb.
1933 (NAI, D/Taois. S8208).

nationality were primarily concentrated.[58] Although Arthur's energies were often focused on the American tours, he was dissatisfied with the Abbey's response to the new climate. Older and frailer, Yeats was increasingly detached from the running of the Abbey, while Arthur believed that the death of Lady Gregory in 1932 – 'She never liked me particularly but that did not matter, she was a great person' – had also eroded the directorate's authority. Overlooking how similar tensions had always characterised the Abbey, he attributed the theatre's creeping conservatism (which he identified with 'a predominance of plays in Gaelic') to the subsidy:

> It always means that somebody will be brought in as ... the managerial director, who must answer to whatever Government is in power. The wonderful thing about the Abbey in the old days was that it was completely without any subsidy. They were without restraint, they wouldn't tolerate restraint ... No censorship whatsoever. Many times we played plays under the most trying circumstances, the people objecting, the money, it was wonderful to play against a crowd like that.[59]

Arthur's dissatisfaction also reflected his growing alienation from post-revolutionary Ireland. De Valera famously depicted his 'ideal Ireland' as a land 'bright with cosy homesteads, whose fields and villages would be joyous with the sounds of industry, with the romping of sturdy children, the contest of athletic youths and the laughter of happy maidens, whose firesides would be forums for the wisdom of serene old age.' Far from living the life that God, and de Valera, desired that men should live, Arthur belonged to a 'wild bohemian demi-monde', an alternative Ireland where hard drinking, partying, adultery, homosexual relationships and other metropolitan practices were pursued (including by some whose day jobs involved the construction of de Valera's rural idyll).[60] While satiating the psychological needs of many Irish Catholics, the imposition of a censorious puritanism made for a cold house for liberals like Arthur, whose commitment to artistic freedom defined his career.

Telephone
Booking Office   44505
Secretary's Office   43412

ABBEY THEATRE
DUBLIN C.8.

Date,   March I   1933

Directors W. B. YEATS, WALTER STARKIE,
LENNOX ROBINSON.
Secretaries J. H. PERRIN, T. J. ROBINSON.

J.J.McHlligott Esq.

Dear Sir

  I have been asked by my fellow-directors to reply to your
letter of February 27th. You state that "representations have
been made to the Minister for External Affairs" by various Irish
persons and Societies in America " to the effect that certain
plays produced by the Abbey Company were, in their opinion, open
to serious objections on various grounds". These plays were
"The Playboy of the Western World", theme of lectures in American
Universities and schools, certainly the most popular play in our
American repertory, a world-famous Irish classic, and "Juno and
the Paycock" which has packed the Abbey Theatre again and again.
In 1911 similar Societies and persons rioted during the production
of the first, and an attack from Press and Pulpit kept Lady Gregory
and me (we had accompanied the Players to America) absorbed in
controversy and drew to our side the powerful support of Theodore
Roosevelt. We had not upon our side at that time all men and
women of Irish birth or descent who had passed through the Universities
Last autumn I was once more in America, and though I lectured on
Irish plays in University after University, delivering my last public
lecture but one in the great Catholic University of Notre Dame, and
invited questions after every lecture, I heard not one word of
protest, nor did a single New York newspaper, nor a newspaper anywhere
so far as I know, speak of such protest. I, at any rate, heard
nothing of it either in public or in private. I heard of it for
the first time the day after my arrival in Ireland from a reporter
of "The Irish Press": cows beyond the water have long horns.
Had however the protest been as formidable as in 1911 it would not
have disturbed us in the least. There has never been an imaginative
or intellectual movement that has not faced and fought such opposition.

  Your letter goes on to say that if we are to retain our
grant we must leave out of our American repertory all plays that
might offend such persons or Societies; that is to say the chief

Splendid defiance: W. B. Yeats
spurns the government's
demands on the Abbey, 1 March
1933 (NAI, D/Taois. S8208).

2

work of Synge and O'Casey.   We refuse such a demand; your Minister
may have it in his power to bring our Theatre to an end, but as
long as it exists it will retain its freedom.   Your letter adds
that "the Minister has consented to the appointment of Professor
W. Magennis of the National University of Ireland as a government
representative on the board of Directors."   Who asked for his
"consent"?   We never heard of Professor Magennis' candidature
until we received your letter.   I find that word "consent"
interesting.   We refuse to admit Professor Magennis to our
Board as we consider him entirely unfitted to be a Director of
the Abbey Theatre.   It is not necessary to state our reasons
for this opinion as my Directors empower me to say in their name
and in my own that we refuse further financial assistance from
your Government.

You ask about the words ☆ by special arrangement with the
Free State Government" printed on the American programmes.   I
saw these words with surprise; they are at once accurate and misleadin
accurate because our tour was undertaken with the consent of the
late Government .   As we were a State Theatre receiving a grant
from the public funds we did not sign our contract until we had
explained to Mr Blythe, then the Minister for Finance, the reasons
that made such a tour imperative.   They are misleading because
some reader may think that we hadthe consent of the Government now
in power.   I have asked the Alber-Wickes Bureau, which has made
all the arrangements for our tour, to omit these words in future.

Yours truly

(signed W B Yeats.)

Central to the creation of a national identity for the new state was the suppression of alternative perspectives. Although Yeats is remembered for his outspoken defence of the Abbey's artistic independence, the theatre's relationship to the Irish state – as Lauren Arrington's valuable research has demonstrated – was inevitably more circumspect.[61] Censorship in de Valera's Ireland was applied not just by the state but, at different times and in different ways, by the Abbey's directors, managers, playwrights, actors and audiences, as well as by interest groups such as the Catholic Church, Irish America and nationalist politicians. Although these prevailing winds were obscured by Yeats's prominent – and sometimes opportunistic – gestures of defiance, the Abbey bent to them. Regardless of the pressures imposed by the subsidy, this shift of tack, as Lionel Pilkington has noted, was 'merely a continuation of the Irish National Theatre Society's already well-established ideological adaptability'.[62]

As an Abbey insider, responsible for some of its most controversial productions, Arthur understood that his theatre practised self-censorship in order to protect or advance its interests. In 1935, having helped to effect a rapprochement between Yeats and O'Casey, Arthur was asked to produce *The Silver Tassie*.[63] The ensuing controversy surrounding the production was driven by a potent cocktail of nationalist intolerance and sectarian grievance. O'Casey's use of Catholic iconography to parody the glamorisation of war revived resentment of the theatre's perceived antagonism to the majority Irish culture. Although the subsidy provided the pretext for the attacks that followed, the troubling secular vista represented by packed audiences attending, without protest, publicly censured plays also troubled many of the theatre's critics.

The boys are back in town: Arthur Shields, Lennox Robinson and Seán O'Casey, 1935 (HL, T13/B/338).

ABBEY THEATRE
— DUBLIN. —

Proprietors - - - - - THE NATIONAL THEATRE SOCIETY, LTD.
Directors - W. B. YEATS, WALTER STARKIE, LENNOX ROBINSON, DR. RICHARD
HAYES, ERNEST BLYTHE, BRINSLEY MACNAMARA, F. R. HIGGINS.
Producer - - - - - - - LENNOX ROBINSON
Assistant Producer - - - - - ARTHUR SHIELDS
Secretaries - - - - ERIC GORMAN, T. J. ROBINSON

All Seats in Theatre with exception of Back Pit may be booked.
Seats Reserved but not paid for, will not be kept later than 7.45 p.m.

Monday, 12th August, 1935, and following nights at
8.15 p.m.

THE SILVER TASSIE

A Tragi-Comedy in Four Acts, by SEAN O'CASEY.

Characters :

SYLVESTER HEEGAN	Barry Fitzgerald
MRS. HEEGAN, his wife	Ann Clery
SIMON NORTON	Michael J. Dolan
SUSIE MONICAN	Eileen Crowe
MRS. FORAN	May Craig
TEDDY FORAN, her husband	P. J. Carolan
HARRY HEEGAN, D.C.M., Heegan's son	F. J. McCormick
JESSIE TAITE	Aideen O'Connor
BARNEY BAGNAL	Fred Johnson
SOLDIERS	Denis O'Dea, J. Winter, Cyril Cusack,
	J. Hand, P. J. Carolan
THE CORPORAL	J. Stephenson
THE VISITOR	Edward Lexy
THE STAFF WALLAH	Tom Purefoy
STRETCHER-BEARERS	W. O'Gorman, M. Finn,
	M. Clarke, B Carey
CASUALTIES	W. Redmond, Edward Lexy
SURGEON FORBY MAXWELL	Tom Purefoy
THE SISTER OF THE WARD	Truda Barling

NOTICE —Ladies sitting in the Stalls are requested to remove their Hats

ACT I.—Room in Heegan's home.
ACT II.—Somewhere in France (later on).
ACT III.—Ward in a Hospital (a little later on).
ACT IV.— Room in Premises of the Avondale Football Club
(later on still).

Settings made in the Theatre from designs by
MAURICE McGONIGAL, R.H.A.

Play produced by ARTHUR SHIELDS.

SMOKING PERMITTED

The Orchestra, under the direction of Dr. J. F. LARCHET, will
perform the following selections :

Overture	Alphonso and Estrella	Schubert (1797-1838)
Irish Airs	Second Suite	J. F. Larchet
Fantasia	Die Valküre	Wagner (1813-1883)
Symphonic Poem	Danse Macabre	Saint-Saens (1835-1922)

ANNOUNCEMENT

Monday, August 19th, 1935, and following evenings at 8 p.m.

JOHN BULL'S OTHER ISLAND
By GEORGE BERNARD SHAW

ABBEY THEATRE PLAY COMPETITION, 1935

The Directors offer a prize of £50 for a play by an Irish Author
who has not had a full length play produced in any professional
Theatre.

Particulars can be obtained from the Secretary, Abbey Theatre.

Following O'Casey's reconciliation with Yeats, Arthur staged *The Silver Tassie* at the Abbey in 1935. The play was condemned as blasphemous by clerical and nationalist commentators (AT).

Seán O'Casey and George Bernard Shaw at the opening night of *Within the Gates* at Royalty Theatre, London, 1934 (NYPL, Berg collection/MSS O'Casey).

What was most revealing about the intemperate response to O'Casey's play was the extent to which Catholicism was presented as synonymous with Irish nationality. The Abbey's plays, as one critic put it, 'reeked with hatred of our faith and people'. The president of the Gaelic League called for the Abbey to be swept away.[64] Describing *The Silver Tassie* as 'a disreputable drama in the sewage of which Christian actors were willing to submerge their Christianity', Father Gaffney told the Catholic Young Men's Society that 'the ideals of Pearse might be buried with his bones in the quick-lime of Arbour Hill.'[65] Criticising the play's 'vigorous medley of lust and hatred and vulgarity', he urged public protests, and called on de Valera to censor the play. Interestingly, the government's appointee to the board remained silent, but Fianna Fáil's distaste for the play was signalled by the description of the production in the *Irish Press* as 'perverted ... blasphemy'.[66] As during the previous controversies, the theatre remained packed throughout the furore despite the play's poor critical reviews. The dispute prompted the resignation of the Abbey's sole Catholic board-member, Brinsley MacNamara, who had not previously objected to the play. He justified his action on the grounds of the offence given 'to the largest section of our audience and to the country from which the Theatre derives its subsidy'. Yeats considered MacNamara to have 'gone over to the enemy'.[67]

Against this background, Lennox Robinson's waning influence at the Abbey increasingly concerned Arthur, as did the giving of priority to commercial success by Yeats's up-and-coming acolyte, F. R. Higgins. A shrewd operator, Higgins, a gregarious poet born in Co. Mayo, had risen swiftly from director to managing director, despite his limited experience of production. A champion of the Abbey's traditional 'PQ' (peasant quality) fare, he had little time for the work of O'Casey.[68] The growing influence of the former minister Ernest Blythe, reputed to regard the Abbey 'not just as a theatre but an instrument of national defence', further troubled Arthur following Blythe's appointment as a director in 1935.[69] Blythe – who over the course of his long tenure as managing director at the Abbey rejected work by Samuel Beckett, Brendan Behan, Brian Friel, Thomas Kilroy and Tom Murphy – was pioneering the Irish-language pantomime when Arthur finally left. That these changes contributed to his subsequent departure from Ireland is clear, even if, as late as 1962, he remained reluctant to criticise the Abbey publicly: 'I couldn't say my prayers, in Gaelic, I would have been out of a job – you needn't put that down,' he told one journalist when explaining his decision to leave.[70]

Arthur's dissatisfaction should be seen in a broader context. That the Abbey was mired in crisis, had lost its way as a playwrights' theatre or had subordinated its artistic independency to political expediency were more or less perennial complaints since its foundation. But what had changed was the context in which these controversies occurred. Before 1922, the Abbey's Protestants, progressives and dissidents – although periodically outraging nationalist opinion – could position the theatre on the side of the nation against

Ernest Blythe (1889–1975), photographed at the Queen's Theatre, 1960. Managing director of the Abbey between 1941 and 1967, Blythe's conservative influence was resented despite the importance of his connections in ensuring state support for the theatre (AT).

the (British) state, not least when its productions brought it into conflict with the state. After independence, confrontation with the (Irish) state became trickier, while the more insular climate narrowed the space for artists to critique society.

Although Arthur preferred to avoid conflict, his unease was voiced by playwrights, such as Seán O'Casey and Paul Vincent Carroll, who railed against 'Dublin's censorious, provincial and pietistic attitude'. As ever, religion and language formed the front line in this cultural war. One of the most distinctive features of the Abbey was that it had been an avowedly 'national' institution conspicuously led by Protestants. The theatre's Protestant identity, and its relationship with the majority culture, remained a source of tension in the 1930s, as Irish-speakers and Catholics began joining the board of an institution that continued to be resented, including by some of its own playwrights, as 'the domain of a Protestant coterie'.[71] The government's escalation of compulsory Gaelicisation made the issue of Irish-language productions particularly fraught. Writing with playwrights such as Carroll in his sights, the writer and senior civil servant P. S. O'Hegarty robustly articulated this issue:

> The prime sin of the present directors is, apparently, that they are 'breaking the tradition' of the theatre by playing plays in 'Gaelic' ... By what process of reasoning can it be held to be inappropriate for the National Theatre Society to produce plays in the national language ... Nor is there any truth in the suggestion that a knowledge of Irish is likely to unfit anybody for acting

> ... The opposition to the Irish language is an opposition
> to the very idea of an Irish nation. It is a hankering back
> to the idea of British domination ... The community for
> which the *Irish Times* speaks, or for which it is presumed
> to speak, has learned nothing in twenty-two years of
> Irish Freedom. It hopes that a government will some day
> arise here which will recede from the principle that the
> Irish language should be taught to all Irish children. It is
> a vain hope.[72]

Against this background, Arthur began to reconsider his future as he prepared for a fourth American tour. The money was good, but the job remained stressful. Administering $2,000 per week in salaries and bills, meeting a tough schedule and managing his players (particularly his brother Barry Fitzgerald) proved challenging: 'He is a terribly selfish man ... Oh this is a terrible life.'[73] However, offers from Broadway and Hollywood were beginning to come, and Arthur's years on the road 'as a sort of Theatre-Manager' gave him the ability and confidence to consider striking out on his own:

> This rush & grind is having a queer effect on me, I find
> myself doing unusual things – being rude, very rude – or
> quite calm when I would ordinarily be flustered. I feel
> I've hardened a good deal, and I feel a certain amount of
> pride at having been able to carry on so far without any
> bad miscalculation in money or other things.[74]

Barry Fitzgerald, moreover, had not returned to the Abbey since filming *The Plough and the Stars* with John Ford in 1936, partly because he felt marginalised by F. R. Higgins, who reportedly regarded him as a 'clown', because of his comic abilities.[75] Signing a seven-year contract with Mary Pickford Productions, Barry began to develop a film career in the United States. Although Barry was eight years older than him, Arthur had a protective attitude towards his brother, while Barry assured him that his talents would be appreciated in Hollywood.

The Abbey on tour, c. 1938. By now, Arthur (preoccupied), and, to his right, Aideen (pensive) were closer than suggested by this photograph (AT).

There was a more personal reason why 'Ireland became impossible' for Arthur.[76] The breakdown of his marriage had soured relations at the Abbey, and Arthur blamed F. R. Higgins ('a swine') for keeping Aideen O'Connor out of work. In 1938 Arthur secured work in New York, directing the rehearsals for Paul Vincent Carroll's masterpiece *Shadows and Substance*. In this 'unsparing attack on populist Catholicism', Aideen played opposite Arthur, as his niece. Arthur had helped to create the part of Canon Skerritt in the original Irish production.[77] That September, Arthur met Yeats at the Kildare Street Club to tell him about his relationship with Aideen, and his plan to leave. Although Yeats valued Arthur – he told his lover, the journalist Edith Shackleton Heald, that he 'incarnates our traditions' – he supported him in his decision. Yeats assured him that a place would remain for him at the Abbey 'as long as he had anything to say about it'.[78] In contrast, Arthur recalled Higgins sneering with disbelief when he told him he was leaving to direct a successful London production, *Spring Meeting*, on Broadway.[79]

Within the year, Yeats had died, and John Ford wanted Arthur for a film role he had written specially for him in *Drums along the Mohawk*.[80] Although Arthur didn't believe in making plans, it was clear where his future lay.

* * *

Chapter 20

Arthur

1939–70

No patty-fingers, if you please. The proprieties
at all times. Hold on to your hats.

—Barry Fitzgerald as Michaeleen Flynn in *The Quiet Man* (1952)

Arthur Shields struggled to make it in America. 'Boss and I have no money
whatsoever,' wrote Aideen O'Connor, in what would become a common
complaint in those early years. Arthur's Broadway production of Paul
Vincent Carroll's *Kindred* flopped in December 1939. Although Carroll's
previous play, *The White Steed* (rejected by the Abbey because of its criticism
of Catholicism), had triumphed, winning the New York Drama Critics'
Circle Award for best foreign play, *Kindred* closed after sixteen performances.
'Kindred – failure!' recorded Arthur in his diary. Verging on bankruptcy,
he sought to recoup his losses by reviving *Juno and the Paycock* off Broadway
the following month. The cast (which included Barry Fitzgerald and the
Abbey veteran Sara Allgood) agreed to take a share of the receipts rather than
salaries in order to get the production off the ground. Although the reviews
were mixed, it performed well enough to offset the debts amassed by *Kindred*.

While *Juno and the Paycock* was running, Arthur was admitted to
hospital with tuberculosis. Although released in March 1940, he never
fully recovered.[1] His lifestyle did not help: 'I hate American picture houses
because one can't smoke in them'.[2] Barry had opted for a less risky and
more lucrative screen career, and it was now his turn to care for Arthur. He
drove his brother from New York to Hollywood, stopping en route to secure
the treatments prescribed by his doctor.[3] Although Arthur picked up small
roles in 1940 in *The Long Voyage Home*, directed by John Ford, and *Little Nellie
Kelly*, starring Judy Garland, he was reluctant to give up his ambitions for
the stage for a career in what he regarded as a lesser medium. Success in
the theatre, however, continued to elude him. In February 1941 he produced
Louis D'Alton's *Tanyard Street* (which, as *The Spanish Soldier*, had performed
poorly in Dublin) on Broadway. Starring Arthur, Barry and Aideen (in her
final appearance on Broadway), the play flopped, prompting Arthur and
Aideen to reluctantly follow Barry out west.

Arthur's collaboration with such writers as D'Alton and Carroll,
whose plays centred on the repressive clericalism of Irish society, might
be read as a quiet form of dissent from de Valera's Ireland. Indeed, during
this period, Shields was criticised in Ireland. According to Aideen, whom
he would later marry, his relationship with her 'rapidly changed in status

from the tolerated, if not completely condoned, stage romance, to the unforgivable sin of desertion of his legitimate wife for another woman'.[4] Others resented his presence in America during the Second World War. Arthur and Aideen, for their part, objected to Irish neutrality, regarding it as a manifestation of parochialism: 'Éire is now so insular, so cut off by her own will from contact from the rest of the world', Aideen wrote. 'It's their own choice I know and it is awful hard to criticise it – but I am all for giving the bases – even my beloved Cove [Cóbh] where my house is'.[5]

Arthur and Aideen struggled to build a life in Hollywood. Aideen had never wanted to settle in America: 'The cities are so big and quick you get run over any day. It is like living in the movies which never seem real to me but just like a fairy world where people can live for a while.'[6] Earlier trips to Hollywood with the Abbey players involved exciting parties with the hard-drinking Hollywood-Irish set, and opportunities to meet film stars like Jimmy Cagney ('very unassuming and terribly interested in Ireland') and Henry Fonda. In one letter home, Aideen recalled attending Una O'Connor's party ('the usual "Hollywood" shambles, Maureen O'Sullivan was there looking beautiful') and a glamorous dinner thrown by John Ford: 'There were a lot of writers and people there – and a cowboy star John Wayne and his wife – who are giving a party for us tonight'.[7]

Settling permanently in Hollywood was a different proposition. Without a work visa, Aideen lacked purpose in life. Despite frequent visits from the Shields' extended family, she grew to hate Hollywood. Lonely, homesick and estranged from her father, who disapproved of her

Abbey players on the Hollywood set of *The Informer*, 1935. The director, John Ford (in sunglasses), can be seen to the right of Shields. An adaption of Liam O'Flaherty's novel, set in the War of Independence, the atmospheric film won four Oscars (HL, T13/B/315).

relationship with Arthur, she became quietly dependent on alcohol. As her biographer Ciara O'Dowd poignantly observed: 'Her love for Arthur Shields both defined and unmade her life'.[8]

Arthur's health also remained fragile. 'He is far from well,' Barry wrote. 'He has had some small jobs here and they have taken a lot out of him.'[9] By the middle of 1942 Aideen felt that their circumstances were improving:

> Boss is somewhat better – much cheerier and very happy
> in his new part in 'Gentleman Jim' at Warners. It looks as
> if he is going to get four weeks on this one – which is (as
> they say here) a 'career' compared with the little bits he
> has been doing. I still hate Hollywood – but at least my
> cooking has improved.'[10]

The position remained much the same in early 1943:

> He did pretty well last year in movies – lots of small parts
> – some of them very small – but, so far this year he has
> not done anything so we are keeping our fingers crossed.
> I wish Boss would get a really decent part. He doesn't get
> a chance to really show what he can do in those 'bits'.[11]

Bazie's death later that year allowed Arthur and Aideen to marry. Further stability came with the purchase of a house at the foot of the Hollywood Hills in 1945. Arthur wrote that the house

> is old – not at all pretentious but when we can find the
> few pieces of furniture and carpet it will be comfortable.
> It cost far too much. I'm broke, but I don't regret it,
> because in the few weeks we have been here we have both
> improved in health & perhaps in disposition.[12]

T13/A/154(6)

1843 North Cherokee Avenue,
Hollywood, Cal.

23rd. August 1941.

Dear Eddie,

    I am writing to you for Boss who is working pretty hard - and
who is a lousey correspondent anyway!   How are you and Iris?
Boss was delighted to get your letter some time ago - indeed we shoul
have written to you long ago but the Californian air gives one such
an attack of inertia that to write a letter sometimes seems the
equivalent of a ten mile walk in the sun.

    The brothers Shields have been engaged as f ollows: Boss
finished in "How Green was my Valley" some weeks ago and on the
16th. this month he went into another one at 20th Century Fox
"Confirm or Deny" and English war picture of London during the
'blitz'.   He plays the part of an oldish,blind telegraphist.   It
is a grand showey part - the best hehas had since "Drums".   I think
he will be very effective.   He has not much diologue but is spotted
all through it and finally has a spectacular death scene during a
bombing.   Fritz Lang started to direct the picture but was taken
very ill and had to go to hospital so Archie Mayo took over.   Boss
likes him very much.   Don Ameche and Joan Bennett are the stars
and Roddy McDowell (a marvellous English kid who is in "How Green
was my Valley") John Loder and Boss have the other important parts.
Boss has nothing else in view after this ø/ø/ picture is over.
And now the famous Will - well, he worked in "How Greenwas my Valley"
- a very tiny prt in which he was terribly unhappy!   It could have
been done in one day but I believe Barry got a three weeks contract
and worked about six days!   Then he went straight into "Tarzan's
Secret Treasure" - in which he wrestled with monkeys, escaped from
crocodiles, rode elephants - and was flung into the lake an average
of three times a day!   Can you imagine his misery?   Boss and I
could hardly keep our faces straight when he would start his tale of
woe every night at dinner.   He worked over five weeks on that and
on Monday he is going away for a holiday to San Fransisco.   He was
wanted for that play "They met at Arques" - now I believe called
"Mr Wookey" but he read and thought it was such an awful script he
wouldn't do it.   Have you read it?   Its incredibly bad and so false.

    Bosses health has been good.   He did give us a scare by getting
a very bad cold and suddenly getting a temperature.   I had a vision
of 'here we go again' and Boss being delerious and hospital etc.etc.
but I took no chances this time and in spite of all protests called
a Dr. and made him go to bed so he was all right in a few days.   A
 week after that Barry really came down with a nasty bout of flu and
I had to move over to his apt. and get a nurse for him.   What a
pair!   Dr. Howson is very pleased with the way Bosses lung is
behaving.   He is going to start easing off on the treatments.
Already Boss can go ten days without any ill effects.   Isn't that
grand?

    I am so glad that you got a good rest this summer Eddie, and
that you are feeling better.   You certainly had a hard winter.
It must be fun for Iris doing stock - its the only way to work in
 the Theatre its so exciting doing a new play every week.   I
nearly got myself a job here but Equity and Lyons ditched it for me,

Aideen O'Connor describes life
in Hollywood in a letter to the
Broadway producer Eddie Choate,
23 August 1941 (HL, T13/A/154). John
Loder, mentioned here as Arthur's
co-star in *Confirm or Deny* (1941),
was the son of General Lowe who
led the British forces at the Easter
Rising. Loder was present, with
his father, at Pearse's surrender.

2.

Gerladine Fitzgerald rang up one day and asked me if I would like to play with her in Selznick's theatre at Santa Barbara.   I went to the Selznick's studio and read the part and they   seemed to like me and asked me if I would start rehearsing.   Then Equity stepped in and said that I would be nine days away from my six months on the opening night.   Houseman (one of the producers) asked for an exemption and they said they would have to convene a special meeting - and then they said they couldn't do that and we would have to wait for the next meeting of the council in New York - a week away.   The play was being done in less than three weeks and was a very difficult one so of course Houseman fumed and foamed but could do nothing.   Then he asked me if I would rehearse for the week and they would take the chance of my getting permission to do it.   I rang up Lyons and told them to ask Equity if I could.   They said yes but that I must not accept any money for it! Well, we started rehearsing and worked like fury - until 2am. most mornings.   My part was lovely it was all with Geraldine and we suited each other very well - the name of the play is "Lottie Dundass" by Enid Bagnold.   Then Lyons suddenly told me to stop rehearsing as they couldn't agree with Houseman on the money question.   I don't blame them! Houseman wanted to pay me $75 and a two weeks quantee.   And that meant that I wouldn't be able to work again for another six months. They squabbled about it for a few days while I calmly went on working - finally it wasmput to me and although I wanted to do it very much Boss was terribly against it as the chances were almost 100 to one that Warner's wouldn't let Geraldine go to New York in it as she wanted to do and Houseman would not look any further than a week in Santa Barbara and IF it was a success there two weeks in San Fransisco.   So I reluctantly left it.   It opened in Santa Barbara and Geraldine got sensational notices.   She is terrific in it.   It a wonderful part.   The girl who got my part is Joanna Roos - I believe she was in "Abe Lincoln".   So I am hoping and praying I will get a part in New York this winter as I am longing to be working again.   I doubt if "Lottie Dundass" will get to New York as the critics seem to think that though Geraldine is super the play is not.   Lyons are supposed to be looking out for a part for me but that means damn all - as you know.   I wish Boss could make a real hit in a play in New York so that he could get the kind of parts in pictures he should be getting.   How was Paul's play?   It sounds as though it might be terrific as he is writing what he is living at the moment. Will you write and tell Boss about it as he is very interested to know.   Although Barry hasn't said much I believe he would do a play if he got the right kind of part.   "Tarzan" has made him feel that the stage is not so bad after all! Wouldn't it be wonderful if we could all be together again in a HIT - something that would run for a year and then tour.   I had better start a novena about it.

        I had a long letter from Liz the other day.   She is in the army now!   A WREN or a FANNY or something.   She says she has to do so much marching and "blitz" work that she has lost 16 lbs and is positively strmamlined.   Her letters are grand so casual and funny.   She is madly in love with an RAF pilot - tall, blond and blue eyed etc.   She asked tombe remembered to you and Iris.

3

Isn't the war awful? We never seem to be able to forget it for a minute. I don't know how the people in the east are but out here they are so indifferent and so apathetic that it is frightenângg. They just don't don't seem to be interested. It looks like being a long business, doesn't it? Boss and I are always feeling we should be back there doing something. Not that we would be any use but we feel its where we whould be. We feâl so useless and SAFE over here - with plenty of food and clothes and amusement when we ought to be sharing the rationing and the anxiety and the work and hardships that the people in Eire are having - or we should be doing something in England. England has become such an inspiration to the world, hasn't she? Have you been reading any of the current books about the war? We are crazy about William L. Shirer's "Berlin Diary". And we also loved Edward R. Morrow's "This is London" and Virginia Cowles "Looking for Trouble". Quentin Reynolds "London Diary" not so much - he is too smart alecky. "I was a Nazi Flyer" was interesting - but is it authentic? Boss is reading "You Can't Do Business With Hitler" at the moment. I read about two books a day - nothing else to do in this god awful town. We have moved into another apt. in this building. It is lovely. Big airy rooms and nice furniture and decorations. Barry has an apt. - a large one - about ten minutes drive from here. He has dinner with us every night. My cooking has become most proficient!

You will be interested to hear that Sally Allgood was distinctly unpopular on the set in "How Green Was My Valley"! Not that one could expect anything else. To the horror of Boss and Will she wore _slacks_ all the time when she was not in costume! Boss didn't care for Maureen O'Hara - she is rather starish and a bit beligerent! He is very fond of little Roddy McDowall. Did you see him in "Man Hunt"? Apparently he is terrific in "Valley". He is a lovely little kid. They also liked Anna Lee very much.

I must stop this gossipy letter now. Please give my love to Iris. I am hoping to see you both soon. Boss sends the very best to you Eddie and you know this letter is really from him - though he would never write all this gossip. I know that if you hear of any part for him you will let him know - unless Jack Kirkland is producing! I don't think that Boss would care to work for him again unless we were destitute. How I hate the little rat. Every time I think of last winter and him and "The Dr's Dilemma" I --- no, I won't say it.

Well, slan leath, Eddie - write soon and I'll get Boss to answer straight away this time.

Lots of love,

Ardee

After the end of the war they brought over Arthur's son, Adam, to live with them, and their daughter, Christine, was born in 1946.

Barry's career, meanwhile, soared to extraordinary levels of success. By the middle of the 1940s, when he won an Academy Award for his role as Father Fitzgibbon in *Going My Way* (1944), starring Bing Crosby, he had become one of the highest-paid stars in Hollywood, reportedly earning $75,000 a picture. Although Arthur picked up work on the set of his brother's films, this success probably reinforced Barry's dependence on Arthur, because of Barry's intense shyness. 'He finds it all rather bewildering,' a *New York Times* profile of Barry noted. 'His old clothes and cloth cap, which once kept him inconspicuous, now make him a marked man.'

Numerous accounts testify to Barry's struggle to adapt to life in Hollywood, such as the time he lost his wardrobe when he forgot which laundrette he used, and his habit of fleeing his house when well-wishers called to visit. In the light of his reputed homosexuality, Barry might also be seen, in a less political sense than his brother, as a refugee from de Valera's Ireland. He shared his home with Gus Tallon, an Iroquois Indian described by press accounts as his 'stand-in', 'valet-companion', 'pal' or 'friend'. A favourite pursuit of theirs was gunning their Harley-Davidsons through the Hollywood Hills.[13] Arthur's attitude to his brother's sexuality, almost as much a taboo in post-war Hollywood as in Catholic Ireland, is not clear. His reply to a letter of consolation from an Irish priest following Barry's death in 1961 suggests a desire to protect his brother's reputation that would accord with their close and mutually supportive relationship. He wrote that Barry was

> a shy little man. He was uncomfortable in crowds
> and really dreaded meeting new people, he was not
> a recluse, and did enjoy certain company ... He never
> married, not that he disliked the company of women,
> but I think he was held back from proposing to
> anyone through shyness.[14]

In 1947 Arthur directed *A Moon for the Misbegotten*, Eugene O'Neill's sequel to *Long Day's Journey into Night*. Arthur, who had successfully staged O'Neill's *Days without End* at the Abbey a decade earlier, was a natural collaborator for the Irish-American playwright whose early plays had transformed American theatre. O'Neill's writing had been deeply influenced by the Abbey Theatre, which he saw on its American tour in 1911: 'The Abbey first opened my eyes to the existence of a real theatre, as opposed to the unreal – and to me then – hateful theatre of my father, in whose atmosphere I had been brought up.'[15] Their first meeting was nonetheless awkward, as O'Neill's ill-health rendered his speech difficult. Arthur recalled that

> for a time nothing was said. I'm not a good conversationalist and I definitely felt that I was being carefully appraised by a very intelligent, kindly person. His eyes were impressive ... the perfect penetrating and understanding look that one could hope to find in a father confessor.

Nor did the rehearsals go smoothly. Neither Arthur nor O'Neill were involved in the casting, and Arthur found the American cast resistant to the Abbey's acting style, with its emphasis on a minimum of movement: 'The eternal moving about! They simply wouldn't stand still.'[16] He was shocked also by the pressure placed on O'Neill by the producers to cut his script: 'My 25 years at the Abbey Theatre – which was definitely a playwrights' theatre – had taught me not to tamper with the work of an established author.'[17]

A Moon for the Misbegotten, a story of deception and guilt set within a dysfunctional family in impoverished rural Connecticut, opened to mixed notices, but it was the police rather than the critics that brought it to an end: 'Too smutty' was the headline in the *Detroit Times*. Appalled that the words 'mother' and 'prostitute' had been used in the same line of dialogue, Detroit's vigilant police censor Charles Snyder informed the press that the play was an obscene 'slander on American motherhood. The play will have to be rewritten before I will let it go on.'[18] Arthur was disappointed more by the acquiescent response of the producers than by the authorities' censoriousness:

> I expected the Guild to fight that kind of censorship and was surprised when word came that the police lieutenant would be allowed to dictate what could be said. The whole episode was so distasteful that the

following morning I left Detroit for the coast.[19]

Arthur had once again been unlucky in his ambition to establish a career on the American stage. Subsequently revived on Broadway five times, *A Moon for the Misbegotten* came to be recognised as one of O'Neill's great late works.

In other respects, Arthur's career was flourishing. Although an attempt to film *Juno and the Paycock* foundered, work was plentiful. He hosted a weekly radio programme and secured a deal to introduce and perform in a television series.[20] Between jobs, however, poor health often confined him to bed, and Aideen's health had also been poor since the birth of their daughter. Although their correspondence indicates a loving relationship, Aideen's loneliness is clear. Disappointed that she could not stay with Arthur in New York, she wrote to him at the Algonquin Hotel: 'all I want is to be with you – even if it's in Timbuctoo.'[21] Ciara O'Dowd has described movingly Aideen's decline as she retreated to the shaded, book-lined Green Room, in the centre of their home:

> Aideen kept her typewriter here, and an easy chair for reading. It was here that she wanted to be when she realised in 1950 that the terrible secret she'd been keeping wasn't a secret, and that her alcoholism was going to kill her. So, they set up a bed there for her – close to the room where Christine's nanny slept and nursed her three-year-old charge. Between sleeping and waking, thinking and dreaming, she could half open her eyes and be anywhere ... even back in the familiar comfort of the Abbey Theatre Green Room.[22]

On 4 July 1950, aged thirty-six, Aideen died of cirrhosis of the liver.[23] Although she was one of the most talented young Irish actors of her day, her short career has been largely forgotten.

Arthur threw himself into his burgeoning film career. Although not auspicious, his screen debut – in John Ford's *The Plough and the Stars* (1936) – inaugurated the most important cinematic collaboration of his career. Hobbled by studio interference (Ford never worked for RKO again) and a script that fashioned melodrama from tragedy, the film was an artistic and commercial failure. Appearing as Patrick Pearse, however, Arthur featured in one of its few effective scenes. Arthur's presence – like that of Wyatt Earp on the set of early silent westerns at which John Ford was present and which years later he would draw on for *My Darling Clementine* (1946) – granted Hollywood's greatest myth-maker a spurious authenticity for his imagined 1916, which bore scant resemblance to the historical event. Some of his cast, Ford told the press,

> Arthur Shields for instance – were really in the Dublin post office when it fell. They were in this pub we've reproduced when the call came to mobilize. I talk with them informally, and get their opinions, and listen to their anecdotes, and as a result get a better picture.[24]

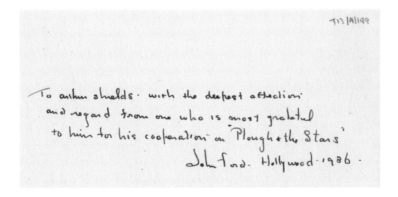

As well as playing the role of Patrick Pearse, Arthur Shields worked as assistant director on the set of John Ford's film *The Plough and the Stars* (1936) (HL, (HL, T13/A/189).

Rather than faithfully reconstructing the Rising, Ford – most notably in a scene in which Arthur, surrounded by the signatories, solemnly intones the Proclamation – depicted it as an Irish re-enactment of the American Declaration of Independence.[25]

Working with Barry, Arthur made six more films with John Ford. Although their range of roles was narrow – they cornered the lucrative market for character parts as priests – the brothers' significance for Ford amounted to more than their minor on-screen presence, as is indicated by the opening credits of *The Plough and the Stars*: 'Directed by John Ford, assisted by Arthur Shields of the Abbey Theatre'. The evocative account by the actor Harry Carey, Jr, of the shoot for the John Wayne western *She Wore a Yellow Ribbon* (1949) makes it clear that Arthur was a respected member of the actors and crew who made up 'Pappy's' legendary personal stock company. Ford, in his characteristically tyrannical way, had insisted that his cast stay on the Navajo Reservation in Monument Valley, in cabins that lacked running water and adequate heating. Despite Ford's reputation for bullying actors, Carey recalled that

> Jack Ford so respected Arthur that he was the only man he would allow to coach his actors off the set. The second night there, Uncle Jack ordered me to get back to my cabin to 'work with Arthur on your part'. [26]

John Wayne, John Ford and Arthur Shields leave Ashford Castle during the filming of *The Quiet Man*, 1952.

In *The Quiet Man*, the Irish-born American boxer Sean Thornton (John Wayne) returns to Ireland to reclaim his family farm, falling for the tempestuous Mary Kate Danaher (Maureen O'Hara). Hollywood's most influential representation of Ireland, this nostalgic romantic comedy won Ford a fourth Best Director Oscar (KC, QUI007CJ).

The transition from the Abbey Theatre to John Ford's Hollywood was less abrupt than it might seem. Working for Yeats may have been a useful apprenticeship for Arthur in his collaboration with Ford, an even more demanding visionary, notorious for his self-aggrandisement, ill-temper and cruelty. There were interesting parallels between these two figures who found in Arthur a foil for their creative genius. As Adrian Frazier argues in his book *Hollywood Irish*, Ford saw himself as continuing the reimagining of Ireland initiated by Yeats's revival. For both men, the process of invention – of nation and self – was central to their work; through their influential representations of their nations, both succeeded in shaping how their mythic histories were understood.

Although partly self-fashioned, Ford's Irish identity was central to his work. As Joseph McBride observed in *Searching for John Ford*, he regarded 'any persecuted group as honorary Irishmen, whether they were dispossessed Okies heading for California in *The Grapes of Wrath*, or Welsh miners drawn together by grief in *How Green Was My Valley*'.[27] This helps to explain the curious oddity that these two Irishmen, Arthur and Barry, became so conspicuous a presence in Ford's redefining of the western as the quintessential American story. In *The Quiet Man* (1952), a film whose significance is increasingly acknowledged by scholars, Ford rooted a heroic Irish-American identity in an imagined Ireland. Strikingly, the two small roles that provide so much of the heart of the film, essentially an American western transposed to the Irish west, are played by the two brothers who, in their own unassuming way, were so quietly subversive of romanticised Ireland. Reflecting on their intriguing collaboration, Frazier proposes Arthur Shields – that 'quiet, modest gentleman' – as an unheralded link between 'the plays of the Irish Revival' and the 'movies of Hollywood's golden age'.[28]

The Quiet Man marked the end of their collaboration, although Ford continued to try to find ways of working with the brothers.[29] In contrast to his life on the stage, for which he continued to pine, Arthur demonstrated little interest in reminiscing about his screen career. He played close to a hundred small, usually typecast roles, in often poorly written films.[30] He was at his happiest performing as Christy in Synge's *Playboy*, but his livelihood came to rest on bit parts in such movies as *Tarzan and the Slave Girl* (1950) and *The Daughter of Dr Jekyll* (1959). The latter role was reported by one Irish newspaper in a feature headed 'Arthur Shields hits a new low – as a film werewolf'. It identified Arthur as

the classic example of a good, perhaps even a great, man of the theatre gone to seed in the Hollywood jungle … Some of his roles have been real shockers … others quite pathetic bit parts that could be filled by a hundred out-of-work small-timers. Now nearly 60, Arthur Shields plumbs a new low with his werewolf character … Well paid let us hope and happy in his Hollywood home, but what a tragic waste of talent.

As Dr E. E. Campbell, Arthur helps to overthrow an evil lion-worshipping cult in *Tarzan and the Slave Girl* (1950), a film described by the *New York Times* as painful to watch. Arthur's film career was increasingly criticised in Ireland (MEPL, 10385109).

Rehearsing what was by then a well-established trope which encompassed other Hollywood Irish stars, such as Sara Allgood and Arthur's brother Barry, this account was more a critique of the Hollywood system for its squandering of Irish talent than it was of Arthur (who would probably not have disagreed with the thrust of it).

This lack of creative opportunities reflected the limitations of the medium at that time. Adrian Frazier notes the irony of an actor committed to the supremacy of the writer ending up in an industry where they notoriously played second fiddle. Arthur's career was further constrained by the limitations of prevailing ideas about Irish identity. Although Barry was far more successful than his brother, in his most popular roles he played the screen equivalent of the stage-Irishman that Yeats's Abbey had sought to consign to history. Revealingly, one of Arthur's few satisfying film roles, his portrayal of the widowed Irish father of a mixed-race daughter in Jean Renoir's *The River* (1951), based on the novel by Rumer Godden, was made far from Hollywood. This intelligent, politically engaged study of unrequited first love – described by Renoir as a 'film about India without elephants and tiger hunts' – could only have been made outside the American studio system, not least because of its challenging of racial taboos. Explaining his decision to cast Arthur, whom he befriended, Renoir told Godden, with whom he collaborated on the screenplay: 'Everybody here admires him but strangely enough this has rarely manifested itself in concrete parts'. Subsequently embraced by such filmmakers as Martin Scorsese, *The River* is now recognised 'as a touchstone for a certain kind of modernity in cinema'.[31] Arthur could shine in the film because it entailed 'a fresh and progressive representation of the Irish character' that challenged Hollywood's Irish stereotypes.[32]

The rise of television saw Arthur's film career dry up in the early 1950s: 'I'm just living on the little fat that remains', he wrote.[33] Although Barry was contracted by Paramount for what Arthur described as an indecent fee to make just one film a year, his career too was coming to an end, whether because of laziness and his love of golf (as Arthur complained) or because of the increasing effects of Parkinson's disease.[34] Arthur accompanied Barry to Rome to care for him on his last major shoot in 1952.

Despite his ambivalence towards the medium, Arthur carved out a successful career in television. He was the narrator of the Emmy Award-winning 'Your Show Time', the first filmed (as opposed to live) network television drama.[35] He became a familiar face in character parts on such shows as 'The Hardy Boys', 'The Mickey Mouse Club', 'Bonanza', 'Rawhide', 'Maverick' and 'Perry Mason'. He was financially comfortable, having invested well in television production. Indeed, he claimed that he moved from Los Angeles to Santa Barbara to make it easier to turn down work.

Arthur married for a third time in 1955. In Laurie Bailey he finally found 'a practical and pragmatic woman who would manage his household without too much artistic temperament.'[36] It was a happy marriage, as Laurie later recalled:

> They were good years we had together. The three of us.
> I had sensed that second marriage had been full of love,
> and no question but that Christine meant the world
> to both of them. Though ours would be a relationship
> uniquely our own, I wanted it to reflect the spirit at
> least, of the Boss-Aideen-Christine union. In large
> measure I believe it did.[37]

They had met after Laurie mistook Arthur for his brother, a common occurrence in his later life. As a result of his role as the public face of the Italian Swiss Colony winery, Arthur became widely known to the public as the 'TV wine announcer Arthur Shields – lookalike brother of actor Barry Fitzgerald'.[38] After a career collaborating with some of the world's greatest dramatists, actors and filmmakers, Arthur appeared resigned to the absurdity of being recognised as 'the man in the wine ad'.[39]

His health failing, Barry Fitzgerald returned to Ireland, where he died in 1961. Ill-health ended Arthur's career the following year.

Arthur Shields died in Santa Barbara, California, on 27 April 1970. Despite his ambivalence about the Irish Republic he had once fought for, Arthur was buried as a patriot in Dublin. His coffin was draped with a Tricolour and escorted to St Patrick's Cathedral by members of the Dublin Brigade of the Old IRA, and the customary shots were fired over his grave by the Defence Forces.[40] He shares a plot with Barry in Deansgrange Cemetery. Although she was buried in California, in Holy Cross Cemetery in Culver City, Aideen O'Connor is not quite alone: her grave lies close to another Hollywood Irish star, the Abbey Theatre veteran Sara Allgood, who was Christine's godmother.[41]

Arthur Shields on the set of an Italian Swiss Colony television commercial, c. 1958. He became a familiar face in California due to his role as spokesman for the wine producers (HL, T13/B/472).

Arthur's decision to be buried in Ireland, Ernest Blythe asserted, 'shows that the fire which burned in him in 1916 was never quenched'.[42] During his final years, Arthur had made several short trips home, where he encountered some ghosts from 1916. At Barry's burial at Deansgrange he spotted Helena Molony at the cemetery gates: 'He made the others wait while she, old and partly crippled, made her way to the graveside.'[43] The times were changing, if glacially: Arthur had been moved to see that there were 'more Catholics in the church than Protestants' at Barry's funeral service at St Patrick's Cathedral. It is tempting to read Arthur's life as a quiet act of dissent. Before his death he received an invitation to Áras an Uachtaráin. He was 'not at all impressed', he reported to Laurie, by his meeting with de Valera: 'God bless us, but he has a lot to answer for.'[44]

* * *
* *
* *
* *

Chapter 21

Remembered for ever:

Memory

Lost revolution? Helena Molony, with 1916 medals (NPA, R24078).

Who wouldn't like to die in the Spring . . .

—From a letter by Crawford Neil, quoted by F. R. Higgins in the preface to

Happy Island: Child Poems (1916)

Dry bones that dream are bitter.

—W. B. Yeats, *The Dreaming of the Bones* (1919)

How did the Abbey's rebels remember their involvement in 1916? How conscious were they that 1916 was, during their own lifetimes, being reshaped in collective memory? To what extent were their recollections of 1916 intended to shape the Rising's legacy?

A remarkable wealth of sources provides answers to these questions, which enable us to understand how the meaning of 1916 evolved over time. In the decades after the Rising, each of the Abbey's surviving rebels recorded accounts of their involvement in it. The most important repository of revolutionary memory, as we have seen, is the Military Service Pensions collection, a product of the government's decision to compensate veterans under a series of acts passed between 1923 and 1953.[1] A successful application for a military pension resulted not only in a detailed account of a veteran's revolutionary actions but also in a record of other aspects of their livelihood until their death. Although the term 'active service' was never clearly defined, applicants were given an incentive to remember those actions that might constitute it. Peadar Kearney, for example, insisted that his position as a prison censor was an intelligence role that required him to be armed.

A parallel but separate project, the Bureau of Military History was established by the state 'to assemble and co-ordinate material to form the basis for the compilation of the history of the movement for Independence'.[2] Those who contributed statements (or refused to) had many motives, but most of those who did felt it was important to record the small role they had played in the most significant event of their lives. Although only Helena Molony of the Abbey rebels submitted a witness statement to the Bureau, the collection also includes correspondence from Máire Nic Shiubhlaigh and hundreds of references (other people's memories) to them. This source reflects some of the problems of retrospective oral evidence, such as subjectivity, Civil War animosities and the accumulation of subsequent information. The investigating officer who recorded Helena's statement, for example, noted that her 'memory is not too good. I am of the opinion that she failed to remember many of the activities in which she took part and that in this respect her statement does not do her justice.' She described her first (oral) attempt at a statement (recorded verbatim in March 1949) as 'unintelligible gabble', and so rewrote and resubmitted her testimony the following May.[3]

These archives are supplemented by unofficial repositories of revolutionary memory. In the 1930s and 40s, for example, Ernie O'Malley 'criss-crossed Ireland in his old Ford, driving up boreens and searching out old companions in order to record, and in a sense relive, the glory days of the revolution'.[4] His voluminous (and nearly illegible) notebooks detail interviews with some 450 Volunteers. In contrast to the Bureau, O'Malley's project was motivated more by post-revolutionary malaise than by the need for material for constructing the state's foundational narrative. Describing his life as 'broken', O'Malley was stoical about the outcome of his revolution: 'I had given allegiance to a certain ideal of freedom as personified by the Irish Republic. It had not been realised except in the mind.'[5] This may have resulted in 'a less sanitized and more embittered memory': although Bob Price's love for a 'half one' was recorded in the Bureau, it was O'Malley's notebooks that made clear its consequences.[6]

Several of the rebels also wrote their own stories. *The Splendid Years: Recollections of Máire Nic Shiubhlaigh*, published by James Duffy in 1955, was the

Abbey 52

Shields contd: times they were. And those things are
bound to affect the people. They affected our "pit
audience" if you like to call it that. Its not said
in any way of daring on. Those were the real people.
Ye, we had other things too I can remember very definitely.
For instance, I can remember that there were certain
people who were "on the run" from the British. We had
Michael Collins.

Gans: Was he the one who starved to death ?

Shields: no, no, that was Terence McSweeney. But
Michael Collins, during the real bad trouble there, would
come into the Theatre sometimes, but nobody ever found
him there, because there were so many people around, who,
when anything strange would happen outside, or anybody
suspicious looking would come along; he could always
get out. There were always people round about to help
him out. Robinson, in his book, talks about the Printing
Press on which the Irish Proclamation was printed,
and he says there is a rumour that it was hidden in the

Like many veterans, Arthur did
not discuss his involvement in the
Rising until late in life. Transcript
of a press interview with Arthur
Shields, c. 1962 (HL, T13/A/392).

Abbey 53 :

Shields contd: Abbey at one time; well I know very
well it was, because I was the one who took it in.
It was a small little hand-press, and of course, it would
have been a great find for the British. It was brought
in by a woman - Miss Helena Maloney - who was played at
the Theatre, and was connected with the movement. She
told me that they had had it in different places, and
these places were constantly being raided - could we
do something with it ? So I was able to hide it down
underneath the stage, among all the old bits of scenery.
It was quite a small thing. And there it lay for a long
time. I was sometimes a bit nervous about it being
down there, when certain people would come in and walk
around the place. But finally she came along with
some other people with a hand-cart one night - late
at night and she said she'd found a regular plce. But
it was with us for, I suppose, nine months, or a year.,
underneath our stage. Most of the people didn't know
about it.

Gans: This is exactly what I mean in reference to the
Irish audience, what I've been trying to get. We had
a wonderful play here on our President that died -

product of a collaboration between Máire and her nephew Edward Kenny. Although written by Peadar Kearney's nephew Séamus de Búrca, *The Soldier's Song: The Story of Peadar Kearney*, published in 1957, also incorporates Peadar's autobiographical reminiscences. Arthur Shields began recording his own story in the late 1960s, drawing on a vast archive of diaries, scrapbooks, correspondence, documents and photos to do so. His papers include hundreds of pages of autobiographical and biographical material (much of it compiled by his wife Laurie after his death). Compared with the state projects, which established guidelines as to what and when should be remembered, autobiography allowed veterans greater latitude in how they remembered their stories, although it was shaped by other pressures, such as family participation.

The Abbey rebels' memories of 1916 also reside in a wealth of letters, reminiscences, interviews and other first-person accounts. Even in the case of Seán Connolly, who could leave no record of his own involvement in 1916, memory was generated by comrades, siblings and descendants. In contrast, veterans whose families did not actively record or preserve their memories have left behind few traces of their lives. Prior to the publication of the Military Service Pensions collection, for example, no first-person testimony was known to exist for Barney Murphy or Ellen Bushell.

What patterns can be discerned from this abundance of memory? A striking feature of the rebels' accounts is the disparity between the importance they attach to remembering their lives before and after the Rising. *The Splendid Years*, for example, comes to an abrupt end as Máire is escorted from Jacob's factory by a polite British officer at the general surrender:

> We walked down the roadway and turned the corner into Camden Street. It was a route I had taken many times through the years. I cannot remember what we talked about – if we talked at all, for there did not seem very much to say. I felt confused and disappointed. All at once, I had begun to feel very tired … Everything looked strange, even the street was different. It was though I had never seen it before. Despite what was going on inside, Jacob's looked very dark, very empty. Dublin seemed unnaturally still.[7]

Although Helena Molony played a significant role in the events of 1917–23, her sixty-page witness statement relegates events after 1916 to a three-page postscript. Similarly, most of de Búrca's biography of Peadar Kearney is devoted to his life before Easter, 1916. In Arthur Shields's voluminous papers there is almost no mention of politics after Easter Week. Although he expressed pride 'that the work of our theatre helped to create our own State', there is no explanation of why he left the republican movement.[8] This chapter seeks to assess not the accuracy of the Abbey rebels' memory of 1916 but rather its meaning.

Why, for example, do their accounts focus on the years before 1916? In them, the Rising, rather than marking the beginning of the story of the new Ireland – as it does in many nationalist histories, as well as in the best-known revolutionary memoirs, by such figures as Tom Barry – marks the end of an era. The shadow cast by the Civil War offers one explanation. By pragmatically discouraging witnesses from discussing events after the Truce, the Bureau of Military History merely reflected a broader reluctance to discuss this divisive period. Although his biography spans Peadar Kearney's life, de Búrca devotes less than one page to Peadar's reminiscences of the 'days of fratricidal strife'.[9] However, this does not explain the rebels' reticence about the War of Independence, which may stem, in part, from the fact that this was an era when violence was both endured and inflicted.

Helena Molony's anxiety about remembering violence is evident from her shifting accounts of the killing of Constable James O'Brien. In an interview recorded by a radical journalist in 1935, Helena emphasised both the rebels' restraint and the momentous impact of their actions:

> They reached the gate of the Castle, and Sean Connolly, who was in command ordered the policeman on duty to stand aside. He refused. Connolly insisted and warned him, presenting the revolver. But this blind tool of imperialism could not believe that the Irish people were demanding their own. Connolly shot him dead, and that bullet destroyed the status quo in Ireland.[10]

However, in her witness statement – recorded for the Bureau of Military History fifteen years later, in the knowledge that it would remain confidential until her death – Helena describes, more sympathetically, a hastier, less considered killing (a version that accords with that of the surviving policeman she mentions in her account):

> When Connolly went to go past him, the Sergeant put out his arm; and Connolly shot him dead ... When I saw Connolly draw his revolver, I drew my own. Across the road, there was a policeman with papers. He got away, thank God. I did not like to think of the policeman dead ... I think the policeman at the gate was killed instantly, because they were quite close. The police did not think the Citizen Army were serious.[11]

When we analyse memory, what is omitted may be as significant as what is included. Despite the shadow (James) Crawford Neil's violent death cast over her family, Máire Nic Shiubhlaigh did not mention it in her memoir. Neil, an actor with the Theatre of Ireland and a popular librarian at the National Library, had turned his life around before the Rising. A dissolute Presbyterian poet, he renounced alcohol and converted to Catholicism after he fell in love with Máire's sister Gypsy. A pacifist republican, he refused to fight at Easter but joined Francis Sheehy Skeffington in trying to avert public looting. On the Tuesday of Easter Week he was shot in the spine, possibly by a looter, in Liffey Street, close to Walker's printing business. When Gypsy eventually found Crawford, lying paralysed in Jervis Street Hospital, the chaplain refused her request to marry them: 'He said he would not perform a wedding where the bride would soon be a widow. Gyp never forgot those words.' He died in her arms two weeks later, on 10 May. His omission from Máire's memoir was not the result of indifference: she published his first, and final, collection of poetry, *Happy Island: Child Poems*, under her own imprint three months after the Rising. The *Irish Times* judged it the work of 'a writer of great promise'.[12] Although Neil's death was noted by contemporary sources, it did not resurface as a narrative told in public until recorded by Máire's great-nephew, Dave Kenny, almost a century later. This parallels a wider silence, only now dissipating, about the civilian dead of Easter Week.

Another act of violence, the execution of the leaders, with whom the Abbey's rebels were intimate, may also account for their reluctance to dwell on events after 1916. Helena Molony's witness statement hints at the traumatic impact of the executions: James Connolly 'was dragged out, unable to stand, and murdered. After that life seemed to come to an end for me.'[13]

The effect of the Easter Rising on the republican movement may also be a factor. Prior to 1916, the Abbey's rebels could view themselves as insiders, never far from the centre of action. As Peadar Kearney put it: 'To be admitted into that magic circle, to be one of the chosen company with whom Tom [Clarke] discoursed without restraint, was something to be worthy of, and a memory to be proud of.'[14] Helena Molony was trusted by the Military Council. Máire Nic Shiubhlaigh spent Easter Sunday at Éamonn Ceannt's house. Barney Murphy was a friend of Tom Clarke and Seán Mac Diarmada.[15] After 1916, they found themselves at the edge of a more popular movement, one with a different leadership, with their role reduced from actors on the main stage to bit players. This was keenly felt, if not necessarily articulated, by the women activists, who played a more significant role before 1916. In her detailed witness statement, Helena made no mention of her extensive efforts to secure representation for women within the leadership of Sinn Féin – efforts which remained forgotten until discovered by feminist historians half a century later.[16]

Post-Rising marginalisation was accompanied by other disappointments. Although a perception that many did well out of 1916 would later emerge, none of the Abbey's rebels benefited materially – leaving aside their modest pensions – from their activism, while several of them suffered considerably as a result of it. Barney Murphy's penury, as we have seen, made remembering 1916 a necessity for him, and most of the others endured poverty in later life. Financial considerations aside, the need to remember was bound up with anxiety about being forgotten, although this did not mean that remembering was a straightforward impulse. Submitting her statement to the Bureau of Military History, Helena Molony was torn between a desire to place on record her story and a reticence shared by many veterans. Helena admitted to the investigating officer, Jane Kissane, to being teased by her partner, Evelyn O'Brien: 'It is Miss Kissane who ought to get a special medal as decoration for dragging information out of a lot of unwilling clams like you all. I doubt if any of you were out in the rebellion at all.'[17]

The Splendid Years, Máire Nic Shiubhlaigh's attempt to write herself back into the 'story of the Irish National Theatre' (her memoir's subtitle), originated in a process of remembering that began with a lecture to women graduates at University College, Galway, in 1947. Máire's fading reputation had not been enhanced by her clash with Yeats, who later overlooked her in his famous Nobel speech of 1923 (which identified her rivals, Sarah Allgood and Máire O'Neill, as the 'players of genius' that made the Abbey a success).[18] A central concern of Máire's narrative was to present her departure as the result of a conscious decision to give priority to politics over art.[19] If we judge from the extent to which her memoir is now cited, she did succeed in writing herself back into the historical record (even if she had yet to escape Yeats's shadow by 1966).

The theme of unrewarded service frequently recurs in the Abbey rebels' narratives. The preface to *The Splendid Years* (written by Máire's nephew Edward Kenny) describes her memoir as 'a story of hard work, for little material reward; of a constant striving for recognition.' In his foreword Padraic Colum notes that 'the young men and women who made these years splendid' gave to and 'got nothing from the Dublin of those days'.[20]

Peadar Kearney recounted how his service impaired his health and reduced his family to charity:

> Twice in my life I left my home never to return to it.
> Books, manuscripts, prints, furniture lost. Personal
> mementoes, autographs of Tom Clarke, Sean McDermott
> and the rest, all destroyed. There was nothing left.[21]

Strikingly, though, rather than Peadar's poverty and obscurity (which de Búrca's narrative juxtaposes with the fame of his ballads) being suppressed out of shame, they became the biography's central themes. De Búrca also drew attention to the destitution of Paddy Heeney, the composer of the national anthem, who was buried in an unmarked grave, and that of such revolutionaries as Phil Shanahan, who fell into poverty after independence. Indeed, the biography proved so successful in foregrounding these themes that they have come to dominate popular memory of Peadar Kearney.[22]

The Soldier's Song attributed Peadar's poverty to unemployment, to his refusal to compromise his trade union principles and to ill-health. It does not record how his prospects had been damaged by the death of Michael Collins. Despite the resentment it must have provoked, Peadar's lengthy legal case against the Free State does not feature in the more stoical narrative crafted by the book: 'There can be no doubt that if Peadar had been a self-seeking man his later life would have been spent in comparative luxury', de Búrca observes. 'But he was content with his humble lot'. In reality Peadar was less sanguine about his fate, as de Búrca noted privately: 'Peadar often said to me: "I got little out of the Soldier's Song, not even fame."'[23] His biography, moreover, contrasts his plight with those (including, presumably, de Valera) who had so clearly benefited from 1916: 'He was never bitter about his lot, which was often hard, though he was bitter against certain old comrades who had turned into self-seeking politicians.'[24]

For Peadar, as for many of his generation, his concern was not merely with being forgotten but with how he would be remembered. The concept of 'postmemory' – a term used to describe how some 'who agonised over how certain domineering events, or causes to which they were deeply devoted, would be perceived by later generations and utilised their privileged position as witnesses of history to assume the role of custodians of memory' – is a useful one.[25] The anxiety experienced by Peadar, a zealous republican who supported the Treaty, about the political triumph of the Civil War's military losers is evident both from de Valera's conspicuous absence from his narrative and from his passionate defence of Collins. 'It is easy for the younger generation to question our motives,' he wrote. 'The generation that will see the Republic will never appreciate the men who gave their all.'[26]

Collectively, these narratives form part of a post-revolutionary literature of disillusionment, encompassing writers such as Seán O'Casey and veterans such as P. S. O'Hegarty, which emerged in the 1930s (alongside a more dominant triumphalist, statist narrative of 1916). From this essentially nostalgic vantage point, the optimism of the 'pre-revolution' was framed by the disappointments that followed.[27] Peadar Kearney's description of republicanism as 'a splendid movement destroyed by scheming politicians' makes it clear that for him, as for Máire Nic Shiubhlaigh, the splendid years lay in the past.[28] Writing to Máire in 1950, Padraic Colum recalled 'days that now seem all summer and poetry'.[29] On learning of Máire's final illness, Colum wrote to her sister Gypsy, recalling 'the lovely times in High Street when we were young and hopeful and enthusiastic'.[30] In her memoir, Máire described the Dublin of her youth (when republicans had rarely been more marginalised) as a city 'full of earnest young people, all of them anxious to do something useful for Ireland'. As Diarmaid Ferriter has observed, this was 'a convenient transference of the personal to the general, but also selective; what were difficult and contested years (reflected in her own theatre career and the intrusion of politics) became instead The Splendid Years.'[31]

The Abbey's rebels formed part of a generation for whom history – particularly historical narratives expressed through drama, literature and biography – was indistinguishable from politics. Peadar Kearney, as we have seen, presented his radicalisation as an epiphany triggered by a sudden understanding of Ireland's history.[32] The Abbey's rebels were radicalised through organisations, such as Inghinidhe na hÉireann and the Fenians, that devoted themselves to sustaining a commemorative political culture. In particular, remembering 1798 had been crucial to imagining 1916. In the light of this, to what extent did their own narratives of insurrection reflect an ideological intent?

The individual whose memory of 1916 most clearly reflected a critique of contemporary society was Helena Molony. Despite her gendered revolutionary service, she emphasised her role as a combatant when applying for a military pension.[33] This was clearly a response to the state's unwillingness to accept that women had fought as soldiers, which in turn reflected its ideologically driven reluctance to acknowledge women's equality as citizens. Although the Army Pensions Act (1923) allowed for pensions to be awarded to individuals who served with the Irish Citizen Army (inadvertently including women), service with Cumann na mBan was not deemed eligible until 1932. However, when Margaret Skinnider – who had been shot three times as she led men in battle during the rebellion – applied on the basis of her injuries, the pensions board ruled that 'the definition of "wound" … only contemplates the masculine gender'. The Treasury solicitor agreed, in a revealingly tortuous formulation: 'the Army Pensions Act is only applicable to soldiers as generally understood in the masculine gender'.[34]

Like Máire, Helena objected to the pension board's refusal to classify much of her revolutionary activism as military service:

Women were recruited into the Citizen Army on the same terms as men. They were appointed to the duties most suitable to them – as were men – and these duties fell naturally into dealing with Commissariat, Intelligence, First Aid and advanced Medical Aid, but their duties were not confined to these.[35]

Helena was 'not primarily concerned with a pension', she told the assessors, 'but with the recognition of women's services rendered to the Republic.'[36] Ill-health, and probably poverty, compelled her to drop these objections, but she continued to criticise the board's policy:

When I was presiding at a meeting in O'Connell St ... (under Army orders) one woman was shot dead, and a boy standing beside me shot through his head, and six others wounded. It is difficult for the ordinary person to understand how such things are not classified as 'military service'. In any regular Army in any civilized country, I never heard of such no[n]-combatants as Army Service Corps, or Intelligence Dept. – being classified as non-Military.[37]

In her submission to the Bureau of Military History fifteen years later, Helena continued to emphasise her military role: 'I had my own revolver and ammunition', she informed them (and posterity): even 'before the Russian Army had women soldiers, the Citizen Army had them'.[38]

Rejecting the Pearsean interpretation of 1916 as a conscious blood sacrifice, Helena attributed the shortcomings of independence to the ideological limitations of the movement that won it. She reflected in 1935 that

perhaps the time was not ripe for success. Our people had not a widespread economic knowledge to cope with social evils. I should have hated to see Padraic Pearse as President of an Irish Republic if the misery and wretchedness of the tenements had still gone on.[39]

Cover of *The History of the Irish Citizen Army* (1943), written by socialist historian R. M. Fox (NLI). An English-born factory worker, and Ruskin College graduate, Fox (1891–1916) was a lifelong labour activist.

In her final years, whether because of her own decline or the conservatism of Irish society, Helena ceased to articulate a radical interpretation of 1916, calling instead for a revival of spiritual values. Her militant friends attributed this, like her rapprochement with de Valera, to her mental frailty: 'she seemed to lose the revolutionary spirit,' Máire Comerford recalled sadly. 'She didn't seem to appreciate what was going on'.[40]

Peadar Kearney's remembering of 1916 makes clear his disappointment at the failure to achieve both Irish unity and the Republic. He articulated a strong sense of class-consciousness, but without a socialist analysis. Like Helena, he was conscious of his generation's ideological limitations:

> We lived as revolutionists in a period of revolution. We had no thought of the morrow. As far as we were concerned, we were simply units in a movement. A fair number of the rank and file were separatists pure and simple, with no idea of economics or the science of politics as such. When the Irish people had the free choice of their own representatives in their own parliament in their own country, our war was ended. Naturally, we hoped it would be a republic.[41]

Arthur Shields's remembering of 1916 can also be seen as a subtle critique of independence. Although the Green Room of his Hollywood home was 'full of souvenirs of the Abbey and of Dublin during the Rising', he rarely discussed his involvement in the Rising.[42] His recollection (recorded by his wife) of his father's disappointment at his decision to join the Volunteers indicates a more nuanced memory of 1916 than those of *The Splendid Years* and *The Soldier's Song*.[43] It is striking also how his memories were often framed by a sense of his otherness. He recalled, for example, how his efforts to remain sane during his political imprisonment by reciting lines from plays were misinterpreted by the old republican in the cell next to his: 'Ah, aren't you the great one for praying, though. It's night and day you never stop!'[44] In India (where he was filming *The River*) when it was proclaimed a republic, Arthur proudly wore his 1916 medal; but, he told the *Irish Press*, when asked by local people he was unable to translate its inscription into English.[45] While reflecting a genuine sense of difference he experienced during the revolution, these ostensibly jocular or self-deprecating anecdotes also represent a retrospective projection of his disillusionment with its legacy. Arthur regarded his subsequent departure from Ireland as being bound up with this failure of revolution, attributing his decision to leave the Abbey to 'a narrow nationalism alien to the spirit of the Rising'.[46]

While the Abbey's rebels exercised varying degrees of influence over their memories of rebellion, the impact of their narratives was largely beyond their control. Most obviously, their reception was conditioned by the changing political context. The transmission (and recycling) of their memories was also shaped, as the biography *The Soldier's Song* demonstrates, by family members. Long before the book's publication, Peadar Kearney's admirers had articulated its principal themes. In 1928, for example, the Dublin historian J. W. Hammond prefaced an essay on him with a quotation attributed to Thomas à Kempis: 'Others shall be magnified in the mouths of men, and on you no one shall bestow a word. Such and such an office shall be conferred on others, but you shall be passed by.' Hammond continued:

> Of the bitterness of life he has quaffed full cup, of the
> sweets he has tasted little. Many who served Ireland
> have been more fortunate. But he bears ill-will towards
> no man. Malice and envy are foreign to his nature, and
> so is egotism … Modest and unobtrusive – an humble

Although reticent about his own role in 1916, Arthur Shields's stage and film career frequently saw him re-enact the Rising (LL, John Ford MSS/16/12). Arthur's reflection can (probably) be seen here, on the set of *The Plough and the Stars* (1936), to the right of John Ford.

> Cincinnatus back at the plough ... this soldier-poet of the new Ireland finds that peace within which the world without cannot give. It is the duty of the nation to ensure that that peace be not fretted by anxiety.[47]

Although *The Soldier's Song* reiterated similar themes three decades later, they were more sympathetically received in the late 1950s. While some reviewers presented Peadar Kearney as an unproblematic exemplar of 'patriotic fervour', most identified the biography's motifs.[48] 'Peadar Kearney contributed more than his share to the National Revolution, and, unlike many others, he got very little out of it', Séamus G. O'Kelly observed: he 'died as he had lived, a poor man.'[49] Both Peadar Kearney and Paddy Heeney, R. M. Fox declared, 'were poor men and hardworking men, who lived lives of self-sacrifice'.[50] Peadar, another reviewer noted, 'made little or nothing from his many poetic works and ... gained equally little from a lifetime of service devoted to the cause of Irish freedom.' The anonymity and neglect endured by Peadar (to which family members, including Brendan Behan, also drew public attention) were noted by many reviewers.

Clearly, the theme of *The Soldier's Song* – unrewarded service – had struck a chord. Its disillusioned subtext was articulated most explicitly by the *Irish Times*, a newspaper that had never sympathised with the state's republican orthodoxy:

> Young people growing up in Ireland at the moment
> cannot be blamed for thinking that some time in
> the early twenties a few hundred men carried out a
> rebellion, were partly successful, took over 26 counties,
> have been running the country ever since, and now
> look on it more or less as their private property. This
> view is not altogether accurate. Quite a few took part
> in the revolution of 1916–23, who sought nothing for
> themselves and who received nothing in return for their
> fight except poverty, derision and broken lives. Such a
> man was Peadar Kearney, the Dublin house painter who
> composed the 'Soldier's Song'.[51]

Here was a narrative of 1916 that chimed with the malaise of the
1950s, reflecting growing resentment of how the Rising's legacy had been
exploited by a political elite for over two generations.

Some sense of how the meaning of 1916 was shifting for a younger
generation can be discerned from a letter sent to Séamus de Búrca about
his book from the Grand-Hôtel du Cap-Ferrat in Monte Carlo by his niece's
husband, the BBC broadcaster Éamonn Andrews:

> I had a strange surge of reactions in the reading of it.
> Perhaps it was because it lay so strangely against a
> foreign background of sunshine and blue sky ... I was
> deeply moved by the ending. Odd is it not that to have
> read it in England would have put me closer to it? Of
> course we realise again the awful apathy that greeted
> the revolution. We are I'm afraid no different from other
> nations ... This is one reason it's wrong to have hate
> against whole nations ... It's only sad that it takes war to
> stimulate heroes.

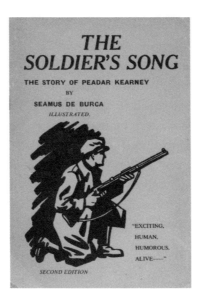

Originally published in 1957, the theme of post-revolutionary disappointment implicit in Séamus de Búrca's biography of Peadar Kearney struck a chord during a period of stagnation.

Andrews's further observations about how patriotism can become 'corrupted to excessive nationalism and love of country to bigotry' are particularly striking, as these ideas are entirely absent from the book's old-fashioned Gaelicist Fenian narrative. As with the *Irish Times* review, there is a sense in Andrews's letter that the story – both Peadar's and the state's – has not ended as it should:

> Did Peadar end his days a saddened man? Was he
> disillusioned by the small men who hide their smallness
> behind the loud talk of wordy patriotism or those who
> think a language is to make a nation small instead of big?[52]

The publication of *The Soldier's Song* also highlights the importance of family networks in constructing, disseminating, preserving and reviving the rebels' stories: de Búrca, Peadar's nephew, wrote and published the biography. He also kept it in print, subsidising, publishing and distributing a second edition. Máire Nic Shiubhlaigh would not have recorded her memoirs, or found a publisher, without her nephew Edward Kenny (whose son, Dave, is preparing a new edition for publication). The biographical treatment, interviews and reminiscences among Arthur Shields's papers were written, recorded or transcribed and – most importantly – preserved by his wife Laurie. Their efforts were not always appreciated. In the 1970s, when the Troubles had diminished the public appetite for remembering 1916, Laurie Shields failed to persuade Gill & Macmillan to publish Arthur's biography.[53] During the same period, de Búrca also failed to publish a third edition of The Soldier's Song.

These books represented just the most visible facet of a broader familial remembering. Working with such like-minded organisations as the Old Dublin Society, Séamus de Búrca solicited reminiscences of Peadar Kearney, published his letters, erected plaques to his memory and ensured that they were maintained by (or, when necessary, protected from) Dublin Corporation. He organised book launches, fund-raising campaigns, parades and other commemorative events; embarked on international lecture tours; presented copies of his biography to writers, diplomats and politicians; secured interviews with journalists; chastised the press, when necessary, for inattention to Peadar's memory; provided sources and interviews to scholars; secured the preservation of papers and recordings in archives; placed books in libraries; donated artefacts to museums and galleries; policed copyright infringements; and rebuked those who slighted the family name. An unfortunate lecturer at the Royal Irish Academy of Music who misattributed the authorship of the national anthem was met with a demand for 'an apology to the sons of Peadar Kearney and the nephews of Peadar Kearney of whom I am one. You have impugned the memory of Patrick Heeney.'[54] Remembering, for some, was an act of love. Laurie Shields sought to stitch the memory of her husband into the fabric of history by arranging interviews with academics, urging scholars to study her husband's life, encouraging writers to place biographical features with such magazines as Life, and archiving his memories.[55]

In Peadar Kearney's case, such efforts formed part of a tradition of familial commemoration which is continued by a fourth generation. In 2013 family members participated in the inauguration of an annual tribute at Peadar's grave, part of a commemorative ceremony honouring 'all who served' in Easter Week, involving Government ministers, British diplomats, the French embassy and the Defence Forces.[56] For some relatives, the family legacy represented both cultural capital and a psychological burden. As Marianne Hirsch has noted, 'to grow up with overwhelming inherited memories, to be dominated by narratives that preceded one's birth or one's consciousness, is to risk having one's own life stories displaced, even evacuated, by our ancestors.'[57] While the rebels' achievements and status could be identified with, and their artefacts and papers auctioned to museums and American libraries, relatives also inherited their disappointments and unfulfilled hopes. Edward Kenny (whose memoir fell out of print after a dispute with the publisher) felt keenly his failure to restore the family name to prominence.[58]

It is not surprising that the rebels' memories of 1916 changed over time. Memory is a social process which shapes our collective understanding of the past's significance. Remembering, particularly of traumatic moments, is also bound up with the construction of social identities.[59] States remember their origins in ways that reflect their contemporary needs, as does society. The Abbey rebels' disappointed memories reflected, in part, 'the sharply conservative aftermath of the revolution, when nascent ideas of certain kinds of liberation were aggressively subordinated to the national project of restabilization and clericalization'.[60] But they also stemmed from the rebels' unrepresentativeness. Radical, urban revolutionaries, they differed in sensibility from the younger, rural and more conservative foot-soldiers of the War of Independence, won over to republicanism as a mass movement. They differed also from more representative members of their own revolutionary generation, such as de Valera, whose post-1916 lives were not framed by disappointment. They helped to light the touch-paper, but exerted little influence over what followed.

Chapter 22

Speaking for ever:

Commemoration

O wise men, riddle me this:
what if the dream come true?
What if the dream come true?
and if millions unborn shall dwell
In the house that I shaped in my heart,
the noble house of my thought?

—Patrick Pearse, 'The Fool', 1916

What did we get for it? A country, if you'd believe
them. Some of our johnnies in the top jobs instead
of a few Englishmen ... What was it for? The whole
thing was a cod.

—Michael Moran, in John McGahern's *Amongst Women* (1990)

The first anniversary of the Easter Rising was marked by a riot. Despite a
week-long ban on assemblies likely to 'promote disaffection', and a heavy
security presence, expectant Dubliners thronged Sackville Street on Easter
Monday, waiting for something to happen. The more defiant among
the crowd wore Tricolour ribbons or black armbands. At noon, they were
rewarded by the sight of a man walking across the parapet of the burnt-
out GPO to raise the Tricolour at half-mast. According to the *Irish Times*, this
occasioned 'an outburst of cheering, and various other demonstrations of
approval on a wide scale'.[1] By late afternoon, as 'the lower element seeking
to let itself loose in honour of Easter Week' began hurling rubble (of which
there was plenty to hand) at the police, the crowd moved on to other parts
of the city.

     The guiding spirit behind the melee was Helena Molony. Working
with other militants ('Cumann na mBan, the Plunkett girls and boys,
well-known extremists'), she orchestrated a series of demonstrations
throughout the city. Flags were flown from each of the rebel garrisons,
facsimiles of the Proclamation – printed by Máire Nic Shiubhlaigh's father,
Matthew – were posted throughout town, and a massive banner proclaiming
James Connolly Murdered – May 12th, 1916 was defiantly unfurled from the roof
of Liberty Hall by Helena and her friends, who prolonged the protest by
barricading themselves in to the building. Her purpose was to highlight the
Proclamation's support for female suffrage, and to make it clear that 'the
Republic still lives'. The way forward, as Helena saw it, was simple: 'For us,

-42-

paper hidden in one of the house-slippers which I was
wearing.   During our conversation, I held out my foot and
showed it to Mrs. Ginnell.   She leaned over from her corner
and, while talking intimately, got it out of my shoe,
without being seen by the wardress.   Then Sylvia Pankhurst
gave it this journalistic splash in the newspapers.   We
were in Aylesbury Jail until the general release - Christmas
Eve, 1916 - when we came home.

Return to Ireland.   Commemoration of the Rising at Easter, 1917.

After our release, our activities were more or less
routine.   For us, it was only a matter of taking up the gun
again.   That feeling, I should say, found its first
expression at Easter, 1917.   We decided to have a
demonstration to commemorate the rebellion - "The Republic
still lives.   A Republic has been declared, has been
fought for; and is still alive".   We had a lot of
discussions.   There were concerts arranged, but what I was
concerned with most was our decision to beflag all the
positions that had been occupied in the 1916 Rising.   We
intended to run up the flags again in all these positions
and to get out the proclamation, and proclaim it again, and
to try to establish the position that the fight was not
over and that the Republic still lives.   That was very
much left to the extremist group in Liberty Hall, who were
indeed the women, including Jinny Shanahan and Winnie Carney.

We made the flags - three, measuring six feet by four
and a half feet.   There was a very nice sailor from Glasgow
called Morran, who looked at the flagstaff in the G.P.O. and
said: "We could get a flag on that.   I will do it, and
they won't get it off in a hurry".   He did it, along with a

Helena Molony describes her
efforts, not appreciated by all her
comrades, to commemorate the
first anniversary of the Easter
Rising (MAI, BMH WS 391).

343

-43-

Fianna boy, Baby Murray, who is still living and is in the
Detective service, I think.   They actually got this big
tricolour out on the large flagstaff, which was out in a
horizontal position in the front of the G.P.O.   This sailor
managed to get it so far out, that it was out of anyone's
reach, and there was no rope coming in.   This was all done
with deliberation, so that it would not be taken down quickly.
So well was it done that the authorities did not get it down
until six in the evening, and the very thing that we were
playing for happened.   They had a cordon of police - while
some men climbed up to this flag and started to fiddle with
it.   Eventually, they had to saw the flagstaff; and they
had to cordon off the people as the staff was falling.   The
place was crowded.

Madeleine French Mullen and I went to the College of
Surgeons for the purpose of hanging out a flag there.   Our
difficulty was to carry the flag, without being noticed.
Madeleine had a loose tweed coat on her, and, being rather
slim, she wrapped it round and round her.   I was rather
slim too, but had no loose coat.   As we were coming by
Clarendon Street, Madeleine thought she felt the flag
getting loose.   I said: "Hold on.   We will go into the
Church" - Clarendon Street Church.   We went in, and, with
a few safety-pins, we made it secure.   I think it was a
false alarm anyway.   As she was always rheumaticy, she had
a stick, and was walking very slowly.   I said: "Don't
disturb it.   You have only a few paces more to go" -
Clarendon Street is only a short distance from the College
of Surgeons.   Someone, observing her outline, remarked:
"God help her.   Doesn't she look very bad".   I said:
"Madeleine, your reputation is gone forever".   We decided
we would call the flag "Madeleine Eimir".   We could not get
into the College of Surgeons.   We went into a lady's flat
in the house opposite, and put the flag out.   She was one

-44-

of our sympathisers, but I forget her name now. We did not
take the same precautions with that flag. If we succeeded
in putting it out the window, and if it hung for an hour, we
felt it would be all right.

Having decided to post up the proclamation, we got
facsimiles of it made. We got that printed by Walker, the
Tower Press man. I did all the ordering for that. When
Walker was printing the proclamation, he was a bit short of
type, and he came to me. As is well known, the
proclamation of 1916 had been printed in Liberty Hall. In
the subsequent destruction of Liberty Hall, the type had been
all smashed up, and thrown about. Nobody had cleared it
up. I said to Walker: "There may be some type in the
corner here". He came down with his son; and he picked
up a number of letters that he was short of. They were
actually used in the 1917 proclamation. An interesting
point about that is that when Mr. Bouch of the National
Library - he is now dead - was afterwards giving a lecture
on the document of 1916, he came to me, asking me to throw
some light on a copy of the proclamation that, he said,
looked like the one he had. He thought it might be a
forgery. He produced magnifying glasses. What was it but
a reproduction of the 1917 proclamation. He asked: "Why
are some letters exactly the same, while others are totally
different?" I said: "It is a reproduction". I explained
how this miracle occurred - because I had supplied the
letters from the heap to Walker. Mr. Bouch said that there
are far more copies of the 1916 proclamation extant than
the 1917 one. He said: "The copy is more valuable than
the original. We have three copies of the 1917 proclamation
and fifteen of the original".

We had the 1917 proclamation printed in two sizes.
We made a special pot of paste for the smaller ones, which

it was only a matter of taking up the gun again'.[2] As we have seen, she would occupy a lonely position in the revolutionary vanguard. Although the Easter Rising's success as an act of propaganda surpassed the wildest dreams of republicans, the movement's new leadership understood that achieving the Republic – not to mention popular support – would require a more cautious strategy than that pursued in 1916.

Its divisiveness would become perhaps the most salient feature of the commemoration of 1916. Concerned to exercise some control over political events, not least with hundreds of prominent rebels languishing in British prisons, the republican leadership had frustrated Helena's efforts to maximise provocation. Her union colleagues were similarly unenthusiastic about her decision to stage another symbolic act of defiance at Liberty Hall, only partially restored following its shelling by the *Helga*. In her witness statement Helena wrongly attributed their hostility to Larkinite influence: 'We knew we had unsympathetic members in the back, and enemies in the front'.[3] In reality, the union was led by the Connollyites William O'Brien and Tom Foran, who revered their predecessor's memory without desiring to emulate his sacrificial tactics. Participation in the Easter Rising, Helena had discovered, did not necessarily ensure influence over how it would be commemorated: in the decades that followed, the valuable capital represented by its legacy would be devoted to more conservative causes than those advocated by militants like Helena.

Commemoration of Seán Connolly, the only Abbey rebel to die in the Easter Rising, offers one example of 1916's shifting legacy. Yeats, inevitably, had a hand in shaping his memory:

> Who was the first man shot that day?
> The player Connolly,
> Close to the City Hall he died.[4]

Although much poetry commemorating 1916 was no more than doggerel – 'At Dublin Castle Sean Connolly dies | As the Republic's flag o'er the city flies'[5] – Yeats characteristically summoned Connolly's legacy to more ambivalent, and prescient, effect, ending his tribute to him on a troubled note:

> And no man knows what's yet to come
> But Patrick Pearse has said
> In every generation
> Must Ireland's blood be shed.

Rarer than the 1916 version, the Easter 1917 proclamation was commissioned by Helena Molony and printed by Máire Nic Shiubhlaigh's father, Matthew. The misspelling of Ceannt's first name mars an otherwise effective replica, although the claim that type from the original Proclamation was used for the 1917 document has been disputed (JC, 61a/12/1917).

JAMES CONNOLLY MURDERED MAY 12ᵀ 1916

Helena Molony ensured that the first
anniversary of the Easter Rising was
defiantly marked at Liberty Hall (GM)

Although the formulation is understandable – 'the second man shot
that day' is rather less poetic – it was not only Yeats who so casually elided
Constable James O'Brien's place in history. Until recently, Seán Connolly
was often described as 'the first Irish fatality' or 'the first nationalist
killed', indicating how those who died on the wrong side were deprived of
their national and political identity. Other accounts, more tidily, describe
Connolly's unarmed victim as a British soldier.[6]

Along with the executed leaders, Seán was instantly memorialised
through ballads, Mass cards, badges, flags, postcards and other
commemorative relics. This public outpouring of grief in the weeks after the
executions offered the first evidence of the seismic shift that the rebellion
had set in train. But, although heartfelt, this wave of mourning was not
entirely spontaneous. As was the case for the widows of the executed rebels,
Christine Connolly's tragic fate transformed her into a powerful source of
republican propaganda. She can be seen in a remarkable newsreel, standing
thirteenth in line in a queue of widows and bereaved mothers waiting
to purchase Republican Loan Bonds from Michael Collins, a transaction
conducted outside Pearse's school, on the block on which Robert Emmet was
beheaded.[7] Later, she joined republican activists like Máire Nic Shiubhlaigh,
touring Ireland to perform in Sinn Féin fund-raising concerts. After the
revolution, Seán's status, her own persistence and perhaps also her public
support for the Treaty ensured that she and her three children received
comparatively generous state support.[8]

Seán Connolly commemorative postcard (NMI, HE/2007/1/726). Icons and relics of the 1916 dead circulated widely throughout Dublin after the Rising.

Sheet music for 'The Jacket's Green', 'As sung by Mrs Sean Connolly', published by the Gaelic Press, c. 1919. Despite the illustration, Michael Scanlan's ballad concerns an Irish woman whose beloved is serving with Sarsfield's Jacobite forces in the Williamite wars. (NMI, HH/1998/54).

The pious nature of the public mourning orchestrated after the Rising had an additional function. Catholic memorialisation of fallen rebels offered a reassuring way of recalling an event engineered by the IRB, an organisation previously condemned by the Church as anti-clerical, in conjunction with a socialist militia. The most overt example of this process occurred in the pages of the *Catholic Bulletin*, where month after month, year after year, the dead of 1916 were depicted as Catholic martyrs, their fate seamlessly woven into a powerful communal narrative of centuries of Catholic resistance to Protestant oppression.[9] In its obituary of Seán Connolly the *Catholic Bulletin* omitted any reference to his socialist beliefs and his membership of the Irish Citizen Army, describing him as 'a member of the Pioneer Total Abstinence Association and of the Sacred Heart Sodality'.[10] This formed part of a deliberate strategy by the journal to omit references to the Fenian and socialist ideologies that had inspired the Rising. The *Bulletin's* hagiographies 'were highly selective, especially with regard to secular activities. The naming of schools attended or sodalities joined implicitly established religious conformity; sometimes a priest's opinion of the individual underscored personal virtue.'[11] The rebels' purported dying words, as in Seán Connolly's case, were published in a further series of essays (accompanied by photographs of their mourning widows and children) in order to highlight their religious devotion. 'If God takes me He will never forsake you or the children,' Seán reportedly told Christine. 'I am giving my life for a noble cause, and I know that you, dear wife, would not keep me from doing my duty.'[12] Although it was not owned by the Catholic Church, the *Catholic Bulletin* led the way in its sacralisation of Irish republicanism. After 1916, enthusiastic young clergy and – rather more reluctantly – elderly bishops got on with the necessary business of 'baptising the Fenians'. In the political sphere, meanwhile, Seán Connolly's legacy was subsumed within a nationalist rather than socialist tradition. Desiring to honour a 1916 martyr with a local family connection, the Sinn Féin cumann that emerged in Naas named itself after Seán Connolly, and a Sinn Féin hall was named in his honour in Dublin.

Having long outlived the Easter Rising, the Abbey's other rebels were rarely, if ever, commemorated prior to the Abbey Theatre's 1966 ceremony. The partial exception was Peadar Kearney, whose most famous song became an essential part of the Rising's commemoration and, in time, the anthem of the state the rebellion had helped to bring about. Even this song was reconfigured by post-independence ideology. By the 1930s it was not the words written by Peadar – and so fervently embraced by his revolutionary generation – that were heard in public but those of Liam Ó Rinn's post-1916 translation, 'Amhrán na bhFiann', which began to displace the original song due to its popularity at GAA matches. So complete was this process that Peadar's song began to be referred to as the English translation

Oil painting of Peadar Kearney by Maurice F. Cogan, exhibited at the Royal Hibernian Academy in 1937 (NMI, HE/EW/279).

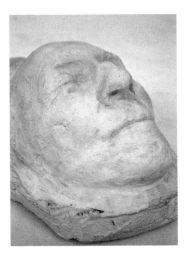

Commissioned by Martin Walton and Seán Farrelly, Peadar's death mask was made by Albert Power RHA, 1942 (NMI, HE/EW/410).

of 'Amhrán na bhFiann'.[13] On the other hand, now that 'the Saxon foe' no longer 'out yonder waits', public unfamiliarity with Peadar Kearney's original words has almost certainly extended his song's shelf life as the national anthem.

Such changes indicate how the event remembered in 1966 was not the one that occurred in 1916. Despite the presence of Helena Molony and one or two other radical veterans at the Abbey Theatre in 1966, their revolutionary world was as distant a memory as was Ireland under British rule. The purpose of the ceremony at the Abbey, however, was not to remember that lost world: commemoration of 1916 in 1966 formed part of a process that subordinated the radicalism of the original event to a conservative vision of revolution. That Yeats's myths, although framing the commemoration, required delicate handling was understood by the politicians and Abbey cognoscenti who orchestrated the ceremony. The state's organising committee had already declared publicly its opposition to 'the inclusion of O'Casey's plays as part of any 1916 Commemorative Programme', while a Government minister had urged his colleagues to steer clear of Yeats's poetry in media interviews. Despite lauding the Abbey's commitment to 'free expression' at the ceremony, the Taoiseach, Seán Lemass, had told the Minister for Posts and Telegraphs to ensure that the state's cultural institutions offered 'suitable' content in 1966: 'This means in particular no O'Casey', Lemass clarified.[14] For its part, the Abbey had its own reasons for reasserting its patriotic credentials at the opening of its new state-funded, modernist building (which replaced the original structure that had to close following a fire in 1951).[15] The memory of the state's past conflicts with the theatre could also be discerned in Lemass's hope that the memorial would remind all 'of the national purpose' that the Abbey's founders had in mind, which he sought to ensure by providing for greater state representation on its board so 'that their advice and guidance might be at the disposal of the directors'.[16]

Although it is easy to criticise such ceremonies, the significance of the Easter Rising, Róisín Higgins argues, has never been 'primarily in its official commemoration'.[17] Other, less visible forms of remembering – such as collective, cultural and family memory – have also shaped its legacy. By the late 1980s, when the state's desire to remember 1916 had reached a low point, the Yeatsian narrative that framed the Abbey's memorial no longer seemed so compelling, prompting Paul Muldoon to wonder mischievously: 'If Yeats had saved his pencil-lead | would certain men have stayed in bed?'[18] Even in 1966, many in the Abbey's audience were sceptical about the ritual in which they were participating. Christine Shields, who delivered a speech on behalf of her father, Arthur, subsequently confided to him her irreverent thoughts:

The Abbey Theatre was closed after a fire on 18 July 1951. Although it moved its productions to the Queen's Theatre, the Abbey did not return to its home until the completion of Michael Scott's unloved building in 1966 (AT).

We ... also met Ernest Blythe ... Horrid man! He refuses
to read or listen to all the criticisms of himself & is
still holding on with the firm grip. Well anyway the
production was pretty bad. Daddy, you would have been
terribly disgusted with the whole bloody mess! 'Recall
the Years' is nothing more than two or three lines from
practically every play the Abbey ever put on & started
with Lady Gregory and Yeats signing the agreement
for the theatre & ended with firemen racing across the
stage ... Well, last nite, the opening, everybody was
there & to tell you the truth, I think everyone was a bit
disappointed. Dev. made the opening speech ... Well,
both Jack and I both were surprised that there was no
party or anything. That's Blythe's doing ... P.S. Seán
Barlow rang the gong at the beginning of the show –
got best reception of all. [19]

Others who attended, or chose to stay away, resented how they,
or members of their family, had been excluded from the memorial. This is
not to set virtuous family memory against opportunistic official memory;
both shape each other. The impetus that 'led to the erection of the 1916
commemorative plaque' had come from Séamus de Búrca's biography of
Peadar Kearney. [20]

'It is not possible fully to assess the implications of the Easter
Rising', Paul Bew has observed, 'unless we know more about what was in
Irish domestic political terms destroyed by it.' [21] Bew was thinking of the
Irish Party, along with Southern Irish unionism the principal political
victim of the rebellion. But the revolutionary world to which the Abbey's
rebels belonged was also swept away by 1916. Their failure to achieve the
Ireland they dreamed of seems all the more poignant given the sacrifices
they made to achieve it. While they fought together for the Republic
proclaimed in 1916, they defined it differently. For Helena Molony, feminist
and socialist ideals were paramount; Máire Nic Shiubhlaigh was committed
to the restoration of Irish; and Peadar Kearney gave priority to complete
separation from Britain and national unity. Like W. B. Yeats, Arthur Shields
had abandoned nationalism, as narrowly understood, coming to define
'freedom in terms of self-expression'. [22] The eclipse of some of these impulses

Helena Molony and Arthur
Shields's daughter, Christine,
at the 1966 commemorative
ceremony (HL, T13/B/352).

by 1966 was as much a consequence of attitudes after independence as of their marginal status before 1916. The fate of the lost Republic demonstrates how the diverse aspirations embodied by the imagined Irish nation were mediated by the realities of religion, class, gender and power in the independent state.

Against this, the mutability of 1916's legacy ensures its permanent relevance. A century later, in a transformed political context, such radical figures as Helen Molony have been largely restored to the historical record and to popular memory.[23] The centenary will see the Easter Rising reinterpreted in ways that are relevant to the present. Rather than simply re-enacting the past, the most successful commemoration, as the revolutionary generation demonstrated through their appropriation of 1798, draws on its energies to imagine alternative futures.[24] Despite the gap between their aspirations and the Irish revolution's outcome, none of the Abbey's rebels regretted their attempt to change the world. More than two decades after 1916, by which time the myth of the Easter Rising as a Christ-like act of blood sacrifice had been firmly established, Helena Molony continued to advocate a different narrative of struggle:

> 1916 has been represented as a gesture of sacrifice. It is said that those in it knew they would be defeated ... I know how we all felt. We thought we were going to do this big thing, to free our country. It was like a religion – something that filled the whole of life. Personal feelings and vanities, wealth, comfort, position – these things did not matter ... Everyone was exalted and caught in the sweep of a great movement. We saw a vision of Ireland, free, pure, happy. We did not realise this vision. But we saw it.[25]

Allen, Nicholas, *Modernism, Ireland and Civil War*, Cambridge: Cambridge University Press, 2009.

Arrington, Lauren, *W. B. Yeats, the Abbey Theatre, Censorship, and the Irish State: Adding the Half-pence to the Pence* (Oxford English Monographs), Oxford: Oxford University Press, 2010.

Coleman, Marie, 'Military service pensions for veterans of the Irish Revolution, 1916–1923', *War in History*, 20/2 (2013), pp 201–21.

Crowe, Catriona (ed.), *Guide to the Military Service (1916–1923) Pensions Collection*, Dublin: Defence Forces, 2012.

de Búrca, Séamus, *The Soldier's Song: The Story of Peadar Kearney*, Dublin: P. J. Bourke, 1957.

Duggan, Penny, *Helena Molony: Actress, Feminist, Nationalist, Socialist and Trade-Unionist* (Working Paper No. 14), Amsterdam: International Institute for Research and Education, 1990.

Ebenezer, Lyn, *Fron-Goch and the Birth of the IRA*, Llanrwst (Clwyd): Gwasg Carreg Gwalch, 2006.

English, Richard, *Irish Freedom: The History of Nationalism in Ireland*, London: Macmillan, 2006.

Ferriter, Diarmaid, *A Nation and Not a Rabble: The Irish Revolution, 1913–1923*, London: Profile Books, 2015.

Finneran, R. J. (ed.), *The Collected Works of W. B. Yeats, Volume I: The Poems*, New York: Scribner, 1997.

Foster, R. F., *Vivid Faces: The Revolutionary Generation in Ireland, 1890–1923*, London: Allen Lane, 2014.

Foster, R. F., *W. B. Yeats: A Life, I: The Apprentice Mage, 1865–1914*, Oxford: Oxford University Press, 1997.

Foster, R. F., *W. B. Yeats: A Life, II: The Arch-Poet, 1915–1939*, Oxford: Oxford University Press, 2003.

Fox, R. M., *Rebel Irishwomen*, Dublin: Talbot Press, 1935.

Foy, Michael T., and Barton, Brian, *The Easter Rising*, Stroud (Glos.): Sutton, 1999.

Frawley, Oona (ed.), *Memory Ireland, Volume 1: History and Modernity*, Syracuse (NY): Syracuse University Press, 2011.

Frazier, Adrian, *Behind the Scenes: Yeats, Horniman, and the Struggle for the Abbey Theatre*, Berkeley (Calif.): University of California Press, 1990.

Frazier, Adrian, *Hollywood Irish: John Ford, Abbey Actors and the Irish Revival in Hollywood*, Dublin: Lilliput Press, 2011.

Grene, Nicholas, *The Politics of Irish Drama: Plays in Context from Boucicault to Friel* (Cambridge Studies in Modern Theatre), Cambridge: Cambridge University Press, 1999.

Hart, Peter, *Mick: The Real Michael Collins*, London: Macmillan, 2005.

Hay, Marnie, *Bulmer Hobson and the Nationalist Movement in Twentieth-Century Ireland*, Manchester: Manchester University Press, 2009.

Higgins, Róisín, *Transforming 1916: Meaning, Memory and the Fiftieth Anniversary of the Easter Rising*, Cork: Cork University Press, 2012.

Kearney, Peadar (ed. Séamus de Búrca), *My Dear Eva: Letters from Ballykinlar Internment Camp, 1921*, Dublin: P. J. Bourke, 1976.

Kiberd, Declan, *Inventing Ireland*, London: Jonathan Cape, 1995.

Lane, Leeann, *Rosamond Jacob: Third Person Singular*, Dublin: UCD Press, 2010.

Levitas, Ben, *The Theatre of Nation: Irish Drama and Cultural Nationalism, 1890–1916*, Oxford: Clarendon Press, 2002.

McBride, Ian (ed.), *History and Memory in Modern Ireland*, Cambridge: Cambridge University Press, 2001.

McCormack, W. J., *Dublin, 1916: The French Connection*, Dublin: Gill & Macmillan, 2012.

McGarry, Fearghal, *Rebels: Voices from the Easter Rising*, Dublin: Penguin Ireland, 2011.

McGarry, Fearghal, *The Rising. Ireland: Easter, 1916*, Oxford: Oxford University Press, 2010.

Mathews, P. J., *Revival: The Abbey Theatre, Sinn Féin, the Gaelic League and the Cooperative Movement*, Cork: Cork University Press, 2003.

Matthews, Ann, *Renegades: Irish Republican Women, 1900–1922*, Cork: Mercier Press, 2010.

Mikhail, E. H. (ed.), *The Abbey Theatre: Interviews and Recollections*, Basingstoke (Hants): Macmillan, 1988.

Moran, James, *Staging the Easter Rising: 1916 as Theatre*, Cork: Cork University Press, 2005.

Moran, James (ed.), *Four Irish Rebel Plays*, Dublin: Irish Academic Press, 2007.

Moran, James, *The Theatre of Seán O'Casey*, London: Methuen Drama, 2013.

Moran, Seán Farrell, *Patrick Pearse and the Politics of Redemption: The Mind of the Easter Rising, 1916*, Washington: Catholic University of America Press, 1994.

Morris, Catherine, *Alice Milligan and the Irish Cultural Revival*, Dublin: Four Courts Press, 2013.

Morris, Ewan, *Our Own Devices: National Symbols and Political Conflict in Twentieth-Century Ireland*, Dublin: Irish Academic Press, 2005.

Murphy, William, *Political Imprisonment and the Irish, 1912–1921*, Oxford: Oxford University Press, 2014.

Murray, Christopher, *Seán O'Casey: Writer at Work: A Biography*, Dublin: Gill & Macmillan, 2004.

Nic Shiubhlaigh, Máire (as told to Edward Kenny), *The Splendid Years: Recollections of Máire Nic Shiubhlaigh's Story of the Irish National Theatre*, Dublin: James Duffy, 1955.

O'Connor, Emmet, *Reds and the Green: Ireland, Russia and the Communist Internationals, 1919–43*, Dublin: UCD Press, 2004.

Pašeta, Senia, *Irish Nationalist Women, 1900–1918*, Cambridge: Cambridge University Press, 2013.

Pilkington, Lionel, *Theatre and the State in Twentieth-Century Ireland: Cultivating the People*, London: Routledge, 2001.

Regan, Nell, 'Helena Molony', in Mary Cullen and Maria Luddy (eds), *Female Activists: Irish Women and Change, 1900–1960*, Dublin: Woodfield Press, 2001.

Reid, Colin, *The Lost Ireland of Stephen Gwynn: Irish Constitutional Nationalism and Cultural Politics, 1864–1950*, Manchester: Manchester University Press, 2011.

Ritschel, Nelson Ó Ceallaigh, 'James Connolly's Under Which Flag, 1916', *New Hibernia Review*, 2/4 (1998), pp 54–68.

Scully, Séamus, 'The Abbey Theatre 1916 plaque', *Dublin Historical Record*, 41/4 (1988), pp 157–66.

Sherry, Ruth, 'The story of the national anthem', *History Ireland*, 4/1 (spring, 1996), pp 39–43.

Steele, Karen, *Women, Press, and Politics during the Irish Revival*, Syracuse (NY): Syracuse University Press, 2007.

Swander, Homer, 'Shields at the Abbey', *Éire-Ireland*, 5/2 (1970), pp 25–41.

Thompson, William Irwin, *The Imagination of an Insurrection: Dublin, Easter 1916: A Study of an Ideological Movement*, Oxford: Oxford University Press, 1967.

Townshend, Charles, *Easter 1916: The Irish Rebellion*, London: Allen Lane, 2005.

Townshend, Charles, *The Republic: The Fight for Irish Independence, 1918–1923*, London: Allen Lane, 2013.

Trotter, Mary, *Modern Irish Theatre*, Cambridge: Polity Books, 2008.

Ward, Margaret, *Unmanageable Revolutionaries: Women and Irish Nationalism*, London: Pluto, 1983.

Welch, Robert, *The Abbey Theatre, 1899–1999: Form and Pressure*, Oxford: Oxford University Press, 1999.

Wills, Clair, *Dublin, 1916: The Siege of the GPO*, London: Profile Books, 2009.

Wren, James, 'Barney Murphy and the Abbey Theatre 1916 plaque', *Dublin Historical Record*, 51/1 (1998), pp 81–3.

Yeates, Pádraig, *A City in Turmoil: Dublin, 1919–21*, Dublin: Gill & Macmillan, 2012.

Yeats, W. B. (ed. John Kelly), *The Collected Letters of W. B. Yeats*, Oxford: Clarendon Press, 2002.

For permission to reproduce photographs, the author
and publisher gratefully acknowledge the following:

Abbey Theatre: vi-vii, 6L, 7, 8, 14, 31, 39, 40, 44, 94,
198, 269, 272, 272, 282, 297T, 299, 352; Allen Library:
102T; Benjamin Iveagh Library, Farmleigh: 271, 276;
Board of Trinity College Dublin: 46, 241R; Cork City
and County Archives Service. Handbill from the Liam
De Roiste collection, ref. MS. U271/K: 254; Dublin
City Gallery The Hugh Lane: 30; Dublin City Libraries
and Archives: 153; Courtesy of George Morrison: 348;
© Getty Images/SSPL: 29; © Getty Images/Hulton
Archive: 58-59; © Getty Images/Topical Press Agency/
Hulton Archive: 77; Irish Traditional Music Archive:
55; Jackie Clarke Museum: 347; James Hardiman
Library, National University of Ireland, Galway:
2, 28, 86, 110, 174-175, 196, 278T, 279, 280L, 282, 283,
284-287, 288, 296, 301, 305, 307-309, 313, 319, 324,
354; John Butler Yeats, Irish, 1839–1922 / Portrait of
Maire Nic Shiubhlaigh (1883–1958), Actress, 1904 /
Oil on canvas / 91 × 71 cm / Photo © National Gallery
of Ireland, NGI.4621: 3; Courtesy of Kilmainham
Gaol Museum, Dublin: 64, 128, 176, 216L, 216R, 219L,
239; The Kobal Collection/REPUBLIC: 315; Laura
McAtackney, kilmainhamgaolgraffiti.com: 180; Lilly
Library, Indiana University, Bloomington, Indiana:
335; © Mary Evans Picture Library: 316; Military
Archives of Ireland/Defence Forces: 67, 69-72, 143-146,
149-150, 152, 200-201, 203, 204, 219R, 223-224, 226,
232-233, 261-262, 263, 343-345; Courtesy of the National
Archives of Ireland: 290, 291, 292, 294-295; Courtesy
of the National Archives UK: 249-253; Courtesy of the
National Library of Ireland: 5, 6R, 10, 19, 21, 22T, 22R,
26, 27, 33, 34-35, 36, 37, 38L, 38R, 41, 50, 73, 74, 76,
82L, 82R, 90, 100, 102B, 106, 118, 120T, 120B, 123-124,
130, 159, 165, 170, 177, 178, 184-185, 186-187, 208, 211,
240, 241L, 255, 256R, 274, 280R, 322, 333; Courtesy of
the National Museum of Ireland: 4, 47, 51, 52, 75, 78,
80, 88, 89, 91, 103, 105, 107, 114L, 114R, 132-133, 138,
148, 162, 214, 243, 256L, 349L, 349R, 350, 351; New
York Public Library: 192, 278B, 297B; Pearse Museum/
OPW: 97; Private collection: 238, 245; Royal Society of
Antiquaries of Ireland: 81.

We also wish to acknowledge the assistance
of The Abbey Theatre 1904 project
(http://blog.oldabbeytheatre.net/)

The author and publisher have made every effort
to trace all copyright holders, but if any has been
inadvertently overlooked we would be pleased to make
the necessary arrangement at the first opportunity.

Key for archive abbreviations in captions:

AL	Allen Library
AT	Abbey Theatre
BIL	Benjamin Iveagh Library, Farmleigh
CCA	Cork City and County Archives Service
DCLA	Dublin City Libraries and Archives
GI	Getty Images
GM	George Morrison
HL	Hardiman Library, NUIG
HLG	Dublin City Gallery The Hugh Lane
ITMA	Irish Traditional Music Archive
JC	Jackie Clarke Museum
KC	The Kobal Collection
KG	Kilmainham Gaol Museum
LL	Lilly Library
MAI	Military Archives of Ireland
MEPL	Mary Evans Picture Library
NAI	National Archives of Ireland
NAUK	National Archives UK
NGI	National Gallery of Ireland
NLI	National Library of Ireland
NMI	National Museum of Ireland
NPA	National Photographic Archive (part of NLI)
NYPL	New York Public Library
PM	Pearse Museum
RSAI	Royal Society of Antiquaries of Ireland
TCD	Trinity College Dublin

Notes

Chapter 1

1. Hugh Hunt, *The Abbey: Ireland's National Theatre, 1904–1978* (Dublin: Gill & Macmillan, 1979), p. 67.
2. *Irish Times*, 25 July 1966.
3. Richard Kearney, *Transitions: Narratives in Modern Irish Culture* (Manchester: Manchester University Press, 1988), p. 218.
4. Swander, 'Shields at the Abbey', p. 26.
5. W. B. Yeats, 'The Man and the Echo' (1938).
6. Reid, *The Lost Ireland of Stephen Gwynn*, pp 52–3.
7. Bureau of Military History, Witness Statements, WS 1769 (P. J. Little) (Military Archives, Dublin).
8. Nic Shiubhlaigh, *The Splendid Years*.
9. Andrew Murphy, 'Acts of rebellion: Shakespeare and the 1916 Rising', podcast, 26 Feb. 2015 (http://www.ucd.ie/humanities/events/podcasts).
10. Kiberd, *Inventing Ireland*, pp 196–217; Moran, *Staging the Easter Rising*, pp 15–16.
11. Foster, *Vivid Faces*, p. 112.
12. Foster, *Vivid Faces*, p. 112.
13. Moran, *Staging the Easter Rising*, p. 18.
14. Ernest Blythe, *The Abbey Theatre* (Dublin: National Theatre Society, 1963).
15. Arrington, *W. B. Yeats, the Abbey Theatre, Censorship, and the Irish State*, p. 2.
16. Higgins, *Transforming 1916*, pp 162–4; *Sunday Independent*, 24 July 1966.
17. Moran, *Staging the Easter Rising*; Higgins, *Transforming 1916*. Meeting in 1965, for example, the RTE Authority agreed that the rebellion should be portrayed as 'a nationalist and not a socialist rising'. John Bowman, *Window and Mirror: RTE Television, 1961–2011* (Cork: Collins Press, 2011) p. 82.
18. Guy Beiner, 'Making sense of memory', 'Remembering 1916' symposium, Queen's University, Belfast, 27 March 2015; Pierre Nora, cited in McBride, *History and Memory in Modern Ireland*, p. 42.

Chapter 2

1. W. B. Yeats, Nobel Prize acceptance speech, 1923 (http://www.nobelprize.org/nobel_prizes/literature/laureates/1923/yeats-lecture.html).
2. James Pethica, 'Lady Gregory's Abbey Theatre drama: Ireland real and ideal', in Shaun Richards (ed.), *The Cambridge Companion to Twentieth-Century Irish Drama* (Cambridge: Cambridge University Press, 2004), p. 65.
3. Nic Shiubhlaigh, *The Splendid Years*, p. 3.

4. Nic Shiubhlaigh, *The Splendid Years*.
5. Nic Shiubhlaigh, 'Reminiscences' (National Library of Ireland MS 27,634).
6. See National Library of Ireland MS 27,635; David Kenny, 'Romantic Ireland's dead and gone', *The Journal*, 7 April 2011 (http://www.thejournal.ie/readme/column-romantic-irelands-dead-and-gone-117511-Apr2011).
7. Alice Treacey, 'Máire Nic Shiubhlaigh of the Abbey Theatre', *Carloviana*, 2/11 (1962).
8. Nic Shiubhlaigh papers (National Library of Ireland MS 27,635); Bureau of Military History, Witness Statements, WS 889 (James Kavanagh [Séamus Ua Caomhánaigh]) (Military Archives, Dublin); Nic Shiubhlaigh, *The Splendid Years*, p. ix.
9. Nic Shiubhlaigh, 'Reminiscences' (National Library of Ireland MS 27,634). Punctuation added by author in this and subsequent extracts.
10. *United Irishman*, 11 May 1901.
11. Foster, *W. B. Yeats: A Life*, I, p. 262.
12. Nic Shiubhlaigh, 'Reminiscences' (National Library of Ireland MS 27,634).
13. Nic Shiubhlaigh papers (National Library of Ireland MS 27,635).
14. Nic Shiubhlaigh, 'Reminiscences' (National Library of Ireland MS 27,634); Nic Shiubhlaigh, *The Splendid Years*, p. 17.
15. Foster, *Yeats: A Life*, I, pp 261–2.
16. Stephen Gwynn, *Irish Literature and Drama in the English Language: A Short History* (London: Nelson, 1936), p. 158.
17. Nic Shiubhlaigh, 'Reminiscences' (National Library of Ireland MS 27,634).
18. Nic Shiubhlaigh, *The Splendid Years*, p. 20.
19. Adrian Frazier, 'The ideology of the Abbey Theatre', in Shaun Richards (ed.), *The Cambridge Companion to Twentieth-Century Irish Drama* (Cambridge: Cambridge University Press, 2004).
20. *Samhain*, Sept. 1903.
21. *United Irishman*, May 1901.
22. Foster, *Yeats: A Life*, I, p. 263; Pašeta, *Irish Nationalist Women*, p. 58.
23. Foster, *Yeats: A Life*, I, p. 324.
24. W. B. Yeats, Nobel Prize acceptance speech, 1923 http://www.nobelprize.org/nobel_prizes/literature/laureates/1923/yeats-lecture.html).

Chapter 3

1. W. B. Yeats, Nobel Prize acceptance speech, 1923 (http://www.nobelprize.org/nobel_prizes/

literature/laureates/1923/yeats-lecture.html).
2. Foster, *Yeats: A Life*, I, p. 275.
3. Author's interview with Dave Kenny, 17 Feb. 2015.
4. Foster, *Yeats: A Life*, I, p. 296.
5. Foster, *Yeats: A Life*, I, p. 296.
6. Pašeta, *Irish Nationalist Women*, p. 61.
7. Frazier, *Behind the Scenes*, p. 73; *Irish Press*, 10 Sept. 1958.
8. Pašeta, *Irish Nationalist Women*, pp 59–60.
9. Nic Shiubhlaigh, *The Splendid Years*, p. 48.
10. Frances Clarke, 'Annie Horniman', *Dictionary of Irish Biography* (Cambridge: Cambridge University Press, 2009).
11. Nic Shiubhlaigh, 'Reminiscences' (National Library of Ireland MS 27,634).
12. Foster, *Yeats: A Life*, I, p. 328.
13. Nic Shiubhlaigh, *The Splendid Years*, p. 71.
14. Nic Shiubhlaigh memoir (National Library of Ireland MS 27,634).
15. W. B. Yeats, Nobel Prize acceptance speech, 1923 (http://www.nobelprize.org/nobel_prizes/literature/laureates/1923/yeats-lecture.html).
16. Foster, *Yeats: A Life*, I, p. 342; Frazier, *Behind the Scenes*, p. 127.
17. Frazier, *Behind the Scenes*, pp 123, 127.
18. Nic Shiubhlaigh, *The Splendid Years*, pp 48, 72, 73; Nic Shiubhlaigh, 'Reminiscences' (National Library of Ireland MS 27,634).
19. W. B. Yeats, 15 Nov. 1903, cited in Foster, *Yeats: A Life*, I, p. 317.
20. Foster, *Yeats: A Life*, I, pp 278–9.
21. Foster, *Yeats: A Life*, I, p. 338.
22. Foster, *Yeats: A Life*, I, p. 329; Nic Shiubhlaigh, *The Splendid Years*, p. 9.
23. Pilkington, *Theatre and the State in Twentieth-Century Ireland*, p. 3.
24. Nic Shiubhlaigh, *The Splendid Years*, p. 137.

Chapter 4

1. W. B. Yeats (eds William O'Donnell and Douglas Archibald), *The Collected Works of W. B. Yeats, Volume III: Autobiographies* (New York: Scribner, 1990), p. 314.
2. Jim Cooke, 'The Dublin Mechanics' Institute', *Dublin Historical Record*, 52/1 (1999), p. 23.
3. Frazier, *Behind the Scenes*, pp xv–xviii.
4. Jim Cooke, 'The Dublin Mechanics' Institute', *Dublin Historical Record*, 52/1 (1999), p. 30.
5. de Búrca, *The Soldier's Song*, p. 34.
6. de Búrca, *The Soldier's Song*, p. 41.
7. de Búrca, *The Soldier's Song*, p. 47.

8. de Búrca, *The Soldier's Song*, p. 19; Dave Kenny, 'Gypsy and the poet' (http://www.writing.ie/tell-your-own-story/gypsy-and-the-poet-by-dave-kenny).

9. de Búrca, *The Soldier's Song*, p. 25. For Rooney see Matthew Kelly, '… and William Rooney spoke in Irish', *History Ireland*, 15/1 (2007), pp 30–34.

10. de Búrca, *The Soldier's Song*, p. 58.

11. de Búrca, *The Soldier's Song*, p. 86.

12. McGarry, *The Rising*, p. 22.

13. de Búrca, *The Soldier's Song*, p. 89.

14. de Búrca, *The Soldier's Song*, pp 82, 84.

15. Bureau of Military History, Witness Statements, WS 263 (Thomas Slater) (Military Archives, Dublin).

16. de Búrca, *The Soldier's Song*, p. 73; Seamus de Búrca (ed.), *My Dear Eva. Letters from Ballykinlar Internment Camp 1921* (Dublin 1976), p. 2.

17. For Kearney's Fenianism see Bureau of Military History, Witness Statements, WS 263 (Thomas Slater), WS 868 (Patrick Kearney), WS 409 (Valentine Jackson) (Military Archives, Dublin).

18. Bureau of Military History, Witness Statements, WS 397 (Thomas Pugh) (Military Archives, Dublin).

19. de Búrca, *The Soldier's Song*, pp 106–7.

20. de Búrca, *The Soldier's Song*, p. 41.

21. de Búrca, *The Soldier's Song*, p. 43.

22. Frances Clarke, 'P. J. Bourke', *Dictionary of Irish Biography* (Cambridge: Cambridge University Press, 2009).

23. Quoted in Foster, *Vivid Faces*, p. 78.

24. de Búrca, *The Soldier's Song*, p. 51.

25. de Búrca, *The Soldier's Song*, p. 51.

26. de Búrca, *The Soldier's Song*, p. 53.

27. de Búrca, *The Soldier's Song*, p. 53.

28. Foster, *Vivid Faces*, pp 151, 177.

29. Townshend, *Easter 1916*, p. 356.

30. Bureau of Military History, Witness Statements, WS 1004 (Daniel Kelly) (Military Archives, Dublin).

31. Bureau of Military History, Witness Statements, WS 1721 (Séamus Robinson) (Military Archives, Dublin).

32. Bureau of Military History, Witness Statements, WS 1647 (John O'Brien) (Military Archives, Dublin).

33. Townshend, *Easter 1916*, p. 356.

34. Bureau of Military History, Witness Statements, WS 929 (Daniel O'Shaughnessy) (Military Archives, Dublin).

35. Bureau of Military History, Witness Statements, WS 1043 (Joseph Lawless) (Military Archives, Dublin).

36. Bureau of Military History, Witness Statements, WS 838 (Seán Moylan, TD) (Military Archives, Dublin).

Chapter 5

1. Quoted in Regan, 'Helena Molony', p. 143.

2. Frances Clarke and Laurence White, 'Helena Molony', *Dictionary of Irish Biography* (Cambridge: Cambridge University Press, 2009); Regan, 'Helena Molony'.

3. Bureau of Military History, Witness Statements, WS 391 (Helena Molony) (Military Archives, Dublin).

4. Fox, *Rebel Irishwomen*, p. 120. Family influences also played a role in her politicisation: she was encouraged in this 'first active interest in politics' by her brother Frank, an IRB member.

5. Fox, *Rebel Irishwomen*, pp 120–21; Ward, *Unmanageable Revolutionaries*, pp 63–4.

6. Bureau of Military History, Witness Statements, WS 391 (Helena Molony) (Military Archives, Dublin).

7. W. B. Yeats, *Autobiographies* (London: Macmillan, 1955), p. 368.

8. Senia Pašeta, 'Nationalist responses to two royal visits to Ireland, 1900 and 1903', *Irish Historical Studies*, 31/124 (Nov. 1999), pp 488–504; Regan, 'Helena Molony', p. 145.

9. Bureau of Military History, Witness Statements, WS391 (Helena Molony) (Military Archives, Dublin).

10. Ward, *Unmanageable Revolutionaries*, p. 51.

11. 'Irish girls' handbill', n.d., Bureau of Military History CD 119/3/1 (Military Archives, Dublin).

12. Bureau of Military History, Witness Statements, WS 391 (Helena Molony) (Military Archives, Dublin).

13. Bureau of Military History, Witness Statements, WS 909 (Sidney Czira) (Military Archives, Dublin).

14. Bureau of Military History, Witness Statements, WS 391 (Helena Molony) (Military Archives, Dublin).

15. *Bean na hÉireann*, Jan. 1910.

16. Foster, *Vivid Faces*, p. 172.

17. Pašeta, *Irish Nationalist Women*, p. 38.

18. Bureau of Military History, Witness Statements, WS 357 (Kathleen Lynn) (Military Archives, Dublin).

19. Regan, 'Helena Molony', pp 148, 155.

20. Bureau of Military History, Witness Statements, WS 391 (Helena Molony) (Military Archives, Dublin).

21. Duggan, *Helena Molony*, p. 8.

22. Bureau of Military History, Witness Statements, WS 140 (Michael Lonergan) (Military Archives, Dublin).

23. de Búrca, *The Soldier's Song*, p. 93.

24. Hay, *Bulmer Hobson and the Nationalist Movement in Twentieth-Century Ireland*, pp 79–81; Regan, 'Helena Molony', p. 144.

25. Foster, *Vivid Faces*, p. 88.

26. Rosamond Jacob, diary, 4 Nov. 1911, quoted in Lane, *Rosamond Jacob*, p. 64.

27. Pašeta, *Irish Nationalist Women*, pp 213–14; Regan, 'Helena Molony', p. 142.

28. Samuel Levenson, *Maud Gonne* (London: Cassell, 1976), p. 271.

29. Bureau of Military History, Witness Statements, WS 391 (Helena Molony) (Military Archives, Dublin).

30. Bureau of Military History, Witness Statements, WS 264 (Áine Ceannt) (Military Archives, Dublin).

31. Duggan, *Helena Molony*, p. 10.

32. 'Helena Moloney', Special Branch file, CO 904/201/305 (National Archives, London).

33. Bureau of Military History, Witness Statements, WS 391 (Helena Molony) (Military Archives, Dublin).

34. Bureau of Military History, Witness Statements, WS 8 (Seumas Mac Caisin) (Military Archives, Dublin); Regan, 'Helena Molony', p. 148.

35. Fox, *Rebel Irishwomen*, p. 125.

36. Fox, *Rebel Irishwomen*, p. 122.

37. *Bean na hÉireann*, July 1909, quoted in Regan, 'Helena Molony', p. 143.

38. Quoted in Ben Levitas, 'Plumbing the depths: Irish realism and the working class from Shaw to O'Casey', *Irish University Review*, 33/1 (2003), p. 136.

39. Bureau of Military History, Witness Statements, WS 391 (Helena Molony) (Military Archives, Dublin).

40. Fox, *Rebel Irishwomen*, p. 125; Bureau of Military History, Witness Statements, WS 1670 (Séamus Kavanagh) (Military Archives, Dublin).

41. Bureau of Military History, Witness Statements, WS 909 (Sidney Czira) (Military Archives, Dublin).

42. Rosamond Jacob, diary, 11 Dec. 1913, quoted in Lane, *Rosamond Jacob*, p. 66.

43. Bureau of Military History, Witness Statements, WS 391 (Helena Molony) (Military Archives, Dublin).

44. *Irish Citizen*, 9 May 1914.

45. Regan, 'Helena Molony', p. 151.

46. Fox, *Rebel Irishwomen*, p. 125.

47. Bureau of Military History, Witness Statements, WS 705 (Christopher Brady) (Military Archives, Dublin).

48. Bureau of Military History, Witness Statements, WS 705 (Christopher Brady) (Military Archives, Dublin).

Chapter 6

1. Scully, 'The Abbey Theatre 1916 plaque'. For a more detailed account see Wren, 'Barney

Murphy and the Abbey Theatre 1916 plaque'.

2. Bureau of Military History, Witness Statements, WS 1670 (Séamus Kavanagh) (Military Archives, Dublin).

3. Bureau of Military History, Witness Statements, WS 140 (Michael Lonergan) (Military Archives, Dublin).

4. *Irish Independent*, 1 Oct. 1938.

5. For Keegan see James Wren, 'The Abbey Theatre 1916 plaque', *Dublin Historical Record*, 52/2 (1999), pp 108–9.

6. Military Service Pensions, Bernard Murphy, sworn statement, 7 July 1937 (Military Archives, Dublin).

7. Tom Hunt, 'The GAA: Social structure and associated clubs', in Mike Cronin, William Murphy and Paul Rouse, *The Gaelic Athletic Association, 1884–2009* (Dublin: Irish Academic Press, 2009), p.201; Jimmy Wren, *Saint Laurence O'Toole G.A.C., 1901–2001: A Centenary History* (Dublin: 2001).

Chapter 7

1. Bureau of Military History, Witness Statements, WS 833 (Michael Knightly) (Military Archives, Dublin).

2. Scully, 'The Abbey Theatre 1916 plaque', p. 162.

3. *Irish Press*, 12 Aug. 1948; Military Service Pensions, Ellen Bushell (Military Archives, Dublin).

4. de Búrca, *The Soldier's Song*, p. 43.

5. Scully, 'The Abbey Theatre 1916 plaque', p. 162.

6. de Búrca, *The Soldier's Song*, pp 43–4.

7. de Búrca, *The Soldier's Song*, p. 44.

8. Bureau of Military History, Witness Statements, WS 889 (James Kavanagh [Séamus Ua Caomhánaigh]) (Military Archives, Dublin); Nic Shiubhlaigh, *The Splendid Years*, p. 189.

9. Bureau of Military History, Witness Statements, WS 8 (Seumas Mac Caisin) (Military Archives, Dublin).

10. Bureau of Military History, Witness Statements, WS 1670 (Séamus Kavanagh), WS 1666 (Thomas O'Donoghue) (Military Archives, Dublin).

11. Military Service Pensions, Ellen Bushell, sworn testimony, 9 June 1939 (Military Archives, Dublin).

Chapter 8

1. Ritschel, 'James Connolly's Under Which Flag, 1916', p. 58.

2. Lady Gregory (ed. Ann Saddlemyer), *The Tragedies and Tragic-Comedies of Lady Gregory: Being the Second Volume of the Collected Plays* (Gerrards Cross (Bucks): Colin Smythe, 1971), p. 360.

3. Laurence White, 'Sean Connolly', *Dictionary of Irish Biography* (Cambridge: Cambridge University Press, 2009).

4. Sean O'Casey, *Autobiographies, vol. 1* (London: Macmillan, 1963), p. 340.

5. Bureau of Military History, Witness Statements, WS 1746 (Matthew Connolly) (Military Archives, Dublin).

6. W. B. Yeats, 'Three Songs to the One Burden', *Spectator*, 26 May 1939.

7. Lady Gregory (ed. Ann Saddlemyer), *The Tragedies and Tragic-Comedies of Lady Gregory: Being the Second Volume of the Collected Plays* (Gerrards Cross (Bucks): Colin Smythe, 1971), p. 360.

8. Sean O'Casey, *Autobiographies*, vol. 1 (London: Macmillan, 1963), p. 342, cited in Laurence White, 'Sean Connolly', *Dictionary of Irish Biography* (Cambridge: Cambridge University Press, 2009).

9. T. F. O'Sullivan, 'Notes' (National Library of Ireland MS 15,382).

10. Seán O'Casey, *Irish Freedom*, May 1942.

11. Sean O'Casey, *Autobiographies*, vol. 1 (London: Macmillan, 1963), pp 642–5.

12. Laurence White, 'Sean Connolly', *Dictionary of Irish Biography* (Cambridge: Cambridge University Press, 2009).

13. Ritschel, 'James Connolly's Under Which Flag, 1916'; see also Ben Levitas, 'Plumbing the depths: Irish realism and the working class from Shaw to O'Casey', *Irish University Review*, 33/1 (2003).

14. Delia Larkin, 'The newer drama', *Irish Worker*, 16 Nov. 1912, cited in Ben Levitas, 'Plumbing the depths: Irish realism and the working class from Shaw to O'Casey', *Irish University Review*, 33/1 (2003).

15. R. M. Fox, *The History of the Irish Citizen Army* (Dublin: James Duffy, 1944), pp 107–8.

16. The title of Connolly's play comes from a poem by Alice Milligan. On the play see Nelson Ó Ceallaigh Ritschel, 'Shaw, Connolly and the Irish Citizen Army', *Shaw*, 27 (2007), pp 131–2.

17. Moran (ed.), *Four Irish Rebel Plays*, p. 24.

18. Cited in Murray, *Sean O'Casey*, p. 97.

19. Ritschel, 'James Connolly's Under Which Flag, 1916', p. 64.

20. Sean O'Casey, *Autobiographies*, vol. 1 (London: Macmillan, 1963), p. 646.

21. M. Ní Conghaile to J. J. O'Kelly, n.d. (c. 1916), (National Library of Ireland MS 18,555).

22. Murray, *Sean O'Casey*, p. 96.

23. James Connolly, *Under Which Flag?* in Moran (ed.), *Four Irish Rebel Plays*, p. 129.

24. Moran, *Staging the Easter Rising*, p. 18.

Chapter 9

1. Quoted in Reid, *The Lost Ireland of Stephen Gwynn*, p. 127.

2. Cesca Trench to her sister Margot [n.d.], quoted in Foster, *Vivid Faces*, p. 349.

3. Quoted in Frazier, *Hollywood Irish*, p. 243.

4. Laurie Shields, 'Saturday's Child Has Far to Go' (outline), T13/A/512, p. 2 (Shields family papers, Hardiman Library, NUI, Galway). Most of the biographical details that follow derive from this outline of a proposed biography, written by Laurie (Arthur's third wife), and from her related research notes (T13/A/505).

5. Laurie Shields, 'Saturday's Child Has Far to Go' (outline), T13/A/512, pp 2–3 (Shields family papers, Hardiman Library, NUI, Galway); for Adolphus's activism see also T13/A/524–5; *Irish Times*, 28 Sept. 1964.

6. James Connolly (ed. Donal Nevin), *Between Comrades: James Connolly: Letters and Correspondence, 1889–1916* (Dublin: Gill & Macmillan, 2007), pp 654–5.

7. *Irish Times*, 28 Sept. 1964.

8. Laurie Shields, 'Saturday's Child Has Far to Go' (outline), T13/A/512; T13/A/511(1) (Shields family papers, Hardiman Library, NUI, Galway).

9. Laurie Shields, 'Saturday's Child Has Far to Go' (outline), T13/A/512, pp 2–3 (Shields family papers, Hardiman Library, NUI, Galway).

10. Laurie Shields, 'Saturday's Child Has Far to Go' (outline), T13/A/512, p. 2 (Shields family papers, Hardiman Library, NUI, Galway). Arthur's sister Marie, a member of the ITUC National Executive and the wife of the socialist R. J. P. Mortished, helped to organise nurses.

11. 1911 census returns. None of the family spoke Irish.

12. Laurie Shields, 'Saturday's Child Has Far to Go' (outline), T13/A/512, p. 3 (Shields family papers, Hardiman Library, NUI, Galway); Frazier, *Hollywood Irish*, pp 101–3.

13. Reid, *The Lost Ireland of Stephen Gwynn*, p. 67.

14. Military Service Pensions, Arthur Shields, summary, 9 June 1938 (Military Archives, Dublin).

15. *Irish Times*, 3 July 1964; Laurie Shields, 'Saturday's Child Has Far to Go' (outline), T13/A/512 (Shields family papers, Hardiman Library, NUI, Galway).

16. *Irish Times*, 28 Sept. 1964.

17. Laurie Shields, 'Saturday's Child Has Far to Go' (outline), T13/A/512, p. 4 (Shields family papers, Hardiman Library, NUI, Galway).

18. Laurie Shields, 'Saturday's Child Has Far to Go' (outline), T13/A/512, p. 3 (Shields family papers, Hardiman Library, NUI, Galway).

19. Swander, 'Shields at the Abbey', pp 27–8.

Chapter 10

1. W. B. Yeats (ed. Colton Johnson), *The Collected*

Works of W. B. Yeats, Volume X: Later Articles and Reviews (New York: Scribner, 2010), p. 88.

2. Quoted in D. George Boyce, *Nationalism in Ireland* (London: Routledge, 1991), p. 308.

3. Quoted in Moran, *Staging the Easter Rising*, p. 3; Kiberd, *Inventing Ireland*, p. 204.

4. Foster, *Vivid Faces*, pp 80, 104.

5. Foster, *Vivid Faces*, p. 85.

6. Trotter, *Modern Irish Theatre*, p. 30.

7. Foster, *Vivid Faces*, p. 91; Nelson Ó Ceallaigh Ritschel, 'The alternative aesthetic: The Theatre of Ireland's urban plays', in Stephen Watt, Eileen Morgan and Shakir Mustafa (eds), *A Century of Irish Drama: Widening the Stage* (Bloomington: Indiana University Press, 2000), p. 26.

8. Nic Shiubhlaigh, *The Splendid Years*, pp 72–3.

9. Nic Shiubhlaigh, *The Splendid Years*, pp 145–6, 147–54.

10. Nic Shiubhlaigh, *The Splendid Years*, pp 140–41.

11. Quoted in Foster, *Vivid Faces*, pp 80–81.

12. Levitas, *The Theatre of Nation*, pp 228–9.

13. Matthews, *Revival*, p. 146.

14. Bureau of Military History, Witness Statements, WS 779 (Robert Brennan) (Military Archives, Dublin).

15. Bureau of Military History, Witness Statements, WS 155 (P. S. Doyle) (Military Archives, Dublin).

16. Unpublished draft of *On Another Man's Wound*, quoted in Nicholas Allen, *Modernism, Ireland and Civil War* (Cambridge: Cambridge University Press, 2009), pp 43–4.

17. Martin Maguire, 'Harry Nicholls and Kathleen Emerson: Protestant rebels', *Studia Hibernica*, 35 (2008), pp 153, 162, 164.

18. Bureau of Military History, Witness Statements, WS 1765 (Seán T. O'Kelly) (Military Archives, Dublin).

19. Martin Maguire, 'Harry Nicholls and Kathleen Emerson: Protestant rebels', *Studia Hibernica*, 35 (2008), p. 164.

20. Nic Shiubhlaigh, *The Splendid Years*, p. 100.

21. Bureau of Military History, Witness Statements, WS 328 (Gary Holohan), WS 327 (Patrick Egan), WS 419 (Mrs Martin Conlon), WS 1244 (Joseph O'Rourke) (Military Archives, Dublin). After the Civil War the stage was used as a resting-place for the bodies of executed republicans released by the National Army.

22. Bureau of Military History, Witness Statements, WS 889 (James Kavanagh [Séamus Ua Caomhánaigh]) (Military Archives, Dublin).

23. Bureau of Military History, Witness Statements, WS 848 (Harry Phibbs) (Military Archives, Dublin).

24. Kiberd, *Inventing Ireland*, p. 204.

25. Foster, *Vivid Faces*, p. 112.

26. Patrick Maume, 'Terence MacSwiney', *Dictionary of Irish Biography* (Cambridge: Cambridge University Press, 2009).

27. *Irish Times*, 12 Nov. 2014.

28. Lawrence White, 'Thomas MacDonagh', *Dictionary of Irish Biography* (Cambridge: Cambridge University Press, 2009).

29. Moran, *Staging the Easter Rising*, pp 24–5

30. Cited in Levitas, *The Theatre of Nation*, p. 222.

31. Moran, *Staging the Easter Rising*, p. 19; Levitas, *The Theatre of Nation*, p. 223.

32. Moran, *Patrick Pearse and the Politics of Redemption*, p. 159; J. J. Lee, 'Patrick Pearse', *Dictionary of Irish Biography* (Cambridge: Cambridge University Press, 2009).

33. Moran, *Staging the Easter Rising*, pp 26–7; Levitas, *The Theatre of Nation*, p. 222; Thompson, *The Imagination of an Insurrection*.

34. Nic Shiubhlaigh, *The Splendid Years*, p. 156.

35. Levitas, *The Theatre of Nation*, p. 222.

36. Nic Shiubhlaigh, 'Reminiscences' (National Library of Ireland MS 27,634).

Chapter 11

1. Acc. letter 3013, W. B. Yeats (ed. John Kelly), *The Collected Letters of W. B. Yeats* (Oxford: Oxford University Press, electronic edition, 2002).

2. Nic Shiubhlaigh, *The Splendid Years*, p. 162.

3. Nic Shiubhlaigh, *The Splendid Years*, pp 164–5.

4. Bureau of Military History, Witness Statements, WS 241 (Charles Walker) (Military Archives, Dublin); Military Service Pensions, Charles Walker (Military Archives, Dublin).

5. Laurence White, 'Sean Connolly', *Dictionary of Irish Biography* (Cambridge: Cambridge University Press, 2009).

6. Bureau of Military History, Witness Statements, WS 192 (Fionán Lynch) (Military Archives, Dublin).

7. Bureau of Military History, Witness Statements, WS 585 (Frank Robbins) (Military Archives, Dublin).

8. Bureau of Military History, Witness Statements, WS 391 (Helena Molony) (Military Archives, Dublin).

9. Bureau of Military History, Witness Statements, WS 258 (Maeve Cavanagh McDowell) (Military Archives, Dublin).

10. Bureau of Military History, Witness Statements, WS 421 (William Oman) (Military Archives, Dublin).

11. Bureau of Military History, Witness Statements, WS 733 (James O'Shea) (Military Archives, Dublin).

12. Duggan, *Helena Molony*, p. 16.

13. Bureau of Military History, Witness Statements, WS 288 (Charles Saurin) (Military Archives, Dublin).

14. Military Service Pensions, Arthur Shields, sworn statement (Military Archives, Dublin).

15. Bureau of Military History, Witness Statements, WS 288 (Charles Saurin) (Military Archives, Dublin).

16. Peadar Ó Cearnaigh, 'Incidents of Easter Week (1916)' (Trinity College Library, MS 3560/1).

17. Bureau of Military History, Witness Statements, WS 139 (Michael Walker) (Military Archives, Dublin).

18. Peadar Ó Cearnaigh, 'Incidents of Easter Week (1916) (Trinity College Library, MS 3560/1).

19. Peadar Ó Cearnaigh, 'Incidents of Easter Week (1916)' (Trinity College Library, MS 3560/1); Bureau of Military History, Witness Statements, WS 139 (Michael Walker) (Military Archives, Dublin). Walker, who manned a barricade with Kearney, describes the shooting and bayoneting of one man.

20. Peadar Ó Cearnaigh, 'Incidents of Easter Week (1916)' (Trinity College Library, MS 3560/1).

21. Peadar Ó Cearnaigh, 'Incidents of Easter Week (1916)' (Trinity College Library, MS 3560/1). Not all were hostile: some civilians 'handed in supplies of milk and cigarettes – a veritable Godsend'.

22. Bureau of Military History, Witness Statements, WS 1746 (Matthew Connolly) (Military Archives, Dublin).

23. McGarry, *The Rising*, p. 2.

24. Bureau of Military History, Witness Statements, WS 421 (William Oman), WS 391 (Helena Molony) (Military Archives, Dublin).

25. Bureau of Military History, Witness Statements, WS 1746 (Matthew Connolly) (Military Archives, Dublin).

26. Bureau of Military History, Witness Statements, WS 357 (Kathleen Lynn) (Military Archives, Dublin).

27. Bureau of Military History, Witness Statements, WS 391 (Helena Molony), WS 1746 (Matthew Connolly) (Military Archives, Dublin), Despite the tragic circumstances of Seán's death, its details were subsequently embellished. Numerous accounts, perhaps as a result of his role in *Under Which Flag?* claim that he was killed raising the Green Flag over City Hall. He is also described as dying in the arms of his girl-friend or fiancée (although it is possible that Molony was the former). For an early version of the flag story see Francis Jones, *History of the Sinn Fein Movement and the Irish Rebellion of 1916* (New York: P. J. Kenedy, 1917). Other similar accounts appear to have made their way from novels – Morgan Llywelyn, *1916: A Novel of the Irish Rebellion* (New York: Tom Doherty, 1998), p. 444; Peter de Rosa,

Rebels: The Irish Rising of 1916 (New York: Doubleday, 1990), p. 278 – to history texts.

28. Fox, *Rebel Irishwomen*, p. 131.

29. R. M. Fox, *The History of the Irish Citizen Army* (Dublin: James Duffy, 1944), p. 154.

30. Bureau of Military History, Witness Statements, WS 391 (Helena Molony) (Military Archives, Dublin).

31. Townshend, *Easter 1916*, p. 164.

32. Matthews, *Renegades*, pp 129–30.

33. McGarry, *The Rising*, pp 161–2.

34. Nic Shiubhlaigh, *The Splendid Years*, p. 168.

35. Author's interview with Dave Kenny, 17 Feb. 2015.

36. Military Service Pensions, Ellen Bushell, sworn testimony, 9 June 1939 (Military Archives, Dublin).

37. Bureau of Military History, Witness Statements, WS 280 (Robert Brennan) (Military Archives, Dublin).

38. Quoted in McGarry, *The Rising*, p. 164.

39. Military Service Pensions, Bernard Murphy, personal statement, n.d. (Military Archives, Dublin).

40. Foy and Barton, *Easter Rising*, p. 128; Bureau of Military History, Witness Statements, WS 351 (Fergus O'Kelly) (Military Archives, Dublin).

41. Townshend, *Easter 1916*, pp 201–2.

42. Peadar Ó Cearnaigh, 'Incidents of Easter Week (1916)' (Trinity College Library, MS 3560/1).

43. Nic Shiubhlaigh, *The Splendid Years*, p. 177; McGarry, *The Rising*, p. 156.

44. Nic Shiubhlaigh, *The Splendid Years*, p. 177.

45. Nic Shiubhlaigh, *The Splendid Years*, p. 174.

46. Nic Shiubhlaigh, *The Splendid Years*, p. 175.

47. Peadar Ó Cearnaigh, 'Incidents of Easter Week (1916)' (Trinity College Library, MS 3560/1).

48. Bureau of Military History, Witness Statements, WS 312 (Seosamh de Brún) (Military Archives, Dublin).

49. Peadar Ó Cearnaigh, 'Incidents of Easter Week (1916)' (Trinity College Library, MS 3560/1).

50. Extract from letter by Nic Shiubhlaigh, n.d., Bureau of Military History, Witness Statements, WS 302 (Máire Ó Brolcháin) (Military Archives, Dublin); Nic Shiubhlaigh, *The Splendid Years*, pp 175–6.

51. Peadar Ó Cearnaigh, 'Incidents of Easter Week (1916)' (Trinity College Library, MS 3560/1).

52. Bureau of Military History, Witness Statements, WS 288 (Charles Saurin) (Military Archives, Dublin).

53. Bureau of Military History, Witness Statements, WS 1754 (Mrs Tom Barry) (Military Archives, Dublin).

54. Bureau of Military History, Witness Statements, WS 258 (Maeve Cavanagh McDowell) (Military

55. *Kerryman*, 3 June 1916.

56. Bureau of Military History, Witness Statements, WS 588 (Father J. M. Cronin) (Military Archives, Dublin); English, *Irish Freedom*, p. 274.

57. Bureau of Military History, Witness Statements, WS 1746 (Matthew Connolly) (Military Archives, Dublin).

58. Kiberd, *Inventing Ireland*, p. 209.

59. McGarry, *The Rising*, pp 159–61.

60. Extract from letter by Nic Shiubhlaigh, n.d., Bureau of Military History, Witness Statements, WS 302 (Máire Ó Brolcháin) (Military Archives, Dublin).

61. Peadar Ó Cearnaigh, 'Incidents of Easter Week (1916)' (Trinity College Library, MS 3560/1).

62. Bureau of Military History, Witness Statements, WS 734 (Thomas Meldon) (Military Archives, Dublin).

63. Peadar Ó Cearnaigh, 'Incidents of Easter Week (1916)' (Trinity College Library, MS 3560/1).

64. Nic Shiubhlaigh, *The Splendid Years*, p. 183.

65. Nic Shiubhlaigh, *The Splendid Years*, p. 177.

66. Nic Shiubhlaigh, *The Splendid Years*, p. 182.

67. Bureau of Military History, Witness Statements, WS 724 (Desmond Ryan) (Military Archives, Dublin).

68. McGarry, *The Rising*, p. 205.

69. Bureau of Military History, Witness Statements, WS 388 (Joe Good) (Military Archives, Dublin).

70. Bureau of Military History, Witness Statements, WS 889 (James Kavanagh [Séamus Ua Caomhánaigh]) (Military Archives, Dublin).

71. Bureau of Military History, Witness Statements, WS 288 (Charles Saurin) (Military Archives, Dublin).

72. Bureau of Military History, Witness Statements, WS 288 (Charles Saurin) (Military Archives, Dublin).

73. Bureau of Military History, Witness Statements, WS 288 (Charles Saurin) (Military Archives, Dublin).

74. Bureau of Military History, Witness Statements, WS 288 (Charles Saurin) (Military Archives, Dublin).

75. Military Service Pensions, Bernard Murphy, sworn statement, 7 July 1937 (Military Archives, Dublin).

76. Military Service Pensions, Bernard Murphy, personal statement, n.d. (Military Archives, Dublin).

77. Peadar Ó Cearnaigh, 'Incidents of Easter Week (1916)' (Trinity College Library, MS 3560/1).

78. Extract from letter by Máire Nic Shiubhlaigh, n.d., Bureau of Military History, Witness Statements, WS 302 (Máire Ó Brolcháin) (Military Archives, Dublin).

79. Nic Shiubhlaigh, *The Splendid Years*, p. 185.

80. Peadar Ó Cearnaigh, 'Incidents of Easter Week (1916)' (Trinity College Library, MS 3560/1).

81. Peadar Ó Cearnaigh, 'Incidents of Easter Week (1916)' (Trinity College Library, MS 3560/1).

82. Peadar Ó Cearnaigh, 'Incidents of Easter Week (1916)' (Trinity College Library, MS 3560/1).

83. Peadar Ó Cearnaigh, 'Incidents of Easter Week (1916)' (Trinity College Library, MS 3560/1).

84. Peadar Ó Cearnaigh, 'Incidents of Easter Week (1916)' (Trinity College Library, MS 3560/1).

85. Nic Shiubhlaigh, *The Splendid Years*, pp 184–5.

86. Bureau of Military History, Witness Statements, WS 399 (Mrs Richard Mulcahy) (Military Archives, Dublin).

Chapter 12

1. Padraic Colum, Introduction, in Padraic Colum and Edward J. O'Brien (eds), *Poems of the Irish Revolutionary Brotherhood* (Boston: Maynard, Small, 1916).

2. David Fitzpatrick, 'Instant history: 1912, 1916, 1918', 'Remembering 1916' symposium, Queen's University, Belfast, 27 March 2015.

3. *Daily News*, 10 May 1916.

4. Military Service Pensions, Ellen Bushell, sworn statement, 9 June 1939 (Military Archives, Dublin).

5. Bureau of Military History, Witness Statements, WS 288 (Charles Saurin) (Military Archives, Dublin).

6. Bureau of Military History, Witness Statements, WS 585 (Frank Robbins) (Military Archives, Dublin).

7. McGarry, *The Rising*, p. 259.

8. Bureau of Military History, Witness Statements, WS 288 (Charles Saurin) (Military Archives, Dublin).

9. Bureau of Military History, Witness Statements, WS 288 (Charles Saurin) (Military Archives, Dublin).

10. Townshend, *Easter 1916*, pp 316–7.

11. Arthur Shields to family, 30 May 1916, T13/A/8 (Shields family papers, Hardiman Library, NUI, Galway).

12. Arthur Shields to family, 30 May 1916, T13/A/8 (Shields family papers, Hardiman Library, NUI, Galway).

13. Charles Saurin to William Shields, 5 June 1916, T13A/9 (Shields family papers, Hardiman Library, NUI, Galway).

14. Hart, *Mick*, pp 99–111; Townshend, *Easter 1916*, pp 319–22.

15. Frazier, *Hollywood Irish*, p. 106; Tom Feeney, 'Arthur Shields', *Dictionary of Irish Biography* (Cambridge: Cambridge University Press, 2009).

16. Ebenezer, *Fron-Goch and the Birth of the IRA*, pp

123–39.

17. Quoted in Foster, *Vivid Faces*, p. 51.
18. Transcript, 'Gans interview for Irish press', c. 1962, T13/A/392, pp 24–5 (Shields family papers, Hardiman Library, NUI, Galway).
19. *Irish Times*, 28 Sept. 1964; Frazier, *Hollywood Irish*, p. 242. Séamus McGowan, considered the inspiration for Donal Davoren in *The Shadow of a Gunman*, was another Protestant internee.
20. *Irish Press*, 28 April 1970.
21. *Irish Times*, 28 Sept. 1964.
22. Bureau of Military History, Witness Statements, WS 391 (Helena Molony) (Military Archives, Dublin).
23. Bureau of Military History, Witness Statements, WS 357 (Kathleen Lynn) (Military Archives, Dublin).
24. Bureau of Military History, Witness Statements, WS 391 (Helena Molony) (Military Archives, Dublin).
25. R. M. Fox, *Green Banners: The Story of the Irish Struggle* (London: Secker and Warburg, 1938), p.298; Bureau of Military History, Witness Statements, WS 357 (Kathleen Lynn) (Military Archives, Dublin).
26. Quoted in William Murphy, 'Political imprisonment and the Irish, 1910–21', PhD thesis (UCD, 2007), p. 99.
27. Foy and Barton, *The Easter Rising*, pp 225–6.
28. Townshend, *Easter 1916*, p. 286.
29. 'Helena Moloney', Special Branch file, CO 904/201/305 (National Archives, London).
30. Townshend, *Easter 1916*, p. 285.
31. Duggan, *Helena Molony*, p. 19.
32. Helena Molony to Ellen Bushell, 22 Aug. 1916 (National Library of Ireland MS 20,702).
33. *Kerryman*, 3 June 1916.
34. Bureau of Military History, Witness Statements, WS 246 (Marie Perolz) (Military Archives, Dublin).
35. Helena Molony to Nell Ryan, 22 Jan. 1917, quoted in Foster, *Vivid Faces*, p. 369.
36. Pašeta, *Irish Nationalist Women*, p. 196.
37. Bureau of Military History, Witness Statements, WS 826 (Maeve MacGarry) (Military Archives, Dublin).
38. Pašeta, *Irish Nationalist Women*, p. 212.
39. Duggan, *Helena Molony*, p. 16.
40. Bureau of Military History, Witness Statements, WS 391 (Helena Molony) (Military Archives, Dublin).

Chapter 13

1. Quoted in Foster, *Yeats: A Life*, II, p. 44.
2. 'Passion and cunning: An essay on the politics of W. B. Yeats', in Conor Cruise O'Brien, *Passion and Cunning and Other Essays* (London: Weidenfeld and

Nicolson, 1988), p. 8, quoted in Foster, *Vivid Faces*, p. 147.
3. Lady Gregory to W. B. Yeats, 8 May (Lady Gregory papers, Berg collection, New York Public Library).
4. St John Ervine to Lady Gregory, 5 May 1916, quoted in Arrington, *W. B. Yeats, the Abbey Theatre, Censorship, and the Irish State*, p. 16.
5. St John Ervine to Lady Gregory, 5 May 1916, quoted in Arrington, *W. B. Yeats, the Abbey Theatre, Censorship, and the Irish State*, p. 16.
6. W. B. Yeats to St John Ervine, 8 May 1916, quoted in Foster, *Yeats: A Life*, II, p. 46.
7. Lady Gregory to W. B. Yeats, 8 May (Lady Gregory papers, Berg collection, New York Public Library).
8. Lily Yeats to John Butler Yeats, 7 May 1916, quoted in Foster, *Yeats: A Life*, II, p. 49.
9. Lily Yeats to Ruth Lane Pole, 16 May, quoted in Foster, *Yeats: A Life*, II, p. 50.
10. Lady Gregory to W. B. Yeats, 13 May (Lady Gregory papers, Berg collection, New York Public Library).
11. Maud Gonne and W. B. Yeats (eds Anna MacBride White and A. Norman Jeffares), *The Gonne-Yeats Letters, 1893–1938* (London: Hutchinson, 1992), p.377.
12. Foster, *Yeats: A Life*, II, p. 51.
13. Foster, *Yeats: A Life*, II, pp 59–64; Kiberd, *Inventing Ireland*, p. 213.
14. *Daily Chronicle*, 9 May 1916, Yeats papers (National Library of Ireland MS 30714), quoted in Nicholas Allen, 'Cultural representations of 1916', Remembering 1916' symposium, 27 March 2015, Queen's University, Belfast.
15. Augustine Birrell, *Things Past Redress* (London: Faber and Faber, 1937), p. 214.
16. *Sinn Fein Rebellion Handbook* (Dublin: Irish Times, 1916), p. 163.
17. Peter Kavanagh, *The Story of the Abbey Theatre* (Orono (Maine): University of Maine, 1984), p. 104.
18. Grene, *The Politics of Irish Drama*, p. 69.
19. Levitas, *The Theatre of Nation*, pp 221–2.
20. Kiberd, *Inventing Ireland*, p. 200.
21. Patrick Pearse, *The Spiritual Nation* (Jan. 1916), cited in Robert Tracy, '"A statue's there to mark the place": Cú Chulainn in the GPO', *Field Day Review*, 4 (2008), p. 214.
22. Foster, *Vivid Faces*, p. 77; Dorothy Macardle, *The Irish Republic* (London: Corgi Books, 1968), p. 58; Thompson, *The Imagination of an Insurrection*, p. 116.

Chapter 14

1. *Irish Independent*, 20 Feb. 1926.
2. Coleman, 'Military service pensions for veterans

of the Irish Revolution, 1916–123'. On the Military Service Pensions collection, see Crowe, *Guide to the Military Service (1916–1923) Pensions Collection*.
3. Military Service Pensions, Edward Keegan, Séamus Ó Murchadha to Department of Defence, 27 June 1938 (Military Archives, Dublin).
4. Ferriter, *A Nation and Not a Rabble*, pp 319–40.
5. The highest grade (A) was worth £149 7s (roughly £8,500 today). The lowest, most commonly awarded grade (E) was worth £29 7s 6d (Ferriter, *A Nation and Not a Rabble*, pp 319, 324).
6. W. T. Cosgrave, *Dáil Debates*, 27 June 1924, cited in Crowe, *Guide to the Military Service (1916–1923) Pensions Collection*, p. 67.
7. Ferriter, *A Nation and Not a Rabble*, p. 22.
8. Military Service Pensions, Bernard Murphy, application, 27 Dec. 1935 (Military Archives, Dublin).
9. Military Service Pensions, Bernard Murphy, J. P. L. Murphy, St Vincent de Paul, to Department of Defence, 12 Oct. 1936 (Military Archives, Dublin).
10. Military Service Pensions, Bernard Murphy, Association of Easter Week Men to Military Service Pensions Board, 24 Nov. 1937 (Military Archives, Dublin).
11. Military Service Pensions, Bernard Murphy, Association of Easter Week Men to Military Service Pensions Board, 11 Aug. 1937; secretary, Military Service Pensions, to secretary, Department of Defence, 22 Sept. 1938 (Military Archives, Dublin).
12. Military Service Pensions, Bernard Murphy, Frank Daly to Military Service Pensions Board, 3 Nov. 1938 (Military Archives, Dublin).
13. Military Service Pensions, Bernard Murphy, private secretary, Frank Fahy, to secretary, Military Service Pensions Board, 12 Nov. 1938; Mary Murphy to Military Service Pensions Board, 19 Feb. 1939 (Military Archives, Dublin).
14. Ferriter, *A Nation and Not a Rabble*, p. 331.
15. *Irish Independent*, 1 Oct. 1938.

Chapter 15

1. Frank Gallagher, quoted in Yeates, *A City in Turmoil*, p. 19.
2. David Dickson, *Dublin: The Making of a Capital City* (London: Profile Books, 2014), p. 462.
3. Bureau of Military History, Witness Statements, WS 707 (Michael Noyk) (Military Archives, Dublin).
4. Bureau of Military History, Witness Statements, WS 397 (Tom Pugh) (Military Archives, Dublin).
5. Yeates, *A City in Turmoil*, p. 129.
6. Bureau of Military History, Witness Statements, WS 150 (Gregory Murphy) (Military Archives,

Dublin).

7. Marie Coleman and William Murphy, 'Diarmuid O'Hegarty', *Dictionary of Irish Biography* (Cambridge: Cambridge University Press, 2009).

8. Bureau of Military History, Witness Statements, WS 660 (Tom Leahy) (Military Archives, Dublin).

9. Bureau of Military History, Witness Statements,WS 1739 (Dan Breen) (Military Archives, Dublin); John Reynolds, 'The Templemore miracles', *History Ireland*, 17/1 (2009).

10. Bureau of Military History, Witness Statements, WS 1739 (Dan Breen) (Military Archives, Dublin).

11. de Búrca, *The Soldier's Song*, p. 154.

12. de Búrca, *The Soldier's Song*, p. 157.

13. Liam O'Flaherty, *Two Years* (London: Jonathan Cape, 1930).

14. de Búrca, *The Soldier's Song*, p. 153.

15. de Búrca, *The Soldier's Song*, p. 168.

16. de Búrca, *The Soldier's Song*, p. 170.

17. de Búrca, *The Soldier's Song*, p. 173.

18. Townshend, *The Republic*, p. 208; Yeates, *A City in Turmoil*, p. 206; David Dickson, *Dublin: The Making of a Capital City* (London: Profile Books, 2014), p. 464.

19. Kenneth Griffith and Timothy O'Grady, *Curious Journey: An Oral History of Ireland's Unfinished Revolution* (London: Hutchinson, 1982), p. 321.

20. Murphy, *Political Imprisonment and the Irish, 1912–1921*, p. 201. Further details on Ballykinler derive from this source.

21. Peadar to Eva, 21 July 1921, Kearney, *My Dear Eva*, p.22.

22. Peadar to Eva, n.d., Kearney, *My Dear Eva*, p. 40.

23. Peadar to Eva, 5 June 1921, Kearney, *My Dear Eva*, p.13.

24. Peadar to Eva, 23 Sept. 1921, Kearney, *My Dear Eva*, p.25.

25. Peadar to Eva, 4 Sept. 1921, Kearney, *My Dear Eva*, p.22.

26. Peadar to Eva, 10 Aug. 1921, Kearney, *My Dear Eva*, p.19.

27. Peadar to Eva, n.d., Kearney, *My Dear Eva*, p. 33.

28. Peadar to Eva, 14 July 1921, Kearney, *My Dear Eva*, p 17.

29. Peadar to Eva, n.d., Kearney, *My Dear Eva*, p. 37.

30. Military Service Pensions, Peadar Kearney, handwritten statement, n.d. (Military Archives, Dublin).

31. *Irish Press*, 4 Oct. 1937.

32. Kearney, *My Dear Eva*, p. 4.

33. Ferriter, *A Nation and Not a Rabble*, p. 321.

34. 'The Soldier's Song', 24 Aug. 1926 (National Archives, D/Taois. S7395A).

35. Peadar Kearney, '2nd Statement', 26 Aug. 1926 (National Archives, D/Taois. S7395A).

36. Military Service Pensions, Peadar Kearney, Kearney to Diarmuid O'Hegarty, 11 Oct. 1926 (Military Archives, Dublin).

37. Quoted in Morris, *Our Own Devices*, p. 43.

38. Quoted in Morris, *Our Own Devices*, p. 47.

39. Quoted in Morris, *Our Own Devices*, p. 48.

40. Quoted in Morris, *Our Own Devices*, p. 54.

41. *Dáil Éireann Debates*, vol. 50 (22 Nov. 1933).

42. Morris, *Our Own Devices*, pp 54, 40.

43. Morris, *Our Own Devices*, p. 51.

44. National Archives, D/Taois. S7395A.

45. *Irish Press*, 7 Oct. 1933; National Archives, D/Taois. S7395A; Sherry, 'The story of the national anthem'.

46. *Irish Press*, 10 Oct. 1933.

47. Uinseann Mac Eoin, *The IRA in the Twilight Years, 1923-1948* (Dublin: Argenta, 1997), p. 337.

48. *Irish Press*, 7 Aug. 1938.

49. Brendan Behan (ed. E. H. Mikhail), *The Letters of Brendan Behan* (Montréal: McGill-Queen's University Press, 1992), p. 15. See also Uinseann Mac Eoin, *The IRA in the Twilight Years, 1923-1948* (Dublin: Argenta 1997), p. 513.

50. Morris, *Our Own Devices*, p. 69.

Chapter 16

1. Military Service Pensions, Ellen Bushell, P. O'Connor to Department of Defence, 1 July 1937 (Military Archives, Dublin).

2. Military Service Pensions, Ellen Bushell, sworn testimony, 8 June 1939 (Military Archives, Dublin).

3. Military Service Pensions, Ellen Sarah Bushell, 12 June 1939 (Military Archives, Dublin).

4. Military Service Pensions, Ellen Bushell, sworn testimony, 8 June 1939 (Military Archives, Dublin).

5. Scully, 'The Abbey Theatre 1916 plaque', pp 162–5; de Búrca, *The Soldier's Song*, p. 44; Nic Shiubhlaigh, *The Splendid Years*, p. 65.

6. Patrick Maume, 'Terence MacSwiney', *Dictionary of Irish Biography* (Cambridge: Cambridge University Press, 2009).

7. Military Service Pensions, Ellen Bushell, Joe Larkin testimonial, 26 July 1935; Paddy O'Connor to Department of Defence, 1 July 1937; sworn testimony, 8 June 1939 (Military Archives, Dublin).

8. Military Service Pensions, Ellen Sarah Bushell, 12 June 1939 (Military Archives, Dublin).

9. *Dublin's Fighting Story, 1913–1921: Told by the Men Who Made It* (Tralee: Kerryman, 1949).

10. Military Service Pensions, Ellen Bushell, sworn testimony, 8 June 1939 (Military Archives, Dublin).

11. Military Service Pensions, Ellen Bushell, sworn testimony, 9 June 1939 (Military Archives,

Dublin).

12. Scully, 'The Abbey Theatre 1916 plaque', p. 163.

13. *Irish Independent*, 14 Aug. 1948; *Irish Press*, 12 Aug. 1948.

Chapter 17

1. Crowe, *Guide to the Military Service (1916–1923) Pensions Collection*, p. 70.

2. Joseph Connell, *Where's Where in Dublin: A Directory of Historic Locations, 1913–1923* (Dublin: Dublin City Council, 2006), p. 50.

3. Military Service Pensions, Máire Price, pension application, 28 Jan. 1935 (Military Archives, Dublin).

4. Military Service Pensions, Máire Price, sworn statement, 22 May 1936 (Military Archives, Dublin).

5. Tom Reilly, *Joe Stanley: Printer to the Rising* (Dingle: Brandon, 2005), p. 21.

6. Bureau of Military History, Witness Statements, WS 707 (Michael Noyk) (Military Archives, Dublin). For the court case, including material seized, see 'Appeal case: Máire Nic Shiubhlaigh v. George Love', 1919 (CO 904) (National Archives, London).

7. Author's interview with Dave Kenny, 17 Feb. 2015.

8. Bureau of Military History, Witness Statements, WS 995 (Éamon Price) (Military Archives, Dublin).

9. Bureau of Military History, Witness Statements, WS 150 (Gregory Murphy), WS 392 (Éamon Dore) (Military Archives, Dublin).

10. Bureau of Military History, Witness Statements, WS 1572 (Pádraig Ó Catháin) (Military Archives, Dublin).

11. Joost Augusteijn, *From Public Defiance to Guerrilla Warfare: The Experience of Ordinary Volunteers in the Irish War of Independence* (Dublin: Irish Academic Press, 1996), p. 142.

12. Tom Doyle, *The Civil War in Kerry* (Cork: Mercier Press, 2008), p. 290; Ferriter, *A Nation and Not a Rabble*, p. 287.

13. Fearghal McGarry, *Eoin O'Duffy: A Self-Made Hero* (Oxford: Oxford University Press, 2005), p. 170.

14. Author's interview with Dave Kenny, 17 Feb. 2015.

15. Máire Price to Alice Milligan, n.d. [c. 1950]; Alice Milligan to Máire Price, n.d. [c. 1950] (National Library of Ireland MS 27,624); Morris, *Alice Milligan and the Irish Cultural Revival*.

16. Military Service Pensions, Máire Price, Price to Department of Defence, 28 Oct. 1942 (Military Archives, Dublin).

17. Frances Clarke, 'Máire Nic Shiubhlaigh', *Dictionary of Irish Biography* (Cambridge: Cambridge University Press, 2009).

18. Military Service Pensions, Éamon Price, Máire Price to Department of Defence, 9 July 1951 (Military Archives, Dublin).

19. An extract can be found in Bureau of Military History, Witness Statements, WS 995 (Éamon Price) (Military Archives, Dublin).

20. *Irish Press*, 13 Sept. 1958; *Irish Independent*, 11 Sept. 1958.

Chapter 18

1. Cited in Ben Levitas, 'Plumbing the depths: Irish realism and the working class from Shaw to O'Casey', *Irish University Review*, 33/1 (2003), p 144.

2. Cited in Foster, *Vivid Faces*, p. 316.

3. Ward, *Unmanageable Revolutionaries*, p. 124.

4. Margaret Ward, 'The League of Women Delegates and Sinn Féin', *History Ireland*, 4/3 (autumn, 1996), pp 37–41.

5. Pašeta, *Irish Nationalist Women*, pp 228–9.

6. 'Helena Moloney', Special Branch file, CO 904/201/305 (National Archives, London).

7. Military Service Pensions, Helena Molony, sworn statement, 3 July 1936 (Military Archives, Dublin).

8. Bureau of Military History, Witness Statements, WS 391 (Helena Molony) (Military Archives, Dublin).

9. Regan, 'Helena Molony', pp 155, 157; James Connolly (ed. Donal Nevin), *Between Comrades: James Connolly: Letters and Correspondence, 1889–1916* (Dublin: Gill & Macmillan, 2007), p. 631.

10. Regan, 'Helena Molony', pp 156–7. After 1922 she performed in eight further Abbey plays, the last in 1927.

11. Helena Molony, 'James Connolly and women', in *Dublin Labour Year Book* (Dublin: Dublin Trades Union and Labour Council, 1930).

12. Duggan, *Helena Molony*, p. 21.

13. Frances Clarke and Laurence White, 'Helena Molony', *Dictionary of Irish Biography* (Cambridge: Cambridge University Press, 2009).

14. Rosemary Cullen Owens, *Louie Bennett* (Cork: Cork University Press, 2001), p. 81.

15. Duggan, *Helena Molony*, p. 23.

16. Rosemary Cullen Owens, *Louie Bennett* (Cork: Cork University Press, 2001), p. 67.

17. Regan, 'Helena Molony', p. 164.

18. Rosemary Cullen Owens, *Louie Bennett* (Cork: Cork University Press, 2001), pp 96–100.

19. Mary Jones, *These Obstreperous Lassies: A History of the Irish Women Workers' Union* (Dublin: Gill & Macmillan, 1988), p. 129.

20. Helena Molony to Sean O'Faolain, 6 Sept. 1934, Bureau of Military History, Witness Statements, WS 391 (Helena Molony) (Military Archives, Dublin).

21. Maurice Harmon, 'Sean O'Faolain', *Dictionary of Irish Biography* (Cambridge: Cambridge University Press, 2009).

22. Susan Pedersen, 'Did women getting the vote make a difference?' *Guardian*, 27 Nov. 2014; Jad Adams, *Women and the Vote: A World History* (Oxford: Oxford University Press, 2014).

23. Regan, 'Helena Molony', p. 161.

24. Regan, 'Helena Molony', p. 160; O'Connor, *Reds and the Green*, pp 149, 167–70.

25. 'Miss Helena Moloney', G2/3364 (Military Archives, Dublin).

26. Regan, 'Helena Molony', p. 166; Mary Jones, *These Obstreperous Lassies: A History of the Irish Women Workers' Union* (Dublin: Gill & Macmillan, 1988), p.204.

27. Katherine O'Donnell, 'Lesbianism', in Brian Lalor (ed.), *The Encyclopaedia of Ireland* (Dublin: Gill & Macmillan, 2003), p. 624.

28. Marie Mulholland, *The Politics and Relationships of Kathleen Lynn* (Dublin: Woodfield Press, 2002), pp 6–19.

29. Foster, *Vivid Faces*, pp 115–43.

30. Regan, 'Helena Molony', p. 167; *Irish Times, Irish Independent, Irish Press*, 30 Jan. and 1 Feb. 1967.

31. Levitas, *The Theatre of Nation*, p. 228.

32. Steele, *Women, Press, and Politics during the Irish Revival*, p. 201.

Chapter 19

1. Æ (George Russell), 'Lessons of revolution', *Studies: An Irish Quarterly Review*, 12/45 (1923), pp 2–3.

2. Welch, *The Abbey Theatre*, 1899–1999, p. 79.

3. For a balanced appraisal see Patrick Maume, 'St John Greer Ervine', *Dictionary of Irish Biography* (Cambridge: Cambridge University Press, 2009).

4. Christopher Fitz-Simon, *The Abbey Theatre: Ireland's National Theatre: The First Hundred Years* (London: Thames and Hudson, 2003), p. 43; Peter Kavanagh, *The Story of the Abbey Theatre* (Orono (Maine): Maine University Press, 1984), pp 104–9.

5. *Irish Times*, 29 April 1970.

6. Lennox Robinson, *Ireland's Abbey Theatre: A History, 1889–1951* (London: Sidgwick and Jackson, 1951), pp 100, 119; Laurie Shields, 'Saturday's Child Has Far to Go' (outline), T13/A/512 (Shields family papers, Hardiman Library, NUI, Galway).

7. W. B. Yeats, Nobel Prize acceptance speech, 1923 (http://www.nobelprize.org/nobel_prizes/literature/laureates/1923/yeats-lecture.html).

8. Laurie Shields, 'Saturday's Child Has Far to Go' (outline), T13/A/512 (Shields family papers, Hardiman Library, NUI, Galway).

9. Laurie Shields, 'Saturday's Child Has Far to Go' (outline), T13/A/512 (Shields family papers, Hardiman Library, NUI, Galway).

10. Swander, 'Shields at the Abbey', p. 34.

11. Transcript, 'Gans interview for Irish press', c. 1962, T13/A/392 (Shields family papers, Hardiman Library, NUI, Galway). For details of Shields's career, see http://www.abbeytheatre.ie/archives/person_detail/13635.

12. Transcript, 'Gans interview for Irish press', c. 1962, T13/A/392 (Shields family papers, Hardiman Library, NUI, Galway).

13. Mícheál Mac Liammóir, *Theatre in Ireland* (Dublin: Three Candles, for Cultural Relations Committee, 1950), pp 20–21; Christopher Murray, *Twentieth-Century Irish Drama: Mirror up to Nation* (Manchester: Manchester University Press), p. 123.

14. Shields, 'History of Abbey', T13/A/100 (Shields family papers, Hardiman Library, NUI, Galway).

15. Pilkington, *Theatre and the State in Twentieth-Century Ireland*, pp 9, 90; Ben Levitas, 'Plumbing the depths: Irish realism and the working class from Shaw to O'Casey', *Irish University Review*, 33/1 (2003), p. 147.

16. Pilkington, *Theatre and the State*, pp 90–102.

17. Foster, *Yeats: A Life, II*, p. 305.

18. *Evening Herald*, 12 Feb. 1926.

19. Moran, *Staging the Easter Rising*, pp 30–31.

20. Foster, *Yeats: A Life, II*, p. 306.

21. Robert Hogan and Richard Burnham, *The Years of O'Casey, 1921–1926: A Documentary History* (Newark (NJ), 1992), p. 301.

22. Foster, *Yeats: A Life, II*, pp 306–7.

23. Seán O'Casey (ed. David Krause), *The Letters of Sean O'Casey: Volume 1, 1910–1941* (London: Cassell, 1976), pp 167–8.

24. Handwritten notes, T13/A/394; Laurie Shields, 'Saturday's Child Has Far to Go' (outline), T13/A/512; transcript, 'Gans interview for Irish press', c. 1962, T13/A/392 (Shields family papers, Hardiman Library, NUI, Galway).

25. Moran, *Staging the Easter Rising*, pp 9, 49.

26. Foster, *Vivid Faces*, p. 303.

27. Laurie Shields, 'Saturday's Child Has Far to Go' (outline), T13/A/512 (Shields family papers, Hardiman Library, NUI, Galway).

28. Arthur Shields to Lini Saurin, 30 Dec. 1931, T13/A/68 (Shields family papers, Hardiman Library, NUI, Galway).

29. Transcript, 'Gans interview for Irish press', c. 1962, T13/A/392 (Shields family papers, Hardiman Library, NUI, Galway).

30. Arthur Shields to Lini Saurin, 18 Feb. 1932, T13/A/75 (Shields family papers, Hardiman Library, NUI,Galway).

31. Aideen O'Connor to Vincent O'Connor, 4 March 1935, T13/A/436 (Shields family papers, Hardiman Library, NUI, Galway).

32. Swander, 'Shields at the Abbey', p. 37.

33. Arthur Shields to Lini Saurin, T13/A/72 (Shields

family papers, Hardiman Library, NUI, Galway).

34. Arthur Shields to Lini Saurin, 10 Jan. 1932, T13/A/69(1) (Shields family papers, Hardiman Library, NUI, Galway).

35. Arthur Shields to Lini Saurin, 18 Feb. 1932, T13/A/75 (Shields family papers, Hardiman Library, NUI, Galway).

36. Arthur Shields to Lini Saurin, 6 March 1932, T13/A/76 (Shields family papers, Hardiman Library, NUI, Galway).

37. Barry Fitzgerald to Lini Saurin, 30 Dec. 1931, T13/A/405 (Shields family papers, Hardiman Library, NUI, Galway).

38. Frazier, *Hollywood Irish*, p. 114.

39. I am grateful to Ciara O'Dowd (NUI, Galway) for this information, and for generously sharing her research on Aideen O'Connor and Arthur Shields. For her 'Chasing Aideen' research blog quoted here see https://chasingaideen. wordpress.com.

40. Born Una O'Connor, she adopted the stage name Aideen to distinguish her from her better-known Abbey Theatre namesake.

41. Cited in Turtle Bunbury, 'Aideen O'Connor (1913–1950): The golden girl of the Abbey Theatre' (http://www.turtlebunbury.com/history/ history_heroes/hist_hero_aideenoconnor. html).

42. Arthur Shields to Lini Saurin, T13/A/76(4) (Shields family papers, Hardiman Library, NUI, Galway).

43. Arthur Shields to Lini Saurin, 6 March 1932, T13/A/76 (Shields family papers, Hardiman Library, NUI, Galway).

44. 'Notes', T13/A/500 (Shields family papers, Hardiman Library, NUI, Galway).

45. 'Notes', T13/A/500 (Shields family papers, Hardiman Library, NUI, Galway).

46. Arthur Shields to Lini Saurin, 18 Feb. 1932, T13/A/75; transcript, 'Gans interview for Irish press', c. 1962, T13/A/392; Arthur Shields to Lini Saurin, 2 Dec. 1931, T13/A/65 (1) (Shields family papers, Hardiman Library, NUI, Galway).

47. John McGarry to Arthur Shields, 13 April 1933, T13/A/98 (Shields family papers, Hardiman Library, NUI, Galway).

48. Barry Sullivan to Arthur Shields, 24 April 1933, T13/A/99 (Shields family papers, Hardiman Library, NUI, Galway).

49. Nic Shiubhlaigh, *The Splendid Years*, pp 132–6; *Sunday Times*, 14 Sept. 2014.

50. Catherine Kelly to Éamon de Valera, 9 Feb. 1938 (National Archives, D/Taois. S8208).

51. Andrew F. Sullivan to Éamon de Valera, 1 Nov. 1934 (National Archives, D/Taois. S8208).

52. Louis J. Walsh, 'Not an island of scholars!', *Irish Rosary*, Jan. 1937, pp 22–7.

53. *Irish Press*, 28 Aug. 1935.

54. *Irish Times*, 26 Aug. 1935, cited in Pilkington, *Theatre and the State*, p. 128.

55. President's secretary to Lennox Robinson, 17 April 1934 (National Archives, D/Taois. S8208). Like many revolutionaries in Dublin, de Valera had trod the Abbey's boards (when he replaced a sick actor in *A Christmas Hamper* in 1905); the *Irish Times* reported that he had 'acted capably'. James Wren, 'The Abbey Theatre 1916 plaque', *Dublin Historical Record*, 52/2 (1999), p. 109.

56. J. J. McElligott, Department of Finance to Abbey Theatre, 27 Feb. 1935 (National Archives, D/Taois. S8208).

57. W. B. Yeats to J. J. McElligott, 1 March 1935 (National Archives, D/Taois. S8208).

58. Arrington, *W. B. Yeats, the Abbey Theatre, Censorship, and the Irish State*, p. 107.

59. Transcript, 'Gans interview for Irish press', c. 1962, T13/A/392 (Shields family papers, Hardiman Library, NUI, Galway).

60. Frazier, *Hollywood Irish*, p. 111; Fearghal McGarry, *Eoin O'Duffy: A Self-Made Hero* (Oxford: Oxford University Press, 2005).

61. Arrington, *W. B. Yeats, the Abbey Theatre, Censorship, and the Irish State*, pp 13–14.

62. Pilkington, *Theatre and the State*, p. 131.

63. Swander, 'Shields at the Abbey'.

64. Pilkington, *Theatre and the State*, p. 127

65. *Irish Press*, 28 Aug. 1935.

66. *Irish Press*, 26 Aug. 1935; Arrington, *W. B. Yeats, the Abbey Theatre, Censorship, and the Irish State*, p. 166.

67. Arrington, *W. B. Yeats, the Abbey Theatre, Censorship, and the Irish State*, pp 163–4.

68. Diarmaid Ferriter, 'F. R. Higgins', *Dictionary of Irish Biography* (Cambridge: Cambridge University Press, 2009).

69. Frazier, *Hollywood Irish*, p. 129.

70. Transcript, 'Gans interview for Irish press', c. 1962, T13/A/392 (Shields family papers, Hardiman Library, NUI, Galway).

71. Pilkington, *Theatre and the State*, p. 126.

72. P. S. O'Hegarty, in Mikhail (ed.), *The Abbey Theatre*, pp 173–6.

73. Memorandum of agreement, 14 July 1937, T13/A/43; Arthur Shields to Lini Saurin, 24 Nov. 1931, T13/A/64(4) (Shields family papers, Hardiman Library, NUI, Galway).

74. Transcript, 'Gans interview for Irish press', c. 1962, T13/A/392; Arthur Shields to Lini Saurin, 10 Feb. 1932, T13/A/74(3) (Shields family papers, Hardiman Library, NUI, Galway).

75. Laurie Shields, Arthur Shields biography notes, p. 8, T13/A/505 (Shields family papers, Hardiman Library, NUI, Galway).

76. Frazier, *Hollywood Irish*, p. 6.

77. Pilkington, *Theatre and the State*, p. 131.

78. Laurie Shields, 'Saturday's Child Has Far to Go' (outline), T13/A/512 (Shields family papers, Hardiman Library, NUI, Galway).

79. Laurie Shields, 'Saturday's Child Has Far to Go' (outline), T13/A/512 (Shields family papers, Hardiman Library, NUI, Galway).

80. Frazier, *Hollywood Irish*, p. 245.

Chapter 20

1. Aideen O'Connor to Eddie Choate, 12 Jan. 1943, T13/A/155 (Shields family papers, Hardiman Library, NUI, Galway).

2. Arthur Shields to Lini Saurin, 26 March 1932, T13/A/77 (Shields family papers, Hardiman Library, NUI, Galway).

3. Laurie Shields, 'Saturday's Child Has Far to Go' (outline), T13/A/512 (Shields family papers, Hardiman Library, NUI, Galway).

4. Laurie Shields, 'Saturday's Child Has Far to Go' (outline), T13/A/512 (Shields family papers, Hardiman Library, NUI, Galway).

5. Aideen O'Connor to Eddie Choate, 25 May 1942, T13/A/155 (9) (Shields family papers, Hardiman Library, NUI, Galway).

6. Quoted in Turtle Bunbury, 'Aideen O'Connor (1913–1950): The golden girl of the Abbey Theatre' (http://www.turtlebunbury. com/history/history_heroes/hist_hero_ aideenoconnor.html).

7. Aideen O'Connor to Eileen O'Connor, 4 March 1938, T13/A/443 (Shields family papers, Hardiman Library, NUI, Galway).

8. Ciara O'Dowd, 'Chasing Aideen' (https:// chasingaideen.wordpress.com/2011/08/18/ all-i-want-is-to-be-with-you-even-if-its-in- timbuctoo).

9. Barry Fitzgerald to Eddie Choate, 12 Jan. 1942, T13/A/155 (2) (Shields family papers, Hardiman Library, NUI, Galway).

10. Aideen O'Connor to Eddie Choate, 25 May 1942, T13/A/155 (9) (Shields family papers, Hardiman Library, NUI, Galway).

11. Aideen O'Connor to Eddie Choate, 12 Jan. 1943, T13/A/155 (15) (Shields family papers, Hardiman Library, NUI, Galway).

12. Arthur Shields to Eddie Choate, T13/A/155 (30) (Shields family papers, Hardiman Library, NUI, Galway).

13. *New York Times*, 14 Jan. 1945; Steve Brennan and Bernadette O'Neill, *Emeralds in Tinseltown: The Irish in Hollywood* (Belfast: Appletree Press, 2007); *Milwaukee Journal*, 18 March 1945; *Pittsburgh Press*, 17 March 1945; *Sydney Morning Herald*, 15 Sept. 1945.

14. Frazier, *Hollywood Irish*, p. 241.

15. Robert M. Dowling, *Eugene O'Neill: A Life in Four Acts* (Yale: Yale University Press, 2014); Nelson

Ó Ceallaigh Ritschel, 'Synge and the Irish influence of the Abbey Theatre on Eugene O'Neill', *Eugene O'Neill Review*, 29 (2007), pp 129–50.

16. Swander, 'Shields at the Abbey', p. 32.

17. Arthur Shields, 'Notes on Eugene O'Neill', T13/A/164 (Shields family papers, Hardiman Library, NUI, Galway).

18. Louis Sheaffer, *O'Neill: Son and Artist* (New York: Cooper Square Press, 2002), p. 595.

19. Arthur Shields, 'Notes on Eugene O'Neill', T13/A/164 (Shields family papers, Hardiman Library, NUI, Galway).

20. Arthur Shields to Seán O'Casey, 23 March 1948, T13/A/246; Laurie Shields, 'Saturday's Child Has Far to Go' (outline), T13/A/512 (Shields family papers, Hardiman Library, NUI, Galway).

21. Aideen O'Connor to Arthur Shields, Jan. 1947, T13/A/241 (Shields family papers, Hardiman Library, NUI, Galway).

22. Ciara O'Dowd, 'Chasing Aideen' (https://chasingaideen.wordpress.com/2014/01/14/spaces-behind-between). See also 'Dramatizing the drinking' (https://chasingaideen.wordpress.com/2013/11/17/54-dramatizing-the-drinking-just-a-short).

23. Information kindly provided by Ciara O'Dowd.

24. *Photoplay*, 50/41 (1936), pp 14–15, 98–100, quoted in Antony Sellers, 'Arthur Shields and the politics of Jean Renoir's The River', *Senses of Cinema*, 49/2 (2009).

25. Frazier, *Hollywood Irish*, pp 93–4.

26. Harry Carey, Jr, *Company of Heroes: My Life as an Actor in the John Ford Stock Company* (Metuchen (NJ): Scarecrow Press, 1994), p. 58. I am grateful to Dan Ford for this reference.

27. Philip French, 'The man who shot America', *Guardian*, 5 June 2003; Joseph McBride, *Searching for John Ford: A Life* (New York: St Martin's Press, 2001).

28. Frazier, *Hollywood Irish*, pp 6–10, 243–4; Luke Gibbons, *The Quiet Man* (Cork: Cork University Press, 2002).

29. Because of his emphysema Shields was too ill to accept Ford's offer of work on *Young Cassidy*, a biopic of O'Casey, in 1964.

30. The Internet Movie Database (http://www.imdb.com) lists 97 acting credits for Arthur Shields.

31. Ian Christie, 'The River' (http://www.criterion.com/films/679).

32. Antony Sellers, 'Arthur Shields and the politics of Jean Renoir's The River', *Senses of Cinema*, 49/2 (2009).

33. Arthur Shields to Eddie Choate, 19 May 1952, T13/A/156 (Shields family papers, Hardiman Library, NUI, Galway).

34. *Irish Press*, 29 April 1950.

35. Fergus Fahey, 'Biographical history', Shields Family Archive (http://archives.library.nuigalway.ie/cgi-bin/FramedList.cgi?T13).

36. Ciara O'Dowd, 'Chasing Aideen' (https://chasingaideen.wordpress.com/2014/01/26/61-the-other-woman).

37. Fergus Fahey, 'Biographical history', Shields Family Archive (http://archives.library.nuigalway.ie/cgi-bin/FramedList.cgi?T13).

38. *San Francisco News*, 26 Oct. 1957.

39. Laurie Shields, 'Saturday's Child Has Far to Go' (outline), T13/A/512 (Shields family papers, Hardiman Library, NUI, Galway).

40. *Irish Times*, 2 May 1970.

41. See Ciara O'Dowd, 'Chasing Aideen' (https://chasingaideen.wordpress.com/2011/08).

42. *Irish Times*, 29 April 1970.

43. Frazier, *Hollywood Irish*, p. 241.

44. Frazier, *Hollywood Irish*, p. 242.

Chapter 21

1. Crowe, *Guide to the Military Service (1916–1923) Pensions Collection*.

2. Quoted in McGarry, *Rebels*, p. xii.

3. Helena Molony to Jane Kissane (investigating officer), 29 Sept. 1947, Bureau of Military History, file S164 (Helena Molony) (Military Archives, Dublin).

4. Foster, *Vivid Faces*, p. 310. Selections from Ernie O'Malley's notebooks, held in UCD Archives, have been edited by his son Cormac for Mercier Press in a series entitled *The Men Will Talk to Me*. The volumes so far published are for Co. Kerry (2012), Co. Galway (2013) and Co. Mayo (2014).

5. Ernie O'Malley, *The Singing Flame* (Dublin: Anvil Books, 1978), p. 213.

6. Bureau of Military History, Witness Statements, WS 1572 (Pádraig Ó Catháin) (Military Archives, Dublin); Joost Augusteijn, *From Public Defiance to Guerrilla Warfare: The Experience of Ordinary Volunteers in the Irish War of Independence* (Dublin: Irish Academic Press, 1996), p. 142.

7. Nic Shiubhlaigh, *The Splendid Years*, pp 185–6.

8. Swander, 'Shields at the Abbey', p. 26.

9. de Búrca, *The Soldier's Song*, p. 219.

10. Quoted in Fox, *Rebel Irishwomen*, pp 128–9.

11. Bureau of Military History, Witness Statements, WS 391 (Helena Molony) (Military Archives, Dublin). See also WS 316 (Peter Folan).

12. *Sinn Fein Rebellion Handbook* (Dublin: *Irish Times*, 1916), p. 280. Details on Crawford Neil from the *Irish Independent*, 11 May 1916; Moran, *Staging the Easter Rising*, p. 16; Dave Kenny, 'Gypsy and the poet' (http://www.writing.ie/tell-your-own-story/gypsy-and-the-poet-by-dave-kenny); National Library of Ireland, online exhibition, 'The 1916 Rising: Personalities and Perspectives'

(http://www.nli.ie/1916/pdf/10.3.pdf).

13. Bureau of Military History, Witness Statements, WS 391 (Helena Molony) (Military Archives, Dublin).

14. de Búrca, *The Soldier's Song*, p. 91.

15. Military Service Pensions, Bernard Murphy, sworn statement, 7 July 1937 (Military Archives, Dublin).

16. Ward, *Unmanageable Revolutionaries*.

17. Helena Molony to Jane Kissane (investigating officer), 29 Sept. 1949, Bureau of Military History, file S164 (Helena Molony) (Military Archives, Dublin).

18. W. B. Yeats, Nobel Prize acceptance speech, 1923 (http://www.nobelprize.org/nobel_prizes/literature/laureates/1923/yeats-lecture.html).

19. Nic Shiubhlaigh, 'Reminiscences' (National Library of Ireland MS 27,634).

20. Nic Shiubhlaigh, *The Splendid Years*, p. xii.

21. de Búrca, *The Soldier's Song*, p. 220.

22. As is evident from entering 'Peadar Kearney' and 'poverty' in an internet search engine.

23. Séamus de Búrca to John O'Donovan, 3 Aug. 1962 (National Library of Ireland MS 39,130/5).

24. de Búrca, *The Soldier's Song*, pp 221–2.

25. Guy Beiner, 'Probing the boundaries of Irish memory: From postmemory to prememory and back', *Irish Historical Studies*, 39/154 (Nov. 2014), pp 298–302, 304–5.

26. de Búrca, *The Soldier's Song*, p. 220.

27. Foster, *Vivid Faces*, pp 294–302.

28. de Búrca, *The Soldier's Song*, p. 91.

29. Padraic Colum to Máire Nic Shiubhlaigh, 1 Dec. 1950 (National Library of Ireland MS 49,752/21).

30. Padraic Colum to Gypsy Walker, 28 Feb. 1958 (National Library of Ireland MS 49,752/22).

31. Nic Shiubhlaigh, *The Splendid Years*, p. xvi; Ferriter, *A Nation and Not a Rabble*, p. 27.

32. de Búrca, *The Soldier's Song*, p. 25.

33. Military Service Pensions, Helena Molony, sworn statement, 3 July 1936 (Military Archives, Dublin).

34. Ferriter, *A Nation and Not a Rabble*, p. 340.

35. Military Service Pensions, Helena Molony, Molony to Advisory Committee, 14 July 1936 (Military Archives, Dublin).

36. Military Service Pensions, Helena Molony, Molony to Advisory Committee, 18 Nov. 1936 (Military Archives, Dublin).

37. Military Service Pensions, Helena Molony, Molony to Advisory Committee, 11 Oct. 1937 (Military Archives, Dublin).

38. Bureau of Military History, Witness Statements, WS 391 (Helena Molony) (Military Archives, Dublin).

39. Fox, *Rebel Irishwomen*, pp 127, 131–2.

40. Regan, 'Helena Molony', p. 167; Duggan, *Helena*

Molony, p. 34.

41. de Búrca, *The Soldier's Song*, pp 217–18.

42. *Irish Times*, 29 April 1950.

43. Laurie Shields, 'Saturday's Child Has Far to Go' (outline), T13/A/512, p. 4 (Shields family papers, Hardiman Library, NUI, Galway).

44. Swander, 'Shields at the Abbey', p. 29.

45. *Irish Press*, 29 April 1950.

46. Swander, 'Shields at the Abbey', p. 39.

47. J. W. Hammond, Introduction, in Peadar Kearney, *The Soldier's Song and Other Poems* (Dublin, 1928), p. 6.

48. Ivrea, 'The Soldier's Song', *Midland Tribune*, n.d. (National Library of Ireland MS 39,125/5).

49. Press cutting (National Library of Ireland MS 39,125/5).

50. 'Jottings by M.A.T.' [R. M. Fox], *Dublin Evening Mail*, 12 Feb. 1958.

51. P. MacA. [Proinsias Mac Aonghusa], *Irish Times*, 1957 (National Library of Ireland MS 39,125/5). Mac Aonghusa was a broadcaster whose left-republican politics led to conflict with RTE and the Government.

52. Éamonn Andrews to Séamus de Búrca, 21 June 1958 (National Library of Ireland MS 39,133).

53. Michael Gill to T. Taplinger, 10 Dec. 1974, T13/A/513 (Shields family papers, Hardiman Library, NUI, Galway).

54. Séamus de Búrca to John O'Donovan, 3 Aug. 1962 (National Library of Ireland MS 39, 130/5).

55. Homer Swander to George Hunt, managing editor, Time-Life Inc., 7 Feb. 1966, T13/A/22 (Shields family papers, Hardiman Library, NUI, Galway).

56. *Irish Times*, 5 April 2015. See also: http://www. decadeofcentenaries.com/forthcoming-easter-rising-commemoration-glasnevin-cemetery-20-april-2014.

57. See http://www.postmemory.net.

58. Author's interview with Dave Kenny, 17 Feb. 2015.

59. Guy Beiner, 'Making sense of memory', 'Remembering 1916' symposium, Queen's University, Belfast, 27 March 2015; Oona Frawley, 'Cruxes in Irish cultural memory', in Oona Frawley (ed.), *Memory Ireland, Volume 3: The Famine and the Troubles* (Syracuse (NY): Syracuse University Press, 2014).

60. Foster, *Vivid Faces*, pp 117, 327–32; for retrospective sources, see pp xix–xx.

Chapter 22

1. Donal Fallon, 'How Dublin commemorated very recent history' (http://comeheretome. com/2013/12/18/easter-1917-how-dublin-commemorated-very-recent-history).

2. Bureau of Military History, Witness Statements, WS 391 (Helena Molony) (Military Archives, Dublin); Moran, *Staging the Easter Rising*, p. 34.

3. Bureau of Military History, Witness Statements, WS 391 (Helena Molony) (Military Archives, Dublin). I am grateful to Emmet O'Connor for this observation.

4. W. B. Yeats, 'Three Songs to the One Burden', in Yeats (ed. R. J. Finneran), *The Collected Works of W. B. Yeats, Volume I: The Poems* (New York: Scribner, 1997), p. 336.

5. Éamonn Mac Thomáis, *Down Dublin Streets, 1916* (Dublin: Irish Books Bureau, c. 1965).

6. John Belchem, *Irish, Catholic and Scouse: The History of the Liverpool-Irish, 1800–1939* (Liverpool: Liverpool University Press, 2007), p. 239; Duggan, *Helena Molony*; Joseph McKenna, *Guerrilla Warfare in the Irish War of Independence, 1919–1921* (Jefferson (NC): McFarland, 2011), p. 113.

7. Available to view at https://www.youtube. com/watch?v=5CfrkvE7_hs. Armed Volunteers forced projectionists to screen the film (made by the former Irish Theatre activist John MacDonagh, brother of Thomas). Kevin Rockett, Luke Gibbons and John Hill, *Cinema and Ireland* (London: Croom Helm, c. 1987), p. 22.

8. Mary Christine Connolly to Dept. of Defence, 20 Dec. 1923, M.S.P. (Sean Connolly). Mary received a widow's allowance of £162 per annum, while the state also paid for her children's education at the exclusive Belvedere and Dominican Colleges. Despite this, Mary articulated similar grievances to other veterans. In 1937, when one of her sons reached adulthood, she denounced the state's 'shameful' refusal to continue paying for the education of 'the son of a patriot', informing government minister Frank Aiken of her resentment of the 'petty pinpricks' inflicted by his department 'where there are many people enjoying good positions, made possible by the years of sacrifice spent by common people like me, who gave health and all chances of making a success of their lives to gain freedom for their country'.

9. Wills, *Dublin, 1916*, pp 110–14.

10. *Catholic Bulletin*, July 1916, pp 404–5.

11. McCormack, *1916: The French Connection*, p. 61.

12. *Catholic Bulletin*, Dec. 1916, p. 703. See also M. Ní Chonghaile to J. J. Kelly, editor, *Catholic Bulletin*, n.d. (1916) (National Library of Ireland MS 18,555/7).

13. Sherry, 'The story of the national anthem'. Whether this is evidence of the success of the state's compulsory Gaelicisation policy is debatable. Although the anthem is heartily rendered at Croke Park, fans of the garrison games (as Sherry points out) more tentatively hum along at Lansdowne Road.

14. Higgins, *Transforming 1916*, pp 122, 162–3. Denounced by Ernest Blythe, the organising committee's statement was memorably described by the *Sligo Champion* as 'possibly the most stupid statement to be issued in the Jubilee year' (Moran, *The Theatre of Seán O'Casey*, p. 171). The Abbey, nonetheless, complied with it.

15. For the Abbey's use of its history see Holly Maples, 'Producing memory: A history of commemoration and the Abbey Theatre', in Frawley (ed.), *Memory Ireland, Volume 1*.

16. *Sunday Independent*, 24 July 1966; *Irish Press*, 25 July 1966.

17. Higgins, *Transforming 1916*, p. 12.

18. Paul Muldoon, '7, Middagh Street', *Poems, 1968–1998* (London: Faber, 2001).

19. Christine Shields to Arthur Shields, 19 July 1966, T13/A/486 (2) (Shields family papers, Hardiman Library, NUI, Galway).

20. Gabriel Fallon, cited in *Abbey Theatre: Dublin, 1904–1966* (commemorative booklet) (Dublin: National Theatre Society, 1966).

21. Paul Bew, *Ideology and the Irish Question: Ulster Unionism and Irish Nationalism 1912–1916* (Oxford: Clarendon Press, 1994), p.xviii.

22. Kiberd, *Inventing Ireland*, p. 213.

23. See, for example, Foster, *Vivid Faces*; Pašeta, *Irish Nationalist Women*; Lane, *Rosamond Jacob*; Morris, *Alice Milligan and the Irish Cultural Revival*; Steele, *Women, Press and Politics during the Irish Revival*. Although republican women, like nationalist servicemen in the First World War, are still described as having been airbrushed from history, their experiences have received considerable attention in television documentaries and press coverage during the present decade of centenaries.

24. Declan Kiberd, 'Disappearing Ireland', 'Theatre of Memory' symposium, Abbey Theatre, 18 Jan. 2014.

25. Fox, *Rebel Irishwomen*, pp 131–2.